DOMESTIC GOODS

The Material, the Moral, and the Economic in the Postwar Years

Visions of life in the 1950s often spring from the United States: supermarkets, freeways, huge gleaming cars, bright new appliances, automated households. Historian Joy Parr looks beyond the generalizations about the indulgence of this era to find a specifically Canadian consumer culture. Focusing on the records left by consumer groups and manufacturers, and relying on interviews and letters from many Canadian women who had set up household in the decade after the war, she reveals exactly how and why Canadian homemakers distinguished themselves from the consumer frenzy of their southern neighbours.

Domestic Goods focuses primarily on the design, production, promotion, and consumption of furniture and appliances. For Parr, such a focus demands an analysis of the intertwining of the political, economic, and aesthetic. Parr examines how the shortage of appliances in the early postwar years was a direct result of government reconstruction policy, and how the international style of 'high modernism' reflected the postwar dream of free trade. But while manufacturers devised new plans for the consumer, depression-era frugality and a conscious setting of priorities within families led potential customers to evade and rework what was offered them, eventually influencing the kinds of goods created.

This book addresses questions such as, who designed furniture and appliances, and how were these designs arrived at? What was the role of consumer groups in influencing manufacturers and government policy? Why did women prefer their old wringer washers for over a decade after the automatic washer was made available? In finding the answers the author celebrates and ultimately suggests reclaiming a particularly Canadian way of consuming.

JOY PARR is a Farley Professor of History at Simon Fraser University. She is author of *Labouring Children* (1994) and *The Gender of Breadwinners* (1990), and editor of *A Diversity of Women* (1995).

DOMESTIC GOODS

*The Material, the Moral,
and the Economic in the
Postwar Years*

JOY PARR

UNIVERSITY OF TORONTO PRESS
Toronto Buffalo London

© University of Toronto Press Incorporated 1999
Toronto Buffalo London

Printed in Canada

ISBN 0-8020-4097-7 (cloth)
ISBN 0-8020-7947-4 (paper)

Printed on acid-free paper

Canadian Cataloguing in Publication Data

Parr, Joy, 1949–
    Domestic goods : the material, the moral, and the economic in the postwar
    years

    Includes bibliographical references and index.
    ISBN 0-8020-4097-7 (bound)   ISBN 0-8020-7947-4 (pbk.)

    1. Household appliances – Canada – History – 20th century.   2. Electric
    household appliances industry – Canada – History – 20th century.
    3. Furniture – Canada – History – 20th century.   4. Furniture industry and
    trade – Canada – History – 20th century.   5. Consumer goods – Canada –
    History – 20th century.   I. title.

    TX298.P36 1999   339.4'86436'0971   C99-930385-6

University of Toronto Press acknowledges the financial assistance to its publishing program of the Canada Council for the Arts and the Ontario Arts
Council.

This book has been published with the help of a grant from the Humanities
and Social Sciences Federation of Canada, using funds provided by the Social
Sciences and Humanities Research Council of Canada.

For GJL
and in memory of H

Contents

viii   Contents

Acknowledgments

This work was supported by the Social Sciences and Humanities Research Council of Canada, a Senior Killam Research Fellowship administered by the Canada Council, the Farley Endowment at Simon Fraser University, and between 1992 and 1998 by the Swedish Institute, through the intervention of Ulla Wikander, then of the Economic History Research Institute at Uppsala University, and with assistance from Veronica Nygren of Konstfactskolan in Stockholm. For space to think, to write, and to listen to demanding talk I am grateful to Florence Ladd of the Bunting Institute of Radcliffe College; Peter Ward of the history department and Richard Ericson and the members of Green College of the University of British Columbia, where the Science and Society seminar has discomfited me regularly on Monday evenings over the last five years; the members of Innis College and Massey College at the University of Toronto; and the Fellows of All Souls College, Oxford, particularly Margaret Bent, Margarita Steinby, and quondam fellows Jane Lewis and James McConica.

In a time when there seems so little time to spare, I am grateful to the following people for gifts of commentaries on drafts: Herb Emery, Ron Shearer, Gail Reekie, two anonymous readers from the University of Toronto Press, John Staudenmaier s.j., Nina Lerman, Roger Horowitz, Leslie Oliver, the late Jan Kuypers, Bea Millar, Marilyn Macdonald, Shirley Tillotson, Avner Offer, Lizabeth Cohen, and Victoria de Grazia. For short challenges that prompted long rethinking I happily acknowledge Jonathan Schneer of Georgia Institute of Technology, J.K. Gibson-Graham of Monash University, Caroline Andrew of University of Ottawa, Nicolas Wickenden at the University of Alberta, and Tom Wilson of the University of Toronto Department of Economics. Anita Mahoney, Jeny Hartwick, Ingrid Epp, Roberta McGinn, Alan Rothenbush, Ron Long, Beth Hastie, and Elizabeth Hermann provided research and technical assistance. Margaret Anne

Knowles, now curator of Fort Calgary, refined the oral history protocol and conducted many of the interviews. Gunilla Ekberg used her own wide knowledge to supplement deficiencies in both my Swedish and my understanding of Swedish feminist politics. Happily, Mary Rawlyk granted permission for her award-winning print to appear on the cover. Annette Lorek prepared the index. Gerald Hallowell and Barbara Tessman have been my editors, the former with forbearance, the latter with laughing candour. I thank them both.

For welcome opportunities to hear what others thought of the work, I am grateful to the organizing committees of the Creighton Lecture at the University of Toronto, the Underhill Lecture at Carleton University, the Bronfman Lecture at the Institute of Canadian Studies at the University of Ottawa, the 1997 President's Lectures at the University of Saskatchewan, and the 1997 SHLITS Lectures at Georgia Institute of Technology. I have also benefited from commentaries by members of the 'His and Hers' seminar at the Hagley Library; the History of Science and Technology seminar chaired by Robert Fox and the Economic History Seminar chaired by Charles Feinstein at the University of Oxford; the Western seminar of the Royal Society of Canada; the Western universities exchange seminar at the University of Alberta; the faculty and graduate students at the University of Victoria; presentations at Northern Lights College at Fort Nelson, the College of New Caledonia at Prince George, Malaspina College in Duncan, and the Women's Centre at Terrace sponsored by the Ruth Woodward Travelling Lectureship of the Women's Studies Department of Simon Fraser University; and the Brown Bag Series in the same department organized for several years by Marilyn Macdonald. Finally, I am grateful to colleagues in the history department of Simon Fraser University who have tolerated, selectively, the early drafts I asked to present to our Thursday noon departmental seminar.

I began to write this book among the women fellows of the Bunting Institute, Radcliffe College, Cambridge, Massachusetts, in the winter of 1992, and finished it among the gentlemen gardeners of Bruce County, Ontario, in high summer 1998; in between I have been heartened by the enthusiasms and support of Kay Armatage, Constance Backhouse, Elaine Bernard, Regina Blaszczyk, Suzann Buckley, Leonore Davidoff, Francess Halpenny, Jack Little, Kate McCrone, Lucia Nixon, Alexandra Palmer, Gerry Pratt, Alison and Jim Prentice, Simon Price, Angela Redish, Mary Lynn Stewart, Philip Scranton, Andrea Tone, Carole Turbin, Cynthia Wright, and Greg Levine. May they all, as they please, take ample occasion to turn, in turn, to me.

GONZALES BAY, VICTORIA
AUGUST 1998

DOMESTIC GOODS

The Material, the Moral, and the Economic in the Postwar Years

Introduction

This book is about Canadian homemakers, designers, and manufacturers in the first two decades after the Second World War and the public policy makers who regulated the relationships between them. Formally it is a series of relatively distinct, chronologically ordered essays which explore modern Canadian material culture. Somewhat unconventionally, most essays consider both the technologies and aesthetics which influenced the physical form of things, and the economic and social ideologies which organized thinking about them. Literally and metaphorically, the essays are all about *domestic goods*, how the two words *domestic* and *goods* were understood separately, and how Canadians, weighing the material, moral, and economic needs of the families, firms, and the nation then being remade in the wake of the war, understood these terms in combination.

Because the juxtapositions here may seem odd, I begin by stating some of the questions which piqued my own curiosity a decade ago and explain how these queries connect to previous explorations in economic and design history and the history of consumption – thus to make clear why different questions need to be asked now. An account follows of how the chapters build in sequence, one on another, for perhaps at first encounter this connection may not be entirely clear. This research puts studies of material culture into unaccustomed company, and therefore challenges certain disciplinary conventions. Yet the research is based on familiar questions, ones we all ask sometimes, whether as citizens, consumers, or makers of things. Given our current crises of production, distribution, consumption, and waste, I hope in this book you will find encouragement to ask them more often.

These, then, are some of the questions. What is the source of the aesthetics which make the same goods beautiful, fitting, and useful at one time, and ugly, extraneous, and foolish at another? How much does contemporary technology constrain how goods are made? There is a shifting boundary between what individuals affirm they may have for themselves and what they, as citizens, agree they must share. How is this boundary drawn? The work of government to encourage industry and redistribute income surely influences the access to possessions. But, directly and indirectly, does it influence the form of things as well? How much can citizens talk back to manufacturers and the state about domestic goods? What can and do citizens do when, by gender, class, or nationality, they have little influence over the shape of the material world in which they must live? Are their actions, when they thus are silenced, merely idiosyncratically and ineffectually private, or are they systematically or circuitously consequential? If householders are moved to practise what might be described as a briskly accommodating resistance in their daily lives among goods, what makes this resistance plausible and necessary? What gives these stances moral and ethical force?[1] What can this briskly accommodating resistance, studied historically, tell us now? This last question I leave to you.[2]

Previous Explorations

The term *consumer* gained great currency in the 1950s for the confluence of autonomy, plenty, and compliance it inscribed. Since then, the term has taken on ever greater generality. Now 'consumer' has entered the public discourse as a synonym for 'citizen.' Our present and future prospects are clouded by grim polemics about liberties lost to past spending accumulated as national debt. Our shared legacy of social welfare institutions, built in the decades which are the focus of this book, now is discussed in the diction of commercial contract and strategic management rather than the language of citizenship. These ways of featuring our current predicament presume much about the practices of modernity in the first two decades after the Second World War. They take as stable and known the relationships between producing and consuming, and between making and using in the national, entrepreneurial, and household decisions of that time. Today, the retrospective material culture of the young reworks polyester, chrome, and scarlet lipstick. Our discussions about the future of cities, the state, and the national economy take as their touchstones sequestered suburban bungalows, postwar Keynesian deficit spending, and planned obsolescence. But, both in the popular culture and in public debate, the representation of the modern is curiously unitary. National differences and temporal changes are submerged. What is regarded as 'typical' of the postwar period was in fact found only in the most prosperous parts of the United States in the most prosperous years of the 1950s and 1960s.[3] Our contemporary worried deliberations about how to live daily, perched between the global and the local, may thus be impoverished. Perhaps considering how postwar material life was distinctively made locally will help us articulate what the local could be, as an alternative and response to the global, now.

Certainly the changes in Canadian material culture in the 1950s were part of an international transformation. But you will find in this study a current of comparison with Sweden, another small northern nation, which had its own resolutions to the questions of what was beautiful, what was useful, and how much was enough – and for whom. Was the material culture of the postwar years merely a reflection of a single homogenizing and pacifying consumer culture, or might there also have been processes of rearticulation and refusal at work (and play) in the making of the modern?

The postwar years are commonly characterized as a time when there were more household goods in the market and in more households – in the balance of importance, having things appeared to matter more to more people than lately, or perhaps ever. Household goods were categorized as consumer goods, and a society which set great cultural store on consumer goods was often called a consumer society. The label is applied to many parts of the North Atlantic world in the decades after the Second World War.

Here the nomenclature begins to race ahead of the evidence, for 'consume' does not mean the same thing as 'have' or 'use.' Consume came into English in the fourteenth century carrying prodigal and rebarbative connotations. It meant to waste, devour, or use up to the point of exhaustion, and it carries these inflections still. From the eighteenth century it has been twinned with produce, in discourses of political economy, as the other blade of the scissors in the market, the demand which met supply.[4] Though economists always have insisted that consumers make choices, and in some circumstances might even have 'sovereignty' over producers, the prior connotations of debilitating prodigality persist. Thus, production is a creative endeavour; consumption is a perpetual process of destruction. To characterize a time as dominated by consumption or, more emphatically for the fifties, by mass consumption is to say something derogatory about the time generally, and in particular about those most engaged in consuming.

Changes in the volume and composition of household consumption were invoked to mark the 1950s as a consumer society, yet the conventionally combined terms 'household' and 'consumption' also work at cross-purposes. Both production and consumption include elements of making and unmaking, construction and destruction, 'using for' and 'using up.'[5] For example, between household tools and a tradesman's tools the line is difficult to draw. Indeed they are often the same instruments. The closer we look at what people do (and did) with the things they are (and were) said to consume, the more problematic does the normative discrimination between production and consumption become. Alan Warde goes too far in suggesting that the distinction is redundant,[6] for these two ways of appropriating resources are not the same, as we soon shall have ample occasion to see. Some elements of the distinction between production and consumption should persist.[7] But the simple separate assertions that production creates enduring social and material meaning while consumption creates social dissipation and waste mask many similarities. Neither are we well served, as we try to live ethically amidst things, by the contrasting contentions that our labour, once sold, creates an authentic identity, while our other engagements with the material world merely perpetuate romantic illusions.[8]

For women, in the 1940s and 1950s, domestic consumption was more about labour than leisure. This consumption was 'self-production,' the process by which the household was sheltered and sustained, not depleted or laid waste.[9] Consumption is commonly identified with the market, but grouped within consumption are many different possible provisioning systems, only some of which are organized by the market. Shifts from one mode of provision to another carry considerable social, political, and economic implications which historically bear close attention. When the means of consumption altered, qualities of life changed. Work was redistributed between household members and across the household boundary.[10] The authority that consumers, by comparison with manufacturers and regulators, had over the design of goods altered as well, in response to a variety of relatively independent processes, of which gender was one.[11]

Modern economic and design theories, and the first generation of historical studies, all understand mass consumption centrally as a consequence and requirement of mass production. Here Henry Ford is the model, a manufacturer who recognized working-class men as the market for the cars which workers in his plant produced. From Ford through 1930s Italian theorist Antonio Gramsci, this characterization of modern consumption as a necessary implication, but passive reflection, of mass production comes down to us as Fordism. But because much which was consumed was not made by industrial methods (as, for example, most houses are not, to this day) or by mass production methods (as many manufactured goods were not in Canada in the decades after the war), the theory will need qualification and amplification to explain what households required and why.[12]

More serious is the implication that the motivation to consume is in the thrall of those who produce – dependent, monolithic, and manipulated rather than heterogeneous and diversely derived. Some American popular commentators of the 1950s, Vance Packard, Betty Friedan, and J.K. Galbraith, argued that advanced capitalism constructed 'false needs' and persuaded people to consume against their conscious wills. More recent analyses of modern consumption by scholars from history and the social sciences have focused upon advertising.[13] These studies, too, take what producers wanted as reasonable approximations of what they achieved, and maintain a tactical, interpretive, and moral distance from the consumers themselves.[14]

This analysis of consumption as a dependent, manipulated, conforming, and captive response is deeply gendered. As Ellen Willis noted years ago in a trenchant feminist critique written from within the New Left, theories of consumerism of the 1960s and 1970s depended for their plausibility and palatability to movement theorists on a common portrait of consumers and women as 'passive sexual objects.' Women were theorized as different from the autonomous self-conscious masculine citizens who would make social change. These gendered associations between masculinity and the capacity to resist had become so naturalized by the late 1960s that they entered the debate as if they were empirical observations rather than dogma. Buying could not be what it seemed to many women to be – a rational, self-interested behaviour adapted to the contemporary hierarchical sexual division of labour – and also be compatible with these premises.[15] Nor could it be informed by political reasoning, or refuse, rather than manufacture, consent. From this theoretical perspective, consumption was recognizable only as gratification taken in trade for pliant complicity.[16]

From these assumptions followed a chain of gendered distinctions which linked economic and aesthetic analyses of modern material culture: masculine engineering, feminine styling, his productive and necessary purchasing, her gratuitous and non-productive shopping. Thus was the chronology of postwar commodity culture understood as descent from the solid functionality of manly 'high' modernism to the decorative femininity of consumer decadence.[17] A series of collisions between the manly and the womanly, the rationally new and the personally retrospective, and the mechanical and the bodily, marked the route down. The twin casualties of these theorized collisions were oppositional politics and womanly autonomy. At the end of the road lay the wreckage created by those who knew no better than to shop until they dropped.

In these encounters, as they were related by modern design historians, ordinary homemakers received the same consistent bad press as the Chicago physician Edith Farnsworth had to bear in her prolonged battle with her architect and patient, Mies van der Rohe, over whether she might take 'her' furniture into 'his' celebrated Farnsworth house.[18] Mass culture became associated with leisure, family, and personal life, all commonly in the thrall of commercial seduction. In this thoroughly colonized space, autonomous action based on an independent interest was inconceivable.[19]

The models of the market in neoclassical economic reasoning similarly are less nuanced in their consideration of consumption than production. Consumer demand is understood to be complexly derived and yet convincingly displayed only at the point of purchase. All the reasoning about how wants and needs are constituted, arbitrated, and frustrated must be distilled into the moment at the cash register. Usually, the preferences 'revealed' by purchase are the only effects of demand it is possible to know well enough to consider reliably. Reluctantly economists thus reason tautologically. People want what they buy and buy what they want. What is not available for sale, they effectively do not want. Consumption is thus best knowable as an asymptotic function of production. Deciding what to buy with a given income is a lonely determined search for the one best resolution. Buyer preferences are fixed. They arrive from somewhere outside the reach of the market model.[20]

The bias in existing historical studies works in the same direction. The entrepreneurial archives, upon which most historical research about consumption is based, tell us little about who bought or why, and by extension reveal little about autonomous changes in demand over time. Thus, we know more about Mr Eaton than about Mr Eaton's customers, and are tempted to infer what Mr Eaton's customers thought from what Mr Eaton thought. Buyers' and users' struggles to influence the form, functioning, distribution, and disposition of goods as they were consumed thus have lost significance by comparison with sweeping stories about changes somewhere else, most commonly stories about production and trade.[21]

As problematically, past habits of consumption have been required to be the origin of our current habits, rather than to have distinct patterns of their own. In many historical studies of consumption, the forms in earlier material life most recognizable now – styling for obsolescence, differentiation to build demand, the cultivation of excess – have obscured from view what was obdurately unfamiliar. By paying most attention to the past that is most like the present, this work has missed the more useful opportunity to encounter and assimilate surprising past differences.

Starkly, perhaps too starkly, in the 1980s, theories of consumerism, identified as postmodern, shifted the emphasis from consumption as a corollary of production to consumption as cultural reproduction. Influenced by Barthes, Baudrillard, de Certeau, and more recently Maffelosi, writers in English began to analyse consumption as reappropriation and symbolic remaking. These theories turned analytical attention from the entrepreneurs, who made and marketed commodities, to those who used them and used them up. This theorizing posited a historical transition. The modern world of dependent consumers yielded interpretively to a postmodern world of consumers actively at play with goods offered for sale. Increasingly, consumption was described as a process of mediation rather than destruction. The most dynamic consumption to investigate was no longer the terrain prepared by designers, manufacturers, and elite tastemakers, but the space occupied by those who took goods as their own for their own purposes. People were said to learn about goods not by looking up but by looking around. If life amidst modern material culture made citizens consent to compliance, after the postmodern succession the material world became a political playground in which to act out resistance and chart new paths. Meanings were fragmented, destabilized, and endlessly regenerated. Consumption became a process of energetic disruption rather than pliant subordination.[22]

This more recent writing about consumption took as its first subject of study the disaffected youth cultures of the 1980s, the youth of Margaret Thatcher's England. Here were consumers who took the commodity culture as a script to be rewritten, and made fabulous and carnavelesque recuperations for their own purposes in the gap between how goods were 'supposed to be consumed and how they really are or might be used.' Here the social and historical circumstances in which goods were received became key to understanding how goods were consumed.[23]

We have, then, two antithetical theories of consumption, one of dependence and one of recuperation, which have come to settle as respective characterizations of the modern and postmodern periods. This partition is, of course, overdetermined, probably in part by the way many scholars in the field personally experienced these generational differences. Perhaps we are reluctant to think of the consumers who were our mothers and grandmothers, comforting in their clean aprons and trim fingerwaves, as pointedly sceptical, ironical, even ribald, in their opinions about Mr Eaton and the men selling detergent on the new flickering television screen.

What we need now, as both Victoria de Grazia and Frank Mort lately have argued by rich example, are studies of consumption which are more precisely located in time and in geographical and social space. We need studies which attend to external influences but also allow acts of consumption to 'talk back' in their own terms. There was more than one turn among consumers from the differentiated to the mass, from the utilitarian to the indulgent, from the authoritative to the enthralled. These turns varied temporally with the objects consumed.[24] Much consumption is always a search for the serviceable. Few goods which mark identity do not also satisfy practical needs. People 'play with the signs they can afford.' Sometimes play is the last thing, sometimes the only thing, on their minds. Most of life in the material world is lived somewhere in between.[25]

As the celebration of consumption as resistance shows signs of becoming an orthodoxy of its own, it is prudent to reconsider the politics of this resistance. As a 'stand-off' threatens between approaches to consumption informed by cultural studies and political economy, better to temporize and explore the influences which flowed across the boundaries between national, entrepreneurial, and household decision-making.[26] This book begins as an investigation of a particular time and place, and along the way experiments with a third, less dichotomous way of reading production and consumption.

The Architecture of the Essays

There are three parts in this book, the first focusing most upon economic policy, the second upon industrial design, and the third on household technology, although the common questions with which I began, and which I have asked you to consider, run as common currents through them all.

Part 1 is a series of studies which bring the state back into the analysis of consumption. As Gary Cross has demonstrated for interwar England and France, 'national economic and cultural conditions produced distinct paths to consumerist modernity.'[27] States worked from different assumptions about the associations between income inequality and economic growth, and production and consumption, and about what standard of living should be considered an ordinary entitlement of citizenship. Consider the contrasts between the precedence of heavy industry in eastern Europe and its relative absence in Latin America, products of national strategies for industrial development which placed very different priorities on the production of capital and consumer goods.[28]

Nations also entered the postwar era with different cultural and industrial legacies. Their distinctive experiences of neutrality or active engagement in the war left them with different demographic and debt burdens. As long as trade barriers and exchange controls persisted – which they did despite the fair internationalist aspirations of the mid-1940s – the population, wealth, and scale of industry within each nation influenced the form, quality, and range of goods citizens might consume.

The tendency has been to read postwar consumption standards and practices off the Marshall Plan intentions for the entire North Atlantic, and to naturalize these hortatory American norms as the intrinsic qualities of 'consumer society.' There is no doubt that through cinema and the glossy press, and through much-publicized political moments, such as the encounter between Khrushchev and Nixon in 1959 in Moscow beside a spotlit American stove, American goods took on profound international cultural significance in the 1950s.[29] But decisions about less and more in the world of goods are not linear and quantitative; they are qualitative, ethical, political, and cultural. To assume that all postwar consumer societies were the same, except in so far as their per capita income differed from that of the United States, is not a simplification but a disabling distortion. This misreading is probably more accessible, and thus problematical, for near geographical neighbours such as Canada than for other North Atlantic nations.

Chapter 1 is a thought experiment which uses the experience of the command economy in wartime to consider what domestic goods might have been like outside, or nearer the boundaries of, the market. If household appliances were conceptualized as tools for use, devices maximally to satisfy the need for household production, rather than commodities for sale for a profit, how would the goods themselves have been different? Would the same people have owned them? Would the same technologies have been in use, or would different mechanisms for allocation have effected technological substitutions? Most of this chapter argues from evidence generated by the Consumer Branch of the Wartime Prices Board, and the controllers at the board charged to monitor and meet civilian requirements for household equipment. But the analysis also uses radio broadcast and market surveys, as well as rural householders' discussion group summaries filed in response to the Ontario Farm Forum radio broadcasts, to reclaim fragments of the dreamscapes Canadians drew for themselves as they looked past the war toward what they hoped would be a more equitable peace.

In a similar vein, Chapter 2 explores two actual thought experiments conducted at the end of the war. Then, the path Canadian secondary manufacturing would follow during reconstruction and after seemed prospective, more a public policy choice than a predetermined course. Should a modern Canadian economy adapt to the free multilateral trade promised by the peace by exporting natural resources and the few high-end manufactured wares a small economy could make competitively in short series, and then use these export revenues to pay for least-cost mass-produced imports made by more populous international traders? Or should Canada develop more of its own mass production industries, both to meet the needs of its own citizens and to sell into international markets? The 1945 *Design in Industry* exhibition at the Royal Ontario Museum, sponsored by the Ontario Handicrafts Guild, displayed goods to represent this first proposed industrial strategy. The next year, the *Design in the Household* exhibition at the Toronto Art Gallery, sponsored by the Toronto Board of Trade and the Canadian Manufacturers' Association, with help from the National Film Board and the Museum of Modern Art in New York, presented an imagined Canadian material culture made by the second policy alternative. Things look different depending upon the perspective of the viewer and the context in which they are displayed. The goals of the curators and trustees, more successfully realized at the art gallery than at the museum, were to disrupt visitors' habits of seeing domestic goods on display and make viewers conscious of how the eye edited what the mind absorbed. Chapter 2 explores these tropes of disruption and, so far as is possible from the evidence, their effects upon the members of the public who came to the exhibitions with distinct goals of their own. What about objects as they were displayed revealed them as goods for sale, what as tools for use, what as products of particular processes of production? Could citizens be made aware of these differences, and thus be drawn into a strategic dialogue about the kind of metaphorical domestic goods that should be achieved by the physical domestic goods of Canadian manufacture?

Unlike the United States, with which Canada's postwar patterns of consumption are too frequently conflated, household goods were scarce in the Dominion after the war, and those made of metal remained so for some time. Chapter 3 explores the many reasons why this was so. Neither of the postwar proposed strategies for rebuilding was actually followed.

Instead, until the early 1950s, planners, manufacturers, and householders were caught in a series of crises, which forced the new generation of Keynesians to practise technical micro-management, slowed the reconversion and modernization of consumer goods industries, and schooled householders to think of the culture of mass consumption as a distant, alien, and perhaps dangerous illusion. The deliberate choice, or rather the series of many smaller ideologically connected choices, was to direct the nation's scarce stores of materials and foreign exchange first to rebuilding producer goods industries and industries producing for export. In key ways, the reasoning which guided these decisions drew upon normative gendered assumptions. This chapter charts the force of these hierarchical gendered analogies, in the costs planners were willing to trade for the benefits they sought, and the unintended consequences their policies bequeathed.

Chapter 4 tells the story of the unequal struggle among Liberal, social democratic, and communist women to articulate the consumer interest and, by organization and representation, to influence public policy in the wake of the war. It analyses the contradictions and ironies in the liberal economic theories of consumer sovereignty, the arguments and tactics communist women employed in their attempts to prolong and expand the command economy, and the awkward ethical dilemma and crisis of allegiance this political conjuncture posed for women leaders in the social democratic Cooperative Commonwealth Federation. Early on, and for them as a matter of some urgency, the governing Liberal Party captured control of the Canadian Association of Consumers (CAC) and used it as voice in defence of the government's economic policies. The CAC thereafter argued, its own organizational purposes echoing those of its partisan backers, that there was a single unified consumer interest which transcended regional, class, and sectional differences. This is a claim which, when closely scrutinized, reveals a profound systemic inequality within market economies.

Acquiring goods through the market requires access either to income or to credit. Chapter 5, the last and chronologically latest in Part 1, captures the debate about who was entitled to spend, as Canadian use of consumer credit began to approach that in the United States. In the late 1950s as a recession took hold, weaknesses emerged in the institutional levers through which the Bank of Canada implemented monetary policy. Progressive Roman Catholics and urban social activists began to analyse the inequities in contemporary consumer lending practices. At the same time, four of the five major Canadian banks for the first time began to join finance companies in extending consumer loans. Most provinces launched special investigations into consumer lending. The royal commission convened in the early 1960s to advise on revisions to the Bank Act took the issue as a central concern, and, from the Senate, David Croll pressed yearly for credit reform. Chapter 5 analyses the morality of spending or, more precisely, of borrowing to buy – in these years, an issue in class and gender politics which was linked inextricably with discussions about the Canadian financial system and the effectiveness of monetary policy.

Part 2 is about the aesthetics and interests which informed high modernism in Canadian industrial design, the ways in which these ideologies and practices were implemented by policy makers and manufacturers, and their influences upon how which domestic goods, furnishings in particular, were chosen and used in Canadian homes. This discussion differs from the Canadian design history currently in print in three ways. It situates modernist aesthetics, not as a search for transhistorical abstractions, but as a particular claim for professional aesthetic authority made palatable by its symmetry with contemporary economic reasoning. It treats the interventions of engineers, manufacturers, and advertising executives as contributions rather than impediments to the design process. And it attends to the practices by which householders reworked the goods they brought into their homes from the market, domesticating these things which once were commodities by cleansing them, in measure, of their market referents.

Chapter 6 is a study of the National Industrial Design Committee, a body created by the initiative and political acumen of Donald Buchanan, formerly of the National Film Board, as a conduit through which the conventions of postwar British industrial design could inform a developing Canadian design modernism. The committee came first to rest in the National Gallery, rather than at either of the institutions Buchanan would have preferred, the National Research Council or the Department of Trade and Commerce. The particular modernism Buchanan articulated – in company with the British art historian Herbert Read and the then Canadian expatriate Allan Jarvis – worked at wilful cross-purposes to both engineering and commercial principles. But after the exchange crisis of 1948 his project found unlikely contingent allies in the Department of Finance where economists' abstract and increasingly contested dreams of international free trade cohered for a time with Buchanan's own projections and projects for an international style.

A case study of the maple furniture made by many Canadian firms and found in many Canadian homes in the 1940s and 1950s is the subject of Chapter 7. The analysis focuses upon the engineering, manufacturing, design, and advertising decisions at the Imperial Furniture Company in

Stratford, Ontario, and the lines the late Jan Kuypers designed for the firm from 1951 to 1959. The goal is to examine the synergies among technical, aesthetic, and commercial practices of modernism as they contributed to Kuypers's splendidly successful reworkings of Imperial's stolid and fustian Loyalist lines, and then to explore how these makers' priorities played with and against homemakers' remembered readings of the same goods.

Chapter 8 begins from the premise that homemakers too were designers. Setting aside the once common sociological reading which treated household furnishings as markers of rising class aspiration, this study tries to reclaim from homemakers' recollections, an admittedly compromised possibility, the reasoning which guided them as they created interior domestic landscapes for their homes. It explores household furnishings as markers of stability and identity, and as objects for play, among women facing the particular challenges of domesticity as the baby boom crested in the wake of the war. not copying rich; carving own identity

Part 3 treats another category of household choices, the deliberations about acquiring and using the domestic technologies increasingly present in Canadian homes in the 1950s and 1960s. These chapters are an example of what Pamela Laird lately has called 'stories against the current,' discussions which question the particularly resilient aura of inevitability which surrounds the artefacts of technology and cloaks their contingency in narratives of inexorable progress or descent.[30] These are narratives which weigh the contending factors which informed product design engineering. Within this calculus, these case studies make a modest place for the briskly accommodating resistance which householders, deliberating on their own priorities, deployed as they accepted, used, and refused these Trojan horses waiting portentously to enter their homes.

Chapter 9 is an account of the most formally organized instance I could find in Canada for this period of women 'talking back' to product engineering designers and asserting their own preferences over the commodity form prevailing in the market. This chapter begins with a portrait of the politics of the appliance showroom in the early 1950s, when commission salesmen, by their gender, were given technical authority over cookery, a labour process which most of their women customers believed they themselves had already mastered. On the electric and gas stoves made in Canada in the 1920s and 1930s, the ovens were positioned at the same level as the burners, at waist level. After the war the ovens were moved below the hob, so that their racks were nearer the knees than the waist, far from eye level and accessible only by stooping. On the advice of their members, the Canadian Association of Consumers convinced an Ottawa Valley firm to build and market a high-oven stove, which in due course won a National Industrial Design award. This model was a commercial failure, and the discussion concludes with reflections about the gender and commercial constraints which might have made this so.

Chapter 10 is an analysis of why automatic washing machines came so much later into Canadian than American homes. Here users' resistance to the newer and in many ways superior technology was not organized, but individual, best observed in the high saturation levels and rates of purchase for wringer rather than automatic washers up until the mid-1960s. A plausible hypothesis would be that this technological choice was purely an income effect. Automatics cost more than wringers, and Canadians had lower disposable incomes than Americans. But the process is clearly more complex. Even wealthy Canadians long preferred the technology that makers and marketers believed outmoded. The answer to this conundrum seems to lie in the intersection between the traits of the Canadian manufacturing system, the intricacies of Canadian plumbing, and the ethics of Canadian consumer culture, or so this discussion contends.

With the final essay, Chapter 11, we finally meet Canadian domestic technology formed by mass production. By the late 1950s the many household needs for equipment deferred through the Depression and the war finally had been met. Birth rates, marriage rates, and the volume of immigration ebbed almost in unison, and makers, with plants built to meet peak demands, found themselves with excess capacity. This is the era, rhetorically, of planned obsolescence, when appliances appeared in strong and improbable colours to make them more transient treats for the eye. In this respect, the appliances became more like cars, and coincidentally a larger proportion of Canadian appliances were built by subsidiaries of automobile makers. As the new power projects on the Peace, the Columbia, and the St Lawrence Rivers came on stream and the Trans-Canada pipeline was completed, utilities too were burdened by excess capacity, and thus eager for new technologies and new habits of technological dependence which would expand their domestic markets. Homemakers were now more experienced buyers, and more of them daily were leaving the home for wage-paying jobs. This chapter discusses the commercial priorities which directed the engineering design of the large refrigerators and clothes dryers, new to the market in these years, and the ways that homemakers, in their use of this equipment, mediated the transition that makers had built into this technology.

This book is an archeology of the material, moral, and economic choices and constraints which formed Canadian commodity culture in the first two decades after the Second World War, choices and constraints which then were buried within the resolved solidity of the things themselves. These things were at once domestic goods, and the products of multiple, complicit, and dissenting opinions about what was good for Canadian families, firms, and the nation. This decision making in a small, northern country, cautiously expanding its welfare state, slowly rebuilding a manufacturing base just broaching mass production, only beginning to glimpse the possibility of a stable and prosperous future for a growing and more diverse citizenry, has been covered over by quick sketches taken mistakenly, and by default, for weighty certainties. Resistance comes in many forms. When womanly, by postwar circumstance made accommodating and in private, its brisk resolve was too ordinary and integral to housewifery to bear remark. But there is a politics in this resistance which bears attention, and perhaps even emulation. Or so I shall now seek to persuade you.

PART 1

POLITICAL ECONOMY

1

Domestic Goods in Wartime

'Whoever discovered water, it surely wasn't a fish.' Thinking about markets, goods made for markets, and people navigating the shoals of markets brings this adage to mind, for markets, like water, are surrounding, infusing, transparent. Trying to think about men producing and women using goods made for the market – that is, to think at once about gender hierarchies and market boundaries – compounds the transparency, which, despite appearances, is not a good thing.

This book is designed to explore Canadian material culture in the first two decades after the Second World War. If national cultures of production and consumption were related but distinct across industrial economies, the links will be easier to see in national than transnational firms. In 1945 the country's household furniture and domestic appliances were still made mostly by Canadian-owned companies, adapting to the local manufacturing condition. If producers and consumers thought about goods for sale in the market in different ways, these will be most plain in products engineered and sold by men, to be purchased and used by women. Hence the focus here on furnishings and household equipment, rather than cars, for Canadian cars were by then made in American branch plants rather than Canadian firms, and driven preponderantly by men.[1] If reasoning about material culture derived not only from the conventions of the market but from values which transcended the price system, then households in the forties and fifties will be a good place to look. Homes were places of production as well as consumption, where choices to enter and leave the market and to follow non-market priorities were, in ordinary times, commonly and comfortably made.

Seeking domestic goods was a postwar preoccupation. There were eleven and a half million Canadians in 1941, fourteen million by 1951, and eighteen million a decade later. There were a million more households in 1951 than in 1941, and a million more again by 1961. Household needs were changing. Steadily the proportion of Canadians living in urban areas increased, from 53 per cent in 1941 to 60 per cent in 1961, and the proportion of married women in the labour force rose from one in twenty-five to one in five. Canada, like New Zealand, Australia, and the United States in the postwar years, was a baby-boom country. The crude birth rate rose from 22.4 in 1941 to 24.3 at the end of the war. Never in the years 1946–59 were there less than 27 live births per thousand population.[2]

These were households in a nation much altered by war. There were bills to be paid, for the federal debt increased by 360 per cent during the six years of hostilities. And there were obligations to be met. With the peace, Canadians who had served the nation at home and abroad rethought their entitlements as citizens. While, in their more radical market economy, Americans were elaborating the rights of citizens as consumers, Canadians were building a more expansive welfare state. Between 1947 and 1960 personal disposable income more than doubled in Canada. But surely, if moderately, this national wealth was being redistributed. Financed in part by a three-fold increase in the personal tax burden, social welfare expenditures almost quadrupled.[3]

Canadians and Americans shared a long border, open to common messages about consumer goods from advertisements, films, and popular fiction, but they did not respond in common to these messages. On either side of the border, the boundaries between both the individual and the collectivity and the marketplace and other living space were being differently defined.

These differences probably existed before the war. We know that in 1940 there were twice as many American households with refrigerators and gas or electric stoves as there were in Canada in 1941. But in both countries during the war, a centrally controlled command economy succeeded the market. A short diversion to study domestic goods in wartime – mostly in Canada, but with strategic glimpses across the forty-ninth parallel – lets us look at household appliances, in particular, when they were less surrounded by the market. It's like draining some of the water from around those fish, with whose cognitive predicament we began. What did planners, manufacturers, and householders do when the market was not everywhere around them doing what markets do? What does this tell us about what markets did? What do these responses reveal, for Canada, about state and private reflexes navigating the world of goods?

During the wartime emergency, the market reasoning of ordinary modern times was not sensible. The market directed distribution based on ability to pay, not need. The peacetime economy counted only the value of goods and services exchanged for a price. In wartime, public purposes were more important than private needs, and these public purposes put pressure on supplies of all sorts. To deal with impending shortages, first the price system was frozen: in Canada in November 1940; in the United States a year and a half later in April 1942. Thus, for a longer duration in Canada than in the United States, economic categories were recast. Their ideological justifications in class and gender difference were displaced. Need was separated from demand, access for use from ownership. The value of household labour, and thus of household technology, was differently appraised.

Among household goods, the effects of the command economy were most apparent for domestic appliances made with metals and powered with fuels, both in scarce supply. Often in Canada appliances were imported or made with imported parts, which thus put pressure on foreign exchange reserves. In peacetime these goods were made for sale and styled for selling. In wartime, controllers fought an often losing battle with the public to strip away the allure of appliances as signs of status and objects of desire. For the duration, domestic appliances officially were to be tools and tools alone, allocated only on the basis of the need for goods and services they would produce.

By the early forties these needs were changing. The marriage rate was high, almost twice as high as it had been a decade before, so that over 120,000 new couples a year required at least some cooking and washing facilities. People were moving to be near military bases and war industries, while the stocks of household equipment largely stayed put. Different kinds of households emerged. Single women pressed to take up work in distant places needed at least the rudiments for light housekeeping – an iron, some utensils, and a hot plate. In many households there was now more work to be done, with less labour and a fixed stock of domestic equipment, for both daughters and servants were gone to industry, replaced by tired and hungry boarders with laundry to be done. More than ever, married women who had entered the labour force needed well-functioning household tools.[4]

The command economy changed how these needs would be met. In Canada in the summer of 1941, the controller of supplies for the Wartime Prices and Trade Board (WPTB) restricted the production of refrigerators, stoves, and electric washing machines. Six months later the Office of Price Administration (OPA) imposed similar limits in the United States.

By the fall of 1942 both countries had suspended all production, except by permit, of this and much other household equipment.[5]

Apart from its earlier price controls, two other differences distinguished the command economy of Canada from that of the United States. The first concerns what manufacturers were ordered to restrict. The Canadian controllers limited output, and released only the materials necessary to produce specified numbers of prewar designs. A regulation of 20 November 1940 explicitly forbade the introduction of new models.[6] By contrast, American controllers, while specifying output, pressed manufacturers to redesign. The new models which resulted from these incentives were lighter, for the total amount of iron and steel used in each class of industry was limited, and less bright, because each sector's access to copper, nickel, chrome, and aluminum was similarly restricted. But an American manufacturer who reduced the metal required to make a refrigerator from eighty-five to twenty pounds could increase production, remain within the controllers' quota, and keep his design team nimble in anticipation of the end of the war.[7] In Canada, product innovation in major appliances ceased for the duration.

The implications of controls were also different for Canada because the existing stocks of household equipment were so much smaller as the command economy began. The proportion of household income spent in the United States on consumer durables exceeded that in Canada by 40 per cent at the beginning of the Depression, and by 25 per cent in 1937. At the start of the war in the United States, 95 per cent of households in rural Vermont, for example, already had powered washing machines, a saturation level not reached in the whole of Canada until 1961. American retailers were still holding large inventories late in 1942, so shortages took a good while to become evident. Indeed, of the U.S. home front the Canadian-born economist, John Kenneth Galbraith, recalled, 'never before had there been so much talk of sacrifice with so little actual want.' In spite of controls, there was a splurge of wartime spending in the United States. By 1943 'the war on production' largely had been won. Limited numbers of new stoves and refrigerators began to appear in American stores in the summer of 1944.[8]

In Canada both retail and household holdings of domestic appliances were lower as the war began. Already in the summer of 1940, much of the nation's domestic equipment was of venerable age. Many households had been deferring purchases for a decade. The majority of washers and ranges were at least five years old, and most of these were over ten. By the fall of 1943 most regions were reporting serious supply shortages of washers, ranges, and electric refrigerators. Canadians, like Americans, had more money to spend during the war – personal disposable income rose by 50 per cent – but in Canada there were few goods to buy. Spending on durable goods, as a proportion of disposable income, declined by two-thirds. By contrast with the United States, there was no wartime spending splurge. Rather, 'Shopping became a matter not of what you could afford, as it had been in the Depression, but of what you could find.'[9]

The command economy elaborated established differences between Canadian and American reasoning about domestic goods. But it also displayed the objects themselves in an unfamiliar and revealing light. For Canada, let us look in turn at the three major appliances, washers, stoves, and refrigerators, paying particular attention to what the absence of the market disclosed. How did controllers and householders react as they were drawn into these unfamiliar waters?

First, washers. In Canada gas- or electric-powered wringer washing machines were relatively rare. Most households relied on washboards, galvanised washtubs, and copper boilers. In cities and towns, many Canadians, rich and poor, depended on commercial laundries. In these circumstances, for controllers and for those householders who did not own well-functioning equipment, the unequal distribution of wealth before the war was a lingering impediment.

Historically, the private ownership of machines had not been the first solution to the wearying problem of the wash. Large-scale laundry equipment run by industrial motors was installed in hotels, institutions, and commercial establishments at the turn of the century, and the most obvious way then to domesticate this technology was to organize market or neighbourhood-shared use of the machines. Shared use rather than ownership made good distributional sense, at least in urban areas.

Understandably, in peacetime this was not a resolution domestic appliance builders, eager to sell many machines, favoured. Although sharing often would have cost less, householders too, in a society which valued private possession for its own sake, were prepared, if they could, to pay for the status and perhaps the convenience of owning machines of their own. Once small engines were refined to run sufficiently safely and silently, and with adequate torque to start machines readily in the home, private rather than collectively used domestic technologies gained precedence.[10]

In these circumstances, the unequal distribution of wealth before the war constrained the decisions of controllers during the war. The most, and technically the best, laundry equipment was in the wealthiest homes. Canadian controllers in wartime, whose task made them focus upon the goods and services domestic appliances would produce, were exasperated that these essential machines lately had been luxury wares. This history, they argued, made the existing distribution of washers a reflection of 'irrelevant factors such as new models and advertising pressure' and measured 'only what people want, not what they need.' Plainly, controllers concluded, a new and more fitting distributional logic was required, one which, for example, put machines where 'multiple use' was assured and where alternative technologies were most taxed, and which ranked the machines themselves in terms of the 'essentiality' of the tasks they would perform.[11]

In wartime, when both existing domestic equipment and the materials with which to make more were scarce, controllers would have liked to recuperate the shared use of machines. The market-mediated joint use of washers – that is, the washers in commercial laundries – had been common in Canada before the war. But, even in this most likely case for sharing rather than private ownership of domestic appliances, there were barriers.

The physical capacity of commercial laundries was fixed, and their proprietors were having difficulty holding their employees, let alone expanding staff to use existing equipment more intensively to meet increased demand. Commercial laundries gave precedence to their best and longest-standing customers, often the wealthy, who by preference rather than necessity did not do their own wash. In Canada and the United States,[12] those newly arrived in town to meet the needs of the war effort were the most likely to be turned away at heavily laden commercial laundry counters by hot and harried staff.

In response the WPTB encouraged laundries to change their product mix. The '"fancy" laundering requiring a good deal of labour,' which the wealthy preferred and which commanded the best prices, was displaced. Laundries instead were to offer the bag or wet-wash schemes working people traditionally had used, which required customers to iron, or dry and iron their commercially washed linen and clothing at home. But this merely caused the labour and equipment shortages to relocate from the marketplace back into the household.

In the non-market system of wartime, controllers had to be concerned about shortages of both waged and non-waged labour. The women of Shawinigan Falls pondered the new predicament in which the command economy had placed them. Should the extra work of finishing the laundry at home – whether by war workers or homemakers keeping boarders – be discounted, as it had been in peacetime, because household labour was unpaid? Just what was essential in wartime? Whose labour merited good tools and why? The prewar answer was evident: the wealthy. The existing distribution of laundry equipment made this conclusion plain. But what about during wartime? 'After careful consideration of the various angles, labour, man-power shortage, laundry services,' the recommendation from the women of Shawinigan Falls was clear. 'This home front definitely has its place too. Should the Government not consider washing machines essential to the housewife?' In wartime this labour too had implications for national productivity and morale which could not go unreckoned.[13] And what about when the peace came, asked a woman from British Columbia. Were women to return to homes where prewar, and pre–first war, and nineteenth-century conditions prevailed, and where, if the old industrial order merely were resumed, women would have no say in the economic planning and the design engineering which so affected their lives in the home? There were choices to be made.[14]

The war forced householders to accept technological substitution. The experience made women, and not only the women from Shawinigan Falls, more conscious that the design and distribution of domestic goods was a product of choices. Whose working lives were to be made easier, and in what ways? In measure, in Canada, the wartime technological resolutions were a step back. Production of hand-powered washing machines, now made with wooden tubs, was increased. More gas-powered washers were made. Still, total production of laundry equipment had fallen by more than 55 per cent (see table 1.1). The crisis of the wash was so great by October 1943 that the board released metals for 50,000 new electrically powered machines.[15]

Tools for cooking also had to be rethought. A domestic appliance was sold as a free-standing object, but its functioning depended upon the mechanical systems of the house. After the war, the dispersion of modern ranges followed the provision of electricity, heavy wiring, and dependable supplies of gas; the most labour-saving washers were not useful until dwellings had water systems with good pressure.

In wartime the impediments to technological substitution were more old-fashioned. The few gas and electric ranges which were manufactured were made just as they had been before the war. But, for stoves as for washers, the more common wartime resolution was a step back. Coal-and-wood and gasoline-and-oil cookstoves came to dominate production, for both their materials and fuels were in greater supply. The catch was that only households with a kitchen chimney could be pressed to return to use of solid fuels; and natural and manufactured gas were not uniformly available across the country.

TABLE 1.1
Production and Apparent Consumption of Consumer Durables, 1930–42

Appliance	Year			
Washing machines	1930	1935	1940	1942
production				
electric	67,577	75,121	99,562	51,259
hand	16,038	7,445	8,207	7,064
other power	2,443	2,110	9,742	7,040
total	86,058	84,676	117,511	65,363
apparent consumption	103,416	88,056	131,057	66,266
Cooking stoves	1931	1935	1940	1942
production				
electric ranges	26,441	24,094	30,853	18,411
electric rangettes	4,049	6,312	14,117	5,905
total including combination	32,073	31,953	47,287	25,193
apparent consumption	23,923	16,633	39,625	23,507
production				
gas	31,530	23,939	31,528	19,064
apparent consumption				
including combination	35,040	30,988	45,273	26,412
production				
coal and wood	59,196	83,201	113,592	96,911
apparent consumption	59,196	83,201	111,201	95,217
production		1936		
gasoline and oil	–	14,550	40,317	50,375
apparent consumption	11,654	25,261	58,034	50,500

Apparent consumption = domestic production + imports – exports
Combination units are electric and coal, and gas and coal
Source: National Archives of Canada (NAC), RG 64, Wartime Prices and Trade Board,
Research Division, Economics Branch, 22 Oct. 1943, Apparent Consumption by
Appliance, 1920–42

More vexing for controllers than the stoves' distinctive demands upon the house was their lingering commercial history as a commodity form. Despite wartime polemics to the contrary,[16] fine large electric ranges remained consumer goods. Their stylishness, apart from their actual usefulness, retained value in the public mind. Controllers had many gasoline and coal oil stoves, reasonably priced and adequately functioning, but 'noticeably lacking' in 'style appeal.' They had almost none of the electric ranges, which they lamented were 'still considered a luxury item to some extent and a part of consumption, normally influenced by style appeal and income.' War workers, now with good incomes, longed for the few gleaming, chrome-clad electric ranges still being made. Instead they were offered kerosene cookstoves, which had re-entered the market in large numbers in the Depression and still invoked memories of those hard times. Many households had to make do with hotplates and grills, an accommodation controllers knew compromised their ability 'to cook well balanced and varied meals.'[17] The lessons about how much a decent home life depended on good working tools, but how much their provision entailed collective trade-offs, were hard to mistake.[18]

In the scramble to establish production and distributional priorities which would sustain efficiency and approximate equity among domestic appliances, refrigerators most frequently lost out. Electrical refrigerators were the last of the major appliances to enter Canadian homes. In 1941, only 21 per cent of Canadian dwellings had them. A further 26 per cent had iceboxes, and the rest made do with cold cellars, a solution controllers were inclined to favour for the duration, reasoning that so long as milk was delivered daily, basement storage of perishables would do. But in places where apartments and flats predominated, conspicuously in Quebec, iceboxes were needed. By late 1943 the remaining stock of these consisted, the controllers admitted, of 'rather inferior and high-priced' models 'made from masonite and other wood products.' Maintaining ice supplies and deliveries in the face of labour shortages also was becoming a problem. Most vexing as incomes rose and inventories vanished, the controllers, who had hoped Canadians would again think fondly of their cold cellars, observed that a mechanical refrigerator too had 'become a highly prized possession, for both its usefulness and its prestige value.'

Canada was, and is, a relatively small manufacturing economy by comparison with its southern neighbour. In 1931, 60 per cent of refrigerators sold in Canada were imported. In 1940, 25 per cent of the supply still came in across the American border. Even refrigerators made in Canada relied on crucial imported parts. These were not machines which could be produced economically in small numbers. Controllers found it 'not practicable from an engineering point of view to manufacture as few refrigerators' as they were prepared to authorize. It was deemed more appropriate, as refrigerators were 'definitely luxuries for which substitutes' were available, virtually to suspend production entirely for the duration. Indeed, the decline in refrigerator production was precipitate, in their importation almost total (see tables 1.2 and 1.3).[19] The ten-fold difference in the size of the Canadian and American populations made an engineering difference

TABLE 1.2
Canadian Production of Consumer Durables, 1942–7

Year	Refrigerators		Stoves (all fuels)		Furniture
	No.	$ millions	No.	$ millions	$ millions
1942	45,868	6.0	–		
1943	2,137	0.2	252,520	8.3	38.1
1944	3,442	0.8	331,582	9.4	36.1
1945	3,459	1.0	443,484	12.4	44.2
1946	48,897	8.42	–	20.1	63.6
1947	111,962	20.3	–	29.9	76.2

Source: *Canada Yearbook*

TABLE 1.3
Value of Imports, Refrigerators and Parts, 1939–46

Year	$ millions
1939	0.001
1940	3.868
1941	3.384
1942	1.053
1943	0.153
1946	5.201

Source: *Canada Yearbook*

in what domestic goods production their economics would sustain, in wartime and also thereafter.

If Canadian and American controllers were working with economies of different sizes, where standing stocks of consumer goods were unequal, and the social usefulness of product innovation was differently interpreted, they also came to their tasks from distinct ideological perspectives. As Meg Jacobs has noted, the men heading the U.S. Office of Price Administration were underconsumption theorists. Their lesson from the Depression was that too little spending caused dearth. Their goal was to prepare the way for a high-wage, low-price mass production economy, capable of sustaining mass consumption.[20]

In contrast, the Canadian controllers were, to use lawyers' diction, black-letter Keynesians. Their lesson from the Depression was that inconstant spending caused instability. Their intention was to use the new tools of macroeconomics to tame the economic volatility which had been the experience of a generation. They sought to prepare a path for steady,

modest growth. The booming wartime economy was for them a precarious
aberration, testing sustainable limits, threatening mayhem at every turn.
Given the scale of the Canadian market, it was not clear that mass production was viable, that mass consumption would follow, or that a high-wage,
low-price economy was plausible. Certainly none of these features lay
within their own experience in the small, tariff-sheltered economy of the
dominion.[21]

In the United States, government propaganda 'fueled popular expectations that abundance was not only a reward for winning the war but the
essence of American life itself.' Wartime incentives in that country were
promises of plenty rather than plans against continuing scarcity. American
expectations were for a return to 1920s consumer ideals with updated
products, the Wartime Information Office reported. Postwar homes would
be stocked with 'all things material in a brave new world of worldly
goods.'[22]

The reference point for postwar expectations in Canada was the thirties.
The booming twenties – that is, the American twenties of popular fiction
and film – came to mind as a cautionary tale. Government reports throughout the war focused not on private but social welfare spending as the
means of averting postwar calamity. The wartime debate over reconstruction weighed as alternatives an expansive or a minimalist welfare state. The
unemployment insurance and family allowance payments begun in 1940
and 1943, respectively, were supported as 'stigma-free social entitlements,'
secured in 'defence of common citizenship.' The popularity of the social
democratic Cooperative Commonwealth Federation (CCF) reached new
heights during the war. A November 1943 Gallup poll reported that 39 per
cent of Canadians favoured government ownership of postwar industry;
offered the alternative of private management, 14 per cent remained
undecided. By the war's end the population was restless with controls.
Wooden iceboxes and hand-powered washers were not the stuff of their
dreams. But in the trade-off between shared material security and private
plenty – for this was how the alternatives collectively were configured in
Canada in 1945 – the choice was for security and not for a brave new
world.[23]

The non-market interlude had revealed domestic goods designed for
the market as tools cloaked in stylish ornament, at once treats for the eye
and helps for the hand, utensils but also commodities whose ownership
bespoke social status and displayed private income. Once the war was over
and the non-market interlude had passed, how were women who had
endured so many shared sacrifices going to appraise these increasingly

essential domestic goods, traditionally distributed unequally on the basis of ability to pay? A 1945 Maclean-Hunter survey, *Canada's Market in Home Equipment*, found washing machines, mechanical refrigerators, and cooking stoves, in that order, as the leading purchases housewives intended to make. This potential demand represented seven times the previous peak annual Canadian production for washers, and thirteen times that ever achieved yearly for refrigerators. The goods given highest priority by householders relied considerably both on high quality metals and imported parts. These were hopes manufacturers would not soon be able to fulfil.[24]

After the end of the war in Europe, the materials controllers reported 'a quite encouraging state of affairs,' although the cause for optimism was modest. Most household necessities were available to almost half of those interviewed by controllers' staff. Refrigerators and washing machines were virtually absent everywhere. Only a third of those who needed stoves could get them. Neither would supplies soon be available to meet unrestricted demands. But none of this was discouraging within the contemporary standards defining good news. 'The situation was tolerable or would be fairly shortly' because consumers seemed sufficiently mindful of the domestic and international constraints on supply to defer their demands and mute their complaints. The situation could be made tolerable longer term, controllers argued, if the public could be persuaded to keep placing collective purposes ahead of individual desires, recognizing that shortages of both materials and imported goods 'might not be overcome for some time.'[25]

In this sense, what planners then called the 'psychological motivation of the transition period' in Canada was closer to that in the United Kingdom than in the United States. People wanted to be free from controls and regimentation, but also to avoid the painful transition which had followed the First World War. In the United States, controls were tenable only in wartime. In Canada, the public apparently was willing to accept continuing controls and persistent scarcity, and endure a lower 'initial equilibrium' between demand for and supply of goods, in order to 'consolidate standards of living attained in the war period.'[26]

In their conversations among themselves, Canadians revealed the modesty and independence of their thinking about domestic goods. Across the country as the war drew to a close, householders were looking ahead. But in 1944, without a marketplace yet full of wares to pre-empt their preferences, they imagined their postwar homes in their own terms. Some of this kitchen table talk has entered the historical record: around Ontario, rural neighbours gathered to listen to Farm Radio Forum broadcasts, and then reported on the discussions the programs had prompted. One 1944 broadcast described modern 'functional design (design for use)' and then asked listeners what features they would want in a new house for the farm. The respondents from River Road, near Port Elgin in Bruce County, were looking for 'a different architectural system than our forefathers used,' when 'too many mansions were built that are of little use to us now.' Most emphasized the need for modern mechanical systems, electricity, and well-placed electric fixtures and plugs. Still their aspirations were posed cautiously. Perhaps in time central furnaces might be 'not too expensive and fairly satisfactory.' Perhaps it was time to 'plan for a future bathroom, even if there's nothing in sight now.' 'Running water either by hand pressure or electricity would be nice,' running hot and cold even better. But all domestic improvements had been beyond reach for so long that this was thinking pursued only in cautious prospect.

Though rural couples looked forward to technological change, they saw advantages worth preserving in their existing household systems. A farm woman with both a well in the yard and a cistern by the eaves collecting rainwater could choose between hard water, which was better for drinking, and soft water, which was better for washing. Would a system to provide running water under pressure preserve these alternatives? 'A central heating system' would be helpful so long as the family could retain a cold cellar for winter storage of vegetables and fruit.

In summer a modern electric stove would be better than a woodstove for it would leave the kitchen relatively cool. But in winter, who would want to pay for electricity when wood was about in abundance and free? The better resolution would be a kitchen big enough for both an electric and a wood-burning range and to serve as 'the eating place for large crowds.' Farm couples were looking for new technologies which would accommodate their needs rather than inattentively remake their lives.[27]

In October and November 1946, participants in Ontario Farm Forums were unwilling to talk about amenities for rural homes without emphasizing their concerns about farm prices and incomes. These were couples made prudent by the uncertainty of farm income, unable 'to plan ahead or save for old age and an education for their children without depriving the entire family of small luxuries which make life more pleasant.'[28]

Agencies in the western provinces offering advice on how to modernize farm homes shared these modest expectations. The model kitchens portrayed in their booklets were designed around iceboxes, hand pumps by the sink, and wood stoves with hot water reservoirs, rather than mechanical refrigerators, water supplies under pressure, and modern ranges.

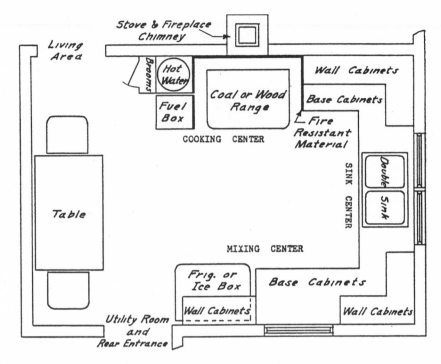

This British Columbia postwar pamphlet, like those prepared in Saskatchewan, was designed to help farm families modernize their homes. These plans did not assume that rural houses would have running water or access to either electricity or gas. The emphasis was on plans for efficient cabinetry which householders could build for themselves, and the best arrangement of coal or wood ranges and refrigerators or iceboxes in the kitchen. A kitchen hand pump and drain were recommended as great savers of time and energy.

Householders were warned to be wary of sales pitches which emphasized 'eye-appeal,' and of grand plans which would make 'the mortgage against the house so large that the family could not enjoy the home because of financial worries.' The way forward would be slow, for the power lines had not yet reached many Canadian farm homes, and the Depression had taught dour lessons about the precariousness of farm earnings.[29]

Equipping households was explicitly about politics for Laura Jamieson, a British Columbian who spent the 1930s as a juvenile court judge for the district of Burnaby, and from 1939 represented Vancouver Centre as a CCF member of the provincial legislature. Writing as the war ended, she asked Canadian women to look about their kitchens for signs of class and gender inequalities. For her the reasoning about who should design and build tools for the home, and who should have them to use, was neither anonymous nor justifiable. 'If industrialisation has reached the farm, why has it not reached the kitchen? If it has reached the factory, why has it not reached the home?'[30] She noted that women had entered war industries in the hundreds of thousands. They had found that they could learn mechanical work easily, and that they liked it. They had helped create aeroplanes and ships, and lay new foundations for Canada as an industrialized country. They had entered the services and risen through the ranks. Yet they were about to be asked to leave these industrial skills and managerial competencies behind and re-turn to what? The prospect was too bleak to countenance.

The modern kitchen Jamieson offered her readers seems ordinary in most respects now. But in 1945 when more than 80 per cent of Canadian households did not own refrigerators, and most of the washers and ranges they were using dated from the late twenties and early thirties,[31] her portrait presented an extraordinary departure. Even for regular readers of Cooperative Commonwealth Federation pamphlets, which from the mid-1930s had depicted all future Canadian homes equipped with the electrical appliances which would set women free to enjoy life more, Jamieson's modern kitchen must have astonished.

Soft lighting illuminates every part of the kitchen needing it. Air conditioning not only keeps the kitchen at an even temperature but carries off all odors. The electric stove has a waist-high oven to save stooping, and has all modern devices. There is a quick freezing unit and storage for fruits and vegetables desirable in fresh form; a dehydrating unit for vegetables best used in that form; and a quick canner. There is a compression cooker, electric mixer, juicer, toaster, waffle iron, etc.; and, of course, an electric dishwasher. Off the kitchen is the laundry, with electric washer, drier with infra-red rays, electric mangle and iron.[32]

All this, she observed, was already possible in the parts of the United States where the New Deal Tennessee Valley Authority had made power and appliances cheap and accessible. Canada had inexpensive, publicly pro-duced power, but household equipment was made by a small number of private firms who sold at high prices. A solution was readily to hand, she suggested. War plants could be converted to publicly owned factories where men and women together could use their skills to make inexpensive domestic appliances 'for the benefit of the people.'[33]

CCF campaign literature late in the war took well-equipped homes for all citizens as an immediate objective and argued that wartime production capacities readily could be turned to peacetime uses. These campaigns borrowed the Swedish social democratic emphasis on civic values which followed from an everyday domestic life amidst beautiful things. As William Irving argued in 'Scarcity or Abundance' in 1944, 'a properly based society in Canada could guarantee a home for every family. That home would be wholesome, comfortable and beautiful; a place to seek and find inspiration and hope; homes in very truth in which the surroundings were clean, bright, cheerful and healthy, and in which a taste for beautiful things might be born and developed in those who inhabit them.'

Looking back, it is not so much Jamieson's long list of tools which astonishes, as her assumptions about women's entitlements as productive workers. Her model kitchen was not a place where goods, bought and paid for, displayed social standing, or where distant manufacturers defined household work as what their products would do. Some women would remain in manufacturing industry. But industrialization would not displace homemakers as producers. Better utilities and equipment would vitalize rather than diminish their productive work in the home.

'Women dry those tears,' she urged, and demand both waged and domestic workplaces where you will be productively employed and have control over your labour. If the cook's work is easier when ovens are high, manufacturers should not built them low. If householders knew that some foods were better preserved dried, some better frozen, others canned, then domestic technologies should be available to respect rather than deny these qualitative distinctions. In Jamieson's model, homemakers were authoritative producers, and domestic technologies were to serve them on their terms.

In the United States, the New Deal vision, made material in parts of the Tennessee Valley, was fading. For its apostles, the Office of Price Administration had been the last outpost. In Canada in certain months of 1943, when CCF popular support was strong, Jamieson might have represented the mainstream. But after the war, the foremost concern would be for security and stability. Valuing and capitalizing household production were fundamentally political issues, but were priorities in postwar Canada acted upon more consistently in the household than at the ballot box.

Wartime rethinking had cast domestic goods in a new light. Officially for the duration, household equipment was to be appraised for what it would do rather than what it would display. Access to new equipment was to be determined on the basis of need rather than demand. So long as these were to be tools for use rather than commodities for sale, their representations of stylishness and their histories in trade were deflections and distortions from what they most ought to be. The value of domestic production was recognized even though it remained without price.

After the war the boundaries between the household and the economy, between goods made for use and goods made for sale, would be re-established. But the transition was not smooth. The succession was not quick. The reasoning of wartime drew on experiences of scarcity and of life outside the market which preceded the war. For at least fifteen years before 1945, most Canadians had had to consider their spending closely

Laura Jamieson's 1945 proposal for the CCF Women's Council of British Columbia showed women's interwar working conditions on the cover. Inside were plans
for a new domestic order with modern housing forms, and multiple labour-saving
devices run by cheap hydro power and made in converted war plants – a plan that
at the war's end the industrial revolution would arrive in Canadian homes.

and temper temptations of style which did not translate into function. They had become accustomed to thinking of technologies as alternatives rather than absolutes. Their household production had been prodigious. They were skilled and seasoned at making do. Whatever the pleasures of dreaming about plenty, this thinking would continue to mark Canadian householders and their goods for some time. The next chapters consider how these values informed public exhibitions, public policy, and associational life. Parts 2 and 3 are excursions into less conventional political terrain, in search of the influence of this politics on the private firms and private households as they, each in their own ways, shaped the material world of domestic goods.

2

Envisioning a Modern Domesticity

In 1945 and 1946, museums and art galleries, rather than houses and stores, were the places people went to look at household furniture and appliances.[1] As the war ended and the peace began, tens of thousands travelled to unfamiliar parts of town, climbed unwelcoming flights of steps, and passed inscrutably ornamented entrances, for the chance to see stoves and chairs, flatware and pots they did not have at home and could not find for sale. The galleries promised to show them contemporary items, not one-of-a-kind works of art but things made in multiples, things a family could put to use. These would be mundane domestic goods a decade later, sooner than that in the United States, but in the mid-forties they were rare. Their inaccessibility made them exciting.

In 1945 household goods were still the stuff of dreams, imaginable in as many different forms as there were dreamers. How these things would look, what they would do, how they would be made, were not so resolved as to make them ordinary. Attending such exhibitions was an adventure, an invitation to look critically at the shape of things, and the political economy which would make them.

In 1945 and 1946, excitement was not difficult to elicit from visitors, even toward goods so everyday as to commonly escape comment. People were accustomed to making for themselves, and making do. Buying goods off the shelf ready-made to someone else's specifications lately had been nearly impossible. The Depression and the war had disrupted habits and encouraged self-reliance and innovation. Household production had been part of the war effort, and household spending promised to save the nation from a postwar recession. The appraisal of household goods in the mid-1940s was less individuated and more contingent than it would become subsequently. The form of things was not just a matter of what retailers offered for sale. At the time, they offered little. Both public signs and private circumstances underlined how much the shape of things was about politics, civic values, and choices in the political economy.

Two Toronto exhibitions, *Design in Industry* which ran at the Royal Ontario Museum through the spring of 1945 and *Design in the Household* at the Toronto Art Gallery through the early winter of 1946, asked visitors to reconsider what household furnishings and equipment should be like in the context of plans to rebuild the nation's industry. Each was a polemic for a particular industrial strategy. By the disjunction between what was being displayed and where and how it was being displayed, these exhibitions unsettled viewers' conventional ways of seeing the distinctions between objects of art, commodities for sale, and tools for use. Both shows were designed to soothe longings too long deferred for household goods but also to make usefully problematic the associations between the appearance of things and the way they would be made.

What prospective purchasers saw when they looked at goods both shaped and reflected power relations in the material world. Depending on whether they focused on style, provenance, or materials, on how the thing was made or how it could be made useful, those who looked found opportunities, banalities, constraints, or obligations. What was seen and what was overlooked, what was made conscious about looking at things and what remained unconscious, influenced whose interest those things would serve.

The gallery display of housewares of modern design was common in Europe or North America during the war. Indeed, it reclaimed, after an interval of deliberate inattention, one of the founding goals for nineteenth-century museums. For example, the Royal Ontario Museum had its origins in the Canadian Institute, established in 1849 as a society 'for the encouragement and general advancement of the Physical Sciences, the Arts and Manufactures.' The Victoria and Albert Museum in London, England, was established to extend 'appreciation of the constituents of good design' in the industrial arts after the 1851 Great Exhibition, when British industrial goods had been compared unfavourably with wares from abroad. Similarly in New York in 1870, founders hoped the collections of the Metropolitan Museum of Art would encourage the 'application of arts to manufactures and practical life,' and raise the standards of retail goods by example.

In Britain and North America, late-nineteenth-century business people and industrialists with practical goals came to museum boards as trustees. They were interested in economic development and earnings. They saw, from European examples, that good design could help persuade buyers at home to reject imports, and buyers overseas to turn to new sources of supply. As the museums' fundraisers, trustees were competing with other worthy causes for the contributions of their fellow philanthropists. As nation-building manufacturers, they were seeking a wide constituency for their own dreams. Trustees wanted museums to be popular institutions filled with streams of visitors carrying lessons away.

But through the first decades of the twentieth century on both sides of the Atlantic, museums turned inward toward connoisseurship and the care of their accumulated collections, growing away from both their citizen-visitors and the pragmatic engagement with industry their charters had prescribed. At the Royal Ontario Museum in these years, the most visited collections were in the natural history department, used by professors teaching students from the University of Toronto next door. Metropolitan art galleries loomed like temples, their architectural conventions befitting their function as final resting place for their patrons' privately amassed collections. As shapers of public taste and arbiters of the new, museums in the interwar period lost precedence to department stores, fairs, and expositions where the commercial intentions of display were explicit and celebrated.[2]

Both the war and the plans for reconstruction shocked museums back into pragmatic present- and future-mindedness. There were once again urgent and explicit nation-building purposes for these fustian and ruminating institutions to address. Weary citizens needed optimistic dreamscapes to console them. In a period of life amidst the ruins, modern industrial design of ordinary useful things was a promising teleology, a way of organizing resources to build a different and better world for the future. This contemporary context gave plausibility, even effervescence, to an ideology of form-giving which lately had seemed abstruse, elitist, and alien. Here were issues about materiality, about ordering, interpreting, and appraising material life, about using objects to represent the essence and immanence of the people and their nation. All about the North Atlantic, trustees and curators warmed to the task.

The ROM *Design in Industry* exhibition argued that Canadian secondary manufacturing after the war should specialize in small-scale production of high-quality goods governed by the design ethos of the crafts. This is how these premises were presented to visitors in May and June 1945:

The greatness of a country does not depend upon the extent of its natural resources but upon its capacity to make effective use of them. Canada is a large country with a small and scattered population. Its industries cannot in consequence hope to prosper greatly by mass production. Its natural resources must be exported raw or primarily processed for others to finish or it must develop high quality but small quantity manufactures capable of competing in design, in workmanship and in material with those of other countries.

The exhibit was to show what Canadian domestic goods would look like if the nation were to specialize in small-scale high-value-added manufactures and resource exports. By this plan, in a postwar reconstruction characterized by freer multilateral trade, mass-produced goods would be imported from foreign makers with larger domestic markets. Mass production and mass consumption would be led from outside the country. Canadian-made consumer goods would compete on quality and workmanship rather than novelty and price. *Design in Industry* made displays of raw materials and household goods into representations of the nation's spiritual wealth and collective purpose and asked visitors to reinvent themselves as modern citizens within this frame.[3]

The idea was not entirely new. Revitalized rural craft production for sale in urban and export markets had been part of regional development programs in Quebec and the Maritimes through the interwar years, and of private women-led charitable enterprises based in Montreal since the early twentieth century.[4] During the war, the crafts had been encouraged to substitute for scarce factory-made goods. A material culture using indigenous resources and talents seemed one way to articulate a national interest transcending 'social, economic, political, religious or racial differences.'[5] Similarly, in wartime the Foreign Exchange Control Board sent investigators searching for crafts-made products of sufficient quality for export or to draw tourists across the American border. Reluctantly they determined in 1940 that craft production in Canada lacked sufficient style, design, and marketing organization to 'command respect and purchasing power' internationally.[6]

Still there were hopeful international demonstrations that craft knowledge could contribute to national economic development. In Europe since the late nineteenth century, the craft worker's attentiveness to materials, and through materials to form, had been assumed and anticipated as a resource for industry. Svenska Slojdforeningen in Sweden and the Wiener Werkstatte in Austria nourished successful decorative arts industries producing high-quality goods in short series for export. In Canada, the wartime president of the Canadian Handicrafts Guild, J. Murray Gibbon, an Oxford student in the heyday of the English Arts and Crafts movement, noted that the Royal Canadian Academy had begun in 1882 with an interest in art as applied to industry. Gibbon argued for 'a rapprochement between the fine arts and the crafts in Canada' to stimulate product development. Given the small size of the market and the ample local supplies of fine woods, leathers, and metals, these European precedents had a certain plausibility for consumer goods industries in Canada which U.S. models of mass production lacked.[7]

Younger Canadian modernists, such as the architect Humphrey Carver, saw the English Arts and Crafts example as a feminizing error, a design doctrine about workshop production which too soon isolated 'itself from the vigorous real world' and 'declined into a reactionary and sentimental spinsterhood.' But, Carver argued, holding fast to his gendered imagery, in 'the postwar reorganization' there could be a 'virile' role for the crafts in the new industrial civilization. In American initiatives under the Works Progress Administration and in urban planning, he saw hopeful alternatives. In Sweden industrial designers continued (and still continue) to be crafts workers through their working lives, using the knowledge refined in the workshop to guide production in the factory next door. In Canada, Carver suggested, the best students from art and technical schools could learn from experience designing for handicraft workers, and 'graduate into the more responsible positions as designers for industry.' 'Industry has done its worst in heaping upon us ugliness and war,' he acknowledged, but through 'handicrafts, designers and industry [could] advance hand in hand in a new creative tradition.' Thus might ethical and design values be linked in the postwar.[8]

The T. Eaton Company, with the Canadian Handicrafts Guild sponsors of the *Design in Industry* exhibition at the ROM, was interested in handicrafts as commodities for sale. From the early 1930s, Eaton's provided the guild with space for a shop in its College Street store in Toronto. O.D. Vaughan, a senior member of the firm, bought European art wares for Eaton's inventory through the interwar years, hoping by example to educate Canadian tastes to Scandinavian and French design standards.[9] In addition to the guild shop, Eaton's made room on its sales floors for craft exhibitions. It sponsored lectures on the history of modern design and low-cost furniture by guild members who were architects. In the early forties Eaton's mixed retailing with design and citizenship education, featuring displays of wartime housing and examples of how to equip a 'Home-in-one-room.' Craft design influences show in the low-cost furniture the company planned to commission from Canadian factories after the war.[10]

The *Design in Industry* exhibition presented in the Armour Court of the

Royal Ontario Museum in May and June 1945 spoke in a voice both clear and conflicted about the interests the crafts guild, the museum, and the retailer shared. The exhibition itself was an argument among the museum curators, the Handicrafts Guild executive, and representatives from the store, about whose expertise should organize how the household goods were offered for view. The curators were accustomed to wielding the authority to explain objects in their care, and to deciding how this knowledge would be edited and articulated for the visiting public. Curators expected that objects to be made fit for museum display must be sacralized – made priceless, above trade, deliberately cleansed of their associations with the commodity market. This was so commonly the intention of museum display that most visitors to a museum expected to see goods remade by this 'museum effect.'

But in many North American museums, trustees had an independent sense of their own interpretive competence and of the appropriate lessons the public ought to learn from the museum's displays. At the ROM in the mid-1940s, trustees and department directors were vying for executive control over the museum. The curators tried through a 1946 motion to limit the trustees' interventions in day-to-day operations. The board scotched the prospect of curatorial autonomy with a 1947 amendment to the museum act, which put the board firmly in control. The 'Design in Industry' exhibition was mounted amidst these heightening tensions.[11]

The dominant trustee in the planning group for *Design in Industry* was Nora Vaughan, graduate student in art and architecture after an honours BA in mathematics at the University of Toronto, and wife of Eaton's O.D. Vaughan, who was a member of the university's board of governors. Nora Vaughan was a serious student of modernism, but she also was well informed about the conventions of retail display. She was frequently in New York where many high-end department stores successfully had been mounting shows of modern crafts and industrial design since the late twenties. She enjoyed buying things, and seeing things for sale. Unlike the curators, she saw the *Design in Industry* exhibition as a way to address concerns about reconstruction using retailers' knowledge about selling.[12]

Whatever their epistemological differences, Vaughan and the curators agreed that the exhibition had a single pedagogical purpose, to convince visitors that Canada's manufacturing future lay with small-quantity, high-quality production for domestic use and export. Their physical plan was unambiguous. They designed the show to fit in the Armour Court of the museum, a long high hall extending from the grand rotunda at the entrance along the width of the building to the west wing, where a large window created a grand illuminated end to the visitor's progress. The location invited an axial composition, urging the visitor along one route from object to object, to a single physical and interpretive conclusion. In the uncertainty between war and peace of the spring of 1945, this space offered potential for a clear storyline, a predictable cadence, and a foreseeable resolution. A series of clusters in sequence along the hall presented materials – leather, wood, glass, silver, and fibres – first unprocessed, then in historical examples from the museum's collections, and finally as they had been used by contemporary designer-crafts people. These displays were intended to illustrate the natural wealth of the nation and the relevance of the museum's collections for a particular path of industrial development. The short accompanying captions emphasized that the crafts worker's knowledge of materials was essential if goods were to be both beautiful and useful. During the age of mechanical reproduction, these texts argued, only the crafts could reclaim 'the relationship of material and form, method of manufacture and use' which industrially made goods ideally required.[13]

The museum curators were not pleased with the results. They were repelled by the way the exhibit blurred the boundaries between retail and museum display, a conflation which had grown common in the great interwar international expositions of industrial design.[14] In their view, looking at things in a museum should not be like looking at things in a shop. 'A good museum show,' they argued, 'must be on a sound scientific basis,' 'with proper continuity and proper explanation,' not mounted in hurried confusion but thoughtfully selected to adhere to a stated interpretation. 'The Design in Industry exhibition had an excellent and timely theme,' they acknowledged, 'good design for objects of everyday use made by machinery,' but many of our visitors must have been completely ignorant of the purpose of the show, thinking only that it was an attractive display of articles, which if they could afford, they might buy for their own use.' Shoppers might be bewitched by goods on attractive display, but a museum participating in the nation-building purposes of reconstruction, they argued, was obliged 'to show how good design grows out of a proper use of material, and a proper respect for the technical limitations of various methods of manufacture.' *Design in Industry*, in their view, embraced the corrupting commodity culture of commerce and thus abrogated the museum's obligation to instruct. It had nothing 'really concrete or constructive to give the person who came seeking knowledge and information whether he was consumer, student, designer or manufacturer.' Rather, the exhibition participated in the modern sellers' convention, presenting the object only as an enticement for the eye, deflecting questions about 'under what conditions it was produced, or whether the design [was] the result of technical limitations, tradition or national taste.' The museum staff noted that only under pressure from visitors, attentive, as the war ended, to national distinctions, were labels stating country of provenance added belatedly to some display cases. To the end of the show, the curators lamented, the innovative glass furniture was left uninterpreted, and was 'simply dismissed' by viewers as an 'exotic and impractical joke.' The 'revolutionary effect on furniture design' of wartime innovations in plywood bending was also left undocumented in display and thus inscrutable to visitors.[15]

But the public came in droves. The museum had ten thousand more visitors during May and June 1945 than in the same months the year before.

The business press was not troubled that the things on display in the museum looked like things for sale. Far from being inscrutable, they reported, the exhibition's message about economic development had come through loud and clear. Wellington Jeffers, financial editor of the *Globe and Mail*, compared the show to the Great Exhibition at the Crystal Palace a century before, when 'far-seeing Britons' had, he claimed, laid the foundations for 'progress and prosperity' based on export trade. Jeffers welcomed the considerable representation of European and American design in the exhibit, hoping for greater international influence of Canadian design and production. The *Board of Trade Journal* echoed the same theme, that if Canada was to be known in future for more than 'maple sugar, wheat and apples,' it must follow the example of those smaller European countries, also late to industrialization, who had found 'mass production ... less important than quality production.'[16]

By contrast, Donald Buchanan, who was with the National Film Board but would soon become chair of the National Industrial Design Committee (latter the National Industrial Design Council), was scathing in his commentary. Buchanan was appalled by what comparison with European and American work in the show revealed about 'the adolescent stage' at which Canadian production remained, 'heavy handed and lacking in both lightness and grace.' 'Do our cabinet makers really believe that stolidity is a virtue?' he inquired, providing what he thought were grim photographic illustrations to demonstrate his point. For Buchanan, the exhibition was misnamed, its premises wrong headed. A show about domestic articles and furnishings could not address the broader questions of art and industry. The future of Canadian industry did not lie in the 'encouragement of very minor crafts.' Where, he asked, were the 'aluminium sheets and magnesium rods, plywood and laminated wood, chemical plastics and cellulose compounds,' the 'new techniques of design' Canadian manufacturers had developed for use in war 'that can be applied in peace as well'? 'Functional utility and grace' were to be found in the 'admirable' materials research of Canadian scientists. Those looking for the way forward, he insisted, should be visiting the laboratories of the National Research Council rather than attempting to learn at the ROM from the 'grotesque root of an Albertan tree, carved into a shape vaguely female in contour, ... proudly displayed in a glass case as a sample of modern Canadian design!'[17]

The *Design in Industry* exhibit had been absolutely plain about the conclusion visitors should reach. Craft was key to the future of design in Canadian industry. But it must have been difficult for visitors to grasp the imputed associations between an internationally appealing look, the use of indigenous materials, and the importance of craft knowledge. The show had been assembled in haste, as craft shows usually were. There were no labels in the exhibit, as there were usually no labels in retail shops. The exhibition was in the museum, bound by the venerating aura of the place, but the objects in view were not interpreted according to curatorial conventions. There was no consistent direction to guide the eye of the visitor reading the goods. The ten thousand patrons, potential shoppers, critics, and voters, had a chance to look at new household goods at a time when there were few elsewhere to see. They came just looking, for just looking had been a pleasure long denied. But except for the protest that the displays did not disclose national origin, they revealed little about what they thought, or whether the exhibition had altered their ways of seeing.

At the museum, politics and time limitations had impaired effective planning, a common dilemma for those in 1945 looking past the end of the war. If the future of Canadian manufacturing did lie in small-scale production influenced by the skills and sensibilities of the crafts, *Design in Industry* had failed to make the case.

But both householders and manufacturers remained eager to dream in public about what would come next. And so, six months later, and a few blocks away, the Toronto Art Gallery (TAG) launched another show of domestic goods. The *Design in the Household* exhibition was initiated by C.S. Band, a gallery board member and Toronto industrialist. Band was not a craftsman or a retailer. As a plastics manufacturer interested in the plastic arts, he wanted to see 'an exhibition that would promote industry.' As a gallery trustee he argued for a show which would inspire corporate donors and their employees and thus aid the current gallery fundraising campaign.[18] Both the Canadian Manufacturers' Association (CMA) and the Toronto Board of Trade offered to support a gallery show about plans for reconstruction and Canadian-made goods by loaning objects and providing publicity. Gallery curator Martin Baldwin, an architect with interests in modernism, aided by Barbara Swann as research assistant, took up the idea in the summer of 1945. Knowing her interests from the shows of modern architectural drawings he had mounted at the gallery in the thirties, Baldwin asked Nora Vaughan to join them.

From the start the CMA influence on *Design in the Household* was clear. The curatorial team set out to find mass-produced goods which were then, or soon to be, available in Canadian cities. These were goods Canadian manufacturers would make for Canadian buyers, and later sell in overseas markets. Whereas the ROM exhibition had argued that under free trade in the postwar, Canada should specialize in the export of raw materials and limited volumes of high-quality manufacturers, while importing mass-produced goods from lower cost makers abroad, the TAG exhibit proclaimed the opposite. 'Her cheap power, her mines and her wealth of raw materials' made 'Canada ideal for quantity production,' and thus had she 'become one of the great manufacturing nations of the world.'

The target visitor for *Design in the Household* was an ordinary citizen seeking low-cost industrially made goods for homes costing less than $8000. The exhibition had two educative purposes: to interest 'a merchandise hungry public' in the design of household articles they soon would be purchasing; and 'by some means' (just how, in the early stages, was not clear), to have that public reveal their attitudes toward modern household goods to the curators and, more importantly, to manufacturers. The exhibit was to refine the sight of both householders and manufacturers, to heighten their capacity to discriminate between goods, and thus raise product standards. Perhaps because the ROM show had yielded so little of apparent use to the discussion about reconstruction, Baldwin, Vaughan, and Swann took their brief from the manufacturers to promote industry as a request for critical engagement rather than agreement. For these public purposes, they set out to find out what the public thought about the objects they chose for display. Perhaps householders could help Canadian industrialists capture world markets through better design. Perhaps visitors as much as curators could be authorities on the objects in view.

This was not to be an ordinary art gallery exhibition. And not all the gallery curators were happy with the prospect. Early on, some of Baldwin's colleagues protested the planned emphasis on the changing social context of design, and the ceding of interpretive voice from curator to visitor. In a memo filled with exclamation marks and bold underlining, one gallery staff member argued that '*the aesthetic criterion should be the only determinative,*' and warned of the 'danger of making the exhibition drift into industrial history *per se.*'[19]

For historically, art galleries, like museums, had functioned as secular temples, places where visitors came to contemplate and absorb an orthodoxy. British industrial design exhibits in the forties followed this mode. *Britain Can Make It,* an exhibition which opened hopeful if ironical at the Victoria and Albert Museum in the fall of 1946, included a design quiz. This quiz was designed to teach rather than inquire. With contrasting examples of household goods, overstuffed chairs beside sleek boxy forms, ornamented lamps beside plain, this quiz pointedly prompted visitors to choose between Bad and Good. Later in the decade, Donald Buchanan used the same technique in exhibition publicity for the Canadian National Industrial Design Committee. By intention these questionnaires departed little from the normative stance of the art gallery as temple. They asked questions, but they were intended to work as catechisms, invoking a prescribed response.[20]

At the Toronto Art Gallery, by contrast and over their colleagues' protest, Baldwin, Vaughan, and Swann had decided to inquire. They designed their exhibit to make visitors conscious of how they reasoned about familiar things, and then asked them to record their thoughts. Thus began a striking experiment in exhibition design.

Four decades later, such a move to reconceptualize the art gallery as forum rather than a temple[21] brought international celebrity to the Toronto gallery, by then renamed the Art Gallery of Ontario (AGO). In the 1980s Douglas Worts, a distant successor to Martin Baldwin, invited the public to post their interpretations of the Canadian Historical collection beside the paintings on the gallery walls. Worts saw this request for visitor reactions, unmediated by curatorial authority, as a way to break down the hierarchies of knowledge which separated the gallery and its collections from 'living culture.'[22] By the 1990s, the claim that an exhibition's form of address should be 'interrogative, inviting response and dialogue' was made frequently in international museum circles. This was part of an argument that citizens, as museum visitors, should be active producers rather than passive consumers of meaning. Thus, the works on view should be treated as products of visible, knowable processes rather than as objects for veneration by believers.[23] In the 1980s and 1990s, a postmodern politics of difference supported these changes, which seemed to be innovations, in museum practice. Significantly, at the TAG/AGO, these practices had not been untried, they were only unremembered in the 1980s.

Four decades earlier, in the forties, modern designers too had believed that objects should be appraised in terms of the materials and the means of their making. As design reformers, they were obliged to acknowledge that the shape of things was revisable, not inevitable but contingent, the recognizable product of conscious decision-making. Certainly modern designers could be rigidly didactic. But in other contexts the modernist voice was more democratic, listening for popular responses in order to interpret the functional needs of users in a paradigmatic best form. Modernists, like postmodernists, were listening, but the modernists' purpose was to refine a single enduring design solution, rather than to honour an evolving postmodern heterogeneity.

At least polemically, modern industrial designers took function as a determinant of form. Making educated choices among objects, whether as a maker or as a purchaser, required knowledge about the processes of use and manufacture, and an understanding of what made materials fitting for both. Those with a pragmatic and commercial orientation, among them Baldwin, Vaughan, and Swann, saw this need for knowledge as an opening for a project of mutual education. Users needed to learn about materials and making; makers needed to learn about users and the uses to which their products would be put. Thus, in one construction, modern design was a dialogue between makers and users reasoning toward a common goal, part of the more equitable civic culture many hoped would be a legacy of the war.

Baldwin, Vaughan, and Swann designed an exhibition to stimulate such a dialogue, mindful that in 1946 Canadians as both citizens and industrial producers were existing in conditions of considerable uncertainty. The way ahead was unclear. Wartime industry would have to be reinvented for the peace. Goods in current production would not serve as prototypes for the future. The task was to stimulate rethinking, to make space for reflection about the future of the economy and the domestic world of goods.

In an exhibition, this goal called not for a strong axial structure, such as had been employed at the ROM, but for display spaces with a considerable ring factor, which allowed visitors to circle back and reconsider, to rework their responses as they collected further information.

The first gallery for the *Design in the Household* exhibition was a large open octagonal space. A four-sided free-standing column in the centre of the hall, about the same height as the display panels on the walls beyond, stated for visitors from the outset in bold lettering the purposes for each room. Wings projecting from the other three sides of this post drew the eye along the multiple sightlines accessible from the entrance way. The panels beyond, about raw materials, industrial facilities, and trade skills, spoke back and forth across the wide angles of the gallery about Canada's multiple potentials for mass production.

From this room opened two other galleries. One introduced visitors to modern design principles through panels Vaughan had borrowed from her associate, Eliot Noyes at the Museum of Modern Art in New York. Below quotations from Socrates and Santayana, modernist design practice was portrayed as a search within the unvarying limitations of use, material, and method of manufacture for timeless forms. The designer would rescue mass production from its potential to debase materials, commodities, and their users. The curators presented this search as urgent within the contemporary political economy, for 'Knowledge of these is essential if we are to take proper advantage of the resources at our disposal.' This room made the case for modern industrial design from the designer's perspective.[24]

The other room off the large central court included examples of household goods, grouped in categories by use, and asked visitors to instruct designers and manufacturers. Goods currently available for sale were displayed, attractively, rather as they might have been displayed in stores, following advice from a retail merchandising display department, but with labels noting their source, designer or maker, and price range. Questionnaires by the displays asked for comment, informed by the lessons learned from Rooms 1 and 2, on the quality of the designs and their practical limitations.[25]

This is how the curatorial goals for this part of the exhibit were described by Humphrey Carver to H.O. McCurry, director of the National Gallery:

The point of view with which all this material is to be presented is: 'Here is a collection of furniture. Some may be good and some not so good. What do YOU like? Please write your opinions on the slips of paper provided.' In this way a kind of public opinion survey will be obtained; it is thought that this will be valuable to manufacturers and merchandisers. This method of presentation evades the whole difficulty of setting a standard and only exhibiting what seems to fulfil faithfully the principles enunciated in the other gallery.[26]

Carver himself may not have been averse to setting a standard or persuading visitors to modernist principles, but in his view there were few well-

This column introduced visitors to the purposes of the *Design in the Household* exhibition and welcomed them to make their own zig-zagging path among the parts of the display, cross-checking the information they had gathered. The column wings initiated the multiple sight-lines which encouraged this way of looking at the exhibit. The purposes of Room 1 were 'To show that our natural resources plus the possibilities of the machine make possible mass production that should lead to right equipment for living.'

The purpose of Room 2 was 'To describe and illustrate the essential elements of design in useful objects.' The room articulated the modernist association of materials, form, and function using didactic panels borrowed from the Museum of Modern Art in New York. Here, on opening night, gallery patrons Mr and Mrs Hugh Allen examine the displayed argument that new materials should remake the forms of commodities.

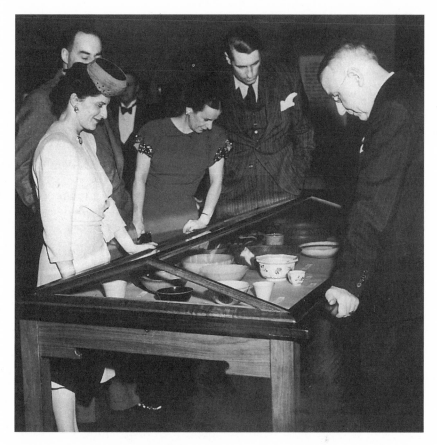

Fine ceramics were displayed in closed cases, as they would have been in an up-scale retailer.

designed Canadian-made goods to display. Thus the need to make teaching tools rather than models of the objects to hand. 'In other words, the Exhibition states principles and invites their application, but does not presume to proclaim that any existing or available furniture fulfils the requirements of good design. Under the circumstances I think this approach is a sound and reasonable one and will succeed in not being too didactic.'

The objects on view in this room had been chosen by Tillie Cowan of the gallery staff, two volunteers, and Carver, who was then preparing an exhibit also called *Design in Industry* for the National Film Board and the National Gallery. They had vetted the products of thirty-one Canadian manufacturers and chosen work from twenty-one, but, unimpressed by either the quantity or quality available, they then supplemented their choices with a thousand dollars worth of housewares from Eaton's and eight pieces of Scandinavian modern furniture from Artek in New York. Carver's concern was about the limitations of Canadian designs, not with possible shortcomings in modernist industrial design principles.[27] But the gallery curators issued a more general invitation for comment in their questionnaires, and visitors, in their responses, launched upon critiques of both principles and objects.

Because in Room 3 the curators wanted to override the museum effect, they used retail conventions in the displays. Plain housewares sat on open tables, pleated drapery samples hung side by side, the best china was showcased in a closed case, all as they would have been in retail display. Living room furniture was positioned in room settings, a Kroehler sectional chesterfield and chair and Eaton's bookcase components circumscribing a corner. Appliances were lined up, like models with like, along the gallery walls, as they would have appeared in a showroom.

These commercial signals disrupted the habits of seeing which a gallery seemed to require. Convention directed visitors to look at all objects on display as if they were art objects, whose interest was primarily visual: being in a gallery prompted viewers to appraise the things before them on aesthetic rather than utilitarian grounds.[28] But the curators who had provided paper, pencils, and writing surfaces on which to prepare critiques, wanted more than commentaries on beauty to transmit from householders to manufacturers. Thus they adopted artifices of display borrowed from commerce. Suggesting that the visitor might as well be in a shop worked against the schooled habits of the gallery spectator. Here the goal was to capture the critical attention of visitors as shoppers, with price tags, brand names, and familiar retail display conventions. For in stores, unlike galleries, people expected to be at liberty to choose for themselves and according to their own lights.

The dilemma was that retail, like museum, display gave precedence to visual effects. Visitors, asked to think of themselves as shoppers, needed to be invited also to respond as deliberating users. To this end, photos of women doing the wash and cooking, actually using the domestic appliances as tools, were positioned on the walls above the washing machines and the ranges, in spaces where banners bearing brand names would have been in a dealer's display. These photographs of women engaged in

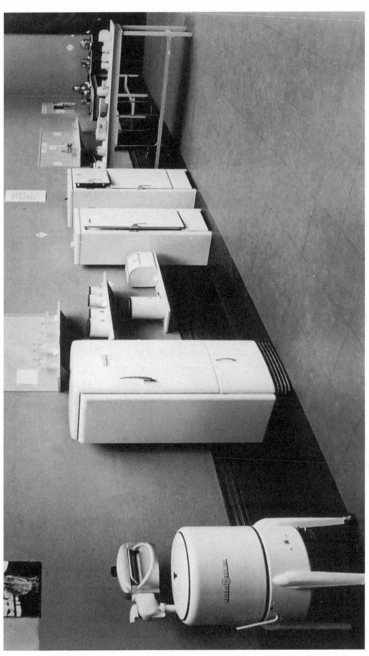

To encourage gallery visitors to feel free to make judgments about the objects on display, the last three rooms mimicked retail conventions. Here iceboxes, a refrigerator, and a washing machine are lined up against a wall, as they would have been in a store, with less expensive household goods accessible on tables to be handled.

domestic work prompted visitors to think of themselves working with the domestic appliances on display. Similarly unsettling of habits of seeing was the row of masterworks from the TAG collection hung above the living room grouping of furniture. These paintings continued by gallery convention on the gallery wall, just as they had before the furniture was moved in, entirely without reference to the new spatial definitions the placement of the household goods suggested. The juxtaposition marked a contrast between what could be enjoyed visually but not taken home, and what would be worth taking home only if it could offer more than visual effect. In the space thus inflected, visitors were asked to speak their minds.[29]

Sixteen thousand people attended the exhibition, and as the curators had hoped, they responded with alacrity – most vigorously to Room 3. Women protested that the gleaming level-topped modern ranges, replacing interwar high-oven stoves, required a person to bend over to attend to baking in the oven. The sectional living room seating, designed to provide flexibility because its parts could be separated and rearranged to fit rooms of different sizes, visitors read as wayward rather than adaptable, unless some method could be found to secure the sections in the chosen conformation.

Retail display liberated gallery visitors to speak their own minds, and was disruptible with visual reminders that exhibition in a store or a gallery was not like use at home. Yet it carried another limitation in its conventions of spectatorship, one that foiled the intentions of curators of modernist convictions. Commercial display separated objects for sale from the means of their making, occluding the processes of production the curators wanted disclosed and appraised. At the TAG, as at the ROM, the public paid little attention to the wartime breakthroughs in product engineering which industrialists and government hoped would drive growth in Canadian manufacturing after the war.

Visitors, following merchandising cues and habits, focused on form. When they appraised function, they read the objects in terms of other household objects they knew. Neither as shoppers nor householders did their visual lexicon encode form and function as a scrutible unity made in engineering. Thus the imported bedroom suite of stacked boxes of drawers mounted on legs made from bent laminated arcs, furniture whose form followed the capabilities of new production methods, was greeted sceptically. So were Dr H. Stykolt and W. Czerwinski's Canadian Wooden Aircraft Company plywood chairs and table, made using techniques practised in aircraft manufacture. The functional masses in these designs seemed to overwhelm their slight supporting members, which made visi-

Above the displays hung panels with photographs of women doing household work, and text questioning how the goods on display functioned as tools. Note that the woman in the display panel photograph has drawn a chair up to the oven door in order to avoid bending as she bastes. The woman visitor points an accusing finger at the low oven. Many questionnaire responses criticized the new stove form.

The Kroehler sectional living room furniture and T. Eaton Company bookcases were arranged in a corner of Room 5 to approximate a home setting, but the Group of Seven paintings hung above them respected gallery display conventions, leaving viewers unsettled about whether to use domestic, retail, or museum conventions in appraising the objects on display.

tors doubt their strength. Reassured by gallery staff about the engineering properties of bent wood, visitors faulted the furniture for its simplicity. Stykolt's plywood arm chair was much sat upon and tested, found comfortable, light, easy to move and clean – in sum practical. But like those European examples which inspired it – Alvar Aalto's Paimo chair for a Finnish sanitarium, or the Isokon short chair Marcel Breuer designed in 1936 for Jack Pritchard's London firm[30] – the chair lacked the visual signs of homeyness householders required. Curators sighed with frustration as their explanations of the creative synergy among material, process, function, and form were so readily dismissed, but then dutifully conveyed the public responses to the trade press.[31]

Both exhibits spoke, as their curators well knew, to dilemmas in the contemporary Canadian world of goods. What was available was in short supply and made by prewar production methods. In the rebuilding which must soon begin, domestic industry and domestic housing forms would need to change, and with them habits of decision making in both industry and the home. Wartime planning for both had been centralized, the abridgement of individual autonomy acceptable to entrepreneurs, workers, and householders so long as the emergency continued. But as the crisis promised to abate, the need for collective action remained, for rebuilding too would require both planning and deferral, and in 1946 the path to a prosperous peace was precarious and uncharted.

In the last months of the war and the first months of the peace, museum and art gallery exhibitions linked the alternative ways of seeing household goods to choices among processes of production and practices of consumption. Curators and trustees asked the public to look actively and critically at the new things they might soon bring into their homes. These things were at once objects of art, tools for use, and commodities for sale. Canada's future as an industrial nation was then prospective, more anticipated than resolved. After the long years of economic depression and war, it was possible to look at these domestic goods with a deliberating eye relatively distanced from conventions about consumption, and to see in their form reflections of power relations in the material world. Trustees, architects, manufacturers, and crafts workers saw the exhibitions as ways to demonstrate the implications of distinctive industrial strategies for the goods Canadians would make for their own use and for export. Curators hoped, variously, to educate or to interrogate public taste so as to direct and improve the quality of Canadian design and the future viability of indigenous manufacturing. Visitors came to these exhibits with a common predicament, that almost everything they might want to buy was not

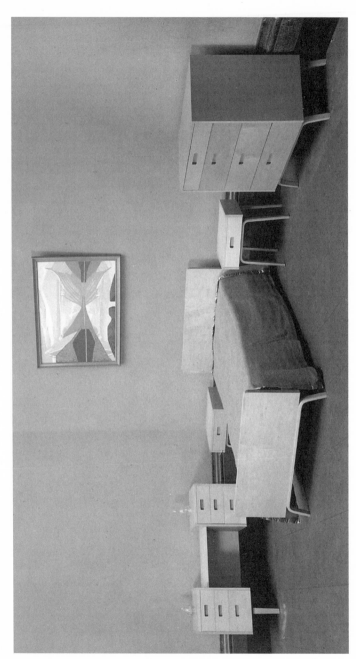

This Scandinavian bedroom suite borrowed from Artek in New York was chosen to show the domestic uses of wartime innovations in plywood bending. Visitors were unwilling to admire domestic goods for their production methods and criticized these pieces for their flimsy appearance, discounting the engineering argument about the strength of moulded wood forms.

available for sale. They arrived largely uninitiated to the aesthetics and practices of modern industrial design, and left disclosing little about what they had learned from Eliot Noyes and his colleagues at the Museum of Modern Art through the teaching panels Nora Vaughan had transported to Toronto from New York.

What did visitors reveal during their interlude in the museum and gallery about how they would choose goods for their homes? At the ROM, only that they wanted to know more than *Design in Industry* told them about where things were made, and which in particular were Canadian-made. At the TAG, as a result of a studied and carefully staged curatorial strategy, members of the public revealed rather more. Visitors' readings of the household goods on display emphasized functionality and familiarity. They filled out the gallery questionnaires by imagining the goods on display put to use inside their homes, and comparing what they regarded as new with what they thought to be proven. They obviously felt at liberty to make choices, as they would on a retail sales floor. But there is little evidence that the thousands who attended these exhibitions broke through the common retail barrier which separated how commodities for sale looked from how they were made. The implications for product design and materials of wartime technological innovations remained elusive, as did the qualitative differences between goods made in short series and those which were mass produced. Thus, curators noted, to their regret, that the crucial and powerful associations between the practices of consumption and the processes of production remained shrouded.

Goods made in short series, emphasizing functionality, workmanship, and materials would look different from goods made for mass production to compete on the basis of price, novelty, and style. Jocularly, and not entirely accurately, design historians invoke this as the distinction between design at Volvo and at General Motors in the postwar years. But in some ways it is true that the mid-forties presented North Atlantic nations with a forked road in the material culture of everyday life, from which the Europeans and the Americans for some decades followed different routes. The choices were not only about what to produce and how to produce it, but about who would have how much, how long things would last, what values would be built into goods, and whose interests the making and selling of those goods would serve. An easy and conventional first guess would be that in the culture of material life, Canadians took a middle path, between the American and the European. Getting to a useful estimation of what happened and why is going to take a little longer.

3

Gender, Keynes, and Reconstruction

Many domestic goods were not available in Canada for a long while after the war ended. This chapter attempts to explain why. Knowing why matters, for the lessons of this experience influenced how Canadian house-holders spent money and how, as citizens, they viewed spending. The focus here is on Keynesian macroeconomic policy, as it embodied and influenced expert and popular thinking about income redistribution, growth, and gender in the first decade after the war. The question here is not whether the best economic policy was implemented for the time and task to hand. Nor is the concern so much with the planners' explicit goals. Rather the focus is upon the unintended consequences of these policies, the costs planners were willing to trade for the benefits they sought. Were there longer term implications of these policies for Canadian household-ers and, by extension, for the economy generally?

This chapter re-examines the commonplace claim that Canadians rushed headlong into the culture of mass consumption soon after the war. That story follows the theories of consumerism of the Frankfurt School, and the American analyses of John Kenneth Galbraith and Vance Packard. The argument is that from the mid-forties the lust for things displaced other priorities. Citizens became acquisitive individuals, unmindful of collective concerns. In a Faustian bargain, consumers traded autonomy for excess without reckoning the political implications. Both Canadian survey texts and careful research studies present these conclusions borrowed from the American literature as if they arose indigenously. But compared with the United States, after the war there was a less lush and less practised com-modity culture to reclaim in Canada, and a much more chequered and lengthy route back.[1] Reasoning from analogy with American mass culture may be unwise here. Better to consider closely what kept people waiting longer for material comforts and pleasures. More than portraits of distant plenty, these values and constraints influenced the culture of consumption which Canadians lived.

But soon after the war came years of instability, the effect, first, of a foreign exchange crisis and then of new demands to rearm. At mid-war, forecasts about reconstruction had been wary recollections of the hard times after 1918.[2] Supply shortages and threats of inflation merged with recollections of unemployment. Keynesian macroeconomic theory, though everywhere still scarcely tried and little tested, gave hope that from these contending possibilities balanced economic growth might be forged. Keynes's Canadian students regarded the man himself with awe and, in arduous circumstances, struggled to make effective policy from the bold clarity of his theory.

At the end of the Second World War, shortages forced choices. Whose plans should be interrupted? Whose should be respected? And by what means? To distinguish among kinds of spending, Keynesian planners turned to direct interventions in the economy, circumventing the operations of the price system. Often, it becomes clear, their discriminations actually turned on technical assumptions about who could and could not be influenced. These, in turn, led to technocratic decisions about which policy levers would work with least turbulence and most direct effect. Systematically spending by government and primary industry was separated from spending by households and the firms which provisioned them. Effective demand was managed by technically distinguishing among those who spent. Thus, hierarchical gendered valuations about public purposes and private desires, and about producing and consuming, were imported into what was broadly called Keynesian postwar planning.

How household consumption came to lose out so consistently in the postwar triage among contending demands is a story not simply told, but worth telling. It is a tale in which characters experience different endings according to their gender and the source of their earnings. There are many twists and turns along the way. Household consumption, once to have been the salvation from postwar recession, was recast at the war's end as a prime threat to economic stability. Government incentives pushed other spending ahead at breakneck speed despite rising prices. Only in retrospect would it be possible even to guess whether the effects of spending called investment and spending called consumption were really so different as reasoning by gendered analogy made them. In the first decade after the war, more was believed than was known about the macroeconomic instruments in which so many hopes were entrusted.

As long as reconversion progressed slowly, or not at all, the peacetime economy retained the producer emphasis of wartime. The consumer goods industries could not make a running start in 1945, even though there were many households in need of basic equipment and with savings to spend. Most firms making industrial equipment and processing basic materials continued in similar work during the war, expanding and modernizing their lines. For the duration most plants manufacturing consumer goods had been retooled radically. Those which continued making household equipment had been prohibited by the 20 November 1940 regulation from producing new lines. By comparison with manufacturing generally, in the consumer goods sector both the way back to producing prewar models and the way forward to making new goods with new materials and new methods presented the most formidable physical and managerial challenges.[3]

Thus appliance sales strategies in the late 1940s were centrally about deferral, for dealers had few goods in stock. Customers were not shopping, but negotiating with retailers for places on waiting lists. Some dealers ran contests for the oldest irons and toasters brought into their stores, displaying these worn-out items in place of non-existent new goods.[4] Trade papers tried to make jokes about the predicament of retailers who had floor models to demonstrate but no inventory to sell. As the first year of waiting faded into the second, makers withdrew their advertisements for the new lines and urged patience. Even the small traffic appliances, waffle irons and sandwich toasters shown at fall fairs across the country in 1947, were not available and would not be available until 1948.[5] Still in 1949 and 1950, both Moffat and Westinghouse, without the metals to build many full-size ranges, tried to divert their 'appliance-hungry' dealers and customers with new stylings of the roaster-adaptable hotplates they had made during the war. For the fair season in 1948, Moffat built a giant mock-up of their diminutive 'handi-chef,' blown-up to almost the size of a regular range. The arrangement of the display mimicked the current supply situation, the 'handi-chef' out front and accessible to visitors, the large two-oven stove spot-lit but out of reach on a podium behind.[6]

The implications were dark on the supply and the demand side. Advocates of free enterprise were embattled. Already in 1943 L.L. Lang, president of the Canadian Manufacturers' Association, was pressing for an early end to the ban on consumer product development in domestic appliances. Without latitude to innovate, he argued, manufacturers of consumer goods would return to their old dies and styles, and not make product changes for some time after the war.[7] This would limit their

"No he isn't proposing – he's trying to get Miss Lovelace to sell him one of our demonstrators."

The shortages created by the postwar scarcity of materials and foreign exchange caused difficulties for householders and for manufacturers and retailers of consumer goods. In these years, manufacturers published periodicals which counselled appliance salesmen on how to keep customers waiting for their particular brand of goods. The gender politics depicted here are anomalous: most salespeople were men; most names on the waiting lists were of women. But the depiction of Miss Lovelace, as buxom and slightly disoriented, conforms to the pattern of trade representations of young women.

In 1948 full-scale ranges were still in short supply in Canada. Here is the display Moffat created for the fair season that year, with their wartime oven adaptation of a hotplate blown up in scale to approximate the two-oven stove for which it was continuing to substitute. The display reproduces the contemporary supply situation, the 'handi-chef' within easy reach, the ranges less accessible on raised pedestals.

growth if freer international trade came quickly, and would deprive Canadian householders of the best modern equipment while tariff barriers remained.[8]

In 1946 C.L. Burton, of the large retailer Robert Simpson and Co., and Floyd Chalmers, from the trade publisher Maclean-Hunter, expressed complementary concerns from the demand side. Imports, the prewar style leaders, were still restricted. Domestic makers continued to specialize in old models and narrow lines. Buyers schooled to make do would not press the 'new frontiers of mass consumption' to sustain mass production or crave 'new satisfactions, new and simpler ways of doing things, and broader and happier ways of living.' In 1947 Canadians still were spending less of their disposable income on consumer durables than they had in 1941.

There were no new frontiers of mass consumption in prospect. Rather, sales and advertising people feared the consequences both for their own trades and for the rebuilding of Canadian secondary manufacturing generally.[9]

If in 1946 more consumer than producer goods plants required reconversion, these were also the industries which regulators granted least access to machinery, equipment, and parts.[10] Householders were kept waiting for washing machines and stoves as a direct and intended consequence of federal government policies while resources went to rebuild machines tools and export capacity.[11]

The Hobson's choice between privileging heavy industry and export earnings or lighter secondary industry for immediate domestic needs faced planners everywhere. The economies of eastern Europe and Latin America represent the catastrophic polar cases here, in their stark emphasis either on iron and steel or luxury consumer goods. A wealthy free market economy, such as the American in the forties, could rebuild its producer and consumer sectors at once. The Swedes too, through a pervasive and effective regulatory structure which made engineers rather than advertisers arbiters of consumer preferences, provided simultaneously for domestic and industrial demands.

The Canadian economy in 1945 was differently constrained – less wealthy than the American, less galvanized to a redistributive consensus than the Swedish, and, while tapped out for cash, respectfully mindful of the needs of a wily imperial parent. The Canadian response was to make rebuilding the capital goods sector easier, and the consumer goods sector more difficult. In this 'first things first' triage, the first things were machines for industry.

This may or may not have been the right choice. Surely those who claim it was dodge a nettlesome question: right for whom? There was no one right choice for all, and in such a chaotic time all chosen paths were inconstantly followed. The question here is not about overall correctness, but about consequences for a particular affected constituency: the domestic producers at the time called 'homemakers,' whose producer goods, stoves, ranges, and washers, were not called capital goods.

A decade later, macroeconomic planners might have used one part of the price system, the rate of interest (the price of borrowed funds and the price paid to those who saved), to dampen or stimulate the economy. Thus might the urgency of demand, expressed through the market, determine spending priorities. But in 1945 real interest rates were at historic lows. Money markets were not yet in place to influence interest rates and spending power gradually. There were no daily offerings of government treasury bills to contract or expand the money supply incrementally. The 1940s option, a sudden sharp rise in interest rates, might imperil the orderly progress of reconstruction or, more grave, tip the economy into depression.

Thus planners turned to direct controls, and first to specific investment incentives. From November 1944 until March 1949, accelerated depreciation allowances lowered and deferred the tax burden on selected investments by firms.[12] For federal planners, these special depreciation privileges had three advantages. They could be finely targeted to encourage specified kinds of capital expenditures. They captured the attention of owners and corporate executives. They worked through fiscal policy and thus commanded the confidence of contemporary Keynesian economists.

Basic industries producing materials for the construction and capital expansion program, and industries producing for export were most clearly within the privileged classes for accelerated depreciation allowances. Utilities, domestic transport, and warehousing, the service and financing sectors, and 'establishments engaged in bridging the gap between producers and consumers' were entirely outside the terms of the program.[13] Of the $1.39 billion in applications for special depreciation allowances approved, the largest portion (26.5 per cent) went to the wood and products industries, the next largest (14 per cent) to food processors, 12 per cent to iron and its products, and 8 per cent to each of chemicals, non-metallic minerals, and textiles. Six per cent was provided to manufacturers of nonferrous metal products and electrical apparatus, which would have included domestic appliances and the equipment utilities needed to expand their service, and 1 per cent to other manufactured products.[14]

The policy had a dual effect on industrial diversification. This was the same order of priority between capital and consumer goods that couples waiting in line to buy household equipment observed. The replenishing of producer goods proceeded more quickly than consumer goods, and makers of consumer goods built products to replace imports at home rather to sell for export. Such increasing import substitution in secondary manufacturing departed from the plan for a strong postwar Canadian economy selling into international markets.[15]

Largely for technical reasons, this plan had been inattentive to householders' concerns. The White Paper on Employment and Income with Special Reference of the Initial Period of Reconstruction, the canonical text of Canadian Keynesianism, was presented to Parliament by C.D. Howe in April 1945. The government's goals then were economic stability, with high levels of employment and income sustained by export growth.[16] After the roller-coaster ride of the interwar years, stability was to be achieved by the management of expenditures, in Keynesian terminology, aggregate demand.[17]

Robert Campbell has argued that because the Canadian version of Keynesianism focused attention on demand as an abstract aggregate 'both analysis and policy were indifferent about the detailed composition of these components.' He concludes that 'Keynesian policy did not appear to have to choose for or against capital, labour, banks, farmers, or any other group.'[18] Yet close attention to how Keynesian instruments were described and deployed in Canada suggests otherwise. Keynesian theory postulated the effects of changes in demand as a whole. But to actually alter aggregate demand, policy makers would have to make technical judgments about the manageability of its separate constituting elements.

Aggregate demand had four distinct parts: public expenditures, export trade, private investment, and consumption expenditures. Each presented the policy maker with distinct challenges. To achieve economic stability by altering the scale and timing of spending, choices would need to be made among these parts. This was apparent from the first articulation of stability as a policy goal in the White Paper of 1945. For within contemporary economic knowledge and with the economic policies then politically accessible, there were great differences in the degree to which the various components of aggregate demand could be influenced by public bodies in the public interest.

Public expenditures were massive and of three types. They funded the service which was government itself, transfer payments including pensions and the newly established family allowances, and public works. Transfer payments would change aggregate demand in so far as they put the tax dollars of the more prosperous in the pockets of lower income groups and larger households more likely of necessity to spend rather than save. In the 1940s government services and income assistance were backed by a civil consensus and politically not easy to cut. Rather, their costs had to be reckoned some time ahead and treated in budget forecasts as fixed. The authors of the White Paper expected that among government expenditures, only spending on public works could be timed to create jobs and thus smooth out fluctuations in the other components of aggregate demand.[19]

Yet start-up times for large public works were considerable, even if a shelf of project plans were kept waiting for the right moment.[20] As soon became clear, public works were too cumbersome to provide the fine tuning that the postwar economy, buffeted by international shocks, would require. As an economic stimulus they were no remedy when, after 1945, the problem to hand was inflation rather than recession.

Historically, export trade had been the dynamic sector in the Canadian economy. In 1945, the government hoped to re-engage and expand these markets rapidly.[21] To this end, from 1943 Canadian delegates to international meetings had been pressing for the multilateral reduction of trade barriers.[22] Wartime planners looking toward the peace considered freer international trade akin to international development assistance. In December 1941 Robert Bryce, a student of Keynes's at Cambridge, who had returned via Harvard to the Department of Finance in Ottawa, argued in New York before the American Economics Association for postwar multilateralism as an extension of policies such as the U.S. New Deal, explicitly its Tennessee Valley Authority (TVA). The multilateralism he advocated was to be a 'benevolent, liberal and far-sighted, if not actually socialist imperialism – a TVA imperialism.' The benefits of expanded trade, he contended, would allow 'the propensity to import full scope in spreading higher incomes from country to country.'[23]

The White Paper also featured multilateralism as mutual aid.[24] But there was much to be done before expanded multilateral trade could bring healing balance. In the longer term, world currencies would have to be made convertible at comparatively stable rates. The war-damaged economies of Europe and Asia would need to be rebuilt. In the shorter term both the debtor nations and their creditors, such as Canada, would need enough stocks of the right currency with which to pay for their imports. Not soon would exports contribute to domestic economic stability.

What remained? In Canada the economy was to be rebuilt by private investment rather than, as in Britain, by the nationalization of key industries. If the government were not going to reconstruct industries by purchasing them outright, then organizing private investment, the component of aggregate demand which would do this work, had to be a public priority. Pent-up demand would create incentives for private investors. Yet an unregulated rush to invest when the most needed skills and materials were still in short supply risked raising prices. The authors of the White Paper believed that 'an inflationary boom' could bring the planned reconstruction 'to an abrupt and abortive conclusion.'[25] But already in November 1944 planners thought that they had found in the special depreciation allowances a way to restrain this inflationary potential and direct private investment to the rebuilding they regarded as most urgent. In this calculus, the needs of householders for consumer goods did not rank high.

As the fourth component of aggregate demand, consumers' long-deferred needs backed by wartime savings presented their own problems and possibilities. Politically, the demand for consumer goods, growing apace as armed forces personnel returned to civilian life, could not be refused. In 1943 this spending had seemed the best national resource with which to stave-off a postwar recession. But by 1945 it seemed menacing. The authors of the White Paper assumed that the demand for consumer goods immediately would drive up prices and only circuitously create employment. This was a part of aggregate demand believed more certain to yield instability than balanced growth. Thus every mention of consumer goods in the White Paper warned of the need for deferral.[26]

If consumer demands were judged postponable, they were also judged pliant. The government would manage stability through the easy cases. They promised 'to use appropriate means to influence' all the components of aggregate demand. But they placed 'particular emphasis on those ... most susceptible of encouragement and control,'[27] those most amenable to policy influence. The partition worked thus. Private investments were most amenable to encouragement. Consumer expenditures, including householders' investments in machinery for home production, were most susceptible to control.

The distinction was partly technical. Consumer expenditures apparently could be influenced by many policy instruments, by direct and indirect taxes and by credit, exchange, and import controls. Whereas public and private investments entrained long-term and invariable financial commitments, householders would be spending from savings accounts or borrowing for short terms. Federal budget makers managing for stability need not treat these purchases as predetermined. Consumers could be influenced, and they could be influenced on short notice, which was all the notice contemporary economic forecasters could offer with confidence.[28]

For the path toward a new international trading order was turning rocky. If the way had been smooth, Canadian consumer goods manufacturers estimated in August 1946 that almost all reconversions would have been complete by the end of 1946, and most modernizations a year later.[29] But current rates soon became unsustainable. Reconversion and modernization depended upon key materials and equipment from outside the country, and thus upon access to foreign exchange. The international monetary system complicated many plans in the years after the war, among them the big plan for multilateral free trade, and many smaller plans to build internationally competitive manufacturing industries.[30]

Historically Canada had sold more to Britain than it bought, bought more from the United States than it sold, and used its British surplus to pay for its American deficit. This pattern served Canada's interest well so long as British buyers had funds, and their pounds were convertible into dollars – which, in the 1940s, they were not.

In 1946 Great Britain still required massive loans from abroad, not only to finance its recovery, but to keep its citizens adequately fed. Sentimentally mindful of the imperial tie and pragmatically hoping to safeguard this leading market for future exports, Canada made an exceptionally large response to British postwar petitions.[31] The Marshall Plan was not yet in place. Although already stretched by war loans and gifts to the United Kingdom, Canada extended a further $1.25 billion loan, a sum a third as large as that provided by the United States from a national output one-fourteenth the size. As Sir Alex Cairncross has noted, the Canadian government undertook to make up this difference 'at considerable risk to its own balance of payments.' The pressure on Canadian stores of international exchange might have been sustainable in different circumstances. The government understood that the loan would be drawn down slowly over five years. They expected that the 1.25 billion outflow of Canadian dollars partly would be offset by an increased trade in commodities between Britain and Canada. They counted on the British to make at least a portion of their Canadian loan repayments in convertible currency. But none of these expectations were fulfilled.[32]

Canada retained a hard currency convertible to U.S. dollars. Canada and Newfoundland, alone among the Commonwealth countries, remained outside the sterling area. Britain was thus eager to collect as much of the Canadian loan as quickly as possible, but unwilling to engage in trade with Canada denominated in dollars. After all, goods could be exchanged within Europe and other parts of the Commonwealth in the soft currencies with which the world was awash. Thus, thwarting Ottawa's expectations, the British government turned increasingly to France for wheat and Denmark for butter. What manufactured goods the British could spare were bartered for other commodities within the sterling area, for Britain had come to favour not multilateralism but an enlarged postwar sterling area, closed off by regulations from the rest of the world.[33]

Canada was thus trice disadvantaged. The British loan drained the convertible currency needed to buy in the United States. Ottawa had huge stores of sterling to buy British textiles and engineering goods. But the British now were selling elsewhere. Canadians thus had to turn to the United States not only for commodities historically obtained there, and

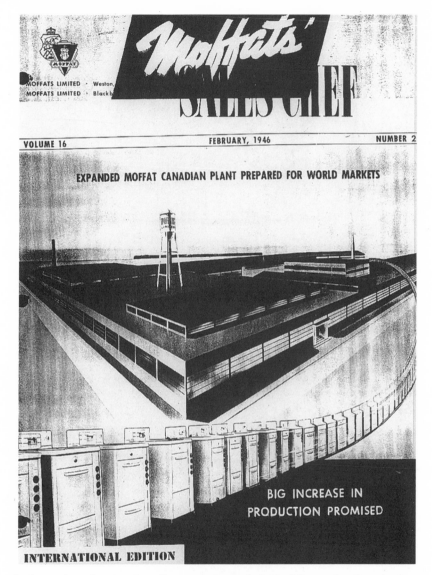

At the war's end, many Canadian manufacturers looked forward to freer international trade and the prospect of creating mass production plants to sell Canadian
goods into export markets. This February 1946 representation shows a huge
single-storey plant of Bauhaus design, from which an endless stream of compact
modern ranges issues forth. These plans soon were dashed.

OUR EXPORT CUSTOMERS NEED OUR PROD-
UCTS BUT THEY HAVE NOT THE FUNDS
WITH WHICH TO BUY THEM.

The national differences behind the British war loan and the postwar exchange crisis depicted in men's clothing, the British customer in top hat and tails, the Canadian producer in an RCMP uniform. The smoke stack and boxed goods in the cartoon mislead in that made-in-Canada manufactured goods were in short supply; it was agricultural production and natural resources which Canadians wished to sell to Britain, and Britons preferred to buy elsewhere using soft currencies.

the consumer goods not yet being made at home, but for those once imported from Britain as well. By late 1947 Canada was in a grave international exchange crisis.

As John Maynard Keynes noted in his last published article in June 1946, these were times in which the 'job for us is to get through the next five years' without 'trying to look ahead further than any one can see.'[34] By November 1947, Canada had to postpone hopes of multilateralism under the pressure of immediate concerns and impose restrictions on imports from the United States.[35]

The Emergency Exchange Conservation Act was, like similar British controls, an attempt to weather a current storm. At the time, these measures were presented as an emergency 'detour' through import-substitution and back toward freer trade once the radically unstable international situation had passed.[36] Exchange controls, unlike tariffs, James Coyne argued, would 'be recognised as essentially temporary measures not intended to give protection to domestic industry' As well, exchange controls, like depreciation allowances, could be used with technical precision to restrain different kinds of expenditures to different degrees.[37]

Here the triage which privileged producer over consumer goods once again applied. Introducing the Emergency Exchange Conservation Act, Douglas Abbott, the minister of Finance, argued that because 'a large proportion of our imports cannot be much restricted without very serious effects on our economic life,' constraints would have to be 'concentrated primarily on finished goods, mostly of a type used by consumers.'[38] Imports of many consumer durables were entirely prohibited. Quotas were set for purchases of foodstuffs and textiles from the United States. By ministerial permit, imports of industrial machinery and parts were allowed selectively.[39]

Abbott's implication, that the absence of consumer durables would not have 'very serious effects' on 'economic life,' later was frequently repeated. By technical definition it was true, for the household was outside 'economic life.' Contemporary economic models measured neither non-waged household labour nor non-priced household production in the national income accounts. But was Abbott making a benign and justifiable assumption about the effects of the new policy? Literally, making do without domestic appliances would have uncounted effects on householders' activities. Would being schooled longer to scarcity leave Canadians' participation in the commodity culture unchanged?

Initially imports of refrigerators, washing machines, stoves, and sewing machines were prohibited on the questionable grounds that they were being produced in sufficient numbers in Canada. Even if this had been true, appliances makers could not continue to produce without imported parts.[40] Manufacture of many consumer durables ceased, for as Abbott noted in a national radio broadcast, it was bootless to ban imports and then expend the foreign exchange savings on parts and materials. The exchange controls worked as intended.[41] The volume of imports categorized under prohibition or quota was reduced by 47 per cent between 1947 and 1948, whereas those favoured with special permits – capital goods and parts – declined by only 17 per cent.[42] Between 1947 and 1949, the value of imports of complete appliances, as opposed to parts, declined for refrigerators from $6.9 million to $.3 million, and for washing machines from $5.5 million to $.025 million.[43]

A month after the controls went into effect, a senior government economist, Louis Rasminsky, publicly justified the ban on imports of domestic

TABLE 3.1
Value of Imports, Refrigerators and Parts, and Refrigerator Imports as
Percentage of Canadian Market, 1947–51

Year	Value refrigerators and parts ($ millions)	Imports as % Canadian market
1947	12.134	28.2
1948	5.816	1.3
1949	7.342	1.0
1950	15.353	2.5
1951	30.620	25.2

Source: *Canada Yearbook*; Institute for Quantitative Analysis of Social
and Economic Policy, University of Toronto, *The Canadian Appliance
Industry*, March 1970, chap. 7, p. 5

appliances and their components because these were 'luxury and non-essential goods' unnecessary for running the Canadian economy or maintaining productivity.'[44] In Parliament, Finance Minister Douglas Abbott faced criticism over such pronouncements. W.R. Thatcher, the CCF member from Moose Jaw, exploded in the House, 'I wonder if the minister would say an electric iron or an electric washing machine is a luxury' rather than 'in the category of an essential to every Canadian housewife.' This was a particularly piquant question as the baby boom grew apace. Of Abbott, John Gibson, who sat as an Independent from Comox-Alberni on Vancouver Island, interjected, 'Perhaps he never used a scrubbing board.' The proportion of personal disposable income spent on consumer durables, which had risen in 1947, dropped sharply in 1948.[45] But, C.D. Howe argued in February 1948, 'if a measure of austerity should result to Canadian buyers, few will complain. Our standard of living is high, perhaps higher than we can afford, and any reduction of that standard that may be the outcome of our dollar conservation programme, will not be serious.'[46] Whether or not he was right in this forecast remained to be seen. Certainly, as soon as the emergency measures of November 1947 were in place, prices of most consumer durables became higher, perhaps higher than many could afford. The import controls were accompanied by an excise tax of 25 per cent on 'less essential' goods, including most electrical appliances. This judgment manufacturers and retailers in the consumer goods sector found difficult to share. They, as much as householders, were being differentially treated.[47]

In 1951, when supplies remained short and spending on durables once more declined as a proportion of disposable income, the Canadian Asso-

TABLE 3.2
Percentage Composition of Retail Sales, First Quarter

Year	Cash	Installment	Charge
1941	60.8	11.4	27.8
1948	63.0	7.2	29.8
1949	62.9	8.1	29.0
1950	62.7	9.1	28.2

Source: NAC, RG 19 Finance E2 C, vol. 32 file 101-102-17,
Control of Consumer Credit, memo on experience with
consumer credit, George Glass to W.C. Clark, 28 Aug. 1950

ciation of Consumers argued for some refinement of the regulations: tax deluxe models but not standard stoves, refrigerators, and washing machines. The drafters of this recommendation, the women of the Nanaimo Branch, apparently agreed that consumer goods built for sale and status should be liable to sumptuary taxes. But taxing standard models built for use, they suggested, only discouraged makers from building better basic tools.[48] The excise taxes continued into the early 1950s, for the Korean War brought forward old justifications for a new round of targeted consumer disincentives. The last of these was removed from electric stoves, refrigerators, and washing machines in April 1952; on electric irons, vacuum cleaners, and other small appliances not until April 1954.[49]

Despite, or some said because of, these interventions, inflation continued. And so, as the demands to rearm for the Korean War heightened, Keynesian planners turned in October 1950 to consumer credit controls. Here ideological judgments about 'good' and 'bad' spending, and planners' technical preferences, entirely displaced close empirical observation.

The wartime restrictions on consumer credit had continued until January 1947. Then consumer debt burdens were not excessive. Personal savings remained high as a proportion of income, even though householders were eagerly buying as goods became available.[50] Instalment sales did begin to rise. Yet, proportionally, 1950 retail instalment sales were notably lower than they had been in 1941. Could this be alarming? Would regulating so small a proportion of total retail sales really have much effect?

In Cabinet documents the arguments supporting this legislation are judgmental and patronizing. Mitchell Sharp, then director of the Economic Policy Division at the Department of Finance, argued that limits on credit buying (he particularly mentioned fur coats) would force consumers to spend savings, and thus dampen demand. Sharp conceded that the anti-inflationary effects of consumer credit controls were difficult to measure. Yet, he continued, these restraints would do no harm. They might instil prudence. They would not be resisted. In the contemporary Canadian culture of consumption, their political effects would be benign.[51]

The first consumer credit regulations of October 1950 kept to the down payments common at the time in the trade for cars, but doubled the usual deposit on domestic appliances.[52] When these limitations had little apparent effect on consumer spending, which in fact was rising in anticipation of shortages, the regulations were tightened overall in March 1951.[53] They were suspended in May 1952, although the federal legislative authority to regulate consumer credit remained in place until 31 July 1954.[54]

In the federal House, opposition members argued that the consumer credit controls did impose hardship. M.J. Coldwell, the CCF leader, objected that they discriminated against those who needed to use credit for necessities while leaving those with cash free to buy cars and refrigerators in multiples. Hazen Argue, CCF member for Assiniboia, recommended an increase in 'the income tax on people in the high income brackets' to curb luxury spending. Why put the farm wife saving egg money for a down payment on a washing machine on the front line of a new war against inflation?

Consumer credit regulations distinguished too much between buyers on the basis of how they paid, and not enough among goods on the basis of the needs they met. The question posed by the women of the consumers association in Nanaimo was asked again, this time by a senior Conservative member of the house. Could all consumer goods really be commonly categorized as non-essential? In Ellen Fairclough's riding of Hamilton West many couples, unable to find city rental accommodation, were moving to unequipped houses in outlying districts. Were their purchases of stoves, refrigerators, and automobiles not essential?[55] Manufacturers and retailers of consumer goods similarly were aggrieved.[56]

Whether the consumer credit controls had any salutary effect stabilizing demand or muting inflation is difficult to know. There were changes in the excise taxes on consumer durables at the same time that the consumer credit controls were implemented and altered. In the early 1950s, price rises and shortages threatened even as household goods became increasingly available. Prospective buyers were having to consider so many interdependent factors, who could know what weight they had given exclusively to consumer credit restrictions? Even Finance Department appraisals of the credit controls later acknowledged as much.[57]

There was a buying spree through 1950 and early 1951, and a decline in consumer spending thereafter. Instalment sales and cash purchases fol-

TABLE 3.3
Wholesale Price Indexes for Producer and Consumer
Goods (1926 = 100)

Year	Producer goods	Consumer goods
1940	78.7	83.4
1941	83.6	91.1
1942	88.3	95.6
1943	95.1	97.0
1944	99.9	97.4
1945	100.7	98.1
1946	105.7	101.1
1947	129.3	117.3

Source: *Royal Commission on Prices, Statistical Supplement* (1948), 3: 315

lowed the same pattern of peak and decline. This suggested that purchasers were responding to broader shared influences as they decided to buy, rather than to the credit regulations.

Yet Finance Department economists yearned to believe that controls on consumer credit were good for the nation. They asserted this even as they acknowledged that there was 'no statistical means of measuring this effect.'[58] What made economists so determined to give consumer credit controls the benefit of the doubt, despite the absence of evidence for any influence, and the tiny proportion of aggregate demand credit limitations might conceivably affect?

The question could be put more generally. Why were so many obstacles put in the way of Canadians who wanted and needed household equipment? Policy makers argued that these barriers were benign. They maintained that their chosen path, rapid reinvestment in primary industry, would build the economy without compromising stability. Restrictions on householder' access to goods would instil prudence without compromising the development of secondary manufacturing. But would these many lessons designed to teach gratification and prudence so differentially really be without costs in the short and long term?

Some economists at the time wondered as much. Federal government policy from 1944 onwards encouraged spending on capital goods and discouraged consumer expenditures, at a time when investment was already exceptionally high as a proportion of gross national product.[59] The accelerated depreciation allowances for producer goods continued in the resource and basic materials sectors even as inflationary pressures mounted.

In 1947 makers and buyers of consumer durables were restrained further by import controls and excise taxes. Yet by then prices for consumer goods were not rising so rapidly as for producer goods (see table 3.3), the sector where government policy encouraging expenditures remained. As Clarence Barber observed in November 1948, the government had fostered a 'capital boom' with its policies 'to discriminate against consumer spending in favor of capital spending.' The government had 'given its tacit approval' to inflation driven by private investment, persisting in these incentives, even adding to them, as prices rose. But surely all inflation, including inflation caused by the accelerated demand for capital goods, created distortions and the risk of a correcting recession.[60]

Inhibiting the reconstruction and revitalization of consumer goods manufacturing had broad effects. Inflation was not the only consequence to be reckoned. Leaders of the Canadian Manufacturers' Association had worried that postwar Canadian product design engineering would be delayed by wartime bans on product improvements. Later restrictions on investment and access to innovations from abroad further limited Canadians to obsolete products made by old-fashioned processes. Already in 1946 Canadian consumers seemed so schooled to prudence and making-do that they would not, and with mounting controls could not, press makers to do better. Looking back in 1952, Harry Eastman argued that the import controls had forced consumers to take what they wanted less in place of what they wanted more, thus diminishing their welfare.[61] In this predicament, consumers were not alone. How consumers participated in the commodity culture influenced retailers, marketers, and makers as well.

As Wyn Plumptre had feared in 1947, the detour away from multilateralism did 'become permanent,' or at least very long-lived. Export levels, of course, declined abruptly at the war's end, by 50 per cent between 1945 and 1946. Then, rather than soaring as reconstruction progressed, export values rose by only 11 per cent in the next five years, and only 24 per cent in the next ten.[62]

There are large questions to be engaged here, and which the rest of this book will engage. What do householders take from their cultural context as they distinguish demands from needs? How do those who use goods deliberate over how much is enough and for whom? How and when do they consider the collective consequences of assuming the ownership of goods?

Those who defended the postwar limitations on consumers' actions offered very simple answers. They responded to their critics on technical grounds: firms could afford to be indifferent to price rises, consumers could not. Capital goods could be distinguished by their end uses, consumer goods could not. Thus the only way to stop luxury spending was to curtail all expenditures on consumer goods.[63] The foundations for these distinctions now seem elusive.

In Canada and elsewhere, the tools of macroeconomic policy were then untested. In the absence of evidence about the direction and dimensions of policy effects, economists muddled through. Often what they presented as technical constraints were fundamentally normative judgments about entitlements. Many postwar controls on consumer spending were, in their ideological foundation, the modern equivalent of early-modern sumptuary laws. Managing economic stability through the technically and politically easy cases in the first decade after the war probably had meant managing too much. These many interventions amplified rather than moderated the sources of instability.[64] These technical choices altered household behaviour, reinforcing past lessons, prompting new judgments, inflecting both the consuming and the manufacturing culture of the 1950s.

4

Consumer Sovereignty

It is absurd to maintain that the private enterprise system is directed towards supplying consumers' needs. Rather, consumers are the pasture on which enterprise feeds. We are used to a system that is run for the benefit of producers, in which the advantage to consumers is merely incidental.

Joan Robinson, *Economics: An Awkward Corner*[1]

Canadian women in the 1950s were described as the nation's purchasing agents, the people who did two-thirds, some said three-quarters, some 80 per cent, of the nation's buying. Those persuaded by liberal economic theory reasoned that in the market the wishes of consumers could be sovereign over makers and sellers. Purchasers' decisions about what goods to buy could determine what manufacturers would produce and what retailers would stock for sale. In the setting of prices, consumers' judgments about how much goods were worth could be as important as sellers' reckonings of how much their products cost to make. *Ceteris paribus*, all other things being equal, as the economic theory always specified, these powers lay within consumers' reach.

Not all citizens in the 1940s were convinced by liberal economic theory, and not all actors in the postwar world of goods were equal. Certainly contemporary regulatory regimes did not treat all consumers and producers as equals. Joan Robinson, a prominent Cambridge economist, called the economic theory of consumer sovereignty absurd. Few consumer activists of the Left, whether communist or social democratic, believed the market would set consumers free or make them sovereign. But for many in the first fifteen years after the end of the Second World War, the liberal idea that the consumer interest could be a powerful directing force in the economy was not an absurdity. Most Canadians absorbed it as part of the dominant ideology of the time, found it comfortable and commonsensical, even if the consumer products around them were neither. This was an idea which had great influence because for many it so convincingly veiled, rather than accurately described, the lines of economic and political power which governed consumption. Liberal consumer activists embraced it.

This chapter is a study of the organizations which in the late 1940s sought to speak for consumers. Each had specific political allegiances – Liberal, communist, or social democratic – some covert, some less so. Did these groups articulate the consumer interest as distinct from other interests? In their programs, how was the lot of the consumer to be bettered? In what circumstances? At whose expense? If being a consumer was not a primary identity, but, within the partisan political reasoning about the re-emerging market capitalism of the forties, always enthralled in other interests, in what context could a self-conscious and self-actualizing consumer exist?

During the war, women had been recruited to the Consumer Branch of the Wartime Prices and Trade Board to represent the concerns of domestic buyers and monitor local changes in the prices, quality, and supply of goods. By the end of the war, over 16,000 women were filing information with the Consumer Branch. Their publication, *Consumers News*, had a circulation of 350,000 and a reputation for being relatively independent of retailers and manufacturers. Through this wartime work women became better informed and more confident to speak out as purchasers.[2] The war effort also intensified, reinvigorated, and ratified household production of more clothing and food, affirming that the work factories did, what was called production, homemakers also did within the household. In life during wartime, if not in economic theory, the distinctions between production and consumption blurred. Both homemakers and domestic manufacturers were producing useful goods, while both had their materials and tools subordinated to the war effort. With the peace, the women who had worked with the Consumer Branch divided about how to proceed.

One matter not in dispute was the representation of the organized consumer as woman. Only once in the twenty-one months planning for the Canadian Association of Consumers, the most enduring successor to the Consumers Branch, was the question of whether consumers might be 'people' rather than 'women' raised, and then, curiously, by a representative of the Canadian Home Economics Association. The other national consumers' organization active in the postwar years bore its gender ascription in its name, the Housewives' Consumers Association. When the social democratic Cooperative Commonwealth Federation considered intervening in consumer issues, the matter was placed before its provincial women's committees. The private proposal for consumer representation circulating in 1947 came from *Chatelaine*, the leading Canadian women's magazine. The Canadian Association of Consumers remained a women's organization until 1961. Thus, the reasoning about the consumer interest in the first fifteen years after the war was always about the rights and responsibilities of people who were women rather than men.[3]

In 1946 prices remained relatively stable. Leaders among the women who had worked with the Consumers Branch then saw the future of consumer activism as an engineering or technical project, an extension of the Standards Division, created at their urging in wartime to monitor changes in product quality. The presidents of thirty-seven national women's organizations surveyed in the spring of 1946 about postwar consumer activism placed more emphasis on product engineering than either economic education or political representation.[4] They argued for consumer protection through independent research, the reasoning which had led Stuart Chase and F.J. Schlink to found Consumers' Research in the United States in the late 1920s.[5] The same priority was pursued in postwar Britain, where a Women's Advisory Committee of the British Standards Institute was formed in 1951.[6]

The most thoroughgoing Canadian proposal for engineering research into women's concerns as homemakers came from Edith Lang, formerly economics convenor for the National Council of Women, and their liaison with the WPTB. Lang proposed that Canadians follow the model of the Swedish Home Research Institute (HRI),[7] founded in 1944, to study both the design of equipment and the efficiency of domestic labour processes. Volunteers from homemakers associations throughout Sweden tested product prototypes. Technical reports from institute laboratories provided the specifications from which appliances manufacturers and interior architects worked.[8]

Lang argued that their wartime experience made 'Canadian housewives conscious of their wants as consumers' and of 'needs far wider' than the existing Canadian standards apparatus could meet. The research bureau she proposed, akin to the National Research Council, would conduct 'wider research on the necessary activities of housewives; how equipment, cleaners, [and] finishes affect the time and energy of those using them; what kind of housing the public wants, what equipment.' Like the Swedish

HRI, this body would intervene fundamentally in the processes of product development in the interest of the user. Local consumer councils drawn from existing women's organizations would define what kind of investigations and products users needed and represent consumer interests to government and industry generally. Lang recognized some hard realities about contemporary product development: that the users of household goods had no effective influence upon their design; that crystallizing effective engineering solutions to production problems within the household was often beyond the expertise of housewives themselves; and that manufacturers' interest could be to disguise the differences between 'what was really valuable and what is merely decorative or sales-making' in their wares.[9]

In April 1947, when representatives of many national women's organizations met under the aegis of the National Council of Women to form a consumers' association, product research was prominent on the agenda. Allan Gill, director of the Standards Division, who was invited to be present, quickly grasped the radical aspect of Lang's plan and spoke against it. He cautioned that the Canadian government had 'not dealt with all aspects of family living' (as the Swedes, spurred by their population crisis, had been doing for more than a decade). There was information on food and very little else.'We cannot put the Government in the position of recommending one man's product against another,' he also noted, thinking of the freedoms the theory of free markets required for men who produced. Furthermore, he doubted both that women would be able to interpret such technical reports on products, and that this was knowledge women could use. Gill had allies, among them many home economists, in the employ of food processors and equipment manufacturers and identified with producers' concerns.[10] The 1947 brief from the group the National Council of Women convened requested government funding for a national consumers' organization but included no budget for a research institute. The quality of consumer goods and housing was listed modestly alongside home markets and foreign trade among the many consumer problems the proposed organization might study.[11]

As price controls were lifted after the war, the cost of food, clothing, and furniture rose rapidly. Protests against Liberal management of the economy grew acute. Consumer issues became less focused on the technical qualities of goods and more broadly partisan. By the spring of 1947 the predominant way of featuring the consumer interest among those in the political mainstream had shifted from goods to growth, or stability and growth. Lang became less influential than Harriet Parsons, formerly On-

CONSUMERS' OPINIONS COUNT

A Program
Based on the Canadian Association
of Consumers

By
(Mrs. W. R.) Edith Lang

In the late 1940s Edith Lang argued that Canadian homemakers should have a government testing agency which would advise them about consumer goods as the National Research Council assisted Canadian manufacturers with materials and production processes. This early pamphlet, however, accurately portrays the Canadian consumer as she was imagined by the Canadian Association of Consumers in these years, as elegantly middle class, and with ample time to attend meetings.

TABLE 4.1
Cost of Living Index, 1940–52 (1935–9 = 100)

Year	Total	Food	Rent	Clothing	Home furnishings	Average annual earnings*
1952	188.4	237.4	147.4	209.4	197.8	2647
1951	185.4	241.4	140.0	203.1	194.4	2434
1950	167.3	210.9	132.9	182.3	169.2	2183
1949	161.6	203.0	123.0	183.1	167.6	2067
1948	155.7	195.5	120.7	174.4	162.6	1960
1947	136.3	159.5	116.7	143.9	141.6	1712
1946	124.5	140.4	112.7	126.3	124.5	1516
1945	120.4	133.0	112.1	122.1	119.0	1538
1940	105.6	105.6	106.3	109.2	107.2	1084

*The average annual earnings are for production workers.
Source: F.C. Leacy, ed., *Historical Statistics of Canada*, 2nd ed. (Ottawa: Statistics Canada, 1983) K1–7 and E44

tario coordinator and educational secretary for the Consumer Branch, and at the time economics and taxation convenor for the National Council of Women. Parsons was a Wellesley College economics graduate who in the 1930s had taught evening courses at the University of Toronto. She was a Liberal, closely in contact with officials both at Trade and Commerce and the Bank of Canada.[12] Lang's concerns were largely with matters economists did not take into account, that is, with qualities of goods which were not reflected in their price, with the productivity of equipment and labour inside the household and thus outside the market, issues which had received serious attention as civilian requirements were appraised during the war. Parsons's interests were more representative of contemporary liberal economists' interests in macro- rather than microeconomics, with factors which affected economic growth and the balance of trade in goods and currency, rather than the goods themselves and the firms which made them. Those working for consumers in wartime had been allies of big government; now those who espoused liberal theory regarded well-functioning markets as consumers' best allies. The same shift in allegiance was occurring within the governing Liberal Party.

The government needed a national women's voice to urge domestic consumers to patience, for it was embarked upon economic policies which, in the short and medium term, gave priority to export and capital goods.[13] They needed voices which would argue, as Harriet Parsons had in her last days at the Consumer Branch, for a calm tackling of 'difficult peacetime problems instead of hysterical rumours, hoarding and wild buying.'[14] The new organization needed an operating grant, and women from the political mainstream, accustomed to working with state-funded Women's Institutes and Home and School groups, argued that public funding would make their work more effective.

Thus it was that the women who gathered to found the Canadian Association of Consumers met in the presence of Graham Towers, governor of the Bank of Canada, M.W. Mackenzie, deputy minister of Trade and Commerce, and the cautious Mr Gill of the Standards Branch.[15] Towers tried to convince his audience that their standard of living depended upon exports. As women in wartime had taught Canadians about inflation and deflation, they should now make clear that 'efficient production and the success of our international trade ... puts us in the best position to maintain employment and improve our standard of living.'[16] In Towers' construction, consumers' wartime legacy was not as advocates and activists but as a stabilizing force.

His audience would have none of it. The women charged to draft a constitution for the new organization instead insisted that the masses of women consumers wanted to hear about practical things, standards of clothing, family spending, marketing through corner stores.[17] But their petition asking the Liberal government for $15,000 in federal funding to establish the Canadian Association of Consumers also strategically made the case that organizing 'on democratic principles such a vast consumption as is controlled by "the ordinary woman"' was 'a matter of vital interest, not only to the customers themselves, but also to national and international trade.' As importantly at that political moment, the CAC claimed to be broadly representative of Canadian women, a 'two way channel' between consumers and both government and industry.[18]

The CAC emphasis on democracy and representativeness was to draw an explicit contrast with the Housewives' Consumers Association (HCA), a group begun in 1937. The HCA articulated the consumer interest through a radical critique of market institutions and capitalist accumulation. Many of their leaders were members of the Labour Progressive Party, the Canadian communists. In Ontario and Saskatchewan a number of social democratic women participated in the Housewives' campaigns.

The HCA had joined in the work of the Consumer Branch during the war. In wartime and after they supported controls as a way to redistribute wealth. Through the summer and early winter of 1946, as the National Council of Women focused on consumers' power to influence product standards, the Housewives organized for continuing price ceilings on basic foodstuffs, locating the consumer interest first in the standard of living.[19] The next spring, the HCA gained the media spotlight with a popular anti-inflationary campaign propelled by street theatre. Their two marches on Ottawa were front-page news. The more Housewives brandishing rolling pins on Parliament Hill became identified with women's concern to roll back prices, the more eager the government grew to encourage and finance the CAC.[20] The Canadian Association of Consumers owed its government grant partly to its willingness to adopt many government priorities as its own, and partly to the Housewives' political work.

The two Housewives' briefs carried to Ottawa, by Margaret Chunn of Winnipeg and her eleven western colleagues in April, and by Lily Phelps on behalf of the HCA of Ontario in June, emphasized the consequences of underconsumption and the contradictions in market allocation. The western Housewives argued that rising prices were eroding the buying power of earnings and wartime savings through consumer demand to maintain employment. 'Every blow to the housewife's purchasing power is a step in the direction of depression,' they argued, and from depression followed war – in current prospect, a war with atomic weapons.[21] Graham Towers and his colleagues in the Department of Trade and Commerce looked to demand in international markets to sustain Canadian living standards. These women of the Left instead wanted directly to stimulate domestic demand by constructing low-income housing, limiting the manufacture of luxury goods, encouraging manufacture of essential household commodities and clothing, and reinstituting controls and subsidies on basic foodstuffs, thus to create jobs.

They defended controls 'because these were means, fair means, of making the public purse do what the individual purse could not do,' insure that the basic needs of all citizens would be met. Markets, they argued, were not free, and did not bring consumers freedom. The government in releasing its regulations had ceded power to and through the market to a new system of controls, 'one which is out of our reach, and we fear out of our interest, and where we have neither rights of approval nor protest.' They denied the market was an unseen hand, an objective and disinterested instrument of allocation, and instead featured it as a whole body, wearing banker's or factory owner's clothes. In choosing to reestablish the market, the Liberals, they argued, had forgotten that 'the first and constant duty of the Government is to its people, not its industrial or financial institutions.'[22]

While Liberal and communist women contended to be the organized voice of women as consumers, women from the Cooperative Commonwealth Federation, after three years of postwar experiment, recrimination,   ·

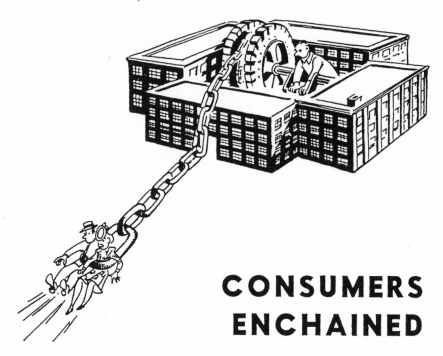

CONSUMERS ENCHAINED

While liberal economic theory suggested that consumers had sovereignty in the market, economic thinking from the Left argued that, without government assistance, householders had few resources with which to counter the power of producers.

and reappraisal, concluded that there was no distinctive consumer interest to represent. The view of Agnes Macphail, who, as the first woman elected to the House of Commons, was a senior woman in the party, was that no consumer organization was any good, that political action was 'the only thing.' The consumer interest was best forwarded by the election of CCF governments. In the metaphor of a contemporary CCF organizing brochure, 'Good homemakers today must take political action. For politics is the key to the kitchen cupboard. Only a CCF government can unlock the door to plenty for every family.' In 1947 and 1948, with prices rising and goods still in short supply, CCF women across the country divided, some joining the Housewives, some the CAC.[23] Those wary of the communists and willing to give the Canadian Association of Consumers the benefit of the doubt argued that women were not yet well informed on consumer matters. They could be politicized as they learned more about the organization of industry and the market through the CAC. Those committed to political action thought the CAC was not committed to genuine change. By late 1948 the choice for social democrats seemed to be between supporting 'Communists in women's clothes' in the Housewives or a 'company union' in the CAC. In neither group were CCF women finding the independent consumers' voice they had hoped might prepare women to hear the CCF platform.[24] By 1949 women of the CCF were convinced that an effective and representative consumers' association no longer was possible, strategically because the two contending national consumer associations had become closely identified with political parties, analytically because consumer identities were so powerfully cross-cut by other loyalties.[25]

By the spring of 1948 the two rival consumer groups had squared off. The Housewives were organizing boycotts and buyers strikes, and attempting to collect a million signatures on a petition asking the prime minister to restore price ceilings on essential foods to January 1946 levels.[26] The CAC, liberal in political philosophy, and loyal to the governing Liberal Party, argued buyers' strikes would cause only unemployment and business failures and that controls were inappropriate in a free market economy.[27]

While the Housewives saw the consumer interest in class-based struggles to defend workers' living standards, the CAC refused the possibility of class and sectional conflict, and emphasized consensus building based on mutual understanding.[28] In this view, the function of a consumer organization was to represent this shared consumer interest before state bodies. The CAC appeared in 1948 before the Commons Special Committee on Prices, and in 1949 before the Senate Banking and Finance Committee and the committee drafting a new trade mark and labelling act. It was instrumental in overturning the federal ban on margarine in 1949 and argued against loss leaders and resale price maintenance as trade practices which restricted the operation of free markets. These briefs presented the consumer perspective as a transcending rather than a distinctive interest.[29] The emphasis on representation, and on fairness and reasonableness, set the CAC apart from the Housewives, and implicitly affirmed its Liberal loyalties.[30] The presumption of conciliation, and the stance which seemed equally to acknowledge all claims, spoke to a membership who saw themselves as consumers in only one aspect of their lives. These were also, in contemporary understandings of gender, womanly attitudes and practices, thus befitting women in their organized work as consumers.

In the early 1950s, the balance in the CAC work shifted from representa-

THE
CANADIAN ASSOCIATION OF CONSUMERS

=

YOUR QUESTIONS

AND

ANSWERS

=

"IN UNITY THERE IS STRENGTH"

The 1948 logo for the Canadian Association of Consumers showed two young women wearing high heels and carrying shopping baskets, speedily pursuing bargains.

tion of consumers before public bodies toward consumer education. For the CAC leadership, many of whom had university degrees in economics, consumer education meant principally education in economics.[31] The focus shifted back from macroeconomic theory to microeconomics, and the theory of the firm. This theory held that consumers could be sovereign, that is, they could determine what firms produced, so long as two conditions applied: that there were many competing sellers in the market, and that consumers behaved rationally. Neither of these conditions could be assumed in Canadian markets in the early 1950s.

The CAC work of representing consumers before tribunals on combines, resale price maintenance, restrictive trade practices, and producer marketing boards had aimed to make the first of these assumptions, of seller competition, more plausible as a description of Canadian markets. But given the weaknesses of Canadian combines legislation, and the increasing consolidation of the Canadian manufacturing sector into fewer, more readily coordinated firms, these hopes were unrealistic.

Consumer rationality was also an elusive goal. For consumers to be sovereign over producers, microeconomic theory held, they must be knowledgeable about the price and qualities of goods offered for sale, and always buy the product of highest quality at the lowest price. In this decision-making they had to be guided by their own independently derived standards of usefulness (utility), rather than by producers' or sellers' attempts to reshape their wants. The Thrift Campaigns sponsored by both the National Council of Women and the CAC in the early 1950s were to persuade women to research their prospective purchases carefully, and postpone buying if necessary until goods of satisfactory quality were offered at reasonable prices. Faced with inflation, this line of argument went, consumers 'must take that sound word "thrift" – take it out of the pages of the dictionaries, dust it off, and PRACTICE IT.' Thus would rational consumption not only limit inflation, but by threats of mounting unsold inventories, chasten makers into producing only the wares consumer wanted.[32]

In the mid-fifties Vance Packard's American revelations of advertisers' power to shape rather than respond to consumers' wants filled the popular press. The CAC campaigns warned that purchasers should be sceptical about the foundations of their own desires. 'Let's not cheat *ourselves* with impulse buying; yield too easily to "greeds" disguised as "needs"; ... most of us have more than our *mothers had,* and most of us buy *more than we really* need. It's the pressure of the Times! But our forebears were stronger than *their* times. Let us manage OURS and not be managed by them.'[33] Women must not seek pleasure but usefulness. Less was better than more. Only self-denial (thrift) could bring women a sense of power as consumers. Ironically in Canada, the civic obligations to postpone consumption, reinforced during reconstruction, made Packard's message at once assimilable and redundant.

From the late 1940s, women from the Cooperative Commonwealth Federation had been sceptical about CAC consumer education campaigns and the possibility that the consumer interest could be pursued through the market. 'This milk and water group,' Marion Harrington of Hamilton scoffed, 'is going to teach the Canadian housewife to adjust herself to the austerity which continuing high prices will bring, ... to prepare her for harder times ahead in order to allay her criticism of the government.' The theory of consumer sovereignty, by making women appear responsible for market processes they could not control, was more likely to make women accept their predicament than strive to change it. 'It is working out very reactionary,' another CCFer worried. 'The Liberals are simply keeping the girls quiet.' After a meeting for drinks with a CAC leader in 1950, Peg Stewart, a CCF woman from London, Ontario, came away 'with a feeling of absolute horror at the cold cynicism and absolute contempt for people,' fearing that these skilled Liberal activists were 'dealing with women who are sound asleep.'[34]

As the Cold War deepened, the comforting concatenation of consumer/ sovereignty/markets/freedom made the CAC way to pursue the consumer interest seem ever more commonsensical. The allure was undeniable. All other things being equal, this doctrine promised, so long as you make your decision on your own and according to your own lights, what you know you most truly want the market will bring it to you. Still the power of 'the individual purse,' as Lily Phelps of the Housewives had called it sceptically in 1947, was diminishing. John Kenneth Galbraith argued in a series of widely read and popularized books that buyers acting autonomously were being overwhelmed by the rising and coordinated market power of makers and sellers.[35] Only by organizing themselves to secure common goals against common adversaries, only by functioning as a countervailing power, could consumers get what they wanted. From its beginning, recollecting the wartime experience of the Consumer Branch and committed to a liberal analysis of how social conflict was best resolved, the CAC had affirmed that such a base for organizing existed, that there was a distinctive and shared consumer interest.

But was there? In a decade of policy discussion, the consumer interest had been framed in so many different and contradictory ways, it retained little creditable life of its own. So frequently had the consumer interest seemed hostage to party political agendas in which it was not paramount, that its autonomy had become suspect whatever cause it was mobilized to champion. Beneath the partisan jockeying were deep and contentious political questions about distribution. Perhaps the consumer interest was not fundamentally about spending, but rather about who would have enough to spend and how much was enough. In most households, the standard of living was more influenced by earning patterns than by spending habits. All citizens were consumers, but all depended upon income earners in order to consume.[36] In the 1950s the dependence of consumers was rhetorically magnified by the assumption that consumers were women and producers were men, consumers, wives and producers, husbands. In these circumstances, how could the consumer interest be a countervailing power?

There had been some inkling of this dilemma from the very beginnings of the CAC, before Liberal women had secured control over the organization or housewifery had lost precedence to growth and markets in discussions of the consumer interest. In the summer of 1947 when asked the very soft question, 'Without committing yourself in any way, would you be inclined to become a member of [a peacetime consumer] organisation if one were set up in your community,' only 53 per cent of women surveyed in Halifax, Montreal, Toronto, Winnipeg, and Vancouver answered yes. The membership campaign of 1948, which aimed to recruit 250,000 members, fell far short of its goal. In 1952 only 1 per cent of that many Canadian women, about 2200, were supporting the CAC by paying dues.[37]

Although the leadership of the CAC claimed roots in the Consumer Branch of the WPTB, in which a wide range of Canadian women had participated, its membership appears to have been closer in composition to that of the National Council of Women, the venerable organization founded in the 1890s by the wife of the governor general, which had summoned it into peacetime existence. At the spring 1947 planning meetings, Allan Gill of the Standards Branch warned of this eventuality, worried that unless the traditional reach of the council were 'enlarged to include low-income groups,' the new consumers' association would not be doing the welfare work which needed to be done. The Housewives' Consumers Association, which claimed a large working-class membership, was not represented within the CAC after the founding meeting of September 1947. Grace MacInnis, a CCF member of the British Columbia Legislature during the war, and later the federal member for Vancouver Kingsway, was not far wrong in concluding by the early 1950s that the CAC 'was too concerned with well-fed, middle-income people and neglectful of the poor' to represent a distinctive national consumer interest.[38]

In the early years of the CAC, Christine White, the labour liaison for the

This CAC pamphlet from the late 1940s refeatures Canadian consumers in fashionable New Look garb, wearing ample yards of fabric and carrying amply filled bags of groceries.

Consumer Branch, daughter of a Clydeside unionist, wife of a printer turned Manitoba factory inspector, herself a scholarship student of accounting and labour legislation and in the 1930s active in consumer co-ops, had kept the dialogue open between the consumers association and labour groups. The Canadian Congress of Labour forwarded resolutions to the CAC for support, in 1949 on ethical standards in advertising, in 1950 on advertising as well as price controls and old age pensions. Mrs Pat Conroy, from the Canadian Congress of Labour, served as corresponding secretary for the CAC in these years, and argued forcefully for these resolutions. But none was carried, those on price controls being defeated as earlier HCL-sponsored resolutions on controls had been, those on advertising being referred back for clarification, and that on old age security ruled 'not a consumer matter.' Despite these rebuffs, the Canadian Congress of Labour matched the contributions of two wealthy donors, one of them Lady Eaton, dowager of the department store dynasty, when the CAC ran into financial difficulty in 1952. But by the mid-1950s active labour representation at the CAC had disappeared. Responding with blame rather than gratitude, Renée Vaudelet, the CAC president in 1956, regretted that 'so far Labor has dealt too lightly with us.' 'We need to enlist more UNION wives in our business of learning and practising consumer economics,' she opined with clear proprietorship, but the claim there was a unified consumer interest across class difference was not standing up under scrutiny.[39]

The tension between the CAC and farm women was sharp from 1947, for the postwar arguments against rising prices were first about foodstuffs and thus about farm earnings. An article in the first issue of the CAC *Bulletin* asked consumers to recognize that farmers' input costs were rising and thus that they could not 'bear the entire burden of providing certain food items at low' prices.[40] But the association's tolerance for farmers' concerns as producers was always more grudging than their sympathy for the business constraints of manufacturers and marketers. The leadership of the CAC was predominantly urban, and more closely tied by marriage to industry and the service sector than to the land. The successful CAC court action to lift the ban on margarine in 1949 widened the rift. Milk producers began to organize marketing boards in the early 1950s to stabilize prices and support farm incomes. The CAC milk committee argued that these 'unfortunately successful' efforts were 'a dangerous threat to the health of the nation because they would raise the price of milk.' When the CAC secured representation on the Ontario and Manitoba marketing boards, farm women were flummoxed. Agriculturalists, they noted, were not given seats as directors of those industries whose products they purchased.[41] An agricultural convenor reported to each CAC annual meeting through the 1950s, trying 'to impress upon the members of the CAC the fact that a stable and prosperous farm population is a major factor in enduring prosperity throughout Canada.' Her voice was always dissonant. While supporting Canadian tariffs on manufactured goods, the CAC resisted agricultural tariffs which would support Canadian agriculture.[42]

In 1955 *Canadian Business* argued that the association, after 'divorcing itself from the "lunatic fringe" and communist-front trouble makers,' had become a purposeful and constructive voice in Ottawa and in industry. And indeed, the leaders of the CAC were welcome as speakers before marketing and manufacturing groups and federal government bodies. The Canadian Association of Consumers claimed to have 16,000 members in 1955, still considerably short of their 1947 goal of a quarter million. The relationship between the CAC and farm women continued to be strained. Of 303 Ontario farm homemakers surveyed in July 1959, only 8 even mentioned the CAC as a possible source for help in buying.[43]

The theory of consumer sovereignty did not describe the world in which Canadian consumers found themselves in the 1950s. Buyers did not have 'perfect' knowledge of the goods for sale in the market, and the possibility that a government agency might help them acquire that knowledge had been ruled out early on as a restraint on competition. In the markets of 1950s Canada, neo-classical economic theory would have predicted with confidence that consumers could not be sovereign, for the conditions which would have made sovereignty possible were not in place. Sellers were few, and growing fewer by comparison with buyers, and were only lightly constrained by regulations from using their greater power in the market. Increasingly buyers did not even buy for reasons that conventional analyses of demand could comprehend. But consumer sovereignty, however chimeric in practice, had become an instrument with impeccable ideological credentials, made commonsensical by the company it kept.

Throughout the 1950s the CAC showed a complex and sympathetic understanding of how consumers' concerns might be tied to the health of the manufacturing sector. Their analyses of labour issues and agriculture were, by contrast, ill-informed and full of suspicion.[44] By class background, by academic training, by loyalty to Liberal government policy, the leaders of the CAC confidently claimed as an objective and unitary consumer interest the perspective of prosperous urban central Canadians, their own perspective.

So long as the concept of the housewife as a producer as well as a consumer had remained vital, there was conceptual apparatus with which to think of the economy as larger than the market. In the forties this authoritative housewife re-emerged, spurred in Canada by the Depression and the war. Later, as non-industrial producers were made invisible in the economy, the household economy, being unmeasured, was called unmeasurable and then of no account. In economic discourse, consumption became less a practice, let alone a knowledge and frame of mind from which to exercise a distinctive influence, than a genderless Keynesian conduit called purchasing power.[45] A public interest group working from this position could not unite consumers nationally or organize them effectively as a countervailing power in a marketplace dominated by powerful manufacturers and retailers. For this analysis accepted that consumers were dependent, in their households on those who earned income, in the nation on those who produced wealth. Where, in these circumstances, would a consumer interest which was self-conscious and self-actualizing exist?

5

Borrowing to Buy

Canadians were saving and spending and borrowing more in the fifties and sixties because their incomes were higher, more stable, and, by individual observation and experience, more secure than in the two previous decades. Among the women with whom I spoke, consumer credit remained anathema for those schooled as girls in what they often called 'depression mentality,' the conviction that only cash buying was prudent and safe. This was especially so if family income depended upon fluctuating earnings from the resource sector or agriculture.[1] Yet by the late 1950s many Canadians were more guided in their decisions to borrow by memories of almost two decades of steady earnings than Depression era recollections of the family phonograph being repossessed. The burden of prudence lifted as the welfare state and private medical insurance plans provided shelter in employment and health crises.[2] And there were more useful and attractive, but expensive, goods to buy.

Personal expenditures on consumer durables trebled from 1948 to 1960, and consumer credit outstanding rose fivefold. By 1967 Canadians were second only to Americans among North Atlantic nations in their volumes of such debt, far ahead of Britons, Germans, and the French as household borrowers.[3] In the late 1950s, how much householders should spend on domestic goods, and how much they ought to be buying with earned or borrowed money, once more became a matter of public and private debate. Yet on the basis of nationwide statistics it was difficult to argue in the fifties and sixties that consumer debt was becoming a burden, even though Canadians' spending on consumer durables rose. As a proportion of disposable income, these expenditures did not increase after 1949. Debt as a proportion of income was the same, on average 10.9 per cent, for both the periods 1948–56 and 1957–65. More purchases of household goods were made using consumer credit as the years went by. But personal savings rates as a proportion of income remained high, as high while the use of consumer credit accelerated in 1965 as they had been since 1948. Did this constitute a debt crisis?[4]

Once again the question was engaged, who was entitled to spend, and on what? Was there a 'morality of spending' to be reckoned when governments expanded public debt either to manage the business cycle or to direct wealth and job creation? Were there ethical issues to be addressed when across the country tens of thousands of householders decided all at once to borrow money to replace furniture or buy freezers? If public and private indebtedness were ethical issues, were they to be judged in the same way? If not, were the two systems of judging how much was enough and for whom necessarily tied or in need of being reconciled? For a decade after 1957, federal governments became more attentive to regional and income inequality. Consumer credit was one focus for public and private deliberation about spending and debt, about how much was enough and for whom.

Savings rates did fall during the late 1950s (see table 5.1). Some then charged that householders were mortgaging the nation's future, diverting for present consumption funds 'which otherwise would have been available for financing Canadian development under Canadian ownership and control.' Such concerns about the relationship between debt and autonomy, both of households and the nation, would linger. But their immediate provocation soon faded. Personal savings burgeoned again in 1962 and remained a significant source of financing for business and government during the boom of the sixties, even as the use of consumer credit grew.[5]

'What has changed,' Gerald Fortin, director of the Social Science Research Institute at Laval University reported in 1962, 'is not the attitude or the norm towards credit but rather the definition of what constitutes the basic needs of the population. What has changed is the consumption norm – the standard package of goods and services which each family wishes to possess.' Hazel Beech of Lake Cowichan, British Columbia, whose letter began by listing the washboard and admirable sawdust burner stove with which she provided for her family of four in the late forties, concluded by describing the sectional chesterfield and upright freezer she bought in the sixties: 'As wages increased we felt justified in owning all the amenities of life for our growing family as opposed to the scarcity of luxuries while growing up in the "Thirties and Forties."' And too, by the later fifties, the constraint that credit was not readily available for working people without collateral was, like Depression memories, fading away.[6]

TABLE 5.1
Canadian Savings Rates,* 1947–67

Year	Rate	Year	Rate
1947	5.6	1958	5.3
1948	10.2	1959	3.3
1949	7.9	1960	3.1
1950	5.7	1961	3.2
1951	9.8	1962	5.4
1952	10.1	1963	5.3
1953	8.2	1964	4.7
1954	4.5	1965	6.1
1955	4.2	1966	6.8
1956	4.9	1967	6.6
1957	4.6		

*Savings rates are total personal savings as
a proportion of total personal income.
Source: Canada, Department of Finance,
Economic and Fiscal Reference Tables
(Sept. 1994) Table 14, p. 25

A common rejoinder to the interview question about borrowing was, 'There wasn't plastic then, you had to save before you bought.'[7] Banks did little consumer lending before 1958. Section 91 of the Bank Act, dating from 1944, limited bank interest on loans to 6 per cent. Though loan policy resulted in an effective rate often nearer 11 per cent, the banks did not seek out personal loans business. The only women I spoke with who 'went to the bank' when they wanted equipment for their homes had savings in bonds which they could put up as collateral.[8]

In 1948, more consumer credit was provided by life insurance companies, extending loans to their policyholders on the basis of accrued cash value, than by banks (table 5.2).[9] As borrowers, those without insurance policies or bonds had limited options. Through the fifties, most people arranged financing for their purchases through the retailer at point of sale. Often the stores then sold these obligations to sales finance companies, firms whose business since the 1920s had been to collect the balance of retail debts. This credit, the loans provided by retailers and sales finance companies in distinct contracts for each item purchased, was more cumbersome and fee-ridden than lender credit, a loan of cash to purchase a group of consumer durables. Consumer loan companies would extend unsecured loans of cash to wage earners, and their share of the consumer loan market doubled between 1948 and 1964. The credit unions and caisses populaires grew apace through the fifties and sixties, though their rates and relations with their borrowers were defined by contrast with the

TABLE 5.2
Composition of Consumer Credit in Canada, 1948–64

	1948	1952	1956	1960	1964
Institution			% of total		
Sales finance companies	8.4	23.0	26.3	20.6	16.7
Consumer loan companies	7.6	9.1	12.4	13.6	14.6
Chartered banks	18.4	14.9	15.2	21.3	29.0
Life insurance companies	18.9	13.1	9.4	8.6	6.4
Retail	40.2	34.0	27.8	23.9	18.5
Credit unions, caisses populaires	6.5	5.8	7.9	10.8	13.6
Total (millions of $)	669	1385	2642	3588	5279

Source: E.P. Neufeld, 'The Economic Significance of Consumer Credit,' in *Consumer Credit in Canada* (Saskatoon: University of Saskatchewan, 1966) 6; Royal Commission on Banking and Finance, *Report* (1964) 204; William C. Hood, *Financing Economic Activity in Canada*, study for the Royal Commission on Canada's Economic Prospects (1958) 133; Bank of Canada, *Statistical Summary* (1965) 676

consumer loan companies. Still most people did their banking with banks and had some aversion to 'getting into the hands of' the finance companies. Thus, once the banks overcame their aversions to the personal loan sector, they quickly became the largest providers of consumer credit, and with their accessible and doughty presence in the field, the volume of consumer credit sought and extended grew rapidly. One bank, the Commerce, had been handling consumer loans since 1936, and all had been permitted to take household property as security for loans since the revision of the Bank Act in 1954. But the others did not enter the field until after the downturn in 1958, when, with more funds to lend than businesses wanted to borrow, the banks began to realize that at some rates of interest handling small loans might be worth their while. By 1964 chartered bank personal loans accounted for 29 per cent of consumer credit in Canada, and any Canadian with a savings or chequing account had an established association with an institution in the business of extending consumer loans.[10]

Despite earlier fears, in the postwar decades consumer expenditures had been a stabilizing influence on the growth of income and employment, while volatility in the economy came from changes in export demand as well as business spending and capital formation financed by borrowing.[11] Now that householders increasingly were borrowers, John Kenneth Galbraith warned in a widely read jeremiad of 1958, their spending compounded the uncertainty created by business.[12]

Though aggregate consumer expenditure generally was stable, the durables portion of consumer spending was responsive to economic cycles.[13] The more commonly credit was used for large household purchases, the more responsive would be demand to rises in income and declines in price. In the presence of credit, the 'bunching' noted in durables purchases (the inclination to buy many, or of many to buy, as times looked brighter; and to buy fewer, or of fewer to buy, as times looked dark) amplified cyclical swings in the economy.

By the time the Royal Commission on Banking and Finance reported in 1964, many Canadian economists agreed that the cyclical effects of buying consumer durables on credit were probably small, tamed by householders' long view of their lifetime income prospects, tranquil beside the volatility of business spending on inventories and fixed investment. But in 1958 when the phenomenon was newer, or at least bank consumer lending was newer, and a downturn was at hand, the worry that increased personal debt might make the economy vulnerable to deflation was not readily assuaged.[14]

If consumer credit was a threat to economic stability, there were tested remedies. Containing consumer credit through selective controls had been tried since the war and was linked at least temporally to the rise in savings rates in the early 1950s (table 5.1).[15] Keynesian economists' instruments of choice for achieving economic stability in the immediate postwar years had been fiscal, changing the sum of all spending by altering the portion of income and wealth drawn away in taxes, or altering the scale of government expenditures. But by the mid-fifties, faith in Keynesian fiscal instruments had faltered.[16] As the economy heated up in 1955 and 1956, more hope was invested in monetary policy.

Monetary policy works by altering the supply and cost of money – that is, the stock of cash or bank deposits readily turned into cash, and the cost of money, the rate of interest. Since 1935, sending out these signals had been the job of the Bank of Canada. At the bank in 1956, consumer credit seemed the delinquent child of the financial sector, without adult obligations and beyond parental control. The central bankers' view was that the extension of consumer credit, particularly instalment credit, was growing too rapidly and, more problematically, was continuing to grow after other lending had been curtailed in response to Bank of Canada constraints. For the chartered banks were closely controlled by the Bank of Canada in the price and the volume of money they might lend to all borrowers, including finance companies.

In 1951 the Bank of Canada attempted to limit instalment lending by stipulating that the chartered banks not increase their lines of credit to finance companies. These were short-term bank loans the sales finance companies in turn lent out as instalment sales contracts to purchasers of goods. These loans stimulated demand. To avoid this central bank limitation on their lending, the finance companies began to raise funds by selling large volumes of high-yielding short-term notes in the money market. Thus they evaded the constraints imposed by federal monetary policy. Having been singled out for special restrictive treatment in 1951, they jauntily used the liberty of being outside the Bank Act to do an irreverent end-run around the Bank of Canada.

The central bank itself was an unwitting accomplice in this evasion. From 1953 it had encouraged the development of the money market to trade the bank's increasing volumes of treasury bills. By their offers of repurchase and sale, these short-term notes were the bank's way to influence the money supply more incrementally. But as William C. Hood noted with irony in 1958, 'Once a corporation treasurer has learned to buy a federal treasury bill, it takes very little more nerve to buy a higher yielding finance company note.'[17] Having been outdone at their own game, the Bank of Canada tried in 1956 to get instalment lenders voluntarily to stabilize the volume of instalment credit. The only concessions came from Eaton's and Simpson's, who agreed to stop selling goods on time without down payments. Otherwise, the retail and sales finance sectors declined the request. This loophole remained open. Acknowledging that the central bank had been bested, in 1964 Gerald Bouey, chief of research at the bank, advised the Parliamentary Committee on Consumer Credit not to look to the Bank of Canada, if 'consumer credit was getting out of bounds'; only Parliament could constrain this renegade route to expanding the money supply.[18]

The 1956 discussion between the bank and the providers of consumer credit did not concern rates of interest. But the issues of the supply and cost of money were linked. Instalment-plan interest was so high that the finance companies could afford to pay money market yields high enough that the studied changes in the bank's treasury bill rates were marginalized. Despite the repeated attempts of Hazen Argue, the CCF member for Assiniboia, to get a maximum interest bill through the federal house, this issue would be deferred for another day.[19]

That day came later in the 1950s when public discussion turned from growth to redistributive concerns. Then the exceptionally high rates householders had to pay for financing gained attention. Louis St Laurent and C.D. Howe's emphasis on growth shared attention during the governing years of John Diefenbaker and Lester Pearson with questions about economic equity and autonomy. Who benefits, who shares, who has a say? The shift in orientation was heralded and informed by the work of the Liberal-led Royal Commission on Canada's Economic Prospects, the Gordon Commission, on the structure and control of Canadian industry. Diefenbaker's election campaigns of 1957 and 1958 reinforced these priorities with promised attention to regional inequalities, Canadian control over Canadian industry, and government funding for immense development projects to reorient growth in economic activity and income.[20]

Because the costs of consumer borrowing were high, who borrowed to buy was a redistributive concern. Although middle-income Canadians were most likely to have some consumer debt, and the poorest Canadians, those with family incomes under $2000 per year, were most likely to have none, outstanding consumer loan obligations pressed most heavily on those with less. In both 1959 and 1964, lower-income families were overrepresented among those whose consumer debts constituted over 20 per cent of their annual income. These were often families of renters without housing debts, but they were borrowing for basics on less advantageous terms than the more wealthy who were house-poor through (often publicly subsidized) mortgages.[21]

On average, families with younger household heads were carrying larger consumer debt loads. The Canadian Retail Federation observed that 'Borrowing varies over the family's life cycle. "Debt rotates through the population."'[22] But not through all the population. In 1959 and again in 1968, Helen Abell found Ontario farm families were making little use of either charge accounts or instalment plans on the grounds that these forms of payment cost money, encouraged overspending, and, in summary, were morally wrong.[23] Recent immigrants borrowed for household goods, but the credit instruments open to them were constrained. In downtown Toronto, 1950s immigrants were less likely to make use of department store credit or be accepted as risks by larger finance companies, and in discussion with university investigators were less likely to report liberal credit terms as a reason for choosing where to buy.[24]

The most consistent and troubling finding about consumer credit sea to sea was that the poorer the Canadians borrowing to buy household goods, the more likely they were to use the most costly instalment plans offered by retailers and sales finance companies.[25] This finding was the focus of intensifying moral concern in the early 1960s because of the power imbalance critics saw between borrowers and lenders. Commentators, such as Betty Lee, writing for the Toronto *Globe and Mail*, found faults on both sides: 'Basically ... the bread-and-butter functions of the mammoth, independent sales finance companies are ... to (a) help get merchandise out of the factory and onto a dealer's floor and (b) to help the consumer move the stuff quickly out of the showroom and into his home without the tedious and unfashionable task of having to save.' But the inequalities observed between the contracting parties were stark.[26]

Jacob Ziegel, a professor of law at Saskatchewan, McGill, and finally the University of Toronto, wanted the law of consumer credit changed. He argued that the assumption of the doctrine of contract, that every person of full age and sound mind bargained on equal terms, was anomalous given the imbalance between the creditor's and the debtor's positions.[27] Neither free markets nor contracts freely entered were necessarily so liberating as liberal dogma claimed. Arthur Moreira, the Portuguese-born Dalhousie law graduate who conducted a Nova Scotia inquiry into the cost of borrowing in 1964 and 1965, contended that there was 'probably no area of commerce in which the public are more vulnerable to exploitation.' 'To dwell on the question whether some people in these businesses are a set of rascally and heartless usurers or not is to miss the point completely. The real point is the extent to which inadmissible practices can be allowed to gain widespread acceptance, so as to commend themselves not only to the few who may be depraved but to the many who are not but simply do not stop to think about them.' Dorothy McArton, director of the Family Bureau of Winnipeg, argued similarly that the 'business of government' was to legislate so that moral businessmen were not forced to collude and deceive to stay in business.[28]

This critique of credit was linked to the critique of a commodity culture adapting in the late 1950s to saturated markets. Contemporary product design was placing more emphasis on styling. Products were being engineered for earlier replacement. This commodity culture and the postwar pattern of younger marriages, the federal joint committee on consumer credit reported, provided 'fertile soil for a system of buying which separates the pleasure of acquisition from the pain of payment.' Thus the Canadian critiques of consumer credit shared something of Vance Packard's *The Waste Makers* and David Caplovitz's *The Poor Pay More*. They were all commentaries on the seduction of commercial bribes-to-buy and the inequitable costs of being seduced.[29]

But the moral burden in Canadian commentaries and proposals for remedy was particularly heavy, and particularly focused upon 'the poor,' whom Senator David Croll, chair of the 1960s federal investigation into consumer credit, characterized as 'more gullible, more easily cheated, less conscious of the quality of the goods they buy,' and thus more in need of being protected from their 'own lack of knowledge and discipline' and 'from operators who take advantage of [their] ignorance and gullibility.' Contrarily, Gerald Fortin, the Laval social scientist, found the education programs so frequently suggested as moral antidotes to the temptations of consumer credit themselves ethically unsound, as their goal was to convince the poor that what was standard for their neighbours was morally bad for them. Better, he argued, with 'more public investment and better income redistribution' to 'guarantee every citizen the standard package.' Croll's own committee suggested a step in this direction with its recommendation that 'hard-pressed low-income wage-earners,' too poor to take advantage of subsidized National Housing Act mortgages and in need of household financing, be given government loans for 'provident and productive purposes ... related to the well-being of home and family.'[30]

That borrowing to buy household goods might be provident and productive was a subversive idea, whose most eager champions, appropriately, were the 'bad boys' of the financial sector, the loan companies and furniture and appliance stores that specialized in instalment sales. Until the 1920s, consumer credit most often had been extended for food and fuel bought on the tick from general merchants, that is, for goods which were literally consumable, 'that disappeared when used.' After the Second World War, consumer credit was offered, instead, for household durables, and credit for consumables became increasingly rare. Yet the terminology invoking ephemerality and disappearance persisted. Consumer goods thus came to be classified by their destination, the household and not the firm, rather than by the duration, none or long, of their value as assets. On close scrutiny, the functional distinction between consumer goods and investment goods became increasingly elusive, as witnessed by this exchange about definitions between members of the parliamentary joint committee and Gerald Bouey of the Bank of Canada in June 1964:

MR MANDZIUK: Mr Bouey is saying that consumer credit is credit extended for things that the borrower consumes. Is that what your definition is restricted to?

MR. BOUEY: Yes, that is right.

MR MANDZIUK: So that the financing of an automobile would not fall into that category?

MR. BOUEY: Yes it would. We would consider an automobile a form of consumption ... Automobiles and furniture and so on are considered as consumer goods.

MR MANDZIUK: But investments are not?

MR. BOUEY: Not investments.

SENATOR STAMBAUGH: It is confined to things that will wear out?

MR. BOUEY: In a reasonably short time, yes, Senator Stambaugh.

SENATOR STAMBAUGH: Furniture and things like that are considered to be consumer goods?

MR. BOUEY: Yes, otherwise you would be left with only things that last for a very short time, such as food.[31]

The distinction was arbitrary, Bouey acknowledged. Its capacity to make expensive, usable, and resaleable goods seem to vanish was most ludicrously apparent to the gentlemen of the parliamentary committee when applied to automobiles – for example, their own.

Retailers and consumer finance company representatives recognized that the categorical differentiation between investment and consumer financing sustained an implicit accusation: instalment sales plans were inducing the households of the nation to feckless dissipation. Upon this differentiation and accusation, regulation might readily follow. Thus, it was in the interest of those who provided householders with loans to refuse the distinctions between investments, automobiles, and furniture, which Senator Stambaugh and his House of Commons colleague had found so difficult to grasp. In their trade papers, and in briefs before royal commissions in the early 1960s, retailers referred to household equipment as 'domestic capital goods,' and parsed the distinction in financing as between investments in 'business capital goods' and 'consumer capital goods.' In these terms, purchases of household goods were investments. Instalment sales plans, they argued, were 'the "trade credit" of the household sector.' The aphorism, 'consumer credit leads to the purchase of things we do not need with the money we have not got,' credit grantors dismissed as 'smug paternalism.' For who but the investor was to judge? A productive household investment, like any investment, was a necessarily 'subjective evaluation' of benefits.[32] The Royal Commission on Banking and Finance incorporated these arguments into its final report, emphasizing the analogies between households and business enterprises: both were making rational appraisals of costs and benefits; both were investing in capital goods to reduce their costs of production.

The economists and bankers on the commission, reasoning through the implications of this position, were then obliged to refuse another distinction which remains contentious and problematically with us decades later. Households, like business enterprises, 'may meet their needs for many goods and services either by buying them or producing them.' Thus when capital goods saved money or labour in the household, the savings were 'real.' They were justifications for the investment. Investment in household durables would 'yield high returns' in as much as it 'replace[d] previous unrecorded but nevertheless real commitments.' 'It is advantageous to employ such capital when its benefits exceed the cost of financing it even though the resulting production is not sold in the market place.' This household production had economic value even though it did not enter into the reckoning of the national income accounts.[33]

Unless the commissioners were assuming that domestic capital goods worked without human intervention, it followed that household labour had economic value even though it was not assigned a market wage. On this unorthodox possibility they strategically evaded comment. Perhaps the next step in the reasoning, that household labour might thus appropriately be waged or at least pensionable, the banking commissioners merely considered to be outside their purview. Minimally, their argument about consumer credit led them explicitly to assert that market and non-market production alike created goods and services of economic value, at least a mild heresy among practitioners who customarily recognized value only through a market price.

Thus had close scrutiny of market reasoning, and the unequal distributional effects 'free markets' brought in their wake, entered policy discussion in Canada in the early 1960s. As a consequence of its ideological origins, the Canadian Association of Consumers, in the late forties a champion of market over non-market resolutions to consumer problems, came late to this transition. Its brief to the Royal Commission on Canada's Economic Prospects in March 1956 stood out for its emphasis on resource exports as the engine of economic growth and its cautionary concern that tariffs on manufactured imports constrained consumers' desires for 'the widest possible variety of goods at the lowest possible prices.' In 1962, the CAC representative continued to make similar arguments, insisting that 'no consumer in her right mind' would pay 'a premium just because the product is Canadian; and no manufacturer in his right mind should expect her to.'

Yet the CAC, too, was beginning to change. Departing from its earlier conviction that free markets made consumers sovereign, its 1963 brief to the Royal Commission on Taxation listed the ill effects imperfect competition and the current tax system had wrought, and urged new fiscal policies which would work toward equity objectives. By mid-decade, a speaker before the CAC annual meeting took, as given, that its goal as an association was to attend to the needs of those 'left behind or left out of the progress of the economy towards higher average levels of consumer income and spending,' among them not only the historically disadvantaged, but the Consumers' own daughters and sons setting up households on starting salaries.[34] In the 1960s, for the CAC (by that time renamed the Consumers' Association of Canada) most conspicuously this meant making common cause with Senator David Croll in his long and often lonely campaign for reform in the regulation of consumer credit.

As David Monod has shown, historically the extension of credit to stores to finance inventories and by stores to customers who bought on time were closely related. In the first third of the twentieth century, suppliers shortened their lending terms. Shopkeepers then could not afford to let shoppers' debts accumulate without prearranged ceilings or payment schedules. The informal bonds which had governed commercial relations between village merchants and neighbours were replaced by strictly denominated commercial exchanges.[35] Yet the full implications of this transition in relations between retailers and householders remained veiled.

For many customers whose practical needs exceeded their limited means in the 1940s and 1950s, the grant of credit remained an acknowledgment, and the repayment of debt a demonstration, of personal worth. Gerd Evans, a Norwegian immigrant, and her husband, a fisherman, lived for the first years of their marriage in trailers and float houses along the British Columbia coast. They bought their first house in 1955, in Vancouver. This is how she described their relationship with Ben Wosk, whose large downtown Vancouver store was a local landmark.

He was the only one who would give us credit. At first the salesman wouldn't so I had heard of him and so I went to Ben Wosk and I said, Mr. Wosk, I said, we don't have money but we will make payments and we've never reneged on a debt of any kind, and I promise we'll pay. So he said, well, I've never had a working man, you know, do me out of anything, so he said you can have it. So that's how we bought. And he was very nice. And we paid it off and we went and thanked him and so it was really nice. And that house was furnished. It had a kitchen table and four chairs, it had a chesterfield and a chair and it had a bedroom set. In fact I've still got it.

In the first decade after the war when household furnishings and equipment cost so much relative to the incomes of working people, getting credit was imperative. 'Someone your age, I don't know if you could even visualize that. But even to have $100 was sometimes quite impossible. And you couldn't borrow it. You couldn't go to the bank and get $100 easily.' So the man on Fourth Street in Kitsilano who sold chesterfields, like Ben Wosk downtown on Hastings Street, seemed an ally in adversity, someone who recognized in the banking system a common adversary. Lily Hansen, the woman who gave me this caution, was the widow of a Vancouver deliveryman and took responsibility for paying her household's bills. Visits to the merchants who had extended them credit were part of her domestic routine. Once a month she went about her rounds – 'It was like an outing' – settling each of the household accounts in cash. Sally Tobe, who kept the books in her parents' furniture store, where instalment sales increased through the fifties, conceded that 'of course there were always the bad debts and the people that skipped town,' but in recollection emphasized the regulars, 'the hard-working guy who's got a wife and family and furniture and he comes in steadily every Saturday to pay his two dollars. And occasionally when he had some extra money he would pay some more but also buy something else.'[36]

Securing credit for basic goods, which were needed now and expected to last a long time, was practical rather than wasteful, a point women emphasized in interviews by showing us 1950s instalment purchases still in use about their homes. Extending credit was seen as akin to extending trust, and the regular personal visits to make payments on the account made debtor and creditor familiars, especially in stores serving immigrant and working-class neighbourhoods.

Instalment sales bore interest as well as other charges, and often an additional cost because credit buyers could not bargain for price discounts. But because credit granting was described and received as a service, retailers commonly called all the financing costs service charges, and evaded clear statements about interest rates.[37] Customers who bought from department stores at advertised prices, with thirty, sixty, or ninety days to pay 'interest-free,' were not reckoning the difference between the immediate and deferred payment prices or the service charges as interest, and in conversation firmly distinguished this buying from buying on credit. More people were entering into financing contracts without legal counsel, assuming unawares costs and obligations which were heavy and unequal: high interest rates, risks of repossession as well as legal liability for the balance of the debt, and the job-threatening possibility of garnisheed wages.[38]

Nor were they likely to realize how close was the relationship between the friendly salesman who wrote up their instalment contract and the sales finance company to whom it soon was sold. Though the fact would have been implausible and counter-intuitive to most shoppers, retailers preferred credit over cash sales. Both salesmen and dealers received a portion of the financing charges. As Arthur Moreira observed for Nova Scotia, these earnings came to constitute an important part of dealers' revenues, up to a third of a retailer's total income.[39]

The transfers between sales finance companies and retailers were called dealers' reserves. Retailers received a finder's fee whenever a buyer purchased on time. The finance company held back some of these fees as reserves against the possibility that the debtors the retailers recruited might default on their contracts. But as William C. Hood described this pattern, in plain language, in 1958, 'after these "dealer reserves" have reached an agreed proportion, perhaps 3 to 10 percent of the dealer's outstanding contracts with the company, then "hold-backs" become "kick-backs" to the dealer.' The dealers negotiated their fees with the finance companies. The dealers and their sales staff, rather than the finance companies, met and recruited loan customers. Competition was between finance companies for the attention of retailers, a situation that tended to bid up the dealer's share of the finance charges and the costs of customers' loans. Dealers financing their own inventories with the same companies focused in this bargaining on rates of interest for their loans, not on terms for their customers' instalment contracts. The shoppers, whose concerns were that financing fees and interest rates be low, were in the thrall of, but not parties to, these negotiations. Moreira called the 'reserves' paid out to the dealers 'bribes.' In this thicket of collusion and deception, when the customer was thankful to be granted credit at all, interest rates for consumer credit remained high, though so shrouded in complex drafting that how high was difficult to discern.[40]

From 1960, Senator David Croll, who had been mayor of Windsor for three terms during the depression of the 1930s, and in the interim the Ontario cabinet minister responsible for public welfare and municipal affairs and then minister of labour, took up the cost of consumer credit as his guiding concern. Croll's bills would have provided consumers as borrowers with the total dollar costs of buying on credit (including interest and fees), and the expression of those costs in terms of simple annual interest. With this information, he argued, 'the consumer who is a borrower, will be able to shop around for credit and compare, as he now shops and compares for the merchandise he wishes to buy.'[41]

There was in the public mind a profound nominal distinction between standard interest rates and usury, the standard being defined by the much-evaded Bank Act loan ceiling of 6 per cent. Thus, all lenders were, for cultural as well as business reasons, deeply committed to using any available means to present their rates as ordinary rather than usurious.[42]

The greater grew the volume of consumer credit, the more worrisome did its clouded, almost unknowable, costs become. Welfare advocates, who realized that the poor were paying more, were concerned. Anyone who believed the price system ought to govern the allocation of resources in the economy disapproved, none more so than the believers in monetary policy for which rates of interest were an effective guiding instrument only if rationally weighed. 'The price system and monetary policy which works through the price system, cannot work if prices are not known generally,' William Hood declared in 1958, an air of desperation seeping into the closing passages of his discussion of consumer finance. Senator Croll and his House of Commons colleague Ron Basford, reporting on the extensive investigation and deliberations of their joint parliamentary committee, expressed the same concern nine years later. The complex technical language which obscured financing costs in sales finance contracts took the brunt of public criticism, but chartered bank contracts for personal loans were little better. A borrower contemplating a personal loan from a bank would have needed to burrow through the minutes of the Commons Standing Committee on Banking for a clear statement of her costs.[43] In the Canadian economy of the 1960s, as all prices rose, the generally fictive quality of all consumer lending rates made anyone troubled by inflationary distortions and the tremulous path of monetary policy increasingly concerned.

In 1957 the Consumers' Association of Canada had passed its first resolution favouring disclosure of total financing costs as simple annual interest, and each year through the early 1960s as Senator Croll's bills went forward and failed, it championed his cause.[44] The association's conviction that 'consumer credit as a service with a price ... can and should be shopped for carefully' remained stalwart. Here the continuity with the founding principles of the association was clear. When full and plainly intelligible disclosure of finance charges was obligatory in all credit contracts, 'consumers would use their purchasing power more efficiently ... Competition in the credit finance business would be stimulated ... Such competition would spur credit finance businesses to greater efficiency and so reduce the cost of this service.' The new emphasis on equity issues became apparent in the CAC's 1963 brief to the Royal Commission on

Taxation. Making common cause with social service agencies, it argued that the interest rate protection under the Small Loans Act of 1939 should cover larger debt consolidation loans, and also instalment sales contracts, lien notes, and chattel mortgages.[45]

The resistance to the disclosure campaign from the financial sector and the Canadian Chamber of Commerce was deep and derisive. R.W. Macaulay, minister of Economics and Development for Ontario, called the proposals 'nuisance legislation,' seeming to invoke images of comfortable ladies in sensible suits as he asked, 'Is it the consumer really asking for it [rate disclosure], or is it somebody who is trying to keep busy by thinking of things to do who is asking for it?'[46] In battle, in parliamentary committee rooms the CAC chose its ground carefully. 'We do not propose to make our Government or this association the custodians of the consumer. The consumer has to use his own intelligence in shopping. We cannot protect him from his own folly, nor do we propose to do so. We want to make as rich a donation as we can to general education in the use of money.' CAC Manitoba representative, June Menzies, presented herself as a candidate for education, working from the student's stance of alertness perked by surprise:

I am baffled that the simple annual interest rate ... can be such a complicated and controversial problem ... Because I am baffled at a straightforward problem I am suspicious ... I am suspicious of the law. The law governing business transactions presupposes a sophisticated consumer – a consumer aware of his rights and responsibilities and aware of the rights and remedies of the lender – a consumer who acts rationally in his own self-interest and who is competent to pit his wits against the men and their lawyers whose business is money.

But, she continued, 'I am not a sophisticated consumer. I am just Mrs. Green or Mr. Jones who would like a new chesterfield or a second-hand car but have to use credit to get it. Now I need protection too. And I need education.'[47]

The Canadian discussions about the culture of mass consumption and the wide use of consumer credit were closely tied, at least temporally. In the late 1950s, the postwar boom in demand for household durables subsided. The most ordinary and serviceable of household goods began to bear more signs of transient stylishness. Makers spoke openly about building obsolescence into their equipment to insure continuing demand. At the same time, the chartered banks began to seek out customers for consumer loans. And sales finance companies found in the newly developing money market their own deep source of financing for growing volumes of instalment sales. By one reading, household goods were becoming more ephemeral even as more were being financed, and on longer credit terms. Those with less were buying more on purchase contracts which would outlast their purchases.

But this concern that mass consumption practices debased consumers as well as their goods was not the dominant strand in the Canadian debate about credit buying. Most Canadian critics of consumer credit wanted the best of modern consumer culture to be more widely shared. Because poorer Canadians were more likely to need to borrow for basics and to seek credit from lenders who charged most for the service, credit practices became an equity issue. They were part of a group of initiatives, dating from the late 1950s and growing more predominant in the 1960s, which aimed to redistribute the wealth of the nation. The campaign for consumer credit reform contained three strands: concern that the cost of borrowing should be stated as simple annual interest; that larger debts should be given interest rate protection; and that there should be subsidies to the poorest Canadians who borrowed to buy basic furniture and equipment, but could not qualify for government-assisted mortgages, benefits on which more prosperous families could rely.

The first goal, disclosure, could be justified on free market principles, that the best allocation decisions were made on the basis of clearly known prices. Though many in the finance and retail sector fiercely resisted these truth in lending initiatives, they were opposed by both consumer and welfare advocates, and central bankers and governments committed to a well-functioning price system.

The latter two goals more plainly required government interventions to constrain the workings of the market and redistribute benefits from private lenders and public revenues to the poor. In the narrowest sense, they relied upon a redefinition: that durable household goods were capital, productive investments rather than profligate expenditures, necessaries in which many should share, not luxuries to remain in the command of the few.

For this redefinition, there was a wide but heterogeneous constituency. Welfare and consumer advocates in the 1960s were becoming forthright: all Canadians were entitled to enjoy the fruits of technological progress and mass production, to own the useful household goods which raised their standard of living and made their lives more comfortable. Those who made and financed consumer durables, eager to sell to more buyers, welcomed terminology which characterized their goods and services as useful and necessary rather than wasteful and predatory. In terms of practical implementation, the latter two goals of consumer credit reform would rely, with the egalitarian social movements of the sixties generally, upon a public will to redistribute income and, until tax reform and non-transfer earnings caught up, to assume greater levels of public debt. The campaign for consumer credit interest rate disclosure was victorious. By the end of 1969 there were truth-in-lending laws in place in all Canadian provinces except Quebec, and the revised Bank Act of 1967 required the same terms of disclosure for chartered bank loans up to $25,000. But the ceiling on cash consumer loans whose interest rates were specified by the Small Loans Act remained unchanged at $1500, and the act was not extended to cover instalment sales financing. Over time these interest rate caps lost significance as the share of consumer credit provided by either consumer loan or sales finance companies decreased.

Borrowers instead turned to banks (table 5.2), where interest rates once had been controlled. This change was not propitious. From January 1968 the long-standing 6 per cent ceiling on chartered bank loans no longer applied. Bank consumer loan rates were disclosed, but they were high and unregulated, in a sector where there was still little competition. Neither was Croll's recommendation accepted that poorer Canadians receive loans to set up their households, akin to the marriage loans established some time before in Sweden. These attempts to make domestic goods more uniformly accessible to Canadian households of all income levels were lost, like the contemporary campaign for guaranteed annual incomes, to concern from the early 1970s with mounting public debt.[48]

PART 2

DESIGN

6

Inter/national Style

Both geometry and machinery can be beautiful. Depending on the circumstances, they can also be useful and, perhaps, fitting. Designers at midcentury saw beauty and usefulness in forms governed by mathematics, and found fittedness, with its echoes of survival and biological succession, in shapes which mirrored the mechanical. These elements were articulated as design principles. There were rules for selecting out certain shapes as good design. Even for everyday goods, there were authorities to consult. The look was identified with modernity in the postwar years, a promise and claim as plausible then as it seems implausible to many now. Most contemporary citizens, if bemused by the need to have rules for homely choices, deferred judgment and went about daily doing what needed to be done.

And well might householders be perplexed. Modernist design, in theory, could come from anywhere and go anywhere. Conventionally, however, whether made by craft or industry, and found in shops, factories, or homes, modernism was identified with industry, rather than the crafts. Its promise was the promise of mass production. Good design was articulated as a single, universal standard, equally applicable to goods made for industry, and those made by industry for the home.

Despite such claims, this design aesthetic was not a timeless essence. It was a chronologically specific form, with a beginning, a constituency, a politics, and an end. First featured as an absolute, it fractured into contingency with time and changing circumstance. Unlike consumer sovereignty, this modernism never became 'common sense' in Canada. It remained a minority concern. But like consumer sovereignty, modern good design was a rallying call for a specific social and economic interest, a timely intervention claiming timelessness, which reveals its era by the company it kept. Its plausibility in the late 1940s was linked to contemporary hopes for freer trade of mass produced goods. Multilateralism as a priority in external trade policy presumed an international style, that there was a geometrically driven, universally acceptable design solution akin to the borderless, optimal free market resolution portrayed graphically in intersecting demand and supply curves.

Modernism was a totalizing ideology and aesthetic, a story about how the whole world would, and some said should, be changed. It was a story usually told in the presence of technology, but, this continuity apart, it was rarely a single or the same story. Rather it was a meta-narrative of paradoxical heterogeneity, sometimes utopian, sometimes dystopic, alternately positioned both as radically right and sociably left, and varying by class, nation, and gender. It focused in uneasy alternation on the machine itself, and on the carnivalesque, the sensual, and the vernacular as refuge and resistance to the machine.

To make the modern sensible historically, we need to scrutinize sceptically the totalizing claims made for this aesthetic, and to reason contextually about a phenomenon frequently asserted to be unconditional. This means considering as parts of one problem both developments which were self-consciously modernist, for example the polemics of good design, and those which were merely modern, or more anonymously contemporary, for example political and economic changes in regulation, production, and distribution.[1] We need to locate the aesthetic within social relations and networks of power, for the dreams about how things should look were related to the dreams about where these looks would find an admiring audience.

Because the modernist aesthetic was a heterogeneous and unstable prescription about one true way, the task demands an ironical stance and a good eye for provenance. For, as executed and displayed, the material culture called modernist was almost always a fragment, the new and wilfully distinct exception to a surrounding accretion made familiar and commonplace by the passing of time. Even in Europe, where the social formations which gave rise to the modernism were indigenous, modern buildings were more often outbreaks than landscapes, and modern goods more often specimens than species. And as Tony Fry has argued for Australia, when models of the modern did not arise locally, but were borrowed from elsewhere, the interpretive problem is more complex still. In colonial and postcolonial settings, modernity was less a 'driving historical condition' than a deracinated 'regime of signs,' a series of solitary examples standing in for distant and 'absent totalities.'[2]

This seems a good stance from which to approach the study of modern design in postwar Canada. This is a pursuit in which weighing instance against incidence, and claim against constituency, could make a real difference. We have already met two fragments offered as guides to reforming modern Canadian industrial strategies and domestic sensibilities: the collection of craft goods displayed as the ethos of industrialism at the Royal Ontario Museum in 1945; and the didactic panels defining industrial design which were borrowed from the Museum of Modern Art for the Toronto Art Gallery show of 1946. We are about to meet more.

In the late 1940s and early 1950s, a federal government agency existed to persuade Canadians, as makers and users of goods, that the visual conventions of industrial design were not merely possibilities but unconditional functional requirements. For a time, securing hegemony for this aesthetic position was taken to be in the public interest, related to contemporary aspirations for the economic health of the nation. The agency which defined this austere purpose as its own, the National Industrial Design Committee (NIDC), was only modestly funded, though its budget was three- and fourfold what the Canadian Association of Consumers received at the same time in government support. The NIDC persisted in this unreconstructed stance for only five years, from 1948 until 1953, when the voices of pragmatism began to challenge modernism's more austere apostles.[3]

The modernism of the National Industrial Design Committee was defined by the influence of three men, Alan Jarvis, Herbert Read, and Donald Buchanan. Jarvis was from Ontario, a Rhodes scholar who studied aesthetics at Oxford and in the 1940s was public relations officer for the British Council of Industrial Design (COID). He later became a controversial head of the National Gallery in Ottawa, the federal agency responsible for the NIDC. Read was a British art historian and theorist whose *Art and Industry*, a book reprinted regularly after it first appeared in 1934, articulated common purposes for abstract art and industrial design. Buchanan was an Albertan, trained in constitutional history at University of Toronto, who like Jarvis was a Canadian scholarship student at Oxford. From 1945 he was supervisor of special projects at the National Film Board, a post which allowed him to explore his interest in industrial design. The aesthetics of these three men, and their beliefs about the appropriate relationship between form giving and form making, determined the institutional arrangements and program priorities which defined design modernism to Canadians in the early postwar years. Their modernism emphasized the machine aesthetic, the beauty of neo-Platonic geometric and abstract forms, and the need to educate popular taste to these ideals.

The machine aesthetic they admired and championed presumed that a distinctive appearance was 'present in the typical products of the machine.' Herbert Read listed these qualities as precision, calculation, flawlessness, simplicity, and economy. Philip Johnson of the Museum of Modern Art in New York, in a contemporary essay on machine art, added smoothness and reproducibility, machine-made traits he said were 'diametrically opposed' to the irregularity, picturesqueness, and decorative value which pertained in the crafts.[4]

Contemporaries recognized that machines could make goods which looked any way imaginable. Indeed design reformers had been railing against this very capability since the days of William Morris. But Jarvis, Read, and Buchanan argued that efficiency, which they quixotically assumed to have a singular and direct relationship to form, had become paramount in postwar mechanical reproduction. The same factors which produced efficiency in a machine, and in objects produced by a machine, produced good design. The traits of the production process carried over into the product itself; by extension, they asserted, 'a design was bound to be good aesthetically if it *worked* well.'[5] The good look inhered in the working well, and this, Donald Buchanan advised in a 1946 address to the Canadian Manufacturers' Association, meant keeping away from 'mere decorative changes in style' and getting down to 'the basic technological problems of design.'

Solving these technological problems, efficiently making goods which would work well, required that the consumers, as the users of goods, adopt the reasoning of machine makers. Consumers were to think about how machines worked, 'assimilate the machine,' reconceptualize their own needs in terms machine makers would recognize, and be 'less prejudiced' by criteria machine makers found unsound. Swedish designers in the 1930s, whose work so impressed Buchanan on his 1935 visit to the Brussels International Exhibition,[6] articulated these premises under the rallying call of 'acceptera,' urging citizens to accept machines into the centre of their lives and define their own potentials through the possibilities machines could open to them. Jarvis called this a 'practical and "engineering approach,"' though it posited a unitary way of resolving problems for which engineering knowledge usually offered a wide variety of possible solutions.[7]

The polemic for a machine aesthetic in the late 1940s was about aesthetics more than about machines. However much being produced efficiently and 'working well' thereafter laid the foundation for good design, beauty lay elsewhere. Material, tools, function, and tradition were four limiting factors on the shape of things, Jarvis counselled the readers of his popular Penguin 1947 paperback, *The Things We See Indoors and Out*, but nearly always a fifth factor dominated the other four, 'the desire to make things beautiful.'[8] Read argued that beauty was not derivable from function but arose relatively autonomously. The aesthetic criteria were independent of social and economic context; they were timeless and universal, detached from industry, commerce, and practical usefulness, and should dominate the form of things.[9] The precedence of influence was clear. The industrial designer was to reconcile 'the necessities of machine production with those standards of beauty which are universally satisfying,' adapting the usable good to the aesthetic standard, by adhering to stated general principles. Only with 'practice, work and effort' were these rules about beauty accessible either to the designer or the public. To not make the effort to distinguish between beauty which was the '*real thing*' and the shallow proliferation of crude synthetics, Jarvis admonished, was to 'boast of our impoverishment,' 'like the spinster of her virtue.'[10] Despite the implicit sensual contrast intended by the mockery of the chaste woman, this modernism was a stern discipline, especially to demand of popular audiences and popular wares.

These general principles were derived from neo-Platonic geometry, rules which promised to reduce the clutter of contingent detail to 'the clarity of essential form.'[11] As Plato found beauty inherent in shapes made by the lathe, ruler, and square, the apostles of this modernist aesthetic featured machines as a 'practical application of geometry.' In so far as machines were formed of straight lines and curves, they were thought capable of reproducing in goods the Platonic laws of symmetry and proportion.[12] Thus, Read argued, machines in the command of a designer sensitive to these 'formal values' could be and could make abstract art. 'Rational abstraction in art is measurable, and resolves into numerical laws ... the machine which works to adjustment and measure, can produce such works with unfailing and unrivalled precision.'[13] Clarity, with purity and integrity, terms of praise in this design discourse, referred to the unmediated geometry of a form, the geometric being posited as the truest shape of things. This is the 'constantly evolving abstract refinement' Virginia Wright has faulted Canadian manufacturers for not pursing with sufficient constancy in consumer goods. The designer's task was to uncover this geometrical essence, anticipated in past forms (hence the classical and oriental references in modernist work, and the exhibition of antiquities in the ROM and TAG shows of 1945 and 1946), and progressively revealed in the increasingly refined abstraction of the modernist project.

For modern industrial design, as it was articulated for Canadians in the late 1940s by Read, Jarvis, and Buchanan, was fundamentally a project to instate artists and aesthetic principles as authorities over the central ground of modern life. This industrial design was specified so as to be a solution to the problem of the modern artist, displaced from form giving by the engineer, displaced from form making by the machine. By defining industrial design by analogy with abstract painting, as a philosophical quest for essences and a physical revelation of absolutes, these art historians tried to establish the refining of aesthetic properties as indispensable to the full realization of the potential of the machine. By a flash of genius, the designer would effect a transcendent synthesis from contending material requirements, and create a machine which functioned by analogy with an abstract work of art, and which similarly should be appraised.[14] This reasoning by analogy effaced the distinctive skills of the engineer and gave the artist precedence. This engineer or technician reconceptualized as abstract artist and designer was above the mundane mediation of manufacturers. 'That is to say,' Read specified, 'designers should not be ... left to the mercy of factory managers and salesmen to adapt to the imaginary demands of the public.' Within the limits of functional efficiency, in this new world prescribed in *Art and Industry*, 'the factory must adapt itself to the artist and not the artist to the factory.'[15] Such reasoning about machines by analogy with abstract works of art could countenance only an abstract and highly idealized concept of function, and a unitary association between how machines worked and how they looked. Both of these simplifications belied the practical limitations of the artist's claim to precedence in design for industry. Formal aesthetics would not resolve complex social needs. Designers and art historians, who featured themselves finding essential solutions for the working of the modern world through industrial design, were finally, in John Heskett's apt phrase, 'a parliament without an electorate.'[16]

Buchanan's challenge in 1946 was to take aesthetics from the galleries to the centre of the stage, to make industrial design authoritative in the engineering laboratories and economic policy consultations where the future of the nation was being made. The modernist goal to bring art to the foreground of decision making in industry could be accomplished only if industrial design became more than an artists' and an art gallery concern,[17] if the abstract refinement in form the design theory promised worked sympathetically with other contemporary ideals, most specifically the ideal of multilateralism.

Buchanan pitched his idea to Brooke Claxton, minister of National

Health and Welfare, and, as minister responsible for the NFB, Buchanan's boss.[18] Claxton circulated this memo to all the prospective players in April 1946. Buchanan's proposal began with a statement of his aesthetic position, that 'Good design in manufactured articles, as we understand it today, means a combination of simplicity, fine proportions and functional utility,' abstract refinement rather than ornament in 'ordinary objects for everyday life.' He then cited the government industrial design agencies in Sweden and Britain, and the competitive advantage that giving 'the most use and the best looks for the least money' would afford exporters. His remedy on the design side was the same one Edith Lang was proposing on the consumer side that spring. Like Lang, Buchanan hoped that a research and coordinating body, modelled on the National Research Council, could establish rule-based uniform verifiable standards for everyday goods, and promote public interest in these standards. Both Lang and Buchanan were seeking a technical authority to distinguish incontestable truths among contending preferences and interests.[19]

The replies to Claxton's query quickly narrowed Buchanan's options. The head of the National Research Council rejected the analogies between systematic thinking in aesthetics and engineering. He called Buchanan's program 'a matter of design rather than research,' not activity any of his staff could supervise.[20] The deputy minister of Trade and Commerce judged the venture more properly a concern of the private sector, perhaps by the Canadian Manufacturers' Association or the Chamber of Commerce. The only favourable response to Claxton's initiative on Buchanan's behalf was from H.O. McCurry of the National Gallery, who embraced the prospect unreservedly.[21]

Buchanan, however, soldiered on. He arranged for Alan Jarvis, who was visiting Canada in the spring of 1946, to meet with the minister of Trade and Commerce, and both Buchanan and Jarvis addressed the Canadian Manufacturers' Association in June, describing European design initiatives and the threat they posed to Canadian exports.[22] Buchanan and McCurry also asked Herbert Read for a report on the future of industrial design in Canada. Read argued that art schools working in the humanist tradition could not prepare designers for a mechanistic world. Machines were not organic but constructivist, their working processes based not on natural but geometric forms. Therefore, abstraction must be the model. Industrial designers must receive 'education on constructivist principles and practice.' Then only if these designers were accorded professional parity with the engineers in decision making about industrial production would the problems of Canadian industry be solved. Only the abstract rigour of essential geometric forms would survive competition in the international market; only an international style would thrive under international trade.[23]

But outside the National Gallery, few believed in the practical value of abstract aesthetics. In the spring of 1947 both the economics ministers, James MacKinnon of Trade and Commerce and C.D. Howe of Reconstruction and Supply, again refused to consider an industrial design division within their departments, insisting the initiative belonged with business associations.[24] Recognizing where the constituency for his vision lay, and where it did not, in early 1947 Buchanan pragmatically joined the staff of the National Gallery as head of its new Industrial Design Department.[25]

There Buchanan pursued two projects, the Design Index and the Design Quiz, both examples of his particular modernist design ideology and practice, unalloyed and uncompromising. The Design Index selection committee used formal modernist aesthetic criteria to eliminate goods, 'not on grounds of inefficiency,' Buchanan noted in 1949, but rather because they lacked the abstract refinement 'which enabled them to come up to the standards set.' In print discussions of the index, Buchanan made plain his loyalties to the British design idealism of Read and his antipathies toward commercially driven American design pragmatism.[26]

The Design Quiz closely followed a model developed by Jarvis's colleagues for the *Britain Can Make It* exhibition in 1946 at the British Council of Industrial Design. Each page showed three design variations on a common household good, with one identified nearby as the good design choice. The purpose of the quiz, as stated with richly revealing inflection by a British-trained architect on the University of Toronto faculty, was to 'raise the I.Q. of the dear-consumer public.'[27] Over ten thousand visitors took the test at the 1948 Canadian National Exhibition in Toronto, and a purse-size version was prepared to reach many others through the Canadian Association of Consumers.[28]

These were gallery projects for educating taste. Their stated goal was to hone visual discrimination, stem the indifference to aesthetic criteria which caused the commodity culture to degrade, and replace crude preferences with a mature taste for timeless things.[29] Beneath was an elite reaction, led in Canada by Buchanan, the stalwart, gnomish Oxonian who kept elegant and powerful company, against the threat that, with mass production, industry might displace art, and discernment give way to accessibility. Buchanan's habit of mind separated sensibility from spectacle and engineering from entrepreneurship.[30] Industrial design, as it was articulated at the National Gallery, featured ideals of materiality which were to transcend materialism in rigorous high-minded opposition to commerce.

The late 1940s in Canada was a sellers' market for many household goods, a time when makers had exceptional autonomy from buyer preferences, and purchasers would take what they could get. A sellers' market would tolerate a measure of experimentation and a certain hauteur from the producer side; goods were rare enough to be thought of as art; new technologies fascinated; the modernist rhetoric of '*beautiful machines*' and '*well-made objects*' fit the moment in a way it would not once the fractious squabble of commerce returned. Were there manufacturers tempted to take a risk with the abstract refinement of modernist aesthetics in their product lines, this would have seemed a propitious time.[31]

For then idealist thinking was prominent in Ottawa beyond the National Gallery. The attempt to will abstract principles into concrete worldly manifestations was almost mandatory in the economics ministries and the Department of Finance. In the economics ministries and at Finance, planners were imagining a new international economy governed by the principles of free market economics. Buchanan's project, to make a particular modern design aesthetic the single universally applicable standard against which all Canadian manufacturing production would be measured, had a certain congruence with these economic development strategies. For if the future of Canada lay in export trade, including the export of secondary manufactured goods, and international trade presently was to be free, then Canadian manufactured goods soon would need to compete in a single world market. The best way to compete in such an international market could be with goods in an international style. Good design, as a claim to a universal rationalist aesthetic of international applicability, met this competitive requirement. This may be why, even though in March and April 1947 Howe and MacKinnon insisted that design advocacy was a matter for business associations, they did not impede the parliamentary grant passed in July[32] for industrial design work at the gallery.

During the period when hopes remained high for a free-trading international economy to lead domestic economic development, there was potential for the economic and aesthetic discourses to merge. Products of good design were to be made by machines of maximum efficiency, goods honed by excision to optimal fittedness. In competition these goods would survive, for the logic of their form, like the logic of the competitive market, purportedly was mathematically derived and governed by rationality. Thus the aesthetic ideal of an essential design was linked to a mythical concep-

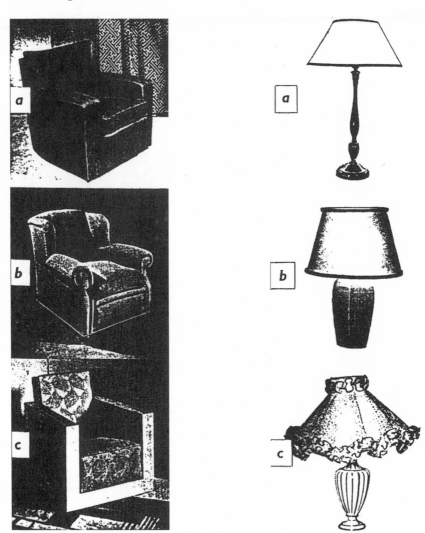

British Design Quiz: In the early years, Canadian official design reform closely followed British models.

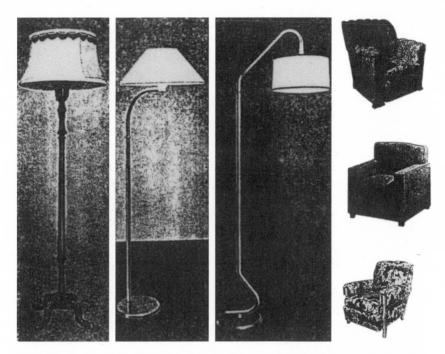

Canadian Design Quiz: In its first decade, Canadian NIDC advice emphasized formal aesthetics rather than commercial or engineering concerns.

tion of efficiency and an idealized relationship between fittedness and
form. This ideal might in turn answer an imagined need in the dream of a
free-trading world for a universally acceptable, industrially made material
culture. Good design and free trade alike were ideological claims whose
appeal, in a time weary of conflict and uncertainty, lay in their presentation as rational and rule-bound technical solutions. Though presently to
be deferred, the prospect of international free trade continued to define
the economic horizon for some years to come, thus sustaining interest in
the properties of modernist good design as an international style.[33]

Pleasing and persistent as this ideological convergence proved to be, the
economics ministries were not won over to industrial design as a government responsibility by either export strategies or dreams of international
free trade. Rather exactly the reverse. Officials in Finance and Trade and
Commerce were persuaded that Canadian industrial design was in the
public interest by the postwar foreign exchange crisis and the imposition

of import restrictions in November 1947. The international style officially came to Canada, carried along on the wake of rising barriers to international trade.

The foreign exchange crisis had clear implications for industrial design. Manufacturers who customarily had commissioned American designers to develop products for the Canadian market – as for example, Moffat had engaged Carl Reynolds, Jr, of Detroit to give form to the handi-chef[34] (see page 68) – now did not have specie with which to pay professional fees denominated in U.S. dollars. Those who previously had bought rights to use American designs and blueprints on licence were in the same predicament. With American tools and parts, whose presence had shaped Canadian design, similarly inaccessible, manufacturers had to fall back on indigenous resources, which would not immediately be sufficient to the task.[35]

Thus did the heavyweights from the economics ministries, Alex Skelton from Reconstruction, R.B. Bryce from Finance, and G.D. Mallory from Trade and Commerce, agree at a meeting convened at the National Gallery on 6 February 1948 to support a permanent publicly financed National Industrial Design Committee.[36] Industrial design had been recognized, institutionally, as part of the government's economic development agenda, although that agenda itself was being remade. Such design was an activity which in the long term might create wealth, and in the short term would at least save scarce foreign exchange. Designers were asked to create Canadian counterparts, just sufficiently divergent from American samples 'to escape patent infringements' and foreign licence fees. Import substitution had become acceptable as a response to the postwar foreign exchange crisis. How long the particular austere vision of good design, which Buchanan and Jarvis had articulated following Read, could persist unmodified as justification for federal spending on industrial design initiatives remained to be seen. A modernism in quest of geometric neo-Platonic ideal forms, aestheticizing the mechanical and reasoning abstractly about function, was an improbable fellow-traveller in company committed to pragmatic calculations of national and commercial interest.

Manufacturers saw the protection as short-term. Soon most of Canadians' deferred demands for household goods would have been met. European producers would recover from the war. A buyers' market, a period when there were more goods than purchasers, would follow.[37] This anticipation kept makers focused on sales. Charles Moffat, a director of the appliance manufacturer Moffat and head of the company's design unit, confidently expected that heightened competition would galvanize the product-development teams in Canadian firms. But he worried that industrial designers 'educated via the Fine Arts' would not be 'willing to compromise the aesthetics of product design' and sacrifice perfection 'in one quality to achieve satisfactory qualities of another sort' – in short, to accept that 'the engineering of any product involves compromises.'[38]

Appropriately then, the NIDC's next project began as an attempt to bridge the gap between designers 'educated via the Fine Arts' and the immediate needs of Canadian industry. An industrial design competition, jointly sponsored by the NIDC, the Aluminum Company of Canada, and the Canadian Lumberman's Association, called for sketches of aluminum and wood products 'of Canadian materials, produced in Canada,' and having 'a ready appeal to the average Canadian.'[39] But Serge Chermayeff, of the Illinois Institute of Technology in Chicago, who reported for the jury, noted that even excellent designers in Canada seemed not to understand the meaning of industrial, in terms of manufacturing 'by machines, in large quantities, requiring knowledge of contemporary technology and production methods.'[40] This was a perceptive critique. 'Industrial,' in Canadian public design discourse, most consistently had been used symbolically, to anchor stylistic references temporally as 'of the machine age,' or to establish abstract geometric forms teleologically as the truest products of the machine. The call for sketches brought forward a goodly number of gadgets and eccentric coffee tables built on 'false analogies' with 'early cubist painting.' Housewives protested that the competition had paid little attention to consumers' needs. The furniture manufacturers' journal, *Canadian Woodworker*, pleaded for design focused on 'market acceptance, saleability and approval of the trade.'[41] By the end of the competition, contemporary Canadian industrial design practice, as mediated by the NIDC, appeared more disconnected than ever from the rest of Canadian life.

Buchanan gamely regrouped. The 1952 competition specifications called for designs for particular objects for defined markets, and required full production specifications. Lawrie McIntosh, who was both a mechanical engineer and a NIDC-sponsored graduate of the Illinois Institute of Technology, won the 1952 competition, a sign dialogue between technique and aesthetic could be possible. By the time this result was announced, however, the ground of the debate had shifted.[42]

For the 1951 competition had crystallized concerns in other quarters. Most Canadian manufacturers of domestic goods were small businesses.

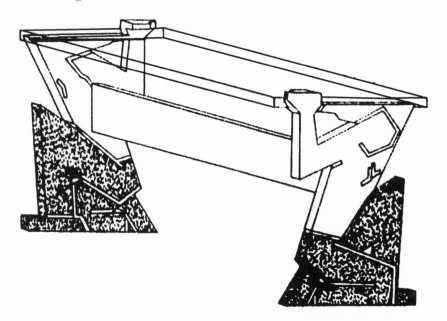

The honouring of geometric forms could be carried to extremes. This is a design submitted to the first NIDC design competition. Many entries were condemned by the international jury as naive about mass production methods. Serge Chermayeff of the Illinois Institute of Technology criticized this coffee table for its false analogies with early cubist painting.

What these makers needed, W.A. Trott, a Winnipeg lighting manufacturer who was then chair of the NIDC, argued in May 1951, was advice on how to use their existing machinery to greater advantage to make staged improvements toward a final design objective, and help from a team which offered balanced design, engineering, and merchandising services. Small firms could not absorb radical design changes in one step, or emphasize appearance in abstraction from tooling capability. Coming from a successful regional manufacturer whose own designs were well regarded at the National Gallery, this was a caution worthy of consideration.[43]

Around the Department of Trade and Commerce, now that the export emphasis in strategic planning had faded, the link between the aesthetics of the international style and international competitiveness for Canadian manufacturers was beginning to lose credibility. Having public advocacy for industrial design associated with the National Gallery appeared to give

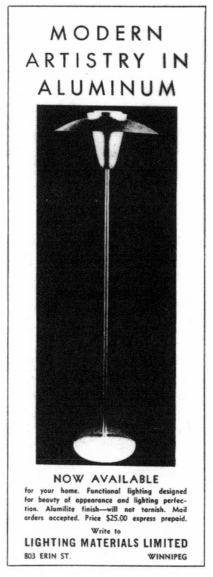
W.A. Trott of Winnipeg designed and manufactured this floor lamp, made from aluminum and thus emphasizing the continuities between wartime research in materials science and making beautiful things for everyday life in the peace. Trott served as president of the National Industrial Design Committee in 1951.

'undue emphasis on the aesthetics and not enough on the practical aspects of good design.'[44] By late 1951 the economics ministries had returned to their 1946 position that industrial design advocacy should be a private sector project. Inside the Canadian Manufacturers' Association, dominated by secondary manufacturers increasingly focused on domestic markets, interest in industrial design in the international style was also extremely muted. By 1954, few outside the National Gallery had much confidence that industrial design advocacy, as articulated by the National Industrial Design Committee/Council, would serve public purposes.[45]

The critics of abstract refinement and industrial referents in everyday goods now included many industrial designers. The bold and imaginative goals Read, Jarvis, and Buchanan had articulated, to remake engineering principles by analogy with aesthetics, and machines by analogy with art, in universal forms which refused time and place, now seemed bull-headed and imperious. Canadian industrial design practice already was being remade from within when import and credit controls ended in 1953. In the process, industrial design was turning from international to national, and from industrial to domestic, referents. Industrial design was coming home.

In what setting manufactured products would be used began to be recognized to be as important, symbolically, as the processes by which they were made. Thus in 1950 affirmed Henry Finkel, a Montreal designer who made his name in plastics, 'A product for living rooms in the home must avoid looking like a machine. The best radio-phono-video combinations close up to look like a cabinet.' Designers began to reinsert function into social space and to reason contextually rather than abstractly about form and function. Jack Luck, a Kingston designer who worked in aluminum, wrote in 1955, 'The "form-follows-function" purists are no longer worth listening to. Today, we are at the point where form is no longer an exclusive expression of function; rather, it is an opportunity to delight the eye. No longer is a chair merely a machine for sitting, or a lamp a machine for lighting. They are objects with the equally important function of gracing the home and satisfying our natural desire for elegance and beauty.'[46] Function was becoming everyday and multiple, and so was form. The universal as a definition of 'good' in design was ceding to the specific, both the specific symbolic systems of the domestic sphere and the specific manufacturing and distributional constraints of the Canadian domestic economy.

Although art historians had defined the public industrial design program for Canada in 1940s, commercial artists defined the practice. While

Jarvis and Buchanan were members of Oxford common rooms in the 1930s, Henry Finkel, for example, having first graduated from architecture school at McGill into the ranks of the unemployed, soon went to work as a commercial artist. Fred Moffatt, later famous for his redesigns of kettles for Canadian General-Electric, was 'laid off' from his post as an engraver's apprentice and did odd jobs for Toronto advertising agencies while attending night courses at the Ontario College of Art, until he got continuing work during wartime with CGE. Sid Bersudsky, who as an infant was brought by his family from Russia to New Brunswick in 1915, left school at seventeen in 1932 to sell his cartoons, and later his package and advertising designs. By the early 1950s his electric kettle, made by General Steel Wares, was competing with Fred Moffatt's CGE design for national sales. John Murray came to industrial design work at Dominion Electrohome after a degree in English and work writing advertising copy.[47]

Their approach to industrial design through commercial art made these men pragmatists. They accepted that industry and commerce had common purposes, and that art in the service of industry was also art in the service of commerce. This was a long way from where Read, Jarvis, and Buchanan had begun, with their arguments that aesthetics should remake industry in its own image, and that style was an untimely commercial deflection from the search for timeless neo-Platonic forms.

George Soulis, who came to industrial design through engineering, forthrightly put these pragmatic propositions before a NIDC conference in 1954. Soulis was then head of the design department at Snyders, a Kitchener, Ontario, firm recognized both in the market and by the Design Council for their modern work. Aesthetics must accommodate engineering, Soulis argued. 'Today furniture must still be pleasing in form, but it must be also suited to our production capacity and to consumer needs.' 'To get low-cost but smart-looking items you have to design to suit your type of machinery and equipment.' Accommodating the machinery was key, if products were to be sufficiently inexpensive to meet the needs of more than the elite. Following notes from his boss, Murray Snyder, Soulis even suggested that a designer 'who put his ideas on the drawing board, regardless of cost' was old-fashioned. More disturbingly for those in the assembled company committed to modern good design principles, Soulis argued that furniture makers had lessons about obsolescence to learn from American car companies, who knew how to make newness a temptation. He candidly described some of Snyders' furniture as 'faddish,' arguing that the faddish lines allowed the firm to produce other forms which were not faddish. 'You must realize that with modern manufacturing methods, mass production is the only way to get costs down, and the only way to have mass production is replacement.' As designers, both Snyder and Soulis plainly found less that was admirable in American automobiles than in Scandinavian furniture, these being the objects often used in contemporary discussions to contrast commerce and formal aesthetics as design influences. But as the prospects for freer world trade faded, so did the relevance of international comparisons: 'It is good to observe what the Scandinavians have done, but let us not kid ourselves, or try to copy the way Scandinavia went about making furniture, it won't work here. We have a different set of conditions, we have a different temperament in the people. We have a different geographical problem. We have to work these problems out for ourselves.'[48] Soulis argued that given the way the postwar economy had developed, Canadians had to design for Canadian circumstances.

For Robin Bush, a British Columbia born furniture designer, increasingly straddling the U.S. border in his work with Charles Eames for the Michigan manufacturer Herman Miller, the turn in industrial design practice toward the particularities of the Canadian market was a continuing challenge. For nation was another specificity which disrupted the promise of good modern design, unassimilable within the philosophical premises which set abstract refinement as the design goal. Yet as the dreams for a free-trading postwar international economy faded, tailoring goods to national circumstances, articulating a national rather than an international taste, fit better with contemporary definitions of citizenship and understanding about how a good standard of living would be maintained. 'People sometimes ask us when we travel back and forth, "Why don't you sit down and make a good indigenous Canadian design that will be nationally produced, that can be identified as a national product?"' Here Bush chose his words carefully, 'We are trying to; but we haven't been able, so far, to produce anything you could put your finger on and say "that is a Canadian design" ... I do not think good design in itself is necessarily indigenous. It is actually fairly international.' And yet he conceded, 'it is affected by the economic, the architectural, the political and other changes going on around us.' Bush had already begun, with many of his British Columbia colleagues in architecture and design, to give his international style a regional inflection, influenced by the sites and the materials of the West Coast. Both commercial and local interests were setting designers along paths which, in their form giving, diverged from good design principles.[49]

While the Design Council remained committed to the international

Snyders of Kitchener, Ontario, made modern upholstered furniture as well as traditional designs. This grouping was made during the time when George Soulis worked for Murray Snyder in the company's design group. Snyder's furniture was sold widely through Eaton's. Snyder emphasized both the need to design for low-cost production and the necessary dialogue between design principles and commercial priorities.

style, by 1955 import substitution was firmly established as a goal in government planning and business practice. Protectionism was no longer a stance for an emergency as it had been in 1948, but a continuing claim to preference for Canadian manufacturers in the Canadian market. Everywhere, plans for international free trade were being deferred. The Europeans were preparing to create a new trading bloc for themselves. If Britain joined, Canadian exports would no longer enjoy Commonwealth preferences. Self-sufficiency in manufactured goods, rather than expanded trade, now seemed the best way to safeguard employment levels and the standard of living in Canada.[50] The Canadian Manufacturers' Association marked this change from an international to a national focus with a new rallying cry, 'Canada can make it.' Fittingly, this slogan, intended to emphasize that Canadians' needs were best met with Canadian-made goods, was borrowed uncredited from the British Council of Industrial Design exhibition of 1946.

The international style had presumed freed international trade and mass production. Protectionism in a country with a population so small as Canada's rather suggested secondary manufacturing in relatively short series. The international style assumed a borderless commonality in aesthetic judgments, a convergence across national boundaries as the abstract essence of forms progressively was revealed and a global economy emerged. Protectionism, in effect if not by intention, presumed that national differences were values to be cultivated rather than vestiges to be transcended. A national economy suggested a national style, though in the Canadian case this suggestion was characteristically unemphatic.

The production constraint on an indigenous Canadian material culture was brutally apparent. Because goods would be manufactured in relatively short runs, costs would be relatively high. The marketing challenge was similarly daunting. By contrast, with Sweden, for example – a relatively culturally homogeneous former imperial power, with a distinctive language and in the 1950s a single television channel – Canada had been a British colony and was a country of immigrants. Its border was particularly open to cultural influences and product information from the south, its manufacturing firms often branches and captives of American concerns. Articulating what was national in such a context would have to be a dialogue between metropolitan and local references, between external and internal constraints, always to some extent the fragmentary 'regime of signs standing in for an absent totality,' in the words with which we began this discussion. Many Canadian postwar manufacturing strategies were intended to appropriate these signs, to find ways to make goods which

By the mid-1950s Canadian industrial strategy for secondary manufacturing had moved from free trade to import substitution. This logo was part of the Canadian Manufacturers' Association campaign, but borrowed from the British Council of Industrial Design *Britain Can Make It* exhibition of a decade before.

looked American, but which were produced under Canadian industrial conditions. From the perspective of producers, this was the cultural burden of import substitution and its immediate design implication: to capture American appearances by adaptations in Canadian engineering, to make goods which bore the signs of mass production but were well suited to manufacture in shorter series.[51] Figuring out what goods would look like if they were designed explicitly to meet the particular constraints of production in Canada, rather than to substitute for goods designed to be produced in American or European plants, was not immediately pressing in the early fifties.[52]

And none of this discussion, despite the many references to function, fittedness, and sales, framed industrial design questions in terms of Canadian purchasers' priorities and Canadian users' satisfactions. The distinctive Canadian problem on the production side was a small domestic market attuned to American commercial references. From the perspective of householders this was a very partial view. To meet the specific requirements of Canadians in their homes, the design discourse would need to engage what was nationally distinctive about household needs.

This is what we need to consider next. How were Canadian household choices influenced by distinctive patterns in household incomes and household factor costs, by household experiences of scarcity and plenty, and by aesthetics framed by household sensibilities? Here, where the borrowed metropolitan fragments of aesthetic dogma and commercial speech engage the pleasures and practicalities of daily domestic life, our real work begins.

7

Maple as Modern

Some Canadian manufacturers of appliances and furniture were involved in the work of the National Industrial Design Committee from its earliest days. We've met Charles Moffat, whose firm made stoves in Toronto, and W.A. Trott, who made lighting devices in Winnipeg. Another early supporter of the committee, for a time its president, for a longer time a friend of Donald Buchanan, was Donald B. Strudley.

Strudley was a University of Toronto graduate in engineering, who had joined his father's firm, the Imperial Furniture Manufacturing Company of Stratford, Ontario, in 1923. By the 1940s, he was Imperial's president. Donald Strudley was a modernist of many parts, socially conscious, technologically sophisticated, and, like many of reformist sympathies, concerned from the early years of the war to plan for the peace. He had been a moving force behind the Ontario Planning Act of 1946, overseen the construction and staffing of a new Stratford hospital, and helped bring the first social housing developments to town. He was knowledgeable and enthusiastic about modern design. Until he hired a full-time industrial designer in 1951, Strudley did the design work at Imperial himself.[1]

Imperial had relocated across the river from Detroit to Walkerville, near Windsor, in 1905. The name Imperial was chosen, company lore holds, to deflect attention from these American origins. Imperial produced rattan furniture until the First World War, after 1910 from Stratford. Imperial never produced the traditional hardwood furniture which was the stock in trade of Ontario manufacturers. They turned from rattan first to willow and hickory, and after 1925 to machine-woven fibre simulating reed, all materials best suited to informal and sparsely ornamented forms. Maple furniture was added to the line in the 1930s. During the war, the Canadian Wooden Aircraft Company, next door, made wing spars for Mosquito bombers. In these years, Imperial produced maple, in lean, sturdy variations, for military hospitals and recreation halls.[2] In later years the firm won a prize at the Milan Triennale, and numerous NIDC awards, though never for their maple. Yet it is to their maple we now turn.

For if most NIDC prize-winners were rarefied specimens rather than familiar species, maple furniture was ubiquitous in the 1950s, a standard, functional familiar of Canadian homes across class and region. While Read, Jarvis, and Buchanan espoused a modernism of abstract refinement, maple was a 'bread and butter' product line for several long-established manufacturers, not only Imperial and Knechtel in Ontario, but Vilas and Thibault in Quebec. This was furniture sold through department store catalogues, by budget as well as high-end retailers, and brought home to both the traditional houses of the wealthy and the compact contemporary bungalows of middle- and working-class couples.

Maple has not received good press. In the standard reference work about postwar communities, *Crestwood Heights*, about Toronto's Forest Hill area, the presence of maple is reported, and described by an appraising neighbour as 'sleazy.' Most design historians have been silent on the subject of maple. Virginia Wright, who regards this furniture with a high modernist eye, condemns it by association with designs 'being politically promoted in Europe as the official Nazi style of home furniture.' To emphasize that it was not 'original, professional design,' in a later study she groups maple with '"do-it yourself" knock-offs or the latest variety of romanticized frippery.' Australian scholars are, in retrospect, no more forgiving of their indigenous Queensland 'colonial' maple.[3]

North American design historians have focused not upon the widely produced popular forms which furnished modern homes in the postwar years, but on what is sometimes called furniture by and for architects, experimental work made in short series, appealing to elite tastes, too costly to be generally affordable. These forms were also the favourites of contemporary arbiters of good design. Yet even the entries made explicitly for Edgar Kaufmann's Museum of Modern Art 1948–50 International Competition for Low Cost Furniture – Don Knorr's hoop of zinc-plated steel, the Eames's fibreglass and steel DAR chair, Marcel Breuer's laminated plywood stacking chairs – never found their way into the homes of ordinary North Americans seeking furniture with which to live a modern life.[4]

Canada's National Industrial Design Council, as we have seen, followed a similar pattern in the 1940s and early 1950s. Design award juries favoured goods made from unconventional materials, shaped in forms which invoked industrial analogies but only rhetorically addressed the priorities of modern production.[5] This furniture was often spare and small-scaled to create the illusion of spaciousness required by those living in small suburban tract housing, and preferred by those inhabiting glass-walled post-and-beam contemporary homes. Scale aside, the household seating and case goods which design authorities praised in the 1950s were not shaped by the practical realities of contemporary family living or the sensibilities, fears, and potentialities modern circumstances had framed.

Succeeding design historians, until recently, have validated and perpetuated the preferences of the postwar good design vanguard. They too have championed modern forms in abstraction from modern life, the genius of the designer and the intention of the maker in abstraction from the domestic contexts in which the goods they created were to be made homely and useful. Women, the nation's purchasing agents for furniture, figure in these accounts as a dreary and wary public whose absence of taste for the new frustrated the modern project. We know more about what furniture they did not buy than about what they chose, and little from their own point of view about how they came to their decisions. For a period often characterized as excessively domestic, we know remarkably little about either the furniture with which the interior domestic landscape was fashioned or the cultural priorities it bespoke.[6]

Lately European students of ethnography and popular culture and British design historians influenced by the new social history have begun to redress this imbalance in studies of modern material culture. They argue that modern popular goods are worth studying precisely because they are popular, and that the popularity of these objects must have something to do with the priorities of those who chose them as well as those who made them.[7] A similar trend has been apparent in American studies of consumer culture, studies which long have read mass culture as the product and instrument of corporate interests for which the public was a passive receptacle. Newer work suggests that the meanings people attribute to choices for their homes derive as much from their own contemporary experience of urban and family life as from stories told by artists, critics, and advertisers. These meanings are multiple rather than unitary, made as much in their owners' mode of dwelling as in the objects' original mode of production.[8] Those who live with goods assimilate them in two senses, by becoming more similar to the objects they select, and in their own lights refeaturing their possessions as similar to themselves. Goods are remade by those who choose them.[9]

For household furniture this process is complex. Furniture is part of the machinery of daily life. But furniture is also akin to art in its place in the home, chosen for the visual satisfactions its form and colour bring, for the tactile pleasures its material invokes. Furniture carries the commercial intentions of its maker, and is reread according to the intended practical purposes of the household. But for those who make it and those who put it to use, furniture holds and generates cultural meanings. Sensually and symbolically, furniture stimulates and organizes responses. These effects, which may be perceived differently by those who shape furniture for the home than by those who shape it in the home, also hold possibilities beyond the intention of either, which arise from physical qualities in the objects themselves.[10] To understand how these goods worked in the home, we need to listen not only to the designers and manufacturers who were articulating modernist principles and experimenting with innovative forms, but to the householders who identified their times as modern, and self-consciously were choosing goods with which to lead a modern life.

The complexity compounds because householders appraised the same line of furniture from different class positions and different regional and ethnic traditions. The wealthy who bought maple for the recreation room or the cottage, and the aspiring who bought maple 'just for now,' saw this furniture differently than those who bought maple to last and have kept it. As Imperial's designers, engineers, and advertising firm will here stand imperfectly for those at Vilas, Thibault, and other makers of maple, these maple Loyalists, recollecting their purchases at four and five decades remove, will stand imperfectly for who purchased and domesticated these forms.

Let us begin, while pledging not to end there, with the men who made the goods – and first among the men, with the engineer. The first indication of Donald Strudley's modernist aspirations for Imperial is the line dating from May 1942 called Imperial Saarinen. These elegant case goods, tables, and chairs, many with curved elements moulded in the steam bending equipment once used to make the wooden structures for rattan furniture, were made in the Stratford plant alongside the commissary maple through the Second World War. The seating was continued for some years in the postwar catalogues as part of the Imperial Modern group.

The provenance of these designs is obscure. Only photos and price lists remain. Strudley regularly visited the Cranbrook Academy outside Detroit, Michigan, where the Finnish architects Eliel and Eero Saarinen were teaching and practising designers. There may have been a generational connection. George Booth, the Detroit publisher who founded the Cranbrook, was Toronto-born, a designer at the Windsor ironworks his

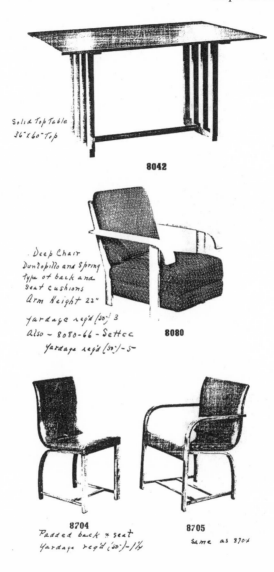

The first modern furniture made by Imperial was this line called Imperial Saarinen, and attributed by Donald Buchanan of the NIDC to Eero Saarinen, then of the Cranbrook Academy in Michigan. The structural members of these pieces were bent with the equipment in the Stratford plant for forming rattan, and were made of Canadian birch.

father managed, and an arts and crafts enthusiast in the years when W.H. Strudley, Donald Strudley's father, was building his rattan firm in Detroit and moving across the river to Canada. It is hard to credit, given his professional training and commitment to developing design standards, that Donald Strudley would have used the Saarinen name or their forms without permission. He apparently felt welcome at the Cranbrook in the early 1950s, for he was eager to introduce his new staff designer to the academy. The Saarinen line was probably not Strudley's own. It was remembered in the plant as difficult to make because its forms had been drawn with the properties of Finnish rather than Canadian birch in mind. Strudley's experience was with North American materials. Strudley's friend, Donald Buchanan of the NIDC, claimed in 1947 that Eero Saarinen had provided Imperial with the designs. However it came to bear the Saarinen name, these 1942 forms indicate the direction Strudley intended to take the firm in the postwar years.[11]

His modern predispositions show not only in the forms he chose to produce but in his production engineering orientation, particularly for the furniture called colloquially 'colonial maple.' Whereas many of the iconic pieces of modern design, despite contemporary claims, were not shaped by the constraints of industrial production, continuing from the 1930s Strudley successively adapted Imperial's colonial line, called Imperial Loyalist, in its material, finishing, and joinery, to make best use of modern machinery and synthetics and of Imperial's existing plant equipment.[12]

Colonial maple begins as an oxymoron, for very little northern maple was soft enough to be worked by the hand-power tools and softer steel blades of the colonial period. Canadian hard rock maple was left standing in the woods into the twentieth century, unusable until modern machinery could meet its formidable density. It continued to be difficult to mill until carbon-tipped blades became generally available in the 1960s. Rock maple was therefore inexpensive, as well as rugged once milled, appealing traits to a maker of popular furniture. Vilas, located in the Eastern Townships of Quebec amidst stands of mineral-stained maple, continued to make 'maple' furniture from maple.

But Strudley began a search for a more fitting alternative to maple. Householders associated solid hardwoods with quality. Modernists valued suitedness to purpose, machinability, and economy. In addition Strudley weighed the expansion-contraction factors of various hardwoods, between summer humidity and winter dryness, as great in Canada as anywhere in the world. On this basis, he chose Canadian yellow birch, both readily available and easier to work than maple. He adapted contemporary hydraulic equipment to compress tenons before they were inserted into open mortises, a modern technical improvement to simulate preindustrial split and wedged joints. These adaptations drew on wartime lessons learned making helicopter blades from compressed laminated birch. Not surprisingly, Imperial furniture began to appear in the trade journal advertisements of yellow birch suppliers.[13]

Birch, like maple, presented technical challenges in the finish. The ruddy, slightly opaque, nail polish quality used in 'colonial' furniture of both woods disguised blemishes made in maple by mineral stains and in birch by irregular penetration of the finisher's pigment. Strudley pioneered the Canadian use of urea-type synthetic varnishes, mastering innovations in industrial chemistry and materials handling to make functionally and visually appealing goods from inexpensive hardwood stock.[14]

Strudley apparently recognized that his own strengths were in engineering rather than design, although he recalled in 1952 that 'for several years after the war everyone could sell everything they could make, and it was so easy to get business.' Furniture makers were little affected by postwar controls on foreign exchange and strategic metals, and furniture relatively quickly became available to meet pent-up domestic demand. But this meant that by the late 1940s, furniture manufacturers faced a buyers' market and risked unused production capacity. Strudley was among those who saw Canada's future in multilateralism. He expected the growth in demand for Canadian furniture to depend upon export sales, particularly into United States markets. As he argued, tariffs were modest for furniture, and limited economies of scale mean that small firms in the industry could produce competitively. If Canadian firms had strong new lines to offer American buyers, rather than 'watered-down editions of designs that had been exploited on the American market for several years already,' in this industry export prospects could be good.

Following this reasoning about the future of Canadian international trade policy, and the competitive prospects of small Canadian firms, in 1951, the year the first NIDC furniture competition foundered in amateurism, Strudley decided to set up a new design department. He hired a professionally trained full-time staff designer and began to 'gradually shift the emphasis' in new designs at Imperial from colonial toward more contemporary forms. In his work with the Canadian Manufacturers' Association and the National Industrial Design Council he attempted to persuade other makers to do likewise. He developed case notes on Imperial's decision to hire a staff designer for use at the University of Western

Ontario School of Business Administration, hoping also to encourage the next generation of Canadian industrialists to reach for export markets through investments in good design.[15]

The designer Donald Strudley hired was Jan Kuypers. Kuypers is a lively legend in Canadian industrial design circles. Born in Nymegan, Holland, in 1925, the son of a craftsman furniture-maker and restorer, Kuypers had studied at the Academy of Arts and Architecture in The Hague during the dark days of the Second World War. He emerged upon graduation in 1947 with both an exemplary training in the design traditions of De Stijl and Bauhaus and a host of hungry dreams.

The conditioning by the war and by the depression was very real. You didn't fool around. You were very serious in your orientation. This dream of creating a new world was very real ... You were part of this society that was starting to get out of the war and get on with life, not only get on with life but actually be active in pursuing what in that respect were old dreams, the dreams of socialism ... But apart from that very strongly, you had to make a living, you had to make the kind of contribution that was viable, was acknowledged by people immediately so that they could pay money for it, and you.

He went first to England and the Rochdale site office of the Grenfell Bains group, where he spent several months on drawings for a daycare centre and a factory sewerage system. In 1948, through the Council of Industrial Design, he found work as a furniture designer with the Glasgow firm H. Morris and Company.[16] Morris was an industry leader in modern design, widely known for research and development in high-technology wood engineering and work with birch, including Canadian yellow birch.[17]

The years in Glasgow from 1948–51, as Kuypers recalled, also 'took a nip at my Bauhaus.' He encountered the work of Charles Rennie Mackintosh for the first time as a revelation of the deep and beautiful wooden roots of modernism. Collecting the prize in a Scottish design competition, he spent some time in Sweden looking at the work of the Scandinavian designers Arne Jacobsen, Finn Juhl, Fitz Hansen, and Hans Wegner, an experience which shows in his later merging of historical and modern forms, and his disposition against formality and 'front-parlour elegance.'[18] In 1951, as he recalled, 'the immediate ardour of postwar, the immediate beliefs of postwar, the glamour around the socialists had faltered a bit,' as had the economics of furniture production at Morris. Kuypers wrote a letter of inquiry to the Canadian Furniture Manufacturers' Association, and Donald Strudley replied offering him a job.[19] Kuypers stayed with

Imperial for nine years, joined in time in the expanding design department by graduates in furniture design from the Montreal Ecole du Meuble
and Toronto's Ryerson Polytechnic. He launched new contemporary lines
and redesigned their 'colonial' Imperial Loyalist forms.

The presentation of colonial as modern, for the designer, was not so
incongruous as the high modernist's scorn or the polar chronological
meanings of the two words might suggest. In the arts industries, particularly in furniture making, ceramics, and glass, technical continuities between craft and industrial production persisted well into the twentieth
century. Certainly the legacy of the arts and crafts movement to industrial
design is ambiguous (see Chapter 2). But many modernists sympathized
with the attentiveness to materials and household purposes shown by
William Morris in Britain, Gustav Stickley in the United States, and Carl
Larsson and Carl Malmsten in Sweden. Although design historians have
placed more emphasis upon the classical or oriental influences on modern forms, collective sensibilities arising from their own communities drew
many modern designers to vernacular precedents.[20]

In the postwar years, the increased emphasis upon practicality, comfort,
even playfulness, in domestic goods led designers to employ more organic
and historical forms, often in combination. Vernacular influences were
prominent in the British utility furniture that Kuypers's mentor, Gordon
Russell, championed at the Council of Industrial Design, and in the work
of the Saarinens and Charles and Ray Eames at the Cranbrook and after.
One need only think of the heart-shaped folk cut-outs on Ray Eames's
plywood chairs, Hans Wegner's Peacock's fan re-rendering of the early
American Windsor, Lena Larsson and Elias Svedberg's play with simple
spindle backs, later so elaborated by Ingvar Kamprad at IKEA. All these are
signs of a general distancing from machine aesthetics after the war, particularly among designers with progressive political sympathies. This interest in vernacular precedents occurred even as they paid more intense and
informed attention to machine production.[21] The modern designers
Kuypers reports as formative influences from the 1940s and 1950s, Juhl,
Gio Ponte, Jacobsen, and Wegner, all experimented updating vernacular
furniture. Their work from the vernacular, like Kuypers's own redrawing
of Imperial Loyalist, honoured craft traditions, but in factory-made furniture accessible to popular buyers.[22]

The 1930s colonial line called Imperial Loyalist quickly surpassed rattan
and loomed reed as the mainstay among Imperial's offerings. Kuypers
characterized the original Loyalist line as very serious and well-constructed
replicas of antiques. The furniture looked heavy, and proclaimed its sturdy

construction in broad solid panels, conspicuously braced rails and tops, and prominently displayed mortise-and-tenon joinery.

Strudley had sketched most of the pieces. Some forms had been bought on licence from Heywood Wakefield in the United States.[23] By the early 1950s, these 'larger and more heavily-scaled pieces,' designed to bespeak quality and antiquity, contrasted unfavourably with the 'general air of grace and elegance' of recent Scandinavian furniture.[24] Sales of Loyalist were falling off. Howard Hemphill, then in charge of sales, remembers Kuypers responding to these signs from the market with a redesign. The objective was to redraw the line as Danish-related and crafts-related. The resulting furniture claimed 'inspiration from Early Canadiana' but 'wed the Colonial idea with the Scandinavian contemporary look.'[25]

Some commentators argued that 'the most likely background for a distinctively Canadian design' lay in early settler furniture.[26] Kuypers took some distance from this stance, wary of self-conscious nationalism as a design ethic, troubled by how such an appeal would be interpreted by stolid Canadian manufacturers. Canadians ought not to 'strive for' their own forms, he argued, or once again 'lift some completely developed form language from some part of the world.' He recommended rather an approach to design which was both forthrightly materialist and tolerant of irresolution. In a 1960 article 'What Next in Canadian Design?' he de-scribed this process as 'to sit down ourselves and try to develop on our own the best product we can out of materials readily available to us, out of our production and distribution system, out of our understanding of the way of living here, and out of all the straws in the wind.' If good products emerged from this process, he told Robert Fulford in 1958, 'the final product might have a character that is Canadian somehow, or which will become Canadian.' This prospective irresolution Fulford found 'not over-poweringly positive.' Yet it was apt as an account of the way in which 'almost accidentally' artists, including designers, created distinctive styles from shared circumstances. Historical referents figured in this process, Kuypers argued, in so far as a firm might recognize 'in their past adapta-tions of a variety of style motifs, some common thread' as 'an embryo style,' and by close attention make it 'commercially profitable.' For Kuypers, the articulation of the historical was many voiced, for if furniture had 'to be useful and comfortable before anything else,' it also must reflect to householders their personalities and their dreams.[27]

Kuypers's redrawing of the Loyalist line tapered the legs and narrowed the rails. By removing or raising the stretchers on chairs, he created the impression that their seats were floating, a technique apparent in Malmsten's

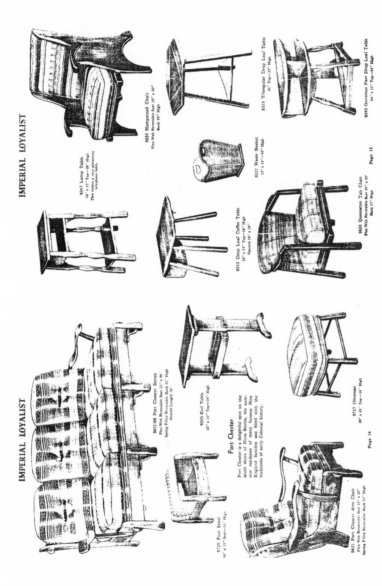

The Imperial Loyalist line before Jan Kuypers's redesign consisted of solid, verging on stolid, invocations of colonial forms, secured by colonial names. The designs were very like the 'colonial' style prized in New Zealand, Australia, and the United States in the 1930s and 1940s.

These two chairs show clearly Kuypers's intention to work from the colonial idiom, making it lighter and more contemporary by borrowing from Scandinavian re-renderings of folk forms. These chairs borrow from Finn Juhl's chieftain arm chair and Arne Jacobsen's egg lounge chair.

interwar seating. By extending the top chair rail outward and upward in an arc, he made the Windsor derivations in the line lighter and more graceful, echoing the use of wings on Finn Juhl's chieftain arm chair and Arne Jacobsen's egg lounge chair. He used the same techniques later on tables and upholstered furniture, recessing and sculpting table aprons and seating rails, minimizing the visual command of structural elements which formerly had been exaggerated. His last Imperial line in the colonial mode, called Sampler, was shaped 'as a "stage setting" exaggerating the historical references,' Kuypers remembers, 'where previously "loyalist" design was a pain, this time it was fun.' This playful liberation was stimulated by Kuypers's volunteer design work with the Stratford Festival.[28] In its cheerful theatricality, Sampler shared many elements with the lines Elias Svedberg and Lena Larsson developed for NK-Bo in Stockholm, and which the world now knows through IKEA.[29]

Industry observers called these lines, and those being similarly rendered by Donald Lapp at Thibault and Paul McCobb at Vilas,[30] cleaner, lighter, leaner, more useful, tailored but not folksy, plain rather than quaint. By the early 1960s, commentators were reversing their appraisal of the design influences. Rather than noting how fustian and stolid colonial was being made modern, they described the basic idea for the forms as modern made more 'livable' by historical references.[31]

More than most Canadian furniture manufacturers, Imperial used magazine advertising to reach and create a market for its furniture. As people scrambled in the early postwar years to get home, and make homes, the Harold Stanfield advertising agency of Montreal and Toronto prepared copy for Loyalist, its power as a totem of permanence and stability: 'When you put a home together around such fine things as Imperial Loyalist furniture, you build for all your years. You give it permanence. You give it a graciousness that grows through the mellowing years. You give it the stability of fine pieces, finely wrought' – stability being used both as a description of the furniture itself and a synecdoche for the home in which it was placed. Through 1945 the ads carried civic-minded anti-inflationary warnings to 'please only buy the pieces you need at once,' to not draw too quickly from 'accumulated war savings,' to 'Remember, Imperial Loyalist is worth waiting for.'[32]

The head lines and subheads of the late forties played on the hybridity of the form, that this was 'Quality Craftsmanship Engineered in Wood,' that these 'authentic recreations of early Canadian styles' simultaneously were 'Designed for Living.' The same models were presented in traditional and modern settings, often in succeeding months, to emphasize the liminality of the designs. 'It is never old, nor new, but always modern,' ran the copy below a curved moderne fireplace oddly fronted by a clutter of colonial in the spring of 1947. By fall Stanfield's were carrying their message better under the punning lead 'Tradition in the modern manor,' having employed the modernist tactic of excision – removing and scaling down the accessories – and pulling the lens back from the subject, to create from the same basic elements the impression of spaciousness.[33] Copy emphasized that Loyalist was 'crafted,' but also that it was 'designed.' The phrase 'the only furniture worth making is furniture you'll want to

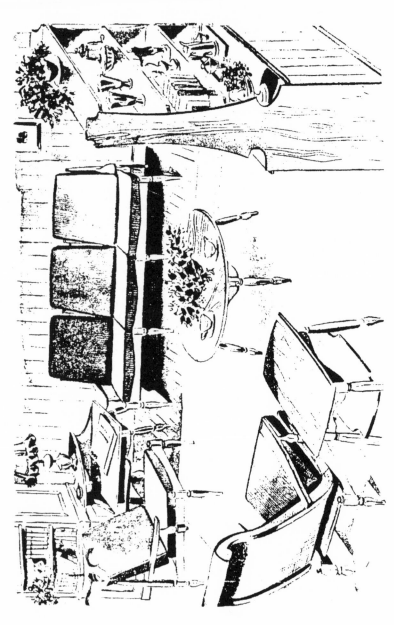

This is Kuypers's last line for Imperial, the Sampler Collection, drawn during a period when he was volunteering time as a set designer at the Stratford Festival and intrigued by the theatrical possibilities of furnishings in domestic settings.

live with all your life' was set sometimes in modernist sans serif lettering to read as a design principle, sometimes in a more ornamented typeface to be read as a homily.[34]

After the redesign in 1955, copy carried more of Kuypers's own emphasis on 'the livable and usable qualities required for modern living' built into the furniture. His last Loyalist line for Imperial, the Sampler Collection, was called an 'interpretation of Colonial design, a basic new format for Canadian furniture for years to come.' Both the room settings and the rhetoric of 'simple grace,' light, and warmth in these later renderings emphasized the affinities between indigenous craft-based forms and the vernacular inflections of Swedish modern.[35]

Maple furniture generally sold best in Ontario, Western Canada, and in the large cities. These were also the best markets for modern furniture.[36] Imperial's dealer records through the 1950s show western Canadian sales for both the contemporary and updated Loyalist lines rising steadily, particularly in Winnipeg, Calgary, and Vancouver. Howard Hemphill, by the late 1950s president of Imperial, estimated that the firm sold over $3 million of Kuypers's Loyalist revisions, a considerable advance on the $365,000 per year the older line had averaged.[37] For all Canadian manufacturers of maple, the Scandinavian and craft-related redesigns of colonial, by professional industrial designers, were popular successes.

What made them popular? Not, it would appear, their colonial design references, nor either, very much, their skilled invocation of modernist idiom. This is not a particularly surprising finding. An American survey twenty years before reported that neither history nor exclusiveness of design held any interest for the vast majority of women buyers.[38] Christine Morley found that English women who furnished their homes in the 1950s did not think stylistic details in furniture significant, nor did they remember them specifically. Other requirements 'short-circuited any design-aesthetic discourse.'[39] Some might argue, as has Pierre Bourdieu, that attention to such formal distinctions, ranking canonical beauty over usefulness, marks and re-creates differences between dominant and dominated classes,[40] and will not be conspicuous in groups which include many middle- and working-class people. But as David Halle rightly notes, Bourdieu's own evidence shows that only a minority in the dominant classes were interested in aesthetics and high culture.[41] It seems more likely, as British design historians lately have argued, that 'design advice made little contact with those it addressed' and that in the postwar period 'the popular aesthetic defined modernity, quality and propriety within its own horizons.'[42]

ITS CHARM INCREASES THROUGH THE YEARS

From the first moment when you see an Imperial Loyalist room, you'll love its sense of well-being. And years later, you'll realize that its charm has mellowed and deepened.

Imperial Loyalist furniture is the re-creation of designing skill that gave the lasting graciousness to early Canadian homes. It is never old, nor new, but always modern. Its charm increases through the years.

IMPERIAL LOYALIST
Made in Stratford, Canada
by Imperial Rattan Co. Limited

LOOK FOR THIS BRAND ON EVERY PIECE

Harold Stanfield advertisements for Imperial Loyalist in 1947, before Kuypers's redesign.

TRADITION
in the
modern manor

▶ The touch of Imperial Loyalist tradition is ever welcome in the modern home. Let Imperial Loyalist reflect your good taste, your keen perception of the quality of fine craftsmanship. Enrich your home by the lasting beauty of Imperial Loyalist . . . the furniture that is perfectly *engineered in wood*.

IMPERIAL LOYALIST

Made in Stratford, Canada
by Imperial Rattan Co. Limited

LOOK FOR THIS BRAND ON EVERY PIECE

Among those with whom I spoke who had chosen maple furniture, none acknowledged its provenance as colonial. Ann Brook, a librarian married to a navy cook, remembered 'It wasn't particularly that I wanted that furniture and furnishings from that period ... that I was going to own something that looked like it was an antique ... No, I saw it as something that was clean cut.'[43] Joan Coffey, the wife of a psychiatric nurse, bought pieces of maple for both her living room and dining room but refused the colonial motif, 'those lamp shades, the little braided rugs,' and rather saw maple as accommodating her own eclecticism.[44] Winnifred Edwards, a British immigrant married to a Canadian-born physician, noted how almost invisible was the cultural diversity of Canada in the 1940s, even in Winnipeg, and spoke of choices for her home: 'I hoped to be representative of Canada. I didn't have any ideas of colonialism but I did expect things to be simpler because of the history and the hardship that so many people encountered. So I think it had the flavour of the country.'[45] This was an argument about maple furniture as somehow indigenous, but anchored in no period, that Jan Kuypers would have recognized as familiar, and Kuypers's Loyalist is the furniture Edwards bought. In many ways Kuypers and Edwards seemed similar to me, educated 1940s immigrants who after a difficult war were, with stout good humour, leading examined lives. These many cultural conjunctures most buyers of maple did not share. When asked if there were historical reference points for colonial, Sally Tobe, who sold the more modestly priced Roxton colonial to working-class postwar immigrants, from her parents' store in downtown Kitchener, Ontario, paused to reflect, and then responded, 'No, as the matter of fact, not at all. Not in the way people collect today from Quebec or Ontario, or back east. [It was] because it was new, brand new. And it was new to them.' New Canadians 'would generally not buy modern, with a hard edge, hard lines'; for them colonial 'seemed to be a modern move.'[46] As displayed in showrooms and glossy magazines, maple furniture was often set in a colonial context. As read by purchasers, and socialized into the household, colonial references were at least attenuated, and often, because incomprehensible, were entirely absent.

Adult Canadians in the 1950s led a modern life in the context of their youthful experiences of depression and war, of change, loss, waste, and destruction. Modern choices were often acts of recuperation framed by the instability of the preceding two decades, choices which were not reclamations of lost forms but reactions to losses. In this context, a modern choice resisted disposability, ephemerality, and stylishness. A Canadian Association of Consumers representative to the National Industrial Design Council reminded retailers and manufacturers in 1954 that there were 'psychological factors' why a shopper would not buy 'sensational' furniture for the home. 'I look for something of good value,' she said of herself, 'for I don't expect to tear my home apart in five or six years.' Certainly no woman who had lived through years of dislocation in make-shift accommodations wished to look forward to more of the same. Sheila Maurice, a nurse and wife of a logger, bought a Vilas bedroom suite in 1955 which she was still using in 1993 because 'We believed in buying good quality and maintaining it.' Generally the 'purchasing frequency of furniture was very low in a lifetime.'[47]

Mary Kippen, the wife of a warehouseman, bought Vilas maple a piece at a time as good, basic wooden furniture, 'something that was going to last for a long time and that I felt that I could live with for a long time.'[48] Many women spoke about acquiring maple gradually piece by piece as an investment, not in resale value but in long-term usableness. This was a pattern good design advocates, who railed against the purchasing of suites, might have welcomed, but that the durable basics being purchased one by one were folkish and maple. Winnifred Edwards saw maple not as 'sleazy' but as a reaction against the 'sleazy politics' of the period and 'sleazy manufactured goods' which went 'along with it.'[49] In this sense, maple was a modern choice, informed by contemporary concerns about planned obsolescence and the degradation of goods, even a modernist's choice for the critique it bespoke of shoddy industrial production. A Canada-wide survey of 504 women conducted by Gruneau Research in 1956 found that 34 per cent were dissatisfied with faulty manufacture in furniture they had chosen, and 26.1 per cent had made purchases which did not wear well. Overall, homemakers' salient advice to manufacturers was to 'devote more attention to construction, make furniture sturdy and durable, not just for looks,' and make it from better quality materials.[50]

Modern, for many women, meant home furniture which was informal, child-friendly, and required little care. Tina Wall, a postwar British immigrant of frugal habits and plain tastes, chose 'modest' maple dining room furniture for both its symbolic and its functional values. A maple dining room would not be 'something formal for Sundays and high days but, you know, just every day.' 'You've got to keep formal things looking very nice. You daren't use them and you daren't sit down. When you're going in and out of the kitchen accidents happen.' For similar reasons, maple was a common choice for boys' bedrooms, steadfast in the presence of rough-housing, requiring little hectoring about due care, sufficiently resilient still to be presentable as guest room furniture years later when the boys were grown and moved on.[51]

Women expected informal modern living also to be comfortable. Maple

A central appeal of maple furniture was that its sturdy construction and resilient finishes made it child-friendly. Homemakers could readily reupholster the cushions. Here are two young British Columbians in a Burnaby household in February 1960. The chair is Vilas maple.

The bottom half of an Imperial Loyalist bunkbed with side rail, from a Calgary household, 1954. This furniture is still in use in the family.

furniture was modern in the sense that it was both – high enough backed to support the head, high enough off the floor for easy egress. In essays written for the Canadian Consumers' Association, homemakers complained about the furniture the NIDC called 'modern,' for its concentration on 'aesthetics to the exclusion of comfort,' and for being more for display than for use. They were describing modernist furniture in terms a turn-of-the-century arts and crafts designer would have used to dismiss the Victorian parlour, as stiff, mannered, and unyielding. Maple, by contrast, was read as modern furniture 'with old-fashioned comfort.' Ann Brook, who first met maple in the barracks and schools of national defence bases, admired Scandinavian furniture but accepted maple as a household compromise because it was wood, because 'it looked, it always looked, good' and because it was comfortable.[52]

Maple accommodated well to the scale and finishing of most housing being built in Canada after the war. It was seen as fitting for these modern homes, literally because it fit. Mary Paine and her husband were raising two boys in Calgary on his earnings selling for Eaton's. They did not have a car. The bedrooms in their 960-square-foot home were very small, and so they bought maple furniture. Canadian Mortgage and Housing Corporation architects thought of the small homes they designed after the war as contemporary in that they were spare, compact, equipped with modern mechanical systems, and planned as mass housing to meet a democratic purpose. Many women read the small scale and practical plainness of their suburban bungalows as cottage-like rather than contemporary. They chose maple because the modesty of its imagery and dimensions made maple sympathetic to the cottages in which they set it to dwell. 'The house we lived in then, and the houses that most people live in are just glorified cottages. I mean, they're not mansions. To see a chandelier in a house like this is ridiculous.' Maple, by contrast, was neither visually nor functionally dissonant with the suburban CMHC bungalow. Indeed the trestle dining tables and benches Imperial and Vilas made in such numbers looked good and worked well in suburban dinettes for the same reasons they had suited North American log cabins and British tenant cottages. They accommodated many eaters around a soundly braced board in a minimum amount of space. The transgressive reading of the modern housing form as cottage directed the furniture choice couples made, and these choices in turn echoed back, making the house as a structure seem more cottage-like on the basis of the elements it contained. Maple accommodated modern domestic life – filled with children and short on room, filled with hope and averse to risk. It secured and stabilized that precarious living space – met a modern need – by being readily recognizable, relatively invulnerable, and inherently companionable.[53]

Modern goods do not hold their stories in their form alone. Modernism was not only an aesthetic project. Modernity was read from many different qualities in a domestic good, the materials from which it was made, the processes by which it was produced, the purposes it was intended to serve, the purposes to which it was put, the messages with which it was imbued, the responses with which it was remade. The modern project in postwar Canada was not only about change, but about making change supportable. In these differing senses, for Strudley and Kuypers and the homemakers who intended to give it decades of houseroom, maple was modern.

8

Domesticating Objects

We live our domestic lives in the presence of objects. Through our relations with them we appraise, assimilate, appropriate, and resist the currents of our time, in a warm and wilful dialogue between self and other. As goods change, and times change, so does this cultural traffic between householders and their goods change – in dominant direction, in relative intensity, in the character of the burden it carries, and in the significance we allow this burden to assume. How much material goods matter in the social and individual reckoning of well-being varies historically. How much consumption matters is a cultural difference, a shared national predicament, a politics grounded in the circumstances of class, and learned as a gendered responsibility.

The history of consumption in Europe and North America is most commonly told as a sweeping meta-narrative about propertied men in the marketplace. In this account, there was once a rural world, which agriculturalists, merchants, and craftsmen shared, where 'thrift, frugality, self-control and impulse renunciation' organized men's relationships with the material goods in their midst, and where studied prudence and otherworldly concerns kept material goods in their proper subordinated place. Then came the market and technological change, and with them abundance. Satisfaction was for sale, and only satisfying in so far as it was displayed. A good gave most pleasure at the moment it was purchased, and quickly thereafter, like all life outside the market, became dreary and outmoded, in need of being replaced according to the next rules the market ordained. Goods once constrained now seduced, possessing the owners who once had possessed them, remaking all social life, deflecting all political energies in the image and interests of the market. In this narrative, the 1950s marked the resounding completion of this transformation.[1]

Such an argument emphasizes the commodification of domesticity rather than the domestication of objects. It is a useful hypothesis, but, as a description, of less general applicability than might be assumed. For the question it asks – 'What influences do goods have, which a market analysis will reveal?' – is not the same question as 'How do people live with goods?' or, for our purposes, 'How do particular people, in a particular time and place, live with goods?'[2]

A wealth of cross-cultural studies, well interpreted by Robert Lane, find 'virtually no relationship between level of national income and ... happiness.' The satisfactions from which well-being arises are not those 'conventionally included in market analysis.' This being the case, as the economist Albert Hirschman has argued, 'extending to all other human activities an analysis that is appropriate to the market' mistakenly generalizes a very weak market association between commodities, income, and sense of well-being. People may find other ways preferable to the market for satisfying their wants for commodities. Studies which examine goods and pleasures only through market relationships do not address this possibility. Whether they come into the household by market or non-market means, it would be unwise to read from the presence of consumer goods alone either their significance or their precedence in the life of the home.[3]

Thus for a student of the postwar years, the anthropologists' distinction between terminal and instrumental materialism is clarifying. The representation of the 1950s in American films and social science, emphasizing accumulation and disposability, acceleration and display, suggests terminal materialism, consumption which becomes an end in itself, an 'autonomous necessity' to possess more things and status. When materialism is instrumental, objects are means to realize common purposes, and people's goals are cultivated through transactions with the object. In this case less may be better than more, because each good a person possesses consumes psychic energy for which there are other known and valued purposes.[4]

If instrumental materialism was a force in the 1950s, it would not be evident in an economic analysis, or in an analysis which presupposed (whether welcomed or dreaded) the precedence of the market. The market model assumes that consumption is terminal rather than instrumental, though the assumptions are not conveyed with these words. In the economists' market model, tastes are fixed: the taste for any good is independent and constant in its relationship to the taste for any other good; preferences among goods do not shift; and the full relationship between person and good is defined by the moment of purchase. The market model captures the purchase decision, but does not comprehend, and thus can be read to deny, the complicated and nuanced reasoning about products and their relation to well-being which might inform and subsequently reappraise that decision. In this sense, the market model depoliticizes consumption by reducing the values which 'constitute a way of life and justify particular choices' to a primitive, unreflexive, unreferential 'liking.'[5] For Habermas and his followers, concerned that politics has been remade in the image of the market, the problem is that market analogies edit public discourse and suppress the rationales for alternative allocation decisions, so that questions about what is 'proper, reasonable and just behaviour generally' will not be asked.[6]

All who live in the presence of the market do not always think through the market, though a thinking device tuned to analyse market reasoning alone leads inexorably, by systematic excision, to this conclusion. The household is a particularly good case in point. Households have multiple members and multiple purposes. Household decision-making is more often satisficing than maximizing, a deliberation among a number of needs rather than a plan to do the best possible according to any single criterion.[7]

Householders deciding to give objects houseroom, for the pleasures and meanings they will provide, deliberate in a broadly contextual fashion. Douglas and Isherwood call this process metaphoric appreciation, a 'prior and pervasive kind of reasoning that scans a scene and sizes it up, packing into one instant's survey a process of matching, classifying and comparing.' This reasoning occurs in the presence of the ideological messages which come from patriarchal consumer capitalism, but goods are not selected and used only within the scripts their producers and sellers write. The elements which women use to fashion the interior landscape of the home may be organized through a vocabulary and syntax only loosely connected to, and not secured by, market relations.[8] /

As J.K. Gibson-Graham have argued in a wise and outrageous book, we need to respecify this capitalist system of market relations currently assumed definitive, substantial, and hegemonic, and to contemplate, as the title of their book makes clear, the end of capitalism (as we knew it). Gibson-Graham note that patriarchy is no longer posited as homogeneous or all-embracing. Why not then also consider capitalism as having many manifestations, not one, as constituted, not foundational? Why not resist fashionable polemics about the globalization of this fractured and contradictory economic form? Thus might we gain conceptual space for non-market ways of thinking about the world, not as romantic remnants or marginal ephemera, but as interpretive possibilities, no more fictive than capitalism.[9]

The goal here is to analyse the making of the landscape inside the home, attempting to reclaim the terms used by those predominantly engaged in the craft, in order to understand the relationship between household goods – here furniture – and contemporary needs and values. These household choices were made, not by professional decorators working according to formal design principles, but by amateurs mediating between their own needs and the needs of those they loved. Theirs is speech about how to live in the world which escapes the bounds of the market and goes its own more multiply referenced way.

Kathleen Stewart, writing about the many forms and uses of nostalgia, argues that these cultural practices are not informed by what Bourdieu would call the 'deliberate naïveté' of 'popular culture,' and are not made explicitly to refuse 'the distancing pure aesthetic of "good taste."' Rather these practitioners thereby bespeak their 'own "sophisticated," or self-conscious, sense' of their own cultural constructions. 'The difference is that the desire is not to act *on* "the world out there" but to act *in* a world that surrounds.' The talk of women in the postwar years about the making of homes sounds like this. Like the discussion of maple, this talk is not governed by distant canonical standards of modern to act *on* the outside world. Nor is it about the converse, a 'haven' made only in the absences created *by* a 'heartless world.' Attending to this talk, by amateur practitioners about decoration, guides the historian through the material, moral, and economic reasoning of their time.[10]

The critics of consumption, more numerous and celebrated in the United States than in Canada, were intellectuals faced with their own losses, who developed analyses with more power to explain the economic system's attempt to control than 'the meaning ordinary people have given to new goods and experiences.'[11] Their portraits emphasize what was dark and disabling, for 'the cultural images that come down to us as history are written by the dissenters,'[12] often male and made myopic as they measure the distance between themselves and the more gullible folk they argue capitalism has remade.

To quote Stuart Hall's plain words, 'ordinary people are not cultural dopes' or 'blank screens.'[13] Claims that consumers were passive creatures of producers' desires have been convincingly contested even in the literature about the United States, where two decades ago such claims were particularly common.[14] In historical writing, the present interpretive challenge is to resist overstating consumption as a sphere of liberty and self-expression.[15] If producers were not paramount in the regulation of post-war consumption, to what intentions, aspirations, and values was commerce subsidiary in Canada in the first two decades after the war?[16]

Conspicuously, Canadian postwar prosperity 'always seemed fragile,' prey to the slightest misstep toward excess. The legacy of the Depression and the Second World War, more than the contemporary Cold War, shaped postwar values. Doug Owram argues that postwar ideas about home were made in a 'search for stability by a generation which had known nothing but instability.'[17] The political and economic conjuncture of the 1940s created a 'defence of common citizenship and shared entitlements,' including a 'moral obligation' to bridge income differences. James Struthers concludes that these priorities were but a transitory social democratic gloss on a liberal foundation.[18] Yet in the 1950s, the combination of a slow and uncertain return to prosperity, a concern for a stability, and a generalized wariness of excess governed Canadians' deliberations about welfare, well-being, and wants.

Their choice of pleasing goods for a home did not necessarily entail a suspension of enlightened self-interest.[19] But in the balance of symbolic trade across the domestic threshold in postwar Canada, it makes more sense to say that women remade their furnishings, than that their furnishings remade them. Their opportunities to do this were many, and the cultural and political authority sustaining them in these practices was secure. Perhaps Alan Ehrenhalt is right for the United States that 'The difference between the 1950s and the 1990s is to a large extent the difference between a society in which market forces challenged traditional values and a society in which they have triumphed over them.'[20] Certainly as Canadian women who set up their households in the postwar years spoke about domesticating objects, to borrow Martine Perrot's apt phrase,[21] their talk was rarely about advertisements and markets. Instead they kept returning to the associations between their decorative household goods and their senses of stability, identity, and play. These discourses and the ways they thought about the specific character of these associations marked them as women of that time.

Stability

Hannah Arendt has written, in a wonderful rumination called the 'Durability of the World,' about the capacity of goods to 'endure, at least for a time, the voracious needs and wants of their living makers and users,' and thus to have 'the function of stabilizing human life.' Humans, 'their ever

changing nature notwithstanding,' she argues felicitously for our purposes here, 'can retrieve their sameness, that is their identity by being
related to the same chair and the same table,' find some steadying possibility of objectivity by comparing the durability of familiar objects with the
'eternal movement' of nature.[22]

In the 1950s, domestic experience more than international Cold War
politics influenced Canadian values.[23] Canadians were concerned that
collective and individual prudence secure stability at home. This mattered
more than displays of consumption and thus capitalist superiority, the
ideological essence of Cold War citizenship in the United States. Among
the goods with which householders in Canada in the 1950s surrounded
themselves, furniture particularly seems to have performed this stabilizing
function. The contrast with automobiles, for example, was stark.[24]

Furniture manufacturers and retailers dreamed of spectacular sales 'if
our industry could ever make homemakers conscious of the need for
more attractively designed furniture to replace their obsolete pieces,' but
through the 1950s complained that 'obsolescence' was 'a sleeping giant'
whom they could not awaken.[25]

In the 1950s, Canadians lived with their furniture, particularly their
living and dining room furniture, for a long time. Few yearned to trade up,
expecting that most furniture would last more than ten years, and that at
least the cabinets they bought would last a lifetime. A 1956 study for
Canadian Homes and Gardens found that most Canadians were 'keepers,' as
the women whose testimony we relied on to interpret maple remembered
themselves to be.

Many women who spoke to me valued traditional furniture, not as a
mark of higher class standing or aspiration, but because, to their minds, it
was relatively unmarked symbolically. Tina Wall, the postwar British immigrant secretary married to an engineer, in 1958 bought a suite she identified as Jacobean, because it 'would not date.' 'This just looks the same,' she
told me in 1994, 'If I had bought modern then,' she argued, 'it would look
old fashioned now.'[26] Sally MacDonald and Julia Porter find a similar
preference for traditional forms and concern about forms which might
'date' in British Mass Observation studies of the fifties, a predilection they
explain on the grounds of economy. Furniture, which its owner thought to
be timeless, would dwell more happily with other household objects, old
and new, and thus not risk making their companion pieces look shabby
and in need of replacement. That the new would cast the old in shabby
shadow was the marketer's hope, the Diderot effect, named for the anx-

TABLE 8.1
Homemakers' Reports on How Long They Had Owned Their Furniture and How Long
They Thought Furniture Should Last (percentage)

						years
	n	less than 5	6–10	11–15	16–20	more than 20	total more than 10
Chesterfield suite							
owned	406	43.5	31.8	12.1	8.7	3.9	24.7
should last	414	9.4	41.3	21.3	15.9	12.1	49.3
Dining room suite							
owned	178	29.8	22.5	17.4	10.7	19.6	47.7
should last	300	2.0	18.7	16.0	24.6	38.7	79.3
Bedroom suite							
owned	415	34.4	26.3	16.4	9.9	13.0	39.3
should last	388	2.6	18.0	18.8	24.6	36.0	79.4

Source: Gruneau Research, *The Furniture Buying Habits of Canadians* (Toronto: Maclean-Hunter, Canadian Homes and Gardens, 1957) 6, 10–11; the study reports on individual pieces of furniture as well, but the data on suites were most complete, perhaps because these were more major expenditures, and thus more likely to attract memories and opinions. Gruneau interviewed 504 'housewives' in twenty-two cities of French and English Canada.

ious predicament the eighteenth-century philosopher Denis Diderot reported, as he compared his new robe with the rest of his possessions and yearned that all be new.[27]

There is a stance of resistance in this preference for traditional forms. Though they would not have known it under this name, the Diderot effect was a possibility these women anticipated, and planned to evade. Patricia Cliff, a retail worker who had come from Saskatchewan to Victoria after the war, made this distinction as between 'good furniture' and 'furniture which was built for a market.' Good furniture was 'substantial. It'll last you for fifty or sixty years if you want it to.' Furniture which endured, which did not wear and did not date, which was not built to readily reveal its need to be replaced, removed itself and its owner, as Cliff observed, from the sense of being 'a market,' and affirmed persisting loyalties to nonmarket values.[28]

When women spoke about the wear-worthiness of their furnishings, they claimed a certain constancy for themselves, important for householders in the 1950s, when modest prosperity was tentatively succeeding two decades of dearth. Winnifred Edwards, the British immigrant of progressive political sympathies who was married to a Vancouver physician, declared goods which would 'self-destruct ... disgusting.' Echoing Ruskin and Morris, she argued 'I don't think people should spend their life work in making trashy things ... it is beneath a man's dignity.' As it was beneath her own dignity to collude in such a process by purchasing 'trashy things.' Distant along the class continuum, but of similar politics, was Gerd Evans, the Norwegian immigrant who wed a fisherman in 1948 and lived in the early years of her marriage on float houses or in boarding houses or trailers, as the work demanded. In 1955 she bought her first furniture on time from Wosk's, a large furniture and appliance dealer on Hastings Street in downtown Vancouver who sold to the broad middle of the market and specialized in instalment sales. The bedroom suite she purchased at that time was with her still in 1994: 'I don't see any reason to get rid of things just because, you know. So I still have it.'[29] Allison Simpson, who as the wife of an RCMP officer also led a peripatetic existence, followed what she recalled as a family rule: 'If you're going to buy anything, either buy the cheapest possible so you can pitch it, or buy the best you can afford ... Don't buy something in the middle because you're apt to be disappointed. It'll be in, it'll be OK for two or three years and then the next thing you know ... I think that was good advice.'[30] Thus she built up a dependable kit of goods with which she could re-establish familiarity for her family as they moved about the Prairie provinces from posting to posting.

Clare Cooper Marcus, a Berkeley architect and Jungian analyst, found – perhaps to her chagrin, given her first profession – that in discussions of dwelling places, it was the 'moveable objects in the home, rather than the physical fabric itself' that people in the California Bay area in the 1970s and 1980s took as 'the symbols of self.'[31] Among postwar households which were mobile, either because they were engaged in resource econo- mies or employed by national organizations which in the practice of the time frequently moved their mid-level staff, holding on to household goods was a way to sustain some continuity for the selves who were the household. As John Seeley and his colleagues found in Toronto's Forest Hill in the 1950s: 'A relatively permanent deposit of material goods re- mains in that house which at any particular time they call "home." Indeed, the presence of these objects in a succession of houses is probably the most important factor in ... [their] concept of home. It is really the moveables which create the air of homeliness, and which are psychologically immove- able, rather than the physically rooted house.'[32]

But women who had been more settled also took pride in the stability of their attachment to their home furnishings. Joan Coffey, who spoke to me in 1994 in a house on the same lot she had occupied since 1946, remembered that her British immigrant mother 'used to change furniture all the time when she lived in Victoria. She used to say, "it's only furniture." I don't feel that way. I sort of get attached to it.' This attachment was savoured for both the stability and the liberty it allowed.[33] For as Tim Putnam argues, in a fine English book called *Household Choices*, 'an understanding of home becomes a means of organizing the world and orienting our passage through it.'[34] Decisions about goods, including furnishings for the home, are ways for people to say something about themselves, their families, their localities and their times, and also part of 'an active process in which all social categories are being continually redefined.'[35] Dwelling among chosen goods is a meditation upon these possibilities, and, particularly in Canada in the 1950s, a way, by ironical understatement, to gain autonomous living space in the shadow of commerce.

Sociological studies of the 1950s and 1960s considered interior decorations, particularly the decoration of the living room, as symbols of social status. Gerry Pratt, in her study of the professionally decorated domestic spaces of wealthy Vancouver and West Vancouver in 1979, showed how acceptable decoration was related to the strength of group identifications and the authority granted formally articulated tastes.[36] Yet, most domestic landscapes were crafted by amateurs rather than professionals, and for houses where entertaining was infrequent and much less important as an activity than the rumble of daily family life. There were no longer front parlours or reception rooms set aside for the practice of social formalities. The evidence women offer about their household choices does not answer questions about social status affirmation when few who were not family, or 'like family,' entered such spaces. But it can tell us a good deal about how women articulated and acted upon values they called personal, and represented those values to their families, thus to reveal chronologically distinctive shared understandings of what homely goods were and what they should do.

Marketers who in the 1950s were interested in the question, 'Why isn't the consumer spending more on home furnishings?' distinguished between two groups, the 'entertainers' and the 'homebodies.' The 'entertainers' were not the marketers' problem. These women used fine furniture and were confident in their command of its shifting nuance. The sellers' and makers' problem lay with the 'homebodies,' women with larger families than their mothers had raised. The 'homebodies' wanted furniture which was 'durable, practical and comfortable,' and were 'wary of furniture salesman,' rather than being willing students of the rules of the trade.[37]

For a complicated set of reasons related to their class position, their family size, and the culture of their time, the women I interviewed and who wrote to me about homemaking in the postwar period seem to have decorated as 'homebodies.' Homebodies, after years of turbulence, were concerned with the home as a symbolic environment sheltering the other people and the objects which would define the self.[38] This circuit between people and things in the home was not closed; goods, once brought into the home, began to do cultural work there; in contemplation, the householders, who daily left and entered the home, reassimilated these recognizable forms; from this milieu of more stable recognition they organized themselves to perceive the world beyond. They remade things for their purposes to mediate this transition between self and other, known, knowable, and unknown.

In part the process of consolidating and remaking depended upon the intrinsic qualities of the objects. In measure, these reactions were physical responses, transhistorical so far as human bodies are transhistorical, to the chill of steel under hand, the glare of light off polished surfaces to the eye, the sound and feel of foot upon carpeted or bare floor. But by their colour, texture, and glean, objects also invoke memories, both those wilfully recalled and those beyond the power of the will to summons or refuse, memories triggered by the sensory contact with the thing itself.[39] In this sense, household objects were both dependable and surprise personal storehouses of memories, holding personal histories of sensations in their materiality. At the same time, reactions to the intrinsic qualities of objects are historically specific and social, collecting shared experiences with goods. Thus was a 1950s reading of chrome or maple different, for example, from later reading of either of these.[40]

It is more useful to attend to these specific special signs than to think of consumers as passive before commercial imperatives, or, by contrast, free from structural constraints to do as they will. Listening to women reading domestic goods is a way to learn about this interaction between the micropolitics of everyday life and politics at the social level, between what the Swedes, who see the significance of this traffic more readily than most modern citizens, call the little life (*det lilla livet*) and the big life of contemporary society and politics. This traffic especially bears watching for the 1950s, when the domestic was a highly charged rather than a residual social category, a terrain marketers and policy makers may have

Ian and the chocolate pudding, 1961. This is a solid hardwood table, the top made of glued-up four-inch boards, by 1961 possibly finished with a resistant urea varnish. Wood appealed for its visual and tactile warmth. The refrigerator is pre-1958, the motor occupying the lower third of the cabinet.

wished to colonize, but where homemakers, like many colonists both peaceable and rebellious before them, often escaped central regulation.

The household furnishings acquired in the first decade and a half after the Second World War, probably more than in later years, were chosen for and served stabilizing functions. In the fifties, most Canadian homemakers were not replacing or redecorating, but were gradually acquiring home furnishings for the first time. Many scoffed, or at least looked mildly bemused, when I asked about how they 'furnished' their homes – not the right word, they thought, to describe the process they had lived. Furniture was bought 'one piece at a time,' so as not to destabilize the household budget. As Pam McKeen, the immigrant wife of an ironworker who settled in the Niagara Peninsula in 1955, remembered, 'You started off with basics that you could afford and gradually over time you added to and built up things.' Mary Paine, the woman who with her husband was raising two boys in Calgary on his earnings as a commission salesman, replied to the 'furnishing' question: 'Well our furniture just sort of grew. I mean we were never in the position to go out and buy everything to match you know. So we sort of had early Salvation Army, mix and match, whatever you want to call it. And so we got to the point where we were putting things together.' This incremental, evolutionary pattern Madigan and Munro also find among working-class homemakers in 1980s Glasgow. Prudent budgeting and the household's sense of security were connected. Even if they were stylistically dissonant, furnishings, by their very signs of having been brought into the household one by one, displayed a continuity of purpose which signified security.[41]

The symmetry in the deliberations which brought these goods into the company of the household was what made them match. Joan Coffey, a homemaker trained as and married to a psychiatric nurse, remembered Coquitlam, near Vancouver, in the 1940 and 1950s,

All our young friends were getting by on a shoestring. And there were many of us starting our families and so many of the people that we knew were building their own houses and they were building them from pay day to pay day ... And every possession that any of us got was really valued because we would have to save up for months ... And I mean we treasured those things because we'd worked so hard, all of us, we were all in the same situation ... We got one thing at a time and we looked after it and treasured it and it was really special to us.

This was the Diderot effect in reverse. The newly acquired furniture was being domesticated into the household's habits of habitation, settling into rather than challenging its new company. Each new piece was expected, like its predecessors, to last. All were made to match by the common intention with which they had been assembled.[42] This is not the pattern some English researchers investigating the same period have reported. Working-class homemakers around London, perhaps reacting to greater

Interwar wood-frame rocker, recovered in 1950s in floral-printed crepe drapery fabric, and still in use in 1997, subsequently covered in leather.

wartime dislocation, found security in the stylistic symmetry of matching sets, and delayed marriage, if necessary, in order to avoid a 'make-shift' start. By contrast, among many Canadians, household furnishings acquired one by one were especially valued and found fitting exactly because they had come into the home in this way – because, to return to Pam McKeen's active language, they overtime had been 'added to and built up,' and had thus become signs of both the stability and the identity of the household.[43] Household goods, which in the market may have been substitutable and ephemerally fashionable, were made to signify stability in the 1950s, made to 'function in another register,' diverted from, while remaining within, the market system[44] once they were brought into the home.

Gender was at work here. Scholars studying the way collectors compose their collections have reported that women, when they think of themselves as nurturing adults, collect 'unemphatically,' paying less attention to the publicly acknowledged qualities of objects than to the ways these objects further the relationships of the household (even though they may be 'serious' and 'discerning' collectors in other aspects of their lives).[45] Similarly homemakers have been reported more accommodating than discriminating in their appraisals of household forms, placing more emphasis upon the subjective judgments about housing, what they have learned from where they are, than upon an objective assessment of what alternative dwelling forms might be ideal. To the product designer, this might seem irrational, but it is so only if the product itself, appraised as an object, is pre-eminent.[46] Few women of ordinary means in the 1950s thought of household goods in this 'objective way,' for the managing of the household involved arbitrating among a wide range of needs, only some of which could be satisfied by objects. Metaphorically, objects must be kept in their proper place. In these circumstances, accommodation and compromise concerning material domestic goods was the active, effective posture, while discrimination, which confused material domestic goods with all domestic goods, was an ineffectual, perhaps disabling, distraction. Joan Coffey distilled this deliberation, between her own priorities and the polemics of the contemporary commodity culture, to a single telling incident:

Some friends of ours bought into a new subdivision ... and [were] buying nice furniture. Then I would have really liked to have been able to spend more money, but I couldn't then because I had the children ... [It] didn't bother me too much but I had a little session there when I know it did. And I'll never forget the lady that made the slip covers for Eatons. She came out and she spent a whole day cutting and measuring. They used to come to the house in those days. I guess they still do ... And she told me – her name was Mrs Smith – and I've never seen her from that day to this, which is about forty years ago and I think she changed my life. She said, 'I'm a widow with two girls ... I have to work, and I go into the most expensive homes, in New Westminster, all those nice places on Queen's Avenue ...' and she said 'I go home to my place and I'm perfectly happy with it. Our house suits us for the girls and myself.' And I thought that's the secret ... You know, this house suits us.[47] In Canada in the 1950s this secret was widely shared and celebrated.

Women were accommodating rather than discriminating in their appraisals of household goods as a consequence of their household roles as mediators. Winning others in the household over to a discourse of 'suitability' (akin to the discourse of 'comfort' Jean Duruz finds at the same period in Sydney, Australia), was part of the homemaker's gendered responsibility to balance irreconcilable demands of other family members for time, space, energy, and autonomy. This womanly obligation to conciliate contending claims included the economic but much else as well.[48]

Suitable often meant familiar, the securing of domestic stability through forms which would be recognizable as 'normal and respectable,'[49] as ordinary and homely. The working-class women I interviewed, like the Glasgow women with whom Madigan and Munro spoke, employed a rhetoric of decency. 'I wouldn't go for something that's nouveau or anything like that,' Gerd Evans said, 'I don't care if it's not the latest trend or anything, but I want it to look halfway decent.' Respectable and decent here were not competitive aspirations to higher status but affirmations or demonstrations of belonging.[50] Nettie Murphy, an immigrant from Holland in 1952 who married young in 1957, reasoned, 'probably what happened was that most of the people around me had the same taste ... And it was not necessarily that I wanted to have the same thing that everybody else had, but still it seems that your taste evolved from what you saw around you. If it feels good to be around that at the time that is what you like.'[51] Storekeepers selling to the popular market understood better than contemporary arbiters of style these 'collective aspects of their customers' tastes and aspirations.'[52]

Sally Tobe learned these lessons about taste, and also about commerce and companionable tolerance, from her parents, in the downtown Kitchener, Ontario, store from which they sold furniture to rural and working-class couples, returning veterans and recent immigrants. Tobe helped her parents sell many large, dark, upholstered living room suites in the postwar years, furniture which has gained a certain retrospective cachet but at the time was scorned by good design experts.

JP: Did working people want to have good taste?

ST: There were times when you would wonder why they would buy something like that because you didn't at that time think it was in good taste, or it was really passé. But they wanted that in particular and that's what they bought. And that's why we continued to carry some of the pieces, or suites, for people long after other people were buying the new things.

Veterans and recent immigrants buying wine upholstered suites at Twin City Furniture found them homey, Tobe recalls, 'the fabric was warm. The form was warm. The form sort of enveloped' because the arms were wide. The demand that these goods speak stability, be normal and recognizable, was most apparent in the customers' strict specifications about colour. 'They were always wine coloured sofas, and then you'd have a chair that was wine, or a chair that was green, or a chair that was blue. It was, you know, a sort of ruby wine colour. And that just seemed to be almost inflexible in terms of those colours. Occasionally you would get someone who wanted one in blue or green, but not very often.'[53]

Imagery of stability permeated homemakers' discussions about home furnishings and the 1950s. The preceding two decades had been years of great disruption. Goods were being acquired after long deliberation and long delay, and usually were expected to see long service. Sometimes the talk was about the hazards to stability of too great emotional or monetary investment in goods. Sometimes goods themselves became signs of the household's security because they had been domesticated according to their owner's fashion, made to fit in and be fitting – in the reverse of the Diderot effect, to leave their newness and their market referents behind and join the assembled household company. Women emphasized the relational aspects of their lives among household goods in the 1950s, that accommodation was a better survival strategy than discrimination, that so long as a good would do, in some subjective sense, its objective qualities might well be overlooked: making do with objects kept these goods in their proper place. This was less a conservative than a conserving impulse, a strategy to resist and subvert market imperatives. In all these distinctive and sometimes contradictory readings, women deployed the intrinsic qualities of household furnishings, their durability and their representation of familiar forms, their capacity to store and spark memory, to secure the domestic goods they valued which were non-material.

Women were arbitrating among contending desires, including their own. This could be called displacement, making virtue of necessity. Duruz suggests that the Sydney homemakers whose recollections of the 1950s included this reasoning were echoing 'an older romantic dream.' Gibson-Graham, by contrast, would describe the non-market reasoning of the household as an alternative rather than an atavism. Coffey, Paine, and other Canadian homemakers did note the pressure of economic necessity in the 1950s. But their resistance to excess, their preference for moderation, was, in life as well as in recollection, also about identity, politics, and pleasure.[54]

Identity

The capacity of household furnishings to store and spark memory is their most readily apparent connection to personal identity. A domestic interior constitutes 'a material memory landscape,' a touchable, observable representation of the subjectivities of those who participate in its composition. Thus does the interior come to serve as a museum of these selves.[55]

As memories are both voluntarily and involuntarily recalled, these museums of the self are both voluntarily and involuntarily composed. Those connections between the self and goods which are unconsciously formed and involuntarily remembered can summon acute responses, both of unquiet and pleasure, and be taken by their serendipity to be particularly defining or redefining of the self. Thus do goods both reflect back the self and become instruments in the processes by which the self is remade. Tina Wall, who had emigrated with her brother after the war to make a firm break with hard circumstances in the north of England and had married but remained childless in Vancouver, discovered on a return visit to Britain years later a cousin's home decorated in the same colours she had used to settle into her house in Vancouver. This discovery became thereafter a continuing reference which established her connectedness and mitigated the rupture of war and emigration. Margaret Shortliffe had found a series of Chinese prints in rural Alberta and stowed them in a cedar chest 'when I was sixteen and had no hope of setting up a house.' That forty years later, after the early death of her husband, a professor of French, these prints, retrieved and used as chinoiserie to decorate a parlour screen, 'all melded so well' in the rooms they had crafted together, reaffirmed their union so untimely severed, made it seem fore-ordained.[56] Both these postwar stories used the recognition of serendipitous affinities among objects to signify the fittedness of relationships between people, these links valued as timely solaces in an era preoccupied by rupture and healing.

The historically specific qualities of the relationships between personal and familial identities and things were also consciously appraised. Women's discussions about the burdens or pleasures of inherited forms were at once reflections on their relationships with their own mothers (and mothers-in-law), and statements about what they felt was required of them, as homemakers, in the particular chronological period when they were creating homes of their own. Grant McCracken has argued that 'modern' families continually have reinvented themselves by new purchases, and that women (such as his study case, Lois Roget) who have surrounded themselves with inherited goods have these capacities to make their own social and personal meanings pre-empted by the tyranny of objects whose significations are 'so fully "pre-recorded."'[57] Yet households accommodate inherited furnishings in ways which 'redefine both piece and place.' Thus ancestral goods brought into the home can be signs of the next generation's power to subvert as much as to revere their predecessors' time and intentions. Even inherited goods and tastes refused houseroom by the next generation leave traces in the 'modern' dwelling in their remembered absence.[58]

The will to 'be modern' was felt acutely in the postwar years. But the pursuit of this state was not straightforward. The meaning of modern was variously inscribed and always echoing with antecedents. In the 1950s George Soulis and John Murray designed a line of lean, low, and light furniture called Young Moderns for Snyders of Kitchener. This furniture was addressed to the needs of young couples with limited means and was sold nationally through Eaton's. Soulis remembers the form as 'partly market driven and partly socially driven in the sense that people who came out of the depression didn't see the past as particularly desirable. If you look at the styles of the depression, Duncan Phyfe, Chippendale, dark mahogany, it all had the connotation of what we wanted to put behind us. Somehow the thought of your living room being furnished with this was to identify with that era ... rather stodgy, over-decorated, not bright, not exciting, not original.'[59]

Mary Paine and her husband bought one of the very first Young Moderns suites, a group of armless sectionals upholstered with conspicuous yellow S's (for Snyders) on a green ground, a presentation piece which finished its national tour in the Calgary Eaton's store where Mr Paine was employed. For her, as for Soulis and Murray, the generational references were clear, but also commanding.

JP: Was it a common form at the time you bought it?

MP: Well as I say it was very modern. Very modern. That's why we liked it cause, you know, we thought we were with it.

JP: What did modern mean?

MP: Well my mother and my mother-in-law had big overstuffed furniture. Big wide arms, big high backs. Sort of a velour, but not as soft as velour. So this was, you know, we thought, very modern.[60]

This suite sat bearing Snyders' monogram, but mutely, over-spoken by a non-commercial dialogue both between the Paines and their mothers, and between their two generations.

For Susan Taylor, raised in the prosperous home of a central Canadian publisher, and 'in rebellion' against a 'very houseproud mother,' furnishing her first home, in a prairie suburb in 1949, presented a daunting challenge. 'We had brought with us a bed, and a crib. That's all I think.' And she determinedly 'had never been a shopper.' Trained as a social scientist, employed in wartime Ottawa planning for a more equitable peace, married to a penurious university professor of progressive sympathies, Taylor, by cheerful avoidance, made furnishing their home a telling and triumphant contemporary ideological affirmation. In 1949 Taylor had one child, one on the way, and the attitude toward having children (she eventually had four) of which the baby boom was made: 'I loved having children – raising children to me was a very interesting occupation, but not housework *per se*' – or shopping. The house was a small storey-and-a-half, in a model suburb where front yards met recreational green spaces and cars were restricted to back lanes. Taylor is the only woman who contacted me for this research who had ever engaged a designer, and she did so only this once, in this most planfully modern Canadian year of 1949. Ed who was twenty-one, an interior design teacher at the university, worked from this instruction: 'We have $500 and a house.'

For this sum, Ed secured two continental beds and a corner table with an upper half shelf to set between their perpendicularly placed heads, two wrought iron Hardoy chairs whose frames he fabricated himself and for which Taylor made canvas sling seats, two Broyhill upholstered chairs, an oak dining table, four side chairs, and a low dish dresser, built to his design by a local carpenter. To the sliding doors of this cabinet Taylor soon added locks, which, she pointed out to me, 'don't add to the beauty. Practicality was terribly important to me.' And there were inquisitive children about. Ed's last contribution, a desk–sewing table of his own design, was made with an extendible leaf to accommodate Taylor's Singer featherweight sewing machine and give her a place to make children's clothing before the living room window. Of these furnishings, the case goods and tables lasted longest, and remained in use in the principal rooms of Taylor's

The living room of a Canadian Mortgage and Housing Small Home in Calgary, 1953. The chair in the corner was part of a Snyders Young Moderns section chesterfield, upholstered in bright yellow S's on a green ground. The chair was sent to Eaton's stores across the country to represent the new Snyders line, and purchased by one of the furniture salesmen at Eaton's Calgary store. The couple were decorating to make the best use of their 800-square-foot home, and valued the chair for its lines, overlooking its advertising iconography.

home forty-five years later, bearing in them the traces of both the principles with which she had begun her adult life and the decades of active domesticity which followed.[61]

Even from the stance of rebellion, the acquisition and domestication of household furniture preserved, edited, and secured the family's history through objects. Sometimes the burden of inheritance ultimately could not be resisted. Joan Niblock, whose own family had been among the original European settlers on Telegraph Trail in the Fraser Valley, ended up living back on this farm, in a house filled with her mother-in-law's furniture. The first furniture she and her husband bought had been 'terribly modern,' chosen to be part of a specific family conversation.

JN: We thought it was wonderful because it was so modern-looking.

JP: Modern?

JN: Well yes, my husband's mother is into antiques, or was ... And we wanted to be different. My mother-in-law wanted to come and live with us and this was sort of something hanging over our heads because she was going to furnish the house and take over. So we wanted something different.

...

JP: How long did that last? It does not seem to have lasted to this very day by the look of this room.

JN: Oh, we inherited my mother-in-law's furniture. We changed our way of thinking. I know, my husband was not too fond of antique furniture. He's not too happy with other people's old junk. But you know.[62]

Sometimes the burden of inheritance became a welcome of continuity across generations. Allison Simpson set great store by the similarity in the tastes of her mother and mother-in-law, and basked in this affinity by contentedly delegating family gift buying for her husband's mother to her own. Each year, early in her marriage, using as collateral for a loan a bond which was a gift from her feminist grandmother, she and her husband bought a piece or two of furniture. Soon, by these choices, their rented home in Meadow Lake, Saskatchewan, 'started to look a little bit more like my idea of home, not someone else's.' By this she meant, 'Something like the home I came from, my mother and father's home, or my husband's home.' Geraldine Pratt found that, in the late 1970s, continuity of taste across generations was assumed among securely established Shaughnessy families, and that women recalled, perhaps in the period Simpson described, having taken careful note of the homes of prospective mothers-in-law as a sign of what might be expected of them. Simpson, the daughter of a mine executive who had begun his career at northern sites and later risen to prominence in Montreal, would have come from the class in which Pratt finds this pattern. But her husband's father was an electrician, her husband a member of the RCMP. Simpson's observation, on a visit back to Ontario from Alberta before her marriage, that her future husband's parents 'lived in a very comfortable home with the kind of furniture that was very much like my mother and dad's,' was a reassurance that she and he had other common ground, besides their experiences at university and in the North, upon which to build a marriage.[63]

For everyone who wrote or spoke to me, the acquiring of furniture included an appraisal of family traditions, and extended, frequently revisited, deliberations about which of these to use and which to refuse.[64] Accommodating these groupings, and finding a compatible place to put them, became a 'problem' and often directed the choice of dwelling away from contemporary forms, a phenomenon which exasperated modern architects of the 1950s. As Suilio Venchiarutti, partner with his brother in a Toronto practice, sputtered in 1954: 'most of the women who worry over this problem don't have authentic period pieces. They just have old furniture. What they don't stop to realize is that the life expectancy of their furniture is only one sixth of the life expectancy of the house ... Besides being inconsistent – my favourite word – you are creating a constant demand on the market for old-fashioned furniture that's just as inconvenient and impractical as old-fashioned houses.'[65] But furniture could not be appraised in these market terms, for the identity of the household was too much tied up in it. These were objects which could be situated historically only by reading through the personal to what was common to the time. Early on, women reviewing the transcripts of our conversations found my pattern of questioning wanting in this respect. They argued that by asking them to comment on objects in sequence, as they had acquired them through time, I had given them less space than they needed to situate their choices within their family traditions. I tried thereafter to mend my ways and listen with a mild expression, waiting as the family tale gradually wound its way back toward the furniture.[66]

In these personal stories of the postwar years, the commonly contemporary element was the insistence, among women with and without children, with large families and small, and of diverse social circumstances, that in that time 'making a home for family' was what furnishing a house was about. After years of economic uncertainty, in makeshift housing, in unfamiliar settings, for women of the 1950s reclaiming delayed plans to bear children and raise families, making a home was a particularly subjective process, internal to the family in its references. For in these times, the need to create a setting which held and specifically interpreted personal histories, which would be resilient in its familiarity, withstanding future moves, compensating for past losses, which could be wrapped up and packed up, transported and reinstalled, was the most important of the many cultural purposes a domestic interior could serve.

A Zest for Making Do

Yet (or perhaps better, and so) these 1950s domestic interiors are remembered distinctively as products and sites of playful, generative, and irreverent creativity. Decorating of the time emphasized making do, a stance which was literally doubly active – *making*, working on materials at hand; *do*, using them to effect. By insisting that the 'made do' were sufficient, householders made these goods cheekily resistant. Making do was a decorative act which talked back to the market, an art which was political in so far as it took charge of what goods would do.

Like a visual artist, a painter, or sculptor 'seeking objective counterparts for ideals or feelings they experience,' a woman decorating a room invokes a state of being.[67] The surfaces she assembles and arranges glint and refract, like a work of art holding more meanings than can be captured in settled lines of text. These decorated interiors have been places where women, through a 'ceremonial oratory of display,' have found means to express themselves when their opportunities for public oratory were limited.[68] The collage women made of the family's living space in the 1950s was not up on the wall, but all around, inflecting the practices of daily life.[69] These rooms, thus, both displayed and made differences. Virginia Woolf's meditation in *A Room of One's Own* catches a tension about this making of difference which has similarities with the recollections of the 1950s: 'The resources of the English language would be much put to the stretch ... before a woman could say what happens when she goes into a room. The rooms differ so completely; ... how could it be otherwise? For women have sat indoors for all these millions of years, so that by this time the very walls are permeated by their creative force, which has, indeed, so overcharged the capacity of bricks and mortar that it must needs harness itself to pens and brushes and business and politics.'[70] In common with the domestic altars and cabinets of curiosities of other places and times, the assembled domestic landscapes of modest postwar interiors had the capacity to speak from private space about the public space beyond.[71]

The goods which gave homemakers most pleasure were those which stimulated creativity, which were redefined as they were used, and which called for intervention.[72] Homes themselves were goods of this order, but women also frequently mentioned sewing machines, radios, record players, musical instruments, and cameras.[73] From sewing machines, most frequently noted of which were the Singer Featherweights, issued streams of clothing, curtains, and crafts. Ella Smith was the wife of a Vancouver factory worker. Their most prized purchase from the 1950s, a movie camera, beat out a formidable but resolutely pragmatic contender for family funds: 'We bought the movie camera. This doesn't really come under furnishings and appliances though. We bought the movie camera before we bought the electric refrigerator. Because we saw a friend who had the use of a relative's camera and the pictures of her baby. Then my husband said 'let's forget about getting the refrigerator. Let's make do with the icebox that we have because the children will be past their babyhood by the time we get the refrigerator paid for.' For Mrs Smith, the camera had been important for the baby pictures it created. With her husband she had then explicitly defined these pictures as more important than an artless, if state of the art, technology. For her retrospectively this recollection was a provocative trace of reasoning from times which were child-rich and cash-poor, when contending wants were muted to maintain peace of mind.

Making do by buying second-hand was both a necessity and, for these couples in the 1950s, a source of accomplishment. The South Asian immigrant couples whom Joy and Dholakia interviewed in a central Canadian city in 1988–9 worried that furniture 'could never be totally appropriated by subsequent owners';[74] postwar English couples linked their independence as newly marrieds with being able to buy new.[75] By contrast, the women who contacted me remembered their postwar participation in the second-hand trade with relish. Although most people buy more second-hand when they are younger than older, the turn to used goods was intensified by particular 1950s conditions. Mary Kippen, whose husband in the 1950s worked as a warehouseman in New Westminster, remembered buying furnishings for her growing family second-hand, partly because her children 'came along fairly quickly,' partly because 'In those days you didn't seem to hesitate too much to purchase second-hand. You were quite happy to go into this because cost was a factor when you only had one income. And credit was not readily available.'[76] Many avoided the market altogether by swapping, or passing goods on to friends or to successors in the continuing transit through northern resource towns.[77] This bartering was helpful. But the acquisitions more often recollected as zestful were those which occurred through the market, and which had allowed the new owner in some way to redefine the terms of trade. Marjorie Barlow, who in 1952 moved from a Manitoba farm to Winnipeg, where her husband began to work as a steam fitter, noted as successful purchases the Aladdin lamp and kerosene iron which had allowed her to read at night on the farm and finish summer laundry without lighting the cookstove. The pleasure in the pursuit of a dark oak dining room table, with her still in 1994, she recalled as of another order: 'I guess the table probably was one of the most thrilling things to buy because I found it. It was stacked away up in a second hand store and it was exactly what I wanted' – 'thrilling' because the table chosen when barely visible was revealed to be exactly right, and because Barlow soon was able to 'complete' it with a find of second-hand complementing chairs.[78]

There was a touch of theatricality in many of the accounts of how second-hand goods were found and made do, but none surpassed the Shortliffes' sense of joyful incorporation and wilful artifice. Perhaps this is not surprising, for Glen Shortliffe was a student of French literature, familiar with contemporary semiotic critiques. But there was also a modern Canadian context to the stance. Shortliffe was a social democrat in Kingston, Ontario, in the 1950s, turned back at the border en route to take up an American university post for his postwar pro-Chinese radio broadcasts. Both Shortliffes were Albertans, raised on family stories of social injustice and personal resilience, for whom making do was making politics as well as making fun. The Shortliffes mostly bought second-hand from Mr Turk, their 'favourite furniture supplier,' on the grounds of both economy and autonomy: 'because he was nice and cheap and you could pick what you wanted and what you didn't want.' From these local finds they crafted 'French' furniture for themselves, rebuilding, refinishing, and reupholstering, turning to nearby immigrant craftsmen for specialized skills, but mostly relying on Glen's own woodworking knowledge. The Shortliffes were unapologetic, indeed resplendent, in their search for effect rather than authenticity.

You are sitting on a chair that we bought from Mr Turk. It was all painted a dark mahogany and it had a beautiful faded rose silk upholstery on it ... We really didn't like the fashions in the catalogues. And we found ourselves going back to second-

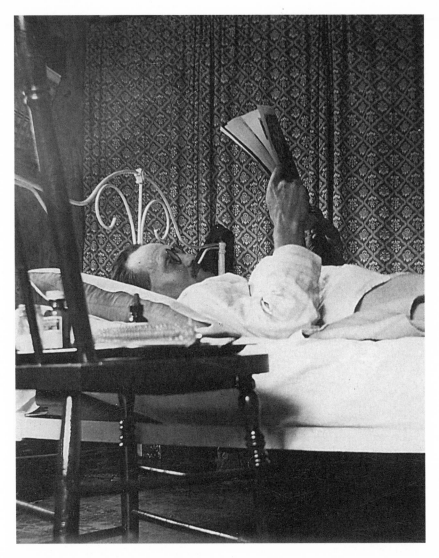

Second-hand furnishings were an important part of the stock of household goods in the years after the Second World War. Here is the Nelson family's first bedstead, an iron frame which would have worked well in the cramped quarters common during the Vancouver housing shortage of the late 1940s. A pressed back kitchen chair doubles as a bedside table and medicine stand. Recumbent, a future member of Parliament.

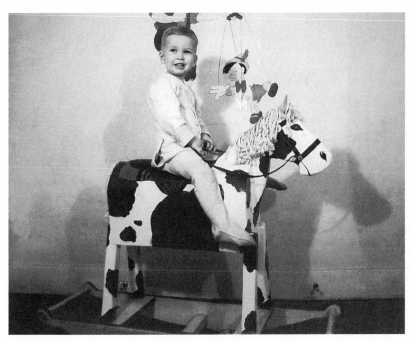

Do-it-yourself skills stretched income and created playful satisfactions. Here the young son of Margaret and Glen Shortliffe enjoys the rocking horse his father made for him for Christmas 1945. The abilities Glen Shortliffe refined during his Alberta boyhood served him well raising a family in Kingston, Ontario. Shortliffe was active in the CCF in Kingston and the Islands. Margaret Shortliffe remembers their excursions to best the market by remaking second-hand goods as both play and politics.

hand stores where we would think that something was beautiful. And then my husband would take it home and refurbish it or refinish it. And that's what we did with this chair. Cause although I knew it wasn't hand carved, it was machine carved, but it still had all the lines I liked and you could hardly see it because it was such a dark colour.

This was play, a game which made getting by into a gleeful festivity for two.[79]

Such studied inattentiveness to authenticity was key to the domestication of furniture, especially in an era when money was scarce and it was not plain that the past, except as a site for imaginative play, had much to recommend it. Through processes of remaking, furniture became special to those who lived with it. The retold account emphasized how each object had been appropriated by succeeding owners and marked with their identities. It was less important to honour past remnants than to capture them and put them actively to work in the present.[80]

When we met in 1994, Allison Simpson, a University of Alberta accounting graduate married to an RCMP constable, pointed out two side chairs which she had come to know were made in Liverpool by a firm in business between 1847 and 1849, but whose story as she retold it took place in Alberta and Australia. While stationed in Moose Jaw, the Simpsons had learned that the antiques in a large house were to be auctioned for their wealthy English immigrant owner, then emigrating to New Zealand. The Simpsons stayed home, expecting that the 'furniture from her house would be way too big for any house we would ever live in,' but the intending emigrant in due course needed to report to the RCMP station for finger-printing, and she and Constable Simpson got to talking about what was fitting, big and small. 'And she said oh she had two chairs in the basement but the upholstery was shot on them. The cat had been sleeping on them. And the back of one was broken although most of the pieces were there. So he went and took a look at them and decided yes he could repair the one that was broken and could reupholster them easily enough. So those are they.' And fine-looking chairs they are. Years later, after Tom Simpson had left the force and joined another organization, he went to keep an appointment with someone at their office in Sydney, Australia. 'When he got there, [this man] turned out to be a Canadian from Moose Jaw. And he told my husband where his family home had been. And Tom said, "is your mother still in New Zealand?" and he almost fell off his chair, because he was, he didn't realize. Anyway, as it happened I had snapshots with me to show our Australian friends what the inside of a Canadian home looked like. And the chairs happened to be in one of the pictures. He was quite surprised.' Allison Simpson read these chairs for what they contributed to a family history of reckoning and refusing what was too ponderously grand to be plausible, seeking out and remaking what was found beautiful and could be made fitting, a history in which the Liverpool chairs of the 1840s became elements in a picture of 'what the inside of a Canadian home looked like.'[81]

The unpainted furniture so commonly available in the 1950s and used furniture of varying quality and antiquity were treated in much the same way, as goods to be remade for the usefulness and fun of making do. Ella

One of a pair of mid-nineteenth-century side chairs made in Liverpool and brought to Moose Jaw as settlers' effects. Tom Simpson purchased them from their owner, who was re-emigrating to New Zealand, and refinished and reupholstered them. They then became part of a photo set the Simpsons carried with them on their travels, to show international friends 'what a Canadian home looks like.'

Smith's story about the unfinished crib which her husband painted pink and decorated with decals, and then reproduced in a miniature replica for his daughter's dolls,[82] shows this pattern, the instant of purchase being made perceptually incidental to the pleasure of remaking and living with the good.[83] This perception, groomed in the postwar years, that the market ought appropriately to be kept at bay, joked with, and obverted, made Tina Wall, after I found and decoded canonically significant design marks and labels she had never noticed on her end tables, turn my attention pointedly to her coffee table:

JP: Some things in this room are of high quality wood.

TW: This is arborite.

JP: And some are arborite.

TW: This is arborite because we put our cups of tea, or books, anything on it and you don't worry.

JP: So this is a round arborite table, about 3 and a half feet in diameter and then it has

...

TW: My husband put casters on. So you can move it around.

She thus reminded me that the logic which governed domestic surroundings that she and her husband composed in the 1950s was pre-eminently their own, made to suit them, to accommodate their pleasures, and that these purposes overrode commercial categories which might have separated walnut from arborite, and living room tables from robust warehouse casters.[84]

There may be something telling in the way generation Xers of the 1990s savour the remains of the popular material culture of the 1950s, something more telling than can be read from the commercial speech, both direct and disguised, of contemporary glossy magazines such as *Chatelaine* and *Canadian Homes and Gardens*. There is a certain symmetry between the ways young people today deploy the postwar plywood and chrome, wrought iron and vinyl – with irreverence, rueful of claims to authenticity, transgressing the commercial succession of obsolescence – and the way Canadians of modest means used these objects to make homes for themselves in the 1940s and 1950s. While the commercial commodity culture of the time strove to commodify domesticity, the women who took primary responsibility for this work in the home decorated explicitly to domesticate the objects they allowed houseroom. Like the generation Xers, most 1950s Canadian homemakers lacked the financial resources to participate in the taste-makers' play. Both groups regarded the market sceptically, generation X from a stance of wary familiarity ecologically tinged with green, the women of the forties and fifties from an innocence, not to be confused with naivety, which could still tune out the clamour of commerce and attend to more pressing and pleasurable concerns.

And yet the generational readings are very different, for the stance of making do in the 1950s was not ironical but optimistic, not aggrieved by the plenty denied but mildly cautious about plenty promised. From these respective vantage points, a wine-coloured sofa and a chrome dining set, a new crib home-painted pink and an early Quebec armoire skinned with a belt sander of all signs of age, are almost unrecognizable as the same domestic goods, so different are they made by the household processes through which they were domesticated. As the market went about its business, the attention of Canadian households was elsewhere. Perhaps refusing market reasoning was self-denial; but surely it was also a denial of certain things. To look beyond the market, to other pleasures and other ways of engaging with the material world, was, in Canada in the 1950s, a contemporary, not a nostalgic stance. Then the promised transformative power of consumer goods was what seemed suspiciously romantic.

PART 3

HOUSEHOLD CHOICES

9

Shopping for a Good Stove

We are accustomed to thinking of women as shoppers and shoppers as women. 'Born to shop' bumper stickers are affixed (whether sardonically, wearily, or proudly) to cars driven by women rather than men. Described for a decade as something women do by nature, that they are born to, shopping lately has been proclaimed by talk-show hosts and writers of mass-market paperbacks a women's addiction, a disease to which women particularly are prone.

There was, of course, a time when no one, either female or male, shopped – when necessaries were found or chased or made or traded – and thereafter a time in Canada's agricultural past when men turned their family's produce or remittances into cash and then goods on their trips alone to town. Women in modern times have been made shoppers by their circumstances rather than their natures. But these circumstances, the changing social setting and experience of shopping, have not been much studied, partly because thinking about shopping, in our time ambiguously work and weakness, at once invisible and obsessional, makes women scholars nervous.

Shopping is not always the same experience. This chapter is about shopping for a stove in the years 1950–5, about trying to find a particular good to meet a clearly but variously defined need; a good made in a limited number of forms by a finite number of firms and sold according to studiously defined practices by well-established stores. The aim is to get to know women of that time better by studying their experience as shoppers: the assumptions about womanliness acted out in the shops, and built into the goods for which women shopped; the ways in which women found out or were kept from what they needed to know in order to buy; and the latitude they had or lacked to get manufacturers to make for them what they wanted to use. This is first a study of women in the early 1950s, and second an experiment in diagnosing the power politics of shopping. It is finally a parable about a stove.

After ten years of depression, six years of war, and five years of disruption in the return to peacetime production, a substantial portion of Canadian households were in need of a stove. In 1950, a stove, unlike a refrigerator, was an undisputed household necessity. Also unlike the refrigerator, it was rarely touched by men, used almost exclusively by women to perform tasks most men had not mastered. Stoves were major purchases, but their principal users were not usually major income-earners. They were manufactured by both Canadian firms and American branch plants to drawings made by male designers, and were sold by male commission salesmen.

Writers in the trade and business press urged their readers to recognize that most of their customers were women, to 'Cultivate the ladies, they do 90% of retail buying.' And, having acknowledged woman as the 'nation's purchasing agent,' businesses were encouraged to 'slant ... sales and merchandising programs to attract the feminine purchaser.' To impress upon their staff that women were important buyers whose 'whims' must be catered to, in 1950 the men in the Merchandise Office at Eaton's in Toronto cited 1948 Illinois shopping data which showed that 41 per cent of all electrical appliances were bought by women alone, and 21 per cent by women and men together. The Illinois study suggested that women did even more of family buying among lower income groups and in larger urban centres. Still from the appliance retailer's perspective, there was at least 'the shadow of a man behind every women who buys,' and in one in five cases the immediate presence of 'an impatient husband who wants to see how his money is being spent but is easily bored by his wife's inability to make up her mind in a hurry.'[1] Retailers assumed that women 'purchasing agents' reported to male bosses.

In the early 1950s major appliances were sold by male commission salesmen. Female sales staff might have carried 'a more convincing story to the customer.' Both the home economics director and the general sales manager at Moffat, the Ontario stove manufacturer, recommended as much in 1952. But the prevailing view in the trade was that 'Saleswomen in the appliance field have fallen flat on their faces. Men don't like them on the selling floor. Women customers don't like to be sold by another woman. Sales girls often dress up too much. Load themselves with expensive hairdos and jewellery. They set up sparks when they came in contact with a poorly dressed housewife dragging two howling kids with her. Some

Gender difference – business suits and bathing suits. This photograph of commission salesmen smiling/leering at a scantily clad model is of a commonly employed genre in the early fifties, when appliance dealers were not franchised, and manufacturers were obliged to compete for the attention of sales staff. University students who modelled to earn their fees in the period report how difficult it was to retain the necessary expression of innocence in the face of cajoling on these commercial assignments. There is an almost identical photo of Beatty salesmen and the two-tone coloured wringer washer in the Provincial Archives of Alberta Blyth Collection, BL 2216/2.

women have succeeded but very few.' What women of the time really thought about buying from appliance saleswomen, or being appliance saleswomen, we do not know. What is clear is that men dominated the well-paid jobs on appliance sales floors, and a shopper stepping on to that floor in search of a stove was entering a place in which masculine assertions and intentions defined womanhood.[2]

The postwar conventions of good salesmanship, 'virile salesmanship,' as it was called in a story about Moffat, were defined man to man.[3] Adapting these conventions for men selling to women mattered to both manufacturers and retailers, in light of the volume and intense competition in appliance sales. But given prevailing gender roles, it was a brisk managerial challenge to make work which required men to serve women both palatable and effective. It was easy enough to advise men, most comfortable thinking of their wares as machines, to adopt women's diction and speak in terms of cooking speeds, not wattages, of how many baking dishes, rather than square inches, an oven would hold.[4] But consider the stalwart principles of the salesman's creed, 'Sell yourself, you are part of the package your prospect buys'; 'Establish some common interest with your buyer'; 'Be a good listener'; 'Arouse your prospect's interest.' These took on a salacious edge when a salesman was making a pitch to a woman. Cecilia Long, a Toronto advertising executive, warned of the dangers out on the sales floor: 'Flattery will get you somewhere but over-familiarity will get you nowhere.'[5]

A woman shopping for a stove was appraising a cooking appliance and trying to estimate future cooking performance. A man trying to sell her a stove had to step outside the prevailing masculine role, to the extent that he must suppress his inclination to explain how the stove was produced, and instead present himself as an authority on what the stove would produce – that is, on cooking. Manufacturers organized cooking schools for salesmen, although these attempts were usually reported as comical failures. In their 'Use Value' campaign of 1950–1, the most Moffat could persuade men to demonstrate was that water poured on top of the range would drain to the spill tray underneath. As one wag noted, the closest the appliance dealer, housewares manager, or salesman 'ever came to basting a chicken was when he spilled champagne on one at the annual company dinner!'[6]

Reckoning that salesmen knew their culinary expertise would not bear scrutiny by an experienced homemaker, manufacturers tried to bolster male confidence by conjuring up a female customer who would not be a threat. They urged salesmen to imagine a dewy customer shopping for

Women customers, especially older experienced homemakers, did not readily credit male sales people with knowledge superior to their own about appliances. Manufacturers attempted to build salesmen's confidence by portraying problem buyers as older, stout, and overbearing, by contrast with more deferential younger women, one here bending to reach a low oven, displaying her buttocks to the smiling salesman behind her.

'the first range in her young life, or her first Moffat range.' Canadian Westinghouse conjured up a new bride, and in 'An open letter to Westinghouse dealers' had her groom reassure salesmen, 'There is nobody in this town who knows more about electrical appliances than you do – and, strictly between ourselves, there is nobody who knows *less* than my bride-to-be.' The fictional groom went on to dismiss the threat of countervailing female authorities by asserting that, 'Like most newly weds my wife is going to be too proud or too shy to ask for advice from her friends or family – but if she feels that you, gentlemen, can guide her in the proper use of home appliances and help her avoid humiliating cooking failures, I think she will probably look upon you as her friend, and will probably buy from you again.'[7] Illustrations in sales guides portrayed

difficult customers as older, ugly, and overbearing, and good sales prospects as younger, attractive, and generously obliging. In this way salesmen
transformed their own fear of their most knowledgeable and discerning
female customers into a negative commentary on the womanliness of the
most skilled women shoppers.

Makers believed that they had more to gain by challenging women's
traditional cooking knowledge than by making salesmen competent cooks
in the estimation of women customers. In a competitive market, each
manufacturer wanted to redefine cooking as the satisfactory *operation* of its
product, to emphasize recently purchased equipment rather than knowledge of ingredients or skills in preparation as the keys to 'baking and
roasting success.' The rhetoric in advertisements redefined cooking as a
competitive, capital-intensive process. Manufacturers and retailers thus
sought to shift credit for fine cookery from the expertise of the housewife
to the engineering of the appliance.[8]

Sales pitches entailed a tactful but firm derogation of what women
already knew about cooking by comparison with what they would need to
know to get the most out of their new investment. Women cooks had to be
persuaded to subordinate themselves to their man-made equipment. The
salesman's job was to

impress upon her [the woman customer] that the full benefits of all the wonderful
things the range can do, all the work it can save, all the perfect cooking it can
achieve are directly influenced by the way the range is handled. This is especially
important with housewives who have long-standing cooking habits based on the
use of old-fashioned or non-electric ranges. They have to be shown, and given
confidence, in how much their Westinghouse Range will do for them – how little
they need do themselves.

Most makers included books of recipes from experts in their 'test kitchens,' adaptations said to be specifically for their stove models, and then
interleaved the recipes with instructions for operation of their equipment.
Women journalists doubted that these tactics would succeed. Abbie Lane,
woman's editor of the Halifax *Chronicle and Star*, told Ontario marketers
that homemakers would not accept 'the test kitchen and the home economist as the originator of recipes,' that for 'ordinary folks' 'recipes have
been in the family for years and that means something.' Other women
flatly denied that what they did in the kitchen was manage an investment.[9]

The elaborate accessorizing of early 1950s stoves, like the scientifically
tested recipe, had more to do with selling than cooking. The accessories at

this stage were a way for manufacturers to differentiate one brand of white metal box from another. More important for the salesman, the features provided content for the sales pitch; a stove with twice as many features had 'twice as much for you to talk about – dozens of special sales features which mean added advantage to you [the salesman] in the days ahead.' But the elaboration of features could undercut the promise that new equipment was easy to use. American studies from later in the decade suggested that while retailers thought customers bought for extra gadgets and style, customers actually were looking most for ease of use, and for service and warranty. D.B. Cruickshank, an Ottawa businessman, and early president of the National Industrial Design Committee, worried about this contradiction in 1949: 'Evidently the average householders' choice is limited to what the average shop offers ... It appears to be sales managers' standards which are being forced on the consumer because the latter has no power of individual choice.'[10]

Manufacturers planned strategies to bring a positive association to stylishness in stoves. Life-size cardboard cut-outs of 'attractive models' in strapless evening dresses were propped up against stoves in the stores, and couturier fashion shows were staged amidst appliance displays at the Canadian National Exhibition in Toronto. Thor's Canadian branch tried historical fashion shows as well, hoping to set women 'reflecting how much better is their lot to be living in a day of simpler and saner fashions – and in a day when manufacturing enterprise removed so much of the household drudgery that plagued their grandmothers.' Westinghouse combined the style and labour-saving messages in a rural before-and-after sequence juxtaposing a harried farm wife, feeding pancakes to a grinning foursome of hired men, with a neatly coiffed woman, playing bridge, smoking, and gossiping with three women friends, the wooden kitchen chairs superceded by Breuer chrome, the wall display of the family patriarch and Lenten bull rushes by a northern landscape, the wood stove by a new Westinghouse electric. Let us count the ways this pitch would have failed: turning out grandfather, and the church, and the working men of the farm, in favour of northern wasteland, female leisure, and a baby crawling unremarked toward the stove. [11]

Women working at home for free were sensitive to criticisms that their days were unproductive and that household tasks required little skill.[12] They were not won over by claims about 'how little they need do themselves' once they had a new range, partly, as a woman marketer noted, 'because they resent being told that a product can do their job better and quicker than they can.'[13] An appliance which 'saved' the labour of a

Yesterday   *... and Today*

The Farmer's Wife

By GEORGE I. HARRISON

The gap between manufacturers' understanding of farm households' domestic priorities and the needs and pleasures of rural women is clearly apparent in this cartoon, contrasting new with old, but not so entirely favourably as the men at Westinghouse may have intended.

woman who did not work for wages cost, but did not save, money. Women whose home work was unmeasured and unpaid were not well positioned to press for purchases on the basis of labour-saving features, even if they could see ways in which the new equipment would improve their work efficiency. As General Steel Wares discovered by 'scientific market research' in 1954 as they planned to launch their new McClary ranges, 'Most housewives would like to own a new automatic range but they feel the money could be better spent on other things of interest to the whole family.'[14]

Many factors, then, made the appliance sales floor a bad place to shop for a stove. A cook could not try out the performance of the range there, even in the limited way in which a driver visiting an automobile dealership could test drive a car. The men selling stoves were not experts in their use, either in their own estimation or in that of their women customers. The manufacturers who provided the sales information about their ranges wrote copy to distinguish their product from that made by rival firms. They sold by looking into a mirror which reflected back other producers, rather than venturing through the looking glass to the distinctive world of the buyers beyond, concentrating on the men who were their competitors rather than the women who were their customers.[15] Retailers sold the idea that new equipment was better than old, following the manufacturers' scripts which emphasized features rather than functioning, attempting to sharpen the distinction between new and old by heightening and justifying sensitivity to surficial styling. Nowhere in this process were the questions the female shopper formulated as a cook satisfactorily addressed. Women protested that they got 'the brush-off' when they went to research their prospective purchase – that is, to shop. They complained that marketers 'slap a great big illustration and just a little reading matter' on their advertisements, 'whereas when we really want to make a big purchase like this women will read advertisements packed with information.'[16] In reaction to the irrelevance of the sales floor to the real work of shopping for a stove, women buyers researched their purchases through word of mouth, enquiring of neighbours and kin about how well the equipment they had purchased was meeting their needs, a route which offered information about the performance of the equipment in the home, so long as acquaintances were willing to be candid about their mistakes. Retailers, exasperated, claimed that all shoppers cared about was price. More likely, by their own observations about the authority women customers accorded the experience of their friends and neighbours, all the shopping for value and performance had been done through more reliable, non-retail routes. At the point of sale, the only questions worth posing of a salesman concerned price.[17]

The processes by which stoves were designed were as far removed from the kitchen as was the appliance sales floor, and equally revealing about the ideology of gender roles in the postwar years. The leading domestic appliance manufacturers had long histories as builders of industrial equipment, turbines for hydro-electric power generation, giant boilers for steam plants. In this work the consumers were sovereign. Manufacturers of producer goods designed to the buyer's specifications. In this work, as Robert Campbell observed in *Canadian Business*, 'the equipment would be built the way the customer wanted it and not the way the manufacturer thought it ought to be.' Yet he observed wryly that large engineering firms setting out to make household equipment departed from this time-honoured convention, assuming that their new client, the housewife, would know 'that her humble role is to select from what is offered and not to advance opinions on what she'd like or why.'[18]

Though thousands of Canadian women had worked in heavy industry during the war, and some – the most well-known the aeronautical engineer Elsie Gregory MacGill – had made important design contributions to forward the war effort, in the urgent national struggle to reconstruct the economy after the war and create new industries through which to recoup Depression losses, the masculinity of machine making was reconstructed unmodified. Honouring machine makers on their own terms became a species of patriotism. The unquestioning faith in the possibilities of the new technologies and materials developed for military purposes became a gesture of faith that peacetime prosperity could be recouped from the wreckage of war. Alan Jarvis, whose influence on British and Canadian industrial design we noted in Chapter 6, used the example of the Mosquito bomber to make this case:

When we go shopping for those things with which we will fill our post-war homes, we ought, therefore, to remember the back-room boys who are trying to solve in the field of industrial design the same *kind* of problem which faced the designer of the Mosquito: how to make use of modern inventions, modern methods of production and newly discovered materials, so that we of the twentieth century shall have in our homes objects which are efficient, inexpensive *and* beautiful.

As we have seen, government industrial design initiatives in consumer goods after the war emphasized the use of new materials, among these light metal alloys, and 'the immediate possibilities of Canadian production,' rather than the functional efficiency of household equipment in the home. The comedic aspects of giving the production engineer free rein wherever he might roam did not go unremarked, as in a cartoon depicting the foibles of a 'production man' in a magazine for Westinghouse employees and their families. But both state and industrial strategic priorities focused upon 'modern' materials and production methods, as men defined them. In this sense, as Stuart Ewan has argued, form followed power, here the power to specify what gains forwarded the national interest.[19]

Functionalism within the modernist's creed did not make the user paramount. 'The hall mark of any well designed, industrially produced object,' Donald Buchanan of the NIDC claimed, was a 'combination of functional efficiency and due proportion in form and structure.' Materials and production processes had most direct influence on form and structure. Functional efficiency, which particularly in household equipment would have required attentiveness to the needs of women workers in domestic settings, consistently lost out in the designer's arbitrage among

"That's what comes of having a production man for a husband."

The production men telling a joke on themselves. Postwar culture venerated war-time innovations in materials science and materials handling to an extraordinary degree, including suggesting that industrial methods and industrially made goods were preferable in domestic production processes. These claims verged on the implausible, as this cartoon in a manufacturer's publication acknowledged.

form, structure, and usefulness. Some even argued that a product was functional if it looked 'its part,' if in the contemporary system of signs it was possible 'to recognize actually what it is.' The criteria for National Industrial Design Awards required only that objects be 'suitable,' rather than optimal for their functions, and drew attention to form rather than performance, to the object itself rather than the task to be done.[20]

Retailers were perplexed that articles which 'had widely established consumer acceptance and appeared to be excellent value' were ranked low by NIDC design experts 'on account of lack of originality of form.' American industrial designers who valued sales appeal tended to leaven

The Nelsons' first stove, a McClary, here pictured in 1950, and a February 1957 photo of their second, still wood-burning, but shorn of its ornamentation. The Nelsons were both school teachers. See page 263 for a photo of the woodyard behind their apartment in the Mount Pleasant district of Vancouver. Solid fuel was more time consuming and less clean to use than electricity or gas. Yet it remained the common fuel for cooking and space heating among working people in the Lower Mainland after the war, because wood was inexpensive, and the solid fuel alternative, sawdust, was free.

the strict formalism of the British theorists whom Buchanan and his colleagues in the national design bureaucracy so admired. But in this leavening the users' needs did not rise to the top. Henry Dreyfuss, who designed appliances for General Electric in the United States, cheerfully argued before the Canadian Manufacturers' Association in Toronto in May 1952 that it was a good thing that industrial design had 'entered the home through the back door,' into the kitchen where 'wear and tear were faster,' and the housewife, 'a gadget-conscious mammal,' could be persuaded to 'have the drab parts of her house brightened-up with handsome bits of machinery.' Dreyfuss found women users too mercurial, or disingenuous, or hedged in by their relationships to the men in their lives, to provide reliable information about what they really wanted. An infrequent user of household appliances himself, he dismissed as retrograde instincts the labour patterns women had developed to manage their work in the kitchen. Monte Kwinter, in the 1950s the managing editor of a Toronto-based product design journal, and later the minister of consumer and corporate affairs in Ontario, stated this view even more strongly, arguing that 'it would be advantageous to General Electric and to industry as a whole to educate people to understand what they should want ... in other words, to give them what they need rather than what they want.'[21]

The women of the Canadian Association of Consumers took a contrary view. Their work with the National Industrial Design Council in the early 1950s put the CAC's optimistic liberal principles to a stern test. From the start, the association's concern was with poor performance in household goods. They began by recruiting suggestions from members, which they expected the Design Council would forward to 'departments of household science for investigation and report.' They hoped this process would allow women, 'instead of stewing over an inconvenience and feeling helpless to improve upon it,' both to complain constructively to 'a source which will take immediate action' and to create 'findings which it will be worthwhile giving to manufacturers.'[22] For its part, as we saw in Chapter 6, the Design Council hoped to convert consumers to modern design principles.[23]

When in 1953 a member of the CAC agreed to serve on the jury for the NIDC annual design awards, the conflicts between consumers' and designers' priorities quickly crystallized. Awards regularly were given to goods which the woman juror and her CAC design committee thought showed evident faults, and withheld from wares they favoured. The award insignia created the impression that products had been performance tested when they had not. Aware that their participation in the judging validated this misimpression, in 1954 and 1955 Kathleen Harrison, chair of the CAC Design Committee, tried to persuade the NIDC to separate household equipment from decorator goods, and withhold awards until the equipment had been tested by an established research group. In the meantime, members of the Ottawa branch began to test goods in their homes, although their work had to be limited to small electrical appliances and housewares, and the volume of the task soon overwhelmed the small group of available volunteers. The NIDC declined to make performance testing part of its own adjudication process, or to require certification of performance testing from manufacturers. Its only response was an extraneous change in the award regulations to require 'evidence of suitability for the Canadian market' – that is, of sales rather than usefulness. Kathleen

Harrison thought she had arranged for a public airing of the dispute through a 'provocative' article in *Canadian Homes and Gardens* entitled 'How Good Is Design Award Merchandise?' but the editorship at the journal changed, and the article never appeared. Their experience with the award jury left the female consumers association knowing that designers and industrialists often wanted their validation rather than their contribution. At the NIDC, a confidential memo linked the breach to the fact that 'the male of the species is not considered a consumer in the CAC!'[24]

Canadian women had strong views about what they wanted in stoves. When the NIDC and CAC in 1954 jointly requested suggestions from CAC members for the improvement of household goods, two-thirds of the responses concerned kitchen equipment.[25]

Women, disenchanted with the existing merchandising system, wanted better ways to get the product knowledge they needed in order to choose among the stoves manufacturers offered for sale. This meant first that they wanted fewer model changes. When appliance manufacturers, following the example of automobile makers, changed their designs every year, they removed from the market the very models, proven by two or three years performance in the kitchens of family and friends, which women wanted most to buy. 'Why,' one woman wrote, don't manufacturers recognize that they would be better off to adopt 'a wait-and-see attitude rather than permit themselves to be dazzled by the immediate selling power of novelty into scrapping models which may be inherently better, as the consumer will, in time, come to recognize?' Second, worn down by 'the sheer physical effort of shopping,' and aware that smaller manufacturers did not have the advertising budgets or the clout with retailers to secure due attention for their products, women suggested that makers 'establish cooperative demonstration rooms' to ensure 'that *everybody's* product could be seen and inspected by prospective purchasers.' Showing a sharp sense of the differences between oligopoly and competition, one woman argued that this change actually would make the market process, which was supposed to allow the best goods to rise to the top of consumer acceptance, work better by ensuring that 'the smaller manufacturer gets every assistance in his struggle to compete.'[26]

On the other hand, women wanted the form of the stoves manufacturers made changed in a fundamental way. They wanted the ovens raised above, in their own terms, waist level, in designers' terms, counter level. 'Why, oh why,' wrote Mrs R.F. Legget of Ottawa, 'do manufacturers persist in placing on the market stoves that are beautiful to look at, with the chromium glistening enamel, but back-breaking to use?'[27] This was a long-standing complaint among women in Ontario. Members of the CAC featured in the NFB film *Designed for Living* raised the same question. Recall that in 1946, the chrome-plated modern table-top range included in the Toronto Art Gallery *Design in the Household* exhibition drew much criticism. Then, visitors' questionnaires showed that consumers wanted 'the oven [to] be restored to its old position above the stove. Housewives find that stooping over to attend to baking is an unwelcome form of exercise.'[28] Historically, the most common Canadian solid-fuel-burning ranges had had ovens set beside rather than below the burners. Early gas and electric stoves followed this form. Donald Buchanan, sceptical when he could find only one Canadian electrical range, a McClary, with the oven at what the housewives claimed was the right height, referred the matter to an authority, Dr J.B. Brodie, head of household science at the University of Toronto. She made common cause with the housewives, arguing that plans 'to "streamline" everything and have a working space around the kitchen at one level ... are evolved by those who do not work in a kitchen and we know that they are not efficient.' Her words were well chosen. Buchanan, stalwart proponent of British good design principles, regarded streamlining as a heresy hatched by American salesmen. He circulated Brodie's report to makers, hoping 'some enterprising manufacturer will devise a better and more functional type of range, that will appeal to the consumer on the grounds of both *appearance* and *ease of handling*,' and through a colleague assigned a group of University of Toronto architecture students to look at the problems of range design 'afresh, without preconceived prejudices as to what is "modern."' But both the students' mock-up and an ungainly one-legged English-style cooker, designed to preserve the plane geometry of the countertop, met with lukewarm responses from members of the public who participated in design quizzes at Toronto and Ottawa exhibitions in the late forties.[29]

When 75 per cent of Canadian Association of Consumers members surveyed in 1951 still favoured high oven ranges, Mrs R.G. Morningstar of Toronto, the CAC representative from the Canadian Dietetic Association, was despatched to interview manufacturers. The results were not encouraging. Though the high-oven mock-ups were no wider than the stoves currently in production, manufacturers declared them too massive. They cited the failures of high-oven models in American market tests. Alexander McKenzie at McClary added that 'he felt that older women were not familiar with modern controls' and when using a high oven would 'keep peeking into the oven to see how the product is baking.'[30]

One Ontario firm, Findlay Stove Manufacturers of Carleton Place, did agree to take up the project. They exhibited a sample high-oven stove at the Toronto exhibition in 1952, and through the next three years conducted surveys of their own and refined their design, working in close concert with the CAC Design Committee. The Findlay Hy-Oven was launched in 1955, and that year duly won an National Industrial Design award and featured billing in an NFB film, *Designed for Living*. The CAC publicity chair in Toronto wrote letters to 279 newspaper and magazine editors and women's radio commentators, under the banner 'From Modernity to Convenience,' and garnered 1666 lines of newspaper publicity. Findlay's ad copy noted that the Hy-Oven ended stooping and bending, took up only 41½ inches of floor space, and with floor plans demonstrated how the new model would fit conveniently into existing kitchens. But the Hy-Oven did not sell, either in Canadian or export markets.[31]

Part of the problem with the Findlay Hy-Oven may have been Findlay's itself. A small if venerable eastern Ontario firm, Findlay's may have lacked the market influence and advertising budget successfully to launch a radically different product in a sector increasingly dominated by large American firms. But there was also a problem with the high-oven design, ways in which its usefulness compromised the ability of the form to satisfy other consumer needs. Mrs G.J. Wherrett, Design Committee chair of the CAC, reported rumours in 1952 that women who saw the Hy-Oven at the Toronto CNE 'liked the convenience of the high oven, but wanted the appearance of the low oven.' In her 1954 NIDC–CAC contest entry, Mrs John M. Dexter of Burritt's Rapids, Ontario, still held the view that women preferred 'the old high-oven stove to the most modern, streamlined one.' Attending to 'manufacturers' complaints that the high-oven stove does not lend itself to good design in a modern kitchen,' she offered a compromise sketch of a range with a retractable oven which could be raised while in use and stowed below counter level at other times.

Henry Dreyfuss argued American high-oven revivals had failed in the market because 'the table-top stove flush with the other cabinets in the kitchen had become such a style factor that the ladies refused to be budged away from it.'[32] The CAC pitch for the Hy-Oven – 'From Modernity to Convenience' – posited too stark a transition. Modernity was not irrelevant to women shopping for convenience. Women were shopping for stoves *and* for the characteristics the presence a particular stove would bring to their kitchen. They were unlikely to see, as they imagined a stove transported from the sales room to their kitchens, exactly the same transformation as, each in their turn, the designer, the manufacturer, and the advertiser had envisioned. It is not that any dysfunctional contraption

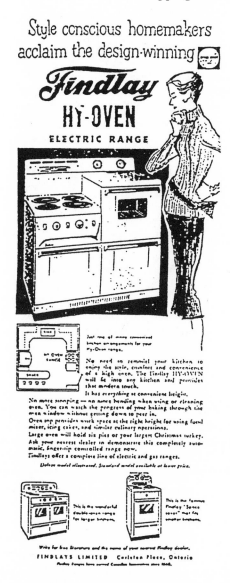

The Findlay Hy-Oven range, in production at Carleton Place in the mid-1950s. The advertising copy emphasized that this design ended stooping and that the oven at convenient height would hold six pies or the largest turkey. This range won an NIDC award but did not achieve commercial success.

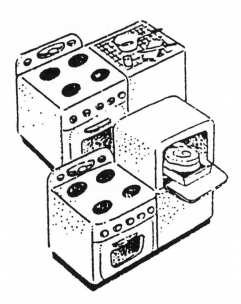

A resolution to the high oven/low oven dilemma submitted to the Canadian Association of Consumers' household improvements competition by Mrs John M. Dexter of Burritt's Rapids, Ontario. Her sketch had both a high and a low oven, the high oven receding to serve as a countertop when not in use.

offered up for sale would have found acceptance with women buyers simply because it was perceived as creating the right cultural effect. But for the woman shopper, as for all the men who had created the array of products from which she would choose, a stove was more than just a stove.[33]

The table-top range, its work surface level with the surrounding counters, was a central feature in the portrait of the kitchen as laboratory, an image which, as Margaret Hobbs and Ruth Pierson have shown, was expounded widely in Canada in the 1930s.[34] With its enamel sparkling cleanliness, its clock and timer and array of knobs promising orderliness and scientific control, the range was the necessity among 'the electrical tools of her trade' which radio announcers for Canadian Westinghouse in 1951 proclaimed were 'rapidly changing the homemaker's kitchen into a convenient, attractive workshop.' In the postwar years, the laboratory kitchen signalled the worth of domestic work to women leaving the paid labour force, and the feasibility of combining waged and non-waged work for those who were not.[35] The messages were not unmixed, for the unyielding regularity of the laboratory aesthetic brought home the imagery of the factory or the office, and the sense of being controlled rather than being in control which some women returning home from the paid labour force had hoped to escape.[36] Later in the decade the once-admired laboratory-look in kitchens was derogated as the 'utility' look, a characterization which in Canada brought to mind the austere minimalism of wartime goods.[37] Wealthier householders then installed conveniently high wall ovens in their custom designed kitchens and traded in the table-top ranges which by the late fifties seemed 'to reflect a greater pre-occupation with the romance of science than with the comforts of home.'[38] But at the time that the men at Findlay's and the women of the CAC were trying to launch their Hy-Oven, they were struggling not only against a machine makers' practice and a national economic strategy which did not take domestic labour into account, but a generation of consumers seeking the signs of science with which to validate their unpaid work within the home.

This is a story which can only be told of Canada in the early 1950s. Then the wartime experience of women in the Consumer Branch, and the relatively unformed practices of mass consumption in domestic durable goods, gave some women confidence to plan ways in which they would shape the design and merchandising of the equipment they would use. The persistence of small Canadian foundries, accustomed to manufacturing in short runs for specialized markets, meant that there was a local firm ready and able to undertake the experiment. By the end of the decade, the small Ontario manufacturers had lost their independence. The CAC had abandoned its attempt to specify the form of household equipment before it was manufactured, and had begun rather to prepare Buyers' Guides to help shoppers sort their way through the goods manufacturers the retailers offered up for sale. The ranks of the appliance salesmen dwindled, their usefulness as intermediaries across the gender gap between makers and consumers disproved. By the late 1950s Canadian appliance retailing was dominated by suburban discounters, with small staffs to write up bills of sale for hopeful if weary women who disembarked from station wagons shopping for a good stove.

10

What Makes Washday Less Blue?

The way Canadian women did their wash confounded the appliance managers of American branch plants in the late 1950s. In 1959 wringer washers, a technology little altered in twenty years, and by contemporary engineering standards a technology entirely superceded, outsold automatics three-to-one in Canada. This was exactly the reverse of the pattern in the United States, where automatics that year accounted for 75 per cent of sales.[1] 'Theoretically there is no market for ordinary washing machines as everyone should be buying the automatic type,' a senior official at Canadian General Electric asserted counter-factually. He added in a bemused attempt at explanation, 'I suppose, however, that the big market for ordinary washing machines lies in less developed countries.' E.P. Zimmerman, who ran the appliance division at Canadian Westinghouse, like his counterparts at Kelvinator and Frigidaire, yearly through the 1950s forecast a breakthrough for automatic machines in Canada, and yearly found that sales of wringer machines remained strong. 'This is strange,' he affirmed, implicitly rejecting the underdeveloped countries explanation, 'because usually Canada is much closer to U.S. trends than this.'[2]

Readers familiar with the literature on domestic technology might share this puzzlement, for the fine work published in the early 1980s by Strasser and Cowan on the United States case has served as the template for understanding household technology in the North Atlantic world. American production of automatics surpassed wringers definitively in 1951. Although Strasser and Cowan are attentive to distinctions between the priorities of makers and users,[3] in the case of washing machine technology they report not conflict but a quick convergence of interest. They find that automatics were accepted into American households as soon as they were made available by manufacturers.[4]

Cowan's justly famous parable about how the refrigerator got its hum,[5] which has the giant electrical apparatus and automobile manufacturers successfully championing the condenser cooling technology over which they commanded proprietary rights, makes the prolonged failure of automatic washers in the Canadian market seem more inexplicable. For it was these same American makers, and for the same reasons, who intended to have Canadian women of the 1950s do their washing in automatic machines. In fact, it was not until 1966, fifteen years later than in the United States, that Canadian automatic sales passed those of wringer washers.[6]

A European observer might not be so befuddled by the Canadian pattern. In the early 1950s when automatics were coming to dominate the U.S. market, fewer than one in five British households owned any washing machine. In 1969 only 5 per cent owned automatics. Most domestic laundry was done either in a copper boiler, a variation on the wringer washer which heated the water and used the boiling action rather than a central agitator to circulate the clothes, or in the modern technology of choice, a twin-tub which housed the washtub and spin dryer side by side in a single casing. Both of these technologies were rare in either Canada or the United States. Even in 1981, there were automatics in only 40 per cent of British homes.[7]

Considering the British case, Christine Zmroczek in 1992 observed, 'if we want to understand women's experiences of technology, it is important to look closely enough to uncover the differences from country to country and culture to culture, even within Western capitalism.' For the interwar period in France, Robert Frost draws similar conclusions, pointing out how ill-fitted were American-modelled domestic appliances for French domestic settings. Manufacturers in search of international mass markets have sought to erase difference. Yet recent cross-cultural studies of household technology clearly show that differences have persisted between men and women, and between makers and users. These distinctions mark cultural differences which *frame*, as surely as they are framed by, historical differences between national economies.[8]

Household technology is centrally different from industrial technology. An industrialist commissions a machine from a producer goods manufacturer, as he might commission a suit from a bespoke tailor. The machine and the suit, having been made to the user's specifications, upon delivery, are promptly put to use. In household technology, this smooth transition cannot be assumed.[9] Makers, a past-president of the Canadian Association of Consumers noted in 1958, tended to think of consumers as 'the buying side' of themselves.[10] In certain conjunctures, the cultural similarities between domestic machine makers and domestic machine users may transcend those differences made by the market economy and gender. Machines offered for sale then may be accepted unproblematically by women seeking tools for their household work. In the United States, for automatic washers, this appears to have been the case, at least for middle-class urban women.[11] But generally, the culture of makers and the culture of users are very different. Machinery which is not made to the specifications of the users, as household technology almost always has not been,[12] often does not satisfy. Here not only gender but also class and national differences are at play. Of laundry technology in particular, the Croatian journalist Slavenka Drakulic recalls, 'it was only when I first washed my clothes in the States, in 1983, in an American washing machine, that I became aware how differences in tradition influence both the industry and my own attitude towards doing laundry.' American machines did not heat the water to ninety-five degrees Celsius and ran for only a third as long. Though the grandmother who had taught her the secrets of washing 'had already passed away,' Drakulic writes that 'I just could not help remembering her, because, strangely enough, I felt as if my clothes were not properly washed at all.'[13]

Understanding what constitutes a proper job is integral to understanding what is acceptable as a proper machine. For many technologies this premise is axiomatic to the design process. For household technologies, particularly domestic technologies used primarily by women, it is not.[14] A discussion of household technological choice must reckon not only how women's technological preferences as users differed from men's technological preferences as makers and sellers, and how engineering and commercial priorities came to prevail, as we did in the last chapter, but the possibility that sometimes *men, as makers and sellers, did not get their way*. The task in this chapter is to set such a broad context for technological choice. How did the traits of the Canadian political economy, and of makers and marketers, work with and against the internal politics and value systems of households to determine which man-made laundry technology women would (agree to) use.

A wringer washing machine consists of a steel tub, either galvanized or porcelain enamelled, upon which the wringer, a pair of wooden or rubber rollers, is mounted. An electric or gas motor suspended beneath the tub drives an agitator to move laundry through the wash water and to revolve the rollers, clamped in tension, to express water from the goods being laundered. The machine was not self-acting. The tub was filled by the operator from a hose or bucket with water heated to the required temperature and then soap or its successor, detergent, and the clothing and linens were added. The woman operating the machine filled a separate tub or pair of tubs with rinse water and then manually lifted the items being washed from the soapy water. She fed them individually through the wringer into the rinse tubs in turn, moving the clothing through rinse waters with a stick. At each rinse she again lifted each piece by hand from the water. After the last rinse she guided the completed washing once more through the wringers, this time into a basket to be carried to the line to dry. After being used for several loads, the soapy water was either siphoned from the tub or disgorged into a floor drain. This process was hard on women's hands and their backs, and except for the ten or so minutes when the agitator was running, required the operator to be actively at work. All in all, this does not seem a technology to inspire devotion among its users.

But by comparison with the technology it replaced in most Canadian homes, the wringer washer was a real improvement. You definitely noticed the difference, Lily Hansen recalled: 'I wasn't very good at scrubbing clothes on the washboard, and wringing them at all. You know, you're trying to wring sheets.' 'When my kids complained about the inconvenient malfunctioning wringer,' Martha Watson wrote, 'I told them they didn't know when they were well off.'[15]

But few denied the limitations of the technology. In rural homes, the machine was stored outside and in winter had to be dragged into the kitchen before washday could begin. In city homes the wringer washer was usually in the basement and, because the machine was not self-acting, 'you were running up and down stairs all morning doing this washing.' In machines without pumps, 'getting the water out of these big tubs, it was heavy work.' Even in the best of circumstances, with a nearby pair of concrete tubs, separate hoses from hot and cold taps, and a mechanical siphon to empty the tub, the routine – washing and rinsing white, coloured, and then heavily soiled work clothes in sequence – was physically demanding. Clothing with buttons or zippers and larger linens had to be folded carefully while still soaking wet before they could be passed through the wringer. Metaphorically, many reported, doing laundry 'was a pain.'[16]

Literally the machines also could cause discomfort. The early wringer rollers were turned manually with a crank, but by the 1950s most rollers were rotated by the gas or electric engine attached to the machine. A woman who had turned on the powered rollers, and was working close to them watching for exposed buttons or trim, might find she had one hand being drawn through the wringer and the other ill-positioned to reach the

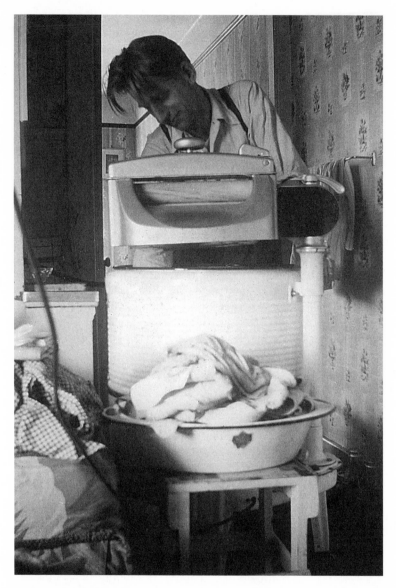

A wringer washer in use in a Vancouver apartment. The Nelsons were able to purchase this machine new in 1948. This made them atypical. They used the washer for twenty-two years until 1970. This made them typical. Greta Nelson was, apparently, the family photographer.

release switch. Removing rings before starting the wash could reduce potential damage for women, but children's fascination with the machine remained a concern. Several women reported rescuing their youngsters' limbs from the wringers, and giving thanks that 'Little kids, you know, their bones are soft.' Longer term, family members speculated that their mother's arthritis was linked to the many hours in cold basements, standing on a wet floor, woman-handling the wash.[17]

Yet for all this, the transition from wringer to automatic technology was not swift in Canada. Allison Simpson, the commerce graduate from the University of Alberta, who spent the fifties in remote northern villages where her husband was posted as an RCMP officer, in winter melted ice on a wood stove for the wash, bringing the water to a boil in her electric kettle. She remembers regretting her accountant's habit of counting as her sons' fifty-four diapers went through each stage of the wash and out onto the line. In her Meadow Lake, Saskatchewan, kitchen in 1955 she tacked up a picture cut out of a magazine of a Bendix duomatic. Four years later she returned to an urban life of modest prosperity, but not until 1973 did she acquire an automatic washing machine.[18]

To understand why right up until the mid-sixties more Canadian women each year bought wringers than automatics, why more considered the wringer the proper machine for the job of doing the wash, we need to look beyond the relative convenience of the machines. We need to consider the broader context in which the consumption decision was made, what Ruth Schwartz Cowan has called the consumption junction.[19] The washer was not a single machine but an integral part of the mechanical system of the house. The buying decision was similarly complex and political. In the home, major household purchases had opportunity costs. They presented opportunities to some household members and denied them to others. Within the Canadian political economy, wringer and automatic machines had very different locations. Wringer and automatic machines both washed clothes, but each of the technologies was built upon and had built in distinct assumptions about the relationships between machines and other resources, both human and natural. These assumptions were to a degree coherent and common among technologies of a given time, as we think of people as bearing affinities of a shared generation. Generational differences among domestic technologies were readily apparent to women of the time, although they are more elusive to us now some forty years distant. To understand the choice between wringer and automatic technology we must disengage from the organizing assumption of Sigfried Giedion's then much read and still much cited *Mechanization Takes Command*[20] and instead feature a history of technology where a good deal more than machinery is at work.

Addressing an appliance marketing seminar at the Canadian Electrical Manufacturers Association meetings in the spring of 1960, A.B. Blankenship, executive vice-president of the leading Canadian consumer research firm, reminded his audience that the images consumers held of household goods were the keys to understanding their market. He characterized these images dichotomously as 'both rational and irrational ... both real and imagined ... both conscious and unconscious.'[21] Marketers promised to bridge these divides by 'getting to really know' the woman longing for a better way to do the wash.[22] But marketers had another pressing promise to keep. Manufacturers wanted them to find – if need be, to create – in the market that desiring female subject, that imagined woman, whom makers already implicitly had invented as they engineered the machines.[23] If sales were to be made, the woman that makers theorized as using their machines must be made plausible to women actually doing the wash. Somehow, what Robert Frost has called the symbolic and the functional or material sides of the machine[24] had to be made to dwell as happy complements in the laundry rooms of the nation.

Fifties advertisements for wringer washers achieved this symbolic and functional resolution relatively readily by emphasizing tradition, for the firms which made wringers were venerable south-western Ontario and Ottawa Valley manufacturers, begun as foundries and boilerworks in the 1840s and 1850s. The name plates affixed to their new washers – McClary, Easy, Beattie, Connor, Clare – were familiar emblems from the fronts of woodstoves and the casings of sinkside kitchen pumps. Thus the ads noted that 'McClary quality' had been 'famous for more than 100 years,' and that Connor had long been a Canadian favourite. Mother and daughter frequently were featured together, their gazes both fixed upon a gleaming new machine – a sensible depiction given the operator attention the wringer washer required. Beatty experimented with pastel yellow, blue, and green machines in 1955, making the machines themselves imagined women by pitching the new model as 'An old friend in new dress.' The same firm struck the combination expected to best sell wringers with its 1958 Copperstyle, a modern wringer clad in the same heat-conducting metal which had sheathed nineteenth-century stovetop laundry boilers. 'Mothers of all ages choose Beatty Copperstyle,' ads proclaimed, as a daughter wearing borrowed high heels hurried to join her smiling mother and applauding grandmother in an admiring circle around the washer.[25]

With automatics the marketer's task was more vexed. Most potential

Beatty appealed to tradition in 1958 with a washer clad in copper, as copper boilers had been. Grandmother and mother keep their eyes on the machine, as they would have had to, for wringers required relatively constant attention from their operators, while daughter rushes to join them.

Central to the wringer washer's appeal was its durability. Beatty experimented with colour in 1953, not as a way to speed replacement, but to make their washers seem more modern. The selected 'neutral' colours, dawn yellow, azure blue, and mist green, were all used in combination with white. Note the offer of a six-year guarantee, and the punning 'Cromatic' at a time when automatic machines were being advertised more extensively.

buyers of automatics already owned a functioning washing machine. Thus, as Susan Strasser has argued in the U.S. case, for the first time the merchandiser was attempting to persuade customers 'to move up from an old-fashioned appliance to the newest latest kind, replacing machines that worked perfectly well.'[26] The wringer washers in most Canadian households in the 1950s were relatively new and highly prized. Many campaigns for automatics therefore emphasized style rather than function, and appealed to (or for) a style-conscious consumer. Stanley Randall, president of the Easy Washing Machine Company and later an influential Ontario cabinet minister, asserted that women bought washers for three reasons, '1. appearance, 2. features, 3. price. Women will pay $40 to $50 more for an appliance if it appeals to the eye, if you don't sell eye appeal, you don't sell.' 'The Canadian housewife likes gadgets,' he added, likening Easy's latest three-dial, twenty-one-setting automatic to a pinball machine: 'it lights up and signs off.'[27] Certainly Randall, who had been a travelling salesman for Easy during the depression of the 1930s, would have known the importance of proper functioning in a washer, would have known that the machine was a first a tool rather than an entertainment. Yet he emphasized gadgetry and eye-appeal, and was silent about function, because in glamour lay the automatic's indisputable advantage over the wringer.

But creating a taste for glamour in the laundry room was a hard sell, as R.J. Woxman, president of American Motors' appliance subsidiary Kelvinator, well knew. If only a washing machine 'was parked in the driveway,' he noted wistfully, 'it would be replaced more frequently.'[28] The manager of the Ontario Appliance Dealers Association fantasized about annual gala evenings to which an audience clad in evening dress would be summoned by engraved invitations, the presentation of each jewel-like new model invoking admiring applause – a fantasy world where women would value washers, as they valued jewellery, for their appearance and symbolic references alone. This was a possibility which, as he stepped down from the podium, he acknowledged was far-fetched.[29]

Marketers best met the concerns and fantasies of real Canadian women with ads which highlighted the self-acting capacities of the automatic machine. Unlike the displays for contemporary wringers (which showed women looking toward the machines), the graphics in advertisements for automatics more frequently showed a woman turned away from the washer, to smile not at the machine but at the child with whom she was playing or the husband with whom she was about to depart.[30] The claim that 'a few things each day keeps "washday" away' – that the automatic 'ended wash-

EASY LIVING .. THE ULTIMATE IN LEISURELY WORKLESS WASHDAYS

Change washday into playday!

THE NEW

EASY

Combination

AUTOMATIC

WASHER - DRYER

WASHES THEN DRIES IN ONE UNIT — YOU JUST PUSH A BUTTON

Just put in dirty clothes   Just imagine life without Washdays! You'd have more time for yourself . . .

Advertisements for automatics promised that washdays would no longer be work days.

day' by making it more feasible to do 'two or three small washes through the week' – may have been the Hobson's choice Susan Strasser described, between 'a weekly nightmare' and an 'unending task.'[31] Yet Ontario Hydro's promise of a machine which would 'do all the hard work' of the wash and promote busy mothers to the position of 'supervisor in the laundry department' could not but tempt women in the home.[32]

Visions of automatics must have danced in the heads of most mothers of infants, for pungent pails of diapers could not be held for a single weekly washday. The woman who owned only two dozen diapers would have been washing them most days by hand. Whatever one's reservations about owning an automatic, who would not have been ready and willing to dream the advertiser's fantasy of a magical machine which all on its own made dirty into clean? Thus, many ads for automatics targeted new mothers. To launch its new washer-dryer set in 1953, Westinghouse worked on the nightmares raised by the thought of arriving twins. Once again the machines were imagined, and introduced to consumers as, people, in this

Many women noted that they bought their first automatic on the arrival of a new baby. Two new babies would have compounded the urgency. This 1953 ad linked the new washer-dryer twin sets with the arrival of baby twins.

case as baby twins. This 'Blessed Event' campaign used ads showing storks delivering new washer-dryer twin sets. Dealers provided birth certificates, tastefully printed in black and gold, to each buyer who took the mechanical twins home. The firm fused the images of the twins they had manufactured and the twins who would create dirty diapers, by offering a free pair of machines to every mother in Canada who bore twins on the launch day of the new model, 17 March 1953.[33] There were echoes of the 1930s Stork Derbys and the celebrated Dionne Quintuplets in the Westinghouse letters to 15,000 doctors, hospitals, and nurses' associations, asking for their intervention to discover lucky candidates and authenticate the births. But the campaign captured well the shared current of pleasure and desperation which flowed about mothers in the midst of the Canadian baby boom. The campaign would also have appealed to a singular predisposition among contemporary manufacturers, at once to feature users in the image of their machines, and to feature the machines they made as human.[34]

Most advertisements for washers addressed a female audience. Men

'Is your Bride still waiting for her Inglis?' If women would not press for automatic washers, could their husbands be shamed into taking the initiative? One of the rare ads addressed to men, this appeared in 1959 as appliance sales generally were down, and sales of automatics remained slow.

were invoked infrequently in any capacity in ads to sell wringers, but they began to appear now and then in the late 1950s in campaigns for automatics. The man in a checked hunting shirt an Ontario Hydro ad showed loading an automatic washer – 'So easy even a *man* can do it' – had only a walk-on part, for the accompanying text quickly turned to address a female reader. But Inglis pitched ads to men twice, first in the 'Wife-Saver' campaign of 1958, which attempted rakish double-entendre, 'urging husbands to "save" their wives by "trading them" in on new Inglis washers and dryers.' The ads the next year – 'Is your Bride still waiting for her Inglis?' – proceeded more cautiously. It combined copy written for husbands – 'We know you are just as anxious as any husband to save work for your bride but honestly ... hasn't the family wash been a labour of love too long?' – with an illustration of a young bride holding a large laundry basket rather than a bouquet, intended to catch women's attention. The timing is interesting here. Men portrayed as patriarchs and providers were targeted directly as buyers in 1958 and 1959 as the recession deepened in Canada and manufacturers found sales into replacement markets more difficult to make.[35]

The differences between the imagined users featured in advertisements for wringers and automatics mirrored differences between the makers of the two machines. Almost every wringer washer used in Canada was Canadian made. The first automatics sold in Canada were imported from the United States, and the Canadian manufacture of automatics quickly was dominated by the branch plants of American firms. The leaders in this sector had diversified either, like Westinghouse and Canadian General Electric, from making electrical apparatus for industry or, like Kelvinator and Frigidaire, from the mass production of automobiles. A few large American subsidiaries dominated the automatic side of the industry. The makers of wringers were smaller, more numerous, and Canadian owned.[36]

Wringer manufacturers in Canada in the 1950s built washing machines using the same labour-intensive batch production methods they used to make water pumps and boilers. These manufacturing processes yielded machines which were heavy and thus durable, simply assembled and thus simply repaired. There was little out-sourcing; as the technology had been relatively static, few parts were covered by proprietary rights. Still wringers could be made efficiently in plants producing 10,000 to 25,000 machines per year, so that economists estimated in the late 1950s and early 1960s that the Canadian market could have supported at least nine, and possibly as many as twenty-two, wringer washer manufacturers.[37] Indeed, the wringers – many sold with twelve-year guarantees by manufacturers who had made their reputations in machines that handled water – became something of a Canadian specialty, and through the mid-sixties Canadian manufacturers reported strong export sales into U.S. and overseas markets.[38]

In its manufacture, the automatic washer was kin not to the water pump, but to the other white boxes, the stove, the refrigerator, the dryer, which in their succeeding seasons kept assembly lines steadily producing. By contrast with the batch methods by which wringers then were made, mass production used less labour and fewer materials, to create lighter, less resilient automatic machines. The automatics' merchandising emphasis on style was linked to this product engineering decision, to build a machine which could be sold more cheaply but would need more frequently to be replaced, to stimulate the mass consumption which would sustain mass production. One analyst using 1960 data estimated the minimum efficient size of a major appliance plant at 500,000 units per year.[39] As Gomez found in her study of the Spanish industry, longer production runs are still seen as key to least-cost production of automatic washers.[40]

But these economies of scale in mass production were not equally accessible to all producers. The whole Canadian market would not have supported a plant making a half million appliances per year. As importantly, the lower input costs for automatics which U.S. manufacturers passed on to their American consumers did not prevail outside the United States. Automatic washer technology had improved rapidly during the 1950s, but much of this knowledge in the fifties and sixties was still proprietorial. Without adequate research and development capacity of their own, U.S. subsidiaries in Canada and Canadian independents had access to these refinements only by purchasing licences to manufacture or by importing finished parts.[41] The long-run effects of licensing arrangements on manufacturing viability are plain in David Sobel and Susan Meurer's recent *Working at Inglis.* Inglis, Whirlpool's Canadian licensee, ended its thirty-year association with the U.S. company with rights to produce only an obsolete machine.[42] Buying components abroad immediately raised prices. Imported finished parts, valued in 1955 at $2.4 million U.S., made parts bills for a Canadian automatic 10 per cent higher than those for an American machine in that year, a difference which persisted through the 1960s.[43] The tariff on washer parts was 22½ per cent. Even in the late sixties, when Canadian automatics finally were selling well, they cost 37 per cent more than similar machines being sold in the United States.[44] The product engineering and merchandising of automatic washers presumed mass consumption, that washers could be offered relatively cheaply so that both a conversion and a replacement market would rapidly develop. But the costs of carrying the technology across national boundaries, which made automatic washers relatively more expensive in Canada (and other jurisdictions) than in the United States, made automatics implausible and impractical as objects of mass consumption. For makers, the washer was an object for sale, reaching out toward an imagined consumer. For prospective users (who may or may not have featured themselves as consumers), neither the price nor the promise was so alluring as the makers assumed.[45]

For most of the forties, as we saw in earlier chapters, washing machines of any sort were woefully elusive commodities in Canada. Late in the decade, a woman who wanted a washer still had to wait her turn on a dealer's lengthy list. Joan Coffey did get a wringer machine in 1947, when her anguished letter struck a cord with an Eaton's department store manager: 'They were just starting to make them and you went on waiting lists for years ... All the neighbours were aghast. They couldn't figure out how I could get a washing machine. And that [machine] was the love of my life.'[46] Many other women turned to commercial laundries, at least for large items such as table cloths and sheets. This was a sensible way to save their own labour, a reality which caused appliance salesmen considerable dismay.[47] Women from both professional and working-class households continued for many years using the 'wet wash' service they had adopted during the war, which returned the laundry damp to be dried and ironed at home. This suggests that in Canada, as in Britain, the issue was not labour-saving alone. The lingering array of post-war shortages – of housing with decent plumbing, of washing machines, of cash – made women seek some compromise which would balance the pressures these various scarcities placed on the household.[48]

Early automatics often were bought by men as gifts for their wives. 'To purchase gadgets that relieve ... drudgery and thus promote domestic affection,' as Marshall McLuhan observed in 1951 in *The Mechanical Bride*, could be seen as a duty, a species of moral choice. The other leading male commentator on technology of the day, George Grant, was generally critical of American influences upon Canada and wary of transnational technology as a threat to liberty. But he made an exception for 'the wonderful American machines' he believed let his wife, Sheila, lead a freer life, acknowledging that 'the practical worth of modern technology' was demonstrated 'every time Sheila washed the clothes in her machine.'[49]

The men who presented their wives with the first automatics were often professionals, geologists or engineers worried about the peripatetic lives their careers imposed upon the family, or university professors who encouraged their wives' dedication to pursuits other than housewifery. They had the income to afford the automatic, enough control over the family budget to make the decision alone, the conviction that manufacturers' promises for the machine would be fulfilled. Beverly Newmarch, in 1948 the wife of a newly hired geology PhD in a British Columbia coal-mining town, remembers how she came to have an automatic in her company duplex:

Chuck decided that with what I had had to use, I should now have an automatic. He began to look at want-ads! – I was horrified, since automatics were so new, I didn't want to start out with one that had experience! He persevered, however, and found himself a new Bendix, still in the wooden crate. The American consul had brought it up to Victoria and for some reason or other they had not been able to obtain permission to install it in their home – something about the plumbing not being adequate.

Ann Brook, married to a navy man frequently away from home, returned from work one day to find the automatic she had declined ('hum, don't need an automatic washing machine, who needs an automatic washing machine?') already installed. Her husband had conferred once more with their customary appliance salesman, Mr Beeton, and he and Mr Beeton had agreed, 'maybe you should try it and see.' Mrs Brook did not decline the gift.[50]

If for the men who bought them in the 1940s and early 1950s, automatic washers were unambiguously desirable objects which bespoke affection and a better life, for children they are recalled as mesmerizing entertainments. The rare front-loading automatics somewhat resembled the even rarer televisions about which most Canadian youngsters had only heard before 1955. Most women who got automatics in the early postwar years tell stories of lines of small spectators gathering to watch the wash.[51] Women as equipment-users had a more complex appraisal to make. Some were persuaded early on. Margaret Shortliffe first had seen an automatic Bendix at Cornell University in 1939, noted the merits of its alternating drum technology, and refused agitator substitutes, either wringer or automatic, instead washing by hand until her husband got a Bendix to Kingston, Ontario, in 1946. Winnifred Edwards, like Shortliffe, got along without a machine until the kind of equipment she had seen in hospital laundries was available for sale in 1952. The consequences of investing in a particular durable tool delayed their purchase of any machine, as it delayed many women's purchase of automatics, for deliberating on an investment takes longer than choosing to consume an object of either personal or altruistic desire.[52]

In such deliberations, price is plainly an important factor. Automatic washers cost more than wringer machines. In 1950, the gap was wide. Standard wringers could cost as little as $90; some automatic models as much as $370. In 1956 the Chatelaine Institute reported best-selling wringer prices ranging from $129 to $259, and automatics from $325 to $469. Over time the gap narrowed, but still in 1966 the average price of wringers advertised in Eaton's mail order catalogue was $146; automatics at an average of $234 cost more than half as much again.[53]

This was not a negligible difference, particularly in the first decade after the war when couples were equipping homes for the first time. Personal incomes in Canada were not high in this period, in 1947–50 they were only about two-thirds of incomes in the United States.[54] Prices for Canadian consumer goods in nominal and real terms exceeded those south of the border. Hard choices had to be made. Credit controls meant that getting everything at once by running into debt was not an option. Deciding what to get first required considerable juggling. For how long should the household get by without a stove, a mechanical refrigerator, or a washer?

Historians of technology sometimes have been surprised by technological choices because they assumed that the choice was between two technologies for performing the same task, rather than among many possible mechanical and non-mechanical improvements. Economists have relied upon the simplifying assumption that like goods are only compared with like. And, for economists, the only benefits the person making the choice weighs are his or her own. These assumptions about non-substitutability do not apply well to households, as feminist economists recently have demonstrated.[55] Buying a wringer rather than an automatic washing machine was a sensible economy. The savings, for example, would have bought a vacuum cleaner or a radio, and the wash would still be done. The washer was the one place in the basic household consumption package where there was a little discretion. Among the 8611 Toronto women Eaton's interviewed about their purchases of furniture and appliances between January 1949 and August 1952, the amount paid for refrigerators ($343–$348) and for stoves ($205–$219) varied little. For washers the range was considerable. Women under twenty-four paid on average $152, women over thirty-five on average $188. More older than younger women were buying automatic machines. New equipment for keeping food cold and making it hot took a relatively fixed amount out of every household budget. A younger homemaker, with more household equipment to acquire at once, could more easily make do with a wringer washer than do without a stove or a mechanical refrigerator.[56] The Central Mortgage and Housing Corporation surveyed 6600 families who had purchased houses between January and May of 1955 in Halifax, Montreal, Toronto, Winnipeg, and Vancouver. The amount spent varied among the cities, on stoves by $62, on refrigerators by $45, but on washers (on average the least expensive of the three appliances) by $127. Only on washers could the new home buyers with the least to spend accrue appreciable savings.[57]

Among the much smaller group of women with whom I spoke and corresponded, a similar pattern emerges. A washer was important, often important enough to risk going into debt for, especially important once children began to arrive.[58] But the choice was not posed in the postwar years as between two laundry technologies, between an automatic and a wringer. Rather women spoke about the other tasks which might be mechanized and the other obligations of the home. The decision about a washing machine was part these other decisions about equipping the household and the household's relationship to the wider world. Buying the automatic, the more expensive machine, when a cheaper satisfactory alternative existed, could easily seem to foreclose more opportunities than it opened, to be less about liberty than constraint.

In rural homes, the needs of the barn and of the house had to be met from the same purse. Investment in labour-saving equipment for the farm took priority, partly because men made these decisions on their own.[59] Perhaps, also, in some parts of Canada, as in Iowa and the Palouse region of Idaho and Washington, women saw investments in farm equipment as saving domestic labour because they eliminated the need for hired men.[60] The priority of the barn is plain in the detailed study of 352 Ontario farm families Helen Abell conducted in 1959. On the most prosperous farms, where investment in all labour-saving equipment exceeded $13,000, less than 10 per cent of this investment was in domestic technology. Paradoxically and surprisingly, the proportion of the farm family's resources invested in household appliances rose among poorer farmers, to 20 per cent for the house when all equipment was valued at less than $7000.[61] Because there were few satisfactory substitutes in domestic technology, the least mechanized of farm families had to allocate the largest share of their equipment budget to the kitchen and laundry basics, at least in Ontario. Choosing a wringer over an automatic reduced these pressures and, for example, might have brought an electric cream separator into the kitchen.[62] In more highly capitalized operations, a farm woman may more readily have been able to justify the purchase of an automatic machine to free her for farmwork outside the house. Jellison finds Iowa women used this argument in the 1950s. The same reasoning may account for why automatic washers more quickly became commonplace in the farms of Quebec, where dairy predominated, than in other Canadian markets.[63]

Both Patricia Cliff and Nettie Murphy linked their purchase of automatic washers to their participation in the workforce. Cliff had twins in diapers and was pregnant again when she went by herself to Eaton's Warehouse in Victoria in 1960 and asked for 'the biggest automatic tub you can give me.' But she explained the decision by noting that she had worked for eleven years before the twins arrived, and thus had a bank account of her own. Murphy bought her first washer many years into her marriage, during a period when she had paid work. 'That made a difference. When you work outside of the home and you have an income, you pack a little more clout.'[64] Manufacturers and marketers expected that wives in the workforce would buy more automatics than women at home full-time. They assumed that two-earner households would have higher incomes, and that wage-earning wives would feel less 'guilty' turning a part of the household budget toward 'short-cuts' for themselves. But as Joan Sangster notes, in Canada in the 1950s and 1960s most married women in the labour force came from families in straightened circumstances. Buying an automatic, when for $100 to $200 less a wringer would do, seemed foolish to a woman earning just to make ends meet. One Canadian study explicitly addresses this question through a comparison of equal numbers of full-time and part-time wage-earning mothers and mothers full-time at home in Guelph, Ontario, in the early 1960s. There Mary Singer and Sue Rogers found that wage-earning homemakers were significantly less likely to own automatic machines than those full-time at home.[65]

Even in good times, the gap between the cost of a wringer and an automatic machine made Canadian women hesitate and consider other household needs. As manufacturers were expanding their production of automatics, the five-year-long recession of the late fifties began. Many a 'wife's pay cheque' was 'merely replacing that of a laid-off husband.' Marketers began to suspect what researchers later would document, that economic uncertainty had an exaggerated effect upon the purchase of major durable goods. In lean times households were 'likely to be cautious about replacing any machine which wasn't "actually breaking down"' and were likely to see the best new machine as the one which put least pressure on other aspects of the family budget.[66]

Makers who featured users making the choice between wringer and automatic washers on the basis of the laundry technologies alone made a more elemental misjudgment. In the early 1950s, the fantasies of Canadian young people were inhabited less by shiny white boxes lined up on showroom floors than by plumbing, wiring, and pipes. The year automatic sales first exceeded wringers in the United States, electrification and running water systems were the stuff of which many young Canadians' dreams were made.[67] As a leading Canadian home economist noted in 1946 and was still noting in 1954, it seemed 'impractical to discuss the dream houses of the future ... until more of our houses, urban and farm, have running hot and cold water.'[68]

The engineering and marketing of tools for household work often proceeded in isolation from consideration of the mechanical systems which would be required for their support, particularly when domestic appliances were launched into international markets.[69] A 1945 survey of the 'Housing Plans of Canadians' found that a third of all Canadian families, two-thirds of those in rural areas, did not have any running water at all. Lever Brothers, anxious to sell large quantities of the laundry detergents it had designed to replace the soap used in washtubs, must have been discouraged to discover for itself that year that only 20 per cent of Canadian farm homemakers had hot running water and thus could do a wash without hefting copper boilers on and off the stove.[70] The early acceptance of automatics in Quebec may be linked to the fact that 63 per cent of farms there had inside running water by 1951, a year when only 40 per cent of those in Ontario, 30 per cent of those in the Atlantic region, and 9 per cent of those in the Prairies were so supplied.[71]

Automatic machines required not only hot running water, but a water supply under strong and steady pressure. Even as the proportion of Canadian homes with hot and cold running water increased over the postwar years (see table 10.1), the proportion not connected to community pressure systems remained considerable. In fact this proportion appears at times even to have risen as new suburban dwellings were built beyond the reach of municipal mains.[72] No Whiggish inexorable succession of technologies here. To invest in equipment which would only function well when attached to a city water system might not be wise aforethought. Women who raised their families in the resource economies of western Canada remember having to trade in new technology for old, electric for gas-powered wringers, washers for washboards, as they moved to islands and remote mining sites, or from city homes to ranches and farms. Less than an hour's drive from Toronto, Kathy Grenswich used a wringer washer until 1975 because this was the machine the household cistern would support. From such perspectives, automatics were a limited technology, more constrained than conventional machines by the plumbing they required to function.[73]

Important as these straightforward economic and infrastructural constraints were, they do not wholly explain the Canadian preference for wringer washers. By the early sixties, many of the economic and infrastructure considerations which favoured wringer washers over automatics had faded. Wages and salaries were rising. Women remembered feeling more prosperous and more confident that prosperity could be sustained.[74] The price gap between wringers and automatics had narrowed. Almost every household had electricity and more than four out of five had hot running water. Yet in 1964 wringers still were outselling automatics by a consider-

TABLE 10.1
Water Supplies of Canadian Homes

Year	Hot running water (%)	Piped from private sources (%)
1955	65.3	22.4
1956	67.9	22.0
1957	70.6	25.3
1959	75.3	21.5
1960	78.8	17.8
1961	80.2	17.8
1962	83.1	18.2
1963	84.8	18.0
1964	86.1	18.1
1965	87.4	16.9
1966	88.3	17.6
1967	89.7	16.7

Source: Dominion Bureau of Statistics, *Household Facilities and Equipment*, 1955–7, 1959–67.

able margin. There was still a mass market for wringers even among higher-income groups in Canada. Women who owned wringers still were more likely to replace them with wringers rather than automatics.[75] While producers and marketers asserted that replacing a wringer washing machine with an automatic was 'trading-up,' it is not at all clear that women doing the wash saw the matter in the same way.

Cultural values attach to goods offered for sale. Product engineers build cultural assumptions into the machines they design. Marketers set out to find or to forge a constituency to whom these assumptions make sense. But as we have already seen, their sales prospects will not necessarily share makers' values, or make their determination on the basis of marketers' assumptions. The purchase of goods is self-implicating. Thus as David Nye notes, the possession of electrical appliances 'engages the owner in a process of self-definition'; in their operation 'the self and object are intertwined.' But the cultural current flows two ways. The machine may remake its user ('I was born to use an automatic'), but the user may also reconstrue the machine ('The automatic is a wasteful extravagance'). Once the constraints of price, plumbing, and income had begun to fall away, it was still not for makers and marketers alone to define how Canadian women would do the wash, or what for them constituted an excellent machine.[76]

Machines are located within moral economies. The tools we use embody values. They may also constrain the field within which we can make moral choices. They widen or narrow our plans and practices, and reveal or conceal the implications of our decisions.[77] Some machines, by their design, seem to operate with resplendent technological autonomy; others, by design, constantly disclose and allow their operator to monitor the demands of the machine upon the provisioning system of which it is a part. Automatic washing machines are of the first sort, wringer washers are of the second. Canadian women making the choice between them in the 1950s plainly distinguished the two kinds of machines in these terms, gave this signification to the distinction.

A woman filling a washer by hauling water, or working a hand pump, or standing by a running hose, knew how much fresh water she was drawing for the task. She saw the character and the quantity of the waste she was disposing into the yard, the septic field, or the sewer mains when the job was done. A homemaker who relied upon a well and septic system knew she must monitor the capacities of these systems and adapt her domestic routines daily and seasonally to accommodate their limits. Any woman who had run a wringer machine had a clearer sense of the relationships between washing, water, and waste, than those of us today who have used only automatic machines which fill and drain through discrete piping, leaving volumes drawn and disposed unobservable and unremarked. For rural women in the 1950s, the new automatics which promised to put each load of laundry through several rinses in fresh water presented an immediate hazard to operation of the farm home. But city women as well had experience with which to recognize the automatics as prodigal, of fuel to heat water, and of water itself. In response to a request for ideas for better washers, Mrs H.G.F. Barr of London, Ontario, wrote thus in 1955:

I have been appalled at the amount of water that seems necessary to do a normal family wash in the new spin-dry type of machine. I believe one brand boasted that it rinsed clothes seven times, and all of them threw the water out after one use. There is hardly a city or town in Canada that does not have some water shortage in summer months. Large sums are being spent on reforestation, conservation and dams. It would appear that this trend towards excessive use of water should be checked now.

Through the 1960s such negative consumer commentaries upon automatic washers remained common, homemakers' rhetoric to describe the new machines more evocative of the manic sorcerer's apprentice in the Disney film *Fantasia* than of the regulated modern domestic engineering manufacturers and marketers sought to portray.[78]

Manufacturers, in both their design decisions and marketing strategies, treated the washer as an isolated object rather than as one element in the production process called 'doing the wash.' It was, after all, the washer alone they had to sell. By contrast, women consumers thought of doing laundry as a task rather than a machine. They appraised the process in the way production processes conventionally are construed, considering their own management priorities and skills and all the non-capital inputs required, as well as the traits of the machinery they might put to work.[79]

In these terms, manufacturers' emphasis on the gadgetry raised alarms among consumers. The early automatics were fragile machines, prone to break down and repairable only by specialized technicians who were not always nearby. 'In the search to provide more and more automatic features,' Mrs W.R. Walton of the Consumers' Association of Canada warned, makers were producing washers 'so sensitive and complex, it will take an engineering expert' to fix them.[80] By contrast, in 1958 many wringer washers were being sold with long guarantees, and supported by a dense network of local dealers who by preference specialized in wringer sales. In an economy where all household appliances lately had been in short supply, where couples still were aspiring to an adequate rather than affluent standard of living, buying a delicate automatic seemed both short-sighted and frivolous.

The promise that an automatic machine would do the wash all on its own seemed a threat. Even when intervention was required, the self-regulating features of the automatics defied operator intervention. Tubs which filled by a timer ran half-empty when water pressure was low. Loads which became unbalanced under lids which locked for the duration of the wash cycle caused the machine to jostle uncontrollably about the room. Women who in the 1950s expressed a preference for simpler machines over which they could exercise a greater measure of control spoke from well-founded technical, managerial, and resource concerns about the operation of the new automatic laundry equipment.[81]

Between the engineering of the wringer and automatic washing machines lay a generational divide. Wringer washers were made in batches, durable and simple to repair. These product characteristics happily complemented a consumer culture habituated to scarcity and schooled to value conservation and thrift. Automatics were mass produced, designed for a consumer culture which would value innovation over durability and be willing to place convenience for the machine operator ahead of household and fuel costs and the social costs of creating more waste. For domestic appliances, at the core of this change was a redefinition of what constituted an excellent machine, a narrowing of the purchasing decision to give priority to labour-saving features over other resource concerns. Many Canadian women in the 1950s and 1960s were unwilling to cross this generational divide. Their loyalty to the wringer washer technology and their scepticism about the new automatics is a sign of this resistance.

The choice between wringer and automatic machines implicated Canadian homemakers in forming distinctions between consumer and user, between gratification and prudence, between production and conservation, between built to last and built to replace. In the circumstances in which they then found themselves, and with the knowledge they then had, it is not hard to see why, red hands and aching backs and wet floors notwithstanding, so many resisted the chromium promises of the new machine.

In the postwar years household technologies increasingly were characterized as consumer goods. The rapid rise of a culture of mass consumption, and the more central place consumer goods came to hold in the definition of personal identities and civic values, is well documented for the United States. Sometimes popular knowledge about these goods effected cultural changes, even when the goods themselves were not widely owned. This is the case Robert Frost makes for interwar France.[82] But the process can also work the opposite way.

Consumer goods can be, and have been, refused because of the cultural values they embody. The degree to which mass consumption became institutionalized differed between regions and nations and across classes. In the first decade following the Second World War, these differences varied with the pace of postwar recovery, the precedence given to export or domestic markets, and household versus industrial needs. Centrally, the plausibility of mass consumption was tied to perceptions of plenty and to beliefs about how the national wealth should be husbanded and shared. For consumer goods which were also working tools, this dialogue was vigorous and many faceted. In measure, manufacturers and marketers remade the material and symbolic functions of their machines to address the resistance of consumers. But so long as the purchasers of household equipment continued to think of themselves centrally as users appraising tools, they were declining to be defined solely as consumers. Their choices of what goods to buy bespoke deeper concerns about how much was enough, and for whom, framed in the politics of the households and the communities to which they belonged.

11

A Caution of Excess

By the late 1950s, the conventions which had organized the domestic world of goods in the immediate postwar years were beginning to break down. What domestic meant had changed in many senses: what was comely, fitting, and useful in the home; how manufacturers in the domestic economy related to their parent companies and competitors internationally; how energy providers construed the domestic, as opposed to the industrial and commercial parts of the demand they serviced. These changes take us beyond the goods themselves to a reconsideration of what Canadians, in their commodity culture and outside it, took to be good.

The scarcities of the forties had passed. In 1958 modern domestic appliances were no longer rarities. Except for the microwave, which was still not far removed from a gleam in the eye of a product design engineer, the major pieces of time-saving equipment we now take for granted in the kitchen and laundry were all known through the marketplace. There were electric or gas ranges in 71 per cent of households, washers in 86.6 per cent, and mechanical refrigerators in 86.3 per cent. The saturations levels for the latest generation of household equipment remained low: chest or cabinet freezers at 8.2 per cent in 1958, dryers at 12.2 per cent when first counted in 1960, dishwashers still at 1.5 per cent in 1961. The two-door large combination refrigerator-freezer, which in the next decade would replace smaller single door models in many households, was just entering the market, in 1957 installed in only 1.6 per cent of the homes of the British Columbia coast and lower mainland, for example.[1] These latest household machines might simplify repetitive tasks, and alter the relationship of domestic work to the weather and the seasons. But none could promise so much as the first major domestic appliances, which had put an end to carrying ice, water, and solid fuels. Henceforth what constituted an improvement – what shade and inflection purported to be an improvement the purchaser would find plausible as a greater good – would be reckoned in smaller and more heterogeneous elements.

Ninety per cent of major appliances in Canadian homes in 1958 were less than ten years old, still young in the span of life for which they had been engineered, still admirably performing the specific functions for which they had been sought.[2] The demographics of the Canadian population were similarly bleak from a market standpoint. By January 1956, the backlog of deferred demand had been met. Soon after, the prospects for new household markets collapsed. The rate of family formation started to decline in 1958 and did not begin to recover until 1965. The trend in immigrant arrivals followed the same pattern. In the decade after 1958, makers would have to count for sales on older, wealthier households developing a taste for luxury goods, for the proportion of Canadians in their twenties and early thirties was small, stable, and not of a mind to marry.[3] From the peaks in the first half of the 1950s, the part of personal income spent on household appliances declined almost without interruption. The postwar boom in the appliance industry had passed. Makers who had scrambled to secure materials and battled against exchange and credit controls to get their products into Canadian homes, looked on in amazement as householders turned away from appliances toward 'clothing, food, haircuts, trips abroad, and thousands of other necessities and luxuries. Would you believe it?' one redoubtable thirty-year veteran of the trade sighed in 1960, '174,000 Canadians visited overseas countries in 1958!'[4]

Some of the appliance makers' wares, for example dryers and freezers, appealed to those with ample discretionary income. But in the late 1950s and early 1960s, most Canadians were no more expecting to accede to sudden wealth than soon to see the sights of Europe. The average number of claimants for unemployment insurance rose sharply from 1957 until 1960 and did not decline to 1957 levels until 1964. Dwelling starts followed to same gloomy arc in reverse, down a third from 1958 to 1960, and rising hesitantly to regain their former ground only at mid-decade.[5] 'Quite frankly,' a dean of Canadian retailing reported in confidence to a federal investigator in 1959, 'we [are] in for pretty rough water any way you look at the situation.' The phenomenon was not Canadian alone. In Britain and the United States as well, consumer confidence plummeted, and the broad middle of the market disappeared. Their warehouses bulging, in 1960 makers began layoffs.[6] Most major household appliances were now in the mature phase of their product cycle. In 1964 only 4 per cent of refrigerators, 15 per cent of automatic washers, and 26 per cent of electric ranges were being sold to meet the urgent needs of new households. Other appliance sales were notoriously difficult to make in hard times. Pat Ellison, a Toronto home economist, noted full-time homemakers' particular aversion to making replacement purchases: 'if the refrigerator works and she can still get all her food purchases into it, the woman of the house makes it do. If her stove is beginning to get to the tired point, she makes allowances for its shortcomings and goes bravely on.' Ellison argued that retailers should begin to target husbands, whom she thought more likely to 'see the need of up-to-date equipment.'[7] As it turned out, dealers' and makers' better prospects lay not with men, but with a different and growing constituency among Canadian women.

Once married women entered the labour force, they began to reconsider the relationship between their work, their household equipment, and the qualities of the goods and services they produced in the home. In 1951 only 11 per cent of Canadian wives were in the labour force. The participation rate for married women in paid work rose 86 per cent between 1951 and 1961, and a further 59 per cent in the next decade. Whereas in 1951 62 per cent of female workers were single women, by 1971 two-thirds of the women in the labour force were, or had been, married.[8]

Any household in which a full-time homemaker was at work effectively placed a high economic value on her domestic activities. When her place there was chosen, rather than forced by want of market opportunities, the household also was making a qualitative decision, outside the market register, which bestowed high moral or ethical value on her non-market work 'creating comfort, beauty and a sympathetic, nurturing and emotional environment for the family.'[9] Women entering the labour force could predict with relative certainty that their household money income would rise, and in times of recession such as the late fifties and early sixties, this was no small consideration. Yet the decision to go 'out to work' was also a decision to shift from producing goods and services for use to producing goods and services for exchange, to forego values and pleasures associated with time at home and homemade goods in favour of cash.[10] As we already have seen, many Canadian women in the first decade after the Second World War personally set great store on their home work *because* it was outside the market, because it reckoned consequences the market would not count, because it honoured worth the market would not weigh. The war and the Depression had been stark lessons in losses, and the promises of the peace were about civil reparations too grave and urgent to be understood solely as terms of trade.

But by the late 1950s times were changing. Familiarity with market goods grew. Their quality increased and their prices fell. Household discretionary income declined (partly because more funds had been committed from each pay cheque to discharge debts owed for housing and household equipment). More women entered the labour force and in the process – Martha Stewart notwithstanding – shifted their revealed preferences from homemade to market-made goods.[11] In the 1940s, rural women had battled against the urban majority in the Canadian Association of Consumers, arguing that farmers were being blamed when city-dwellers foolishly preferred packaged, prepared foods over homely ingredients. A decade later, these same women had begun to buy 'cake mixes, and baker's bread, and creamery butter' in order to make time for other activities. For a woman in the labour force, new equipment which would 'eliminate the unnecessary work that is repetitious and does not satisfy' seemed now to secure rather than compromise her own 'good health and mental stability' and that of her family. The dryer, the dishwasher, and the waiting supply of frozen food to calm the 'suicide hour' before dinnertime promised to mitigate the pressures of being away from home.[12] Girls' toys normalized this transition. The E-Z Bake ovens of the late fifties, for example, came fitted with light bulbs, so that they *really* heated up, and stocked with miniature mix packets with which to make 'real' cakes.[13] A recent review of the international literature suggests that by the early 1960s, employed women were spending less time at housework than full-time homemakers and that this decline followed, if at some lag, the diffusion of the main household appliances.[14]

The character of the market had changed with the times. As Mary Kippen, the wife of a New Westminster warehouseman, remembered, 'Well, by this time we were realizing that, as everybody comes to the realization, that with so many products on the market and so much competition you have to know or find out, OK what are the best things? What are the best products to buy?'[15] Marketers began to report that retail buyers were 'hard-bitten' and 'tougher.' 'These are the customers who have been around. They're buying their *second* washing machine, their *second* house, their umpteenth pair of slacks. They know what they want. They're hard to sell. They pride themselves on wanting the facts, not fancy when they buy.' Both retail outlets and products became more heterogeneous, and ferocious price competition in a predominantly replacement market, as we shall see, made the meaning of quality more biddable. A woman shopping for household equipment in the late 1950s, typically a person in her middle years, needed to be, and was, more savvy and sceptical, but also more willing and able to spend money to save time and to have exactly 'the right' equipment at home.[16]

In their styling, their corporate history, and their place in the domestic landscape and household routines, refrigerators reveal this transition. Mechanical refrigerators were the last of the three basics to become commonplace. In 1941, when there were electric or gas stoves in three-quarters of Canadian homes, only one in five households contained a refrigerator rather than an icebox.[17] The change to mechanical refrigeration was still fresh in the memory of many a decade later, and was momentous, as Irene Newlands of Surrey noted, recalling a transition she must have made in the mid-fifties.

I think the appliance I most appreciated was a second hand fridge. It had a small freezer compartment on one side, several shelves, shelves on the door and 2 drawers for vegetables. I just couldn't believe they made such a marvellous appliance. We had had a wooden ice chest with a lid that lifted up and a tray that sat on the floor under the box to collect the drainage. Everything sat in this box and as the ice melted the bags, boxes and bottles would be wet and dirty with sawdust and sediment. As the ice melted the butter softened as also did the ice cream; the veggies became limp. If you went out & forgot to empty the tray you would return to be greeted with a wet floor. So to think that everything had a place in the frig; the milk stayed cold, the veggies crisp. I just thought it was the greatest and would often stop during the day just to look at it and admire it.[18]

This great leap was dependent on acceptable household levels of safety reached by the mid-1930s when fluorocarbons, by trademark known as freon, replaced sulphur dioxide and methyl chloride as refrigerants.[19] During the thirties and forties, the working elements of the domestic refrigerator, the motor, condenser, and evaporator, evolved rapidly. By the fifties they had become relatively standardized, and industrial designers 'could do little beyond minor modifications of the interior, redesign of the hardware, and other details of styling.' Refrigerators more than any other household appliance came to depend upon style to sustain share and turnover in the market.[20]

The link between refrigerator and automobile manufacture in North America emerged early. Both Kelvinator and the firm that would become Frigidaire began in Detroit in the 1910s. In production, automobiles and refrigerators are similar. Both demand capacity in metal working and require electrical and cooling systems. Both are assembled from similar parts, a crankcase, pistons, cylinders, cam shafts, a pulley, and fan in the compressor. Early in the century both showed mass market promise.[21]

The quest for stylistic obsolescence began in the United States in the 1930s when Sears hired Raymond Loewy to transform their Coldspot refrigerator from a cold four-legged box into a modernist icon. Then and thereafter, refrigerator models changed every year, sold for their symbolic as well as functional values, by turns mimicking skyscrapers, Bauhaus cabinets, and art deco screens. The giants of modern American design, W.D. Teague, George Nelson, Henry Dreyfuss, and Harold Van Doren, followed Loewy to the task. In their design, refrigerators echoed automobiles, their heraldic door shields and handles borrowed almost directly from their corporate parents' lines.[22]

Each year from the early fifties, the industry offered more variety in their refrigerator models than in any other appliance. In 1950 Frigidaire launched four new models. In 1953 International Harvester, a late entrant to the field, tried to use marketing innovations to compensate for their fledgling product-engineering expertise in domestic appliances by introducing ten models. These included the 'Decorator Refrigerator,' featured in the advertisements in both polka dot and plaid. Sales copy promised that a willing housewife, with seven minutes and a yard and three quarters of fabric to spare, could make the door of the refrigerator match her 'kitchen curtains, walls, floors or tablecloths.' In the search for heightened eye-appeal, International Harvester was not alone. Automobile analogies faded after 1958, but in 1965 Frigidaire recuperated the connection for Canadians with the 'Jet Floating Frig,' made to lift off the floor for easy movement when the blower nozzle of a domestic vacuum cleaner was attached to its base. The Jet Frig was featured in promotions with a stiletto-heeled model clutching a steering wheel perched on its top. In the same year, Kelvinator offered the 'Originals, from French Provincial to Pennsylvania Dutch, from humor to hot rods,' including a cowhide-covered model with a spur handle.[23]

Refrigerators, again more than the other first-generation appliances, foreshadowed the continental integration of North American secondary manufactures. In 1956 and 1963, American subsidiaries produced more than half the brand name refrigerators sold into Canadian homes. The market was about evenly divided between branches of the automobile makers and the electrical apparatus manufacturers, Westinghouse, Canadian General Electric, Kelvinator, and Frigidaire. By contrast, the share of these four firms in range sales was closer to a third.[24]

Automobile manufacturers dominated refrigerator production. The 'problem' addressed here was that dirt accumulated under refrigerators. The 'solution' was to give refrigerators the same floating ride offered for cars.

The precedence of style in the refrigerator made it difficult for Canadian independent makers to secure and maintain a firm foothold in the field. From under the shadow of the nearby Kelvinator works, T.W. Fenton of General Steel Wares' London, Ontario, plant reported in 1953, 'Because models and taste in refrigerators change so quickly a large percentage of inventories are held in component parts. These can be assembled to meet changes in demand without too much trouble. It's an expensive way of doing business but when the line includes over 20 different models, you can lose even more on fully assembled models that customers don't want.' His colleague S.W. Allen echoed Fenton in 1961 as he concluded his summary of the latest whipsaw in the market for refrigerators: 'There must be an easier way of making a living than this.'[25] The large proportion of proprietorial parts needed to build a refrigerator, which had to be purchased or made under licence from American firms, amplified Canadian makers' disadvantages. Less predictable and more disabling was the influence of imports, which from the end of controls in 1951 until 1960 always took up at least a quarter and sometimes nearly half of the Canadian market. From early in the fifties, domestic makers suspected that U.S. firms were dumping the tail-ends of their lines over the border at below cost. After 1958, with the Canadian dollar at a 5 per cent premium, the incentive for transborder shipping increased. That year a Moffat official told a visiting federal investigator, 'We don't think there is much future for refrigerator operation[s] in Canada.'[26]

In the midst of this heightening pressure from imports, General Motors introduced a radical (for refrigerators) change in form, the 'sheer look' Frigidaires. The new Frigidaires were designed to appear 'built-in' to contemporary kitchens, their tops square-cornered to meet the cabinetry above, their doors opening flush so that a four-inch gap was no longer required between the machine and the counter on the hinge side. Most importantly in a tight market, they were cheaper to build. Although formed by the same tangent-bending methods introduced to make rotund and castellated shapes after the war, the smaller radii in the new models required much less metal finishing. The design also concealed the spot welds which previously had to be smoothed, individually, by grinding wheels before painting.[27]

In the first instance, however, the sheer look was not easier to sell. William Campbell of Canadian Westinghouse reported in 1957 that the new machines, with their 'shape and style are excellent for built-in applications but they look rather queer when set by themselves. At least, we think so.' L.N. Gill from Frigidaire had the same reservations that year. The 'new models with straight corners, not rounded, and a less massive look' he reported, 'failed to attract public fancy ... Maybe the company should have done some motivational research to discover just what image of a refrigerator customers had. Maybe straight lines don't correspond to customers' images. So far these are only hopes.'[28] Canadian Westinghouse protected itself by initially importing rather than making the square machines, waiting to see 'if these models catch on.' Frigidaire, with a formidable 20 per cent of market share, could bull through buyer resistance.[29] The Canadian independents were preoccupied with the challenge the arrival of natural gas in central Canada posed to electric ranges, where their greatest market share lay. They could less readily protect themselves from the commercial disorder created by the new refrigerator form. General Steel Wares, for example, could afford to retool only part of its line in 1958, and like all makers suffered from deep discounting as retailers who had bet on square models found their customers wanted round, and retailers who had stocked round found their local market was for square.

The first square-cornered refrigerators had a larger frozen-food compartment than the shoebox-sized freezer of their predecessors, but it was still lodged behind a single cabinet door. This design required two evaporators, one wrapped about the freezer and a second mounted on the back of the machine to cool the shelves and drawers below. There was a layer of insulation to separate the two parts of the cabinet, and a sophisticated regulating mechanism to balance the effects of their two separate temperature controls so that the temperature difference between the freezing and cooling parts of the cabinet could be set and sustained. With the colder freezer walls no longer exposed to condense moisture from the cooler below, humidity levels in the cooler remained higher, food there dried out less, and the freezer needed to be defrosted less frequently. But by the 1960s, in continuing price-conscious markets, the cost of the second evaporator and the finer regulator drove this design from production.

Refrigerators began to appear with two doors, the thermostat on the cooler replaced by an adjustable vent cover on the pipe through which cold air was blown by a fan from the freezer into the rest of the cabinet. Henceforward, the food-storage compartment became a passive adjunct to the freezer, its humidity levels once again problematically low because air there was first desiccated as it passed through the colder freezer and then made drier still by the work of the fan. These innovations yielded food-storage conditions markedly inferior to those achieved in the refrigerators of the early 1930s. As one refrigeration engineer notes of this transition period, 'Consumers, although they didn't realize it, were being asked to tolerate considerable compromise in quality of storage conditions in their refrigerators in order to accommodate larger freezers' and ac-

A round-cornered refrigerator in a Kingston, Ontario, kitchen in 1950.

cepted the change in trade for bold promises that frozen food was the way of the future, 'which, for many certainly' it was not.[30]

More apparent were developments in foam insulation, which allowed for thinner walls, increasing the usable space within a given size of cabinet, and in the mechanisms combining controls and fans, which reduced or eliminated the need for defrosting. By the early 1960s, refrigerators were being offered in a dizzying array of models – manual, no frost, and auto defrost; single door or two door with the freezer at the top, bottom, or side, opening to the left or the right – with colours shading from white through yellow, turquoise, and avocado to copper and chocolate brown. As Harold Crooknell of the University of Western Ontario noted late in the decade, 'There can be no doubt that such proliferation leads to lower production efficiency, [but] ... companies who ignore the trends do so at their peril.' The pressure this proliferation in models placed on the smaller Canadian independent makers was acute, and their share of the refrigerator market remained small.[31]

Buyers became attuned to these differentiations. Remember Joan Coffey, loyal to Eaton's since 1948 when a manager, allowing her to jump queue, despatched a wringer washer to her muddy new Coquitlam street. In 1960 Coffey switched dealers to get a Frigidaire with a freezer in the bottom. 'I wanted it that way because you don't go into your freezer nearly as often as a fridge, and it's nice to have the fridge there [in full view].' 'You don't see them very often. It would take about 250 lbs, something like that. So I had a lot of use out of that,' for the mud of a decade before had been turned into a well-developed kitchen garden. Bea Millar, in the sixties head of the Home and Dealer Service Department at BC Hydro and an acknowledged expert in freezer food processing, suggests that the models with the freezer below the food storage compartment sacrificed taste and texture, reasoning that food in the unit's wire basket drawer reached low temperatures more slowly without direct contact with the colder freezer wall. But Susan Taylor also remembers these models and their pull-out drawer as 'a good practical design,' especially 'good for a short person.' The form faded, and later appeared in the Canadian market principally in high-end imports such as the Amana because the design forced the mechanism to work against gravity, pushing colder and heavier lubricants, refrigerant, and air from the colder base of the cabinet to the warmer precincts above. Tina Wall, retaining in later times her keen eye for a bargain, delighted in the accelerating heterogeneity in the market for, by accepting the visual dissonance of 'last year's' turquoise into her kitchen, she secured a higher quality refrigerator at a lower price.[32]

The festival of experimentation with both materials and mechanicals through the decade after 1958 made purchasers more sceptical and discerning in the market. Nettie Murphy, whose work cleaning houses for pay gave her broad experience with the product range, remembers the first generation of the plastic used for cabinet lining and shelving as not *skookum* (the Chinook word for strong), but easily broken and stained, and difficult to clean. The cheaper metals, chosen for handles and trim to get costs down, were prey to metal fatigue. Some of the innovations were flamboyantly counterintuitive. Accepting of limitations in household equipment in the early fifties, Ella Smith, the woman who had agreed to buy a movie camera rather than trade up from her icebox, was appalled that her new refrigerator in 1967 'had to have a heater put in the freezer. Can you believe that? Never heard of a heater in the freezer. Was $365.'[33]

As mass production capacity in the Canadian appliance industry outpaced both current and prospective demand, it became imperative for makers that the person on the other side of the cash register change from someone who *used*, to someone who *used up*, their wares, that the purchaser become a consumer. Goods made for mass consumption were not grey serviceable basics, as one reading of the word 'mass' might portend, but rather just the opposite. Makers encouraging mass consumption sought to train buyers 'to decode the minutiae of distinctions' in dress, housing, recreations, and equipment. Desires must come to supercede needs, and exchange values must replace 'more straightforward appraisals of use.' Goods which became objects for mass consumption might continue to be useful. Certainly refrigerators as they passed through this transformation remained functional, even assumed enhanced utility as they grew more capacious and required less care. But as goods became articles of mass consumption, their appearance of use value became detached to some degree from their actual usefulness, severed from the objects themselves as represented in the rhetoric of commerce. It was the appearance of use value upon which the commercial speech of advertising seized. Morgan Reid of Simpsons saw this change beginning in the mid-1950s in suburban Canada with a 'new emphasis on the fashion element in merchandising – in the broadest sense of the word ... The power mower and the barbecue, the sports shirt and the sunsuit are symbols of this new market. In the consumer goods group, fashion becomes translated into "emotional obsolescence" – a phrase coined to express the sales impact of new models.' Here was a fetishization of commodities which entrained the fetishization of their use. To buyers with desires as well as needs, this connection, forthright and fabulous in its public presentation, was both pleasurable and disconcerting, a change which prompted both wonder and alarm.[34]

For manufacturers who had branched into appliances from specializations in heavy capital goods, turbines for the utilities, boilers for industry, pumps for agricultural uses, the transition to building goods to be replaced was a paradigm shift. But to those who had come to appliances through automobiles, by the mid-fifties 'dynamic obsolescence' was second nature. 'The appliance industry is guilty of not making enough progress product wise,' Roger Keyes, vice-president of General Motors, accused Canadian Frigidaire dealers in 1955. 'General Motors analysed kitchens and became convinced,' he asserted with swelling corporate *noblesse oblige*, 'it wasn't fair for poppa to have a new car if momma did not get a new kitchen.' D.C. Marrs of Canadian Westinghouse echoed these imperatives with less disguised self-interest and plainer gendered imagery in 1961. 'Until we realize and are prepared to act on the realization that it is our responsibility to create a demand for the product we produce, to excite the consumer until we literally *drive* a product through the luxury class, we will not only retard our rate of growth as individual competitors, but also take a diminishing share of the consumer's dollar.' Industry executives insisted that appliance makers had improved their products but had not sold them adequately as goods of mass consumption: they needed to emphasize changing stylish appearances of use rather than their dogged, persisting functionality. Or as R.J. Woxman, president of Kelvinator Canada, framed the issue in 1962: 'It brings home the job that the automotive industry has done in establishing the automobile as a status symbol, and its resulting replacement market. The appliance industry on the other hand, while developing vastly improved products, has not convinced the housewife that today's appliances are really that much superior to those of 8 or 10 years ago.' For an industry worrying that the rumble from overstocked warehouses was a death rattle, the corporate interest in this transformation in the commodity culture was clear.[35]

Purchasers shared the circumstances which effected this change. The Canadian population was mobile. Their time horizons shortened as their family and work circumstances altered. There were more material and cultural pleasures to be savoured. Thus the opportunity costs of spending two months' wages on a range became greater. Why invest in a formidably durable refrigerator which might not fit in the next house, or the next? Perhaps spending less, and planning to replace sooner, could have its advantages.

For makers and retailers, an immediate challenge of trading up was trading in. Salesmen needed to be fired up to persuade shoppers to take their old appliance to the cottage and replace it with top-line new merchandise at home. Their bosses needed to learn enough about second-hand markets to price trade-ins accurately. For buyers there were bargains to be had. As more well-functioning equipment was traded in, the prices of used appliances as a proportion of new declined, for refrigerators from 51 to 40 per cent, for laundry equipment from 35 to 28 per cent, over the period 1948–52 to 1956–7. But the cottage and rural resale markets upon which urban retailers had depended were becoming satiated by 1963. Trade-ins were becoming a problem.[36]

Yet not so much a problem as makers might have hoped, for the Canadian approach to mass consumption commodity culture, perhaps characteristically, and at least for appliances, was cautious. The University of Toronto team reporting in 1970 on their six-year study of the appliance industry noted two differences between Canadian and American markets: income, and what they termed 'genuine peculiarities of Canadian taste and environment.' Canadians were willing to purchase appliances at lower income levels than their American neighbours, but at all income levels they preferred stripped-down models.[37] They resisted the 'dynamic' or 'emotional' obsolescence and the appeal of 'appearance of use value' over usefulness upon which mass consumption depended. The difference emerged early in a Canadian lack of interest in coloured appliances, and persisted. In this respect Canadians seemed more 'conservative' than Americans, more inclined to discount colour as 'a sales gimmick.' Dealers reported that the avocado, turquoise, 'Flamingo Pink,' and 'Woods Brown' makers chose for maximum immediate visual effect, buyers judged too warm, too bright, and too demanding. Rather than being enticed by new features, shoppers were apparently made hesitant. The word retailers used was 'confused.' By the late sixties colour became obsolete in the Canadian market without ever having achieved wide buyer acceptance.[38]

Canada was not the only country to resist the use of refrigerators as fashion statements. The Swedish Home Research Institute refused to endorse colour as a feature in domestic appliances. Hugo Lindstrom, later head of the Industrial Design Department at Electrolux, recalls still the sharpness of his disappointment when the fine red appliance he had imported from New York was dismissed. Swedish domestic appliances would be white and only white. Swedish consumer advocates had set their minds, on ethical grounds, against fashion characteristics in durable goods which would needlessly speed their obsolescence.[39]

In small national markets, other factors were also at play. By the mid-1960s British analysts were arguing that appliance firms in the United Kingdom were making 'too many products in an excessive variety of models,' expending energy on sales which would have been better spent on production and development. Successive presidents of the Consumers' Association of Canada in the early sixties offered similar advice.[40] Canadian firms never had been in the forefront of introducing new products into the appliance market. Yet without competition on features, in which buyers were showing only moderate interest, it was difficult to see how the existing structure of the industry could be maintained.[41] From the late 1940s the debate about the viability of independent Canadian secondary manufacturing had swung between the scorn of C.D. Howe and the enthusiasm of Walter Gordon. During the sixties the tenability of Canadian economic nationalism was battered back and forth between the free-traders' warnings of the Kennedy Round and the adventurism of Expo '67. The changes in commodity culture, so apparent in the story of refrigerators, thoroughly remade the terrain of possibilities. There was little hope for Canadian independent appliance manufacturers, best suited to producing basic equipment in small plants, but to foreswear independence and settle into an uneasy and anxious alliance with the American giants.[42]

Within capitalism, as Judith Williamson observes, a product is often 'wheeled on as the "answer" to a "problem," while in fact the product itself defines the problem it claims to solve.'[43] The problem domestic appliances addressed for electrical utilities was load. Load is the ratio between the electricity a utility actually supplies and the amount of electricity it has the capacity to supply. The capital costs of producing electricity are large and continuous regardless of the amount of electricity generated. For hydroelectric generation, running costs are relatively small. Revenues vary directly with sales, but costs are tied to peak rather than average load. At low loads, rates charged for electricity would necessarily be high, so that building load, in effect smoothing out the drops on either side of the peak, is crucial for suppliers.[44] Historically, industrial and commercial loads peaked at mid-morning and afternoon during the week. Traction loads, drawing people from home to work and back on street cars and electric railways, hastened the onset and slowed the end of these daily peaks. As importantly, industrial, commercial, and traction demands varied in concert through cyclical changes, at their highest when business was good, decreasing in harder times. Usually the scheduling of market and non-market work differed. Mealtimes and bath times fell outside, or during breaks in, the paid work day and week. The relative resilience of domestic demand in the thirties demonstrated that residential load would stabilize revenues in hard times. Between the wars, utilities also began to sell domestic appliances as a way to build load. These retail activities ended in Ontario and British Columbia after the Second World War only when it became clear that private merchants could achieve higher appliance-market saturations faster.[45]

Earlier in the century in the United States, as electric lighting and cooking became more feasible, gas companies lost a considerable part of their market to new firms selling electricity.[46] In central Canada and the West in the late 1950s, electrical utilities, and the parts of mixed fuel utilities selling electricity, faced this problem in reverse. With pipeline construction, natural, as opposed to manufactured, gas became widely available. The most voracious part of the domestic demand for electricity – heating food, water, and (then less frequently) space – was threatened. Gas was cheaper than electricity for these functions, and these were exactly the uses which contributed best to building load.[47]

Thus began in the late fifties, at the same time as the recession deepened, what Paul McKay has called a 'civil war' between providers of electricity and natural gas. Industrial demand for electric power, which had increased by 22 per cent between 1951 and 1955, rose by only about the same amount, 24 per cent, between 1958 and 1962. Even in British Columbia, where a campaign to recruit industrial users of electricity was in full swing, increments were small. Heavy industry, forestry, and mining were developing more energy-efficient production processes. In the medium term at least, electrical utilities could not count on primary or secondary manufacturing to sustain their revenues against competition from gas. Then new sources of hydroelectric power – for British Columbia on the Peace and the Columbia Rivers, for Ontario along the St Lawrence Seaway in the eastern counties – came on stream at higher capital costs, at a greater distance along expensive transmission lines from most power users. None of the alternatives to dams – coal- or oil-fired thermal generators or nuclear plants, using non-renewable or, with contemporary technology, non-disposable fuels – promised relief on costs. Thus was the historical basis for low Canadian electrical rates threatened from both sides. This is where householders and their domestic goods enter the picture.[48]

One response to the problem of declining relative demand and galloping excess supply of electricity was a nationally coordinated campaign to build domestic load.[49] Each spring and fall for the decade after 1958, the manufacturers and the utilities launched joint campaigns pitching the most kilowatt-hungry of domestic appliances, dryers, home chest and cabinet freezers, larger refrigerators with separate freezers and automatic defrost, dishwashers, and automatic washers. Ontario Hydro established a sales promotion department in 1958, a Home Economics Program to equip classrooms in 1959, and a Homemaker Service in 1963 to target women's groups directly. BC Hydro broadened the work of its Dealer and Home Service branch to offer kitchen and laundry design assistance, advising householders how to fit the maximum number of appliances into available space. Electric blankets, fine off-peak load builders, often were offered as a bonus (for whom?) to purchasers of dryers. From 1958 to 1965 electricity sales to residential and farm customers rose by 72 per cent, almost three times faster than in sales to commerce and industry.[50]

The utilities' dryer campaigns played on autumn regret for the fading of the Canadian summer. On particularly wet days, British Columbia dealers were urged to hang clothes on lines outside their stores to be 'drenched by the rain and battered by the wind,' to festoon their windows with ribbons or strips of tin foil to simulate storms lashing down on slicker-clad figures (the Slick Shopper Stopper), and to send out postcards to selected home-makers among their prospects, inquiring solicitously, 'Did your wash get caught in the rain yesterday?' Stretching the trade-in concept past its plausible limit, the utilities urged retailers to offer fifty cents for each clothes pin and foot of clothes line against the price of a new automatic dryer.[51]

Each fall advertising emphasized the threat nature posed and the solution engineering offered. Copy promised a dryer would 'dispose of the weather problem,' grant 'freedom from flying insects, birds, rusty clothes-lines, brambles, wind whipping, sun fading and all other hazards of outdoor clothes drying,' save the miles of walking, the tons (calculated at fifteen pounds per load) of lifting and the twenty eight-hour days outside per year, which using lines required.[52] For a little bit extra, the machines would come fitted with ultra-violet lamps to kill germs, or sprinklers to prepare clothes for ironing, as they dried. Machine-dried clothes were said to last longer, smell sweeter, and require less care. Alternatively, for home-makers wanting more work rather than less, dryer advertisements promised fewer cleaning and laundry bills, if drapes, slip covers, pillows, blankets, and men's wash-and-wear shirts were laundered at home, and further cost savings, because a smaller stock of clothing and linens would be needed if they could be reliably dry for reuse.[53] Editorial copy in magazines directed toward women carried similar themes, that dryers saved clothing, time, money, and even energy (if the homemaker's energy alone were counted), allowed her to have more tasks on the go at once, and reduced the household's dependence on services from the market.[54]

Yet dryers were a hard sell, even in rainy coastal British Columbia. Across the country, questions of whether to buy a dryer and whether to use it once installed were curiously separate. In this dialogue about quality,

Dryers were not an easy sell in British Columbia. Hence these brutal campaigns emphasizing the bleak prospects for drying outdoors on lines on Vancouver Island.

cost, and time, householders weighed the merits of the 'natural' and the mechanical differently than makers and fuel providers would have hoped. Women in the workforce were most readily persuaded of the dryer's utility. 'When you're working, [cost] isn't a prime thing,' Ann Brook noted, 'the prime thing is getting the load of laundry done and dry quickly.' Pam McKeen took a job in the cafeteria at Sears in 1970, and bought a dryer then using her employee discount, though she had used lines when her three children were young. But many remembered buying dryers as their families grew larger, the decision occasioned by the arrival of another infant and the return of diapers, especially if basement space had been converted for tenants to help out with mortgage payments.[55]

That the dryer saved time and made doing the laundry less physically arduous was beyond dispute. 'It really took the drudgery out of Mondays,' Olive Kozicky of Calgary wrote. 'Kind of missed hanging the clothes out and the smell of them fresh off the line,' but, Joyce Cunningham of Victoria noted, her regret was readily assuaged when 'suddenly I found I had three free hours on washday.' Dryers seemed to have dispersed from nodes on certain streets, as neighbours arrived to admire, returned on bad days seeking help, and then managed to buy machines of their own. Northerners were pleased in sub-zero temperatures to have relief from crackling lines, frozen laundry, and freezing fingers. In resource towns before stacks were fitted with scrubbers, and in urban areas where sawdust, wood, and coal still were used as domestic fuels, line drying compromised the effects of the preceding wash. Varieties of Mary Kippen's New Westminster dilemma were common.

I used to hang my clothes out on a line at the back of the house and we lived ... up the hill from the river and down on the river there were pulp mills, with burners. And the beehive burners would deposit all their little bits of sooty grit all over my baby's diapers. And in those days, you used flannelette diapers, right? And so you would have to bring diapers in that were almost as dirty as when you put them out. So having a dryer made a lot of sense ... for two reasons, the weather plus the fallout that we were experiencing ... I had no say in the matter. This was a gift that my husband gave me and it was an excellent choice that he made.

If older industrial processes and household fuels made dryers desirable, new housing forms sometimes had the same effect, for some suburban developments discouraged new residents from installing lines, and some new residents thought laundry lines out of keeping with their modern homes. Across the country a generation of new 'cliff-dwellers' was becoming adapted to dryers in the laundry rooms of high-rise apartments.[56]

In the 1950s Vancouver air quality suffered less from automobile exhaust than from the particles sent into the air by the commonly used woodstoves and sawdust burners in the Lower Mainland. This is the woodpile behind the Nelsons' home in the New Jersey Apartments in the Little Mountain district of Vancouver in the mid-1950s.

Those who did not buy often cited costs. Although dryers could be purchased for between $100 and $200 in the early sixties, in the minds of many they were expensive to run. The figure electrical utilities usually cited was five cents per load. There were installation costs as well because the early models had to vented to the outdoors, and households which had not been using electricity for cooking needed their service upgraded to 220 volts. In 1960 the biggest demand for these machines remained among households with family income greater than $5000. The slow Canadian acceptance of automatic washers may have had a complementary effect upon dryer sales, for clothes emerged from the conventional wringer wetter and thus more expensive to dry mechanically than from the automatic washer's spin cycle.[57]

More who did not buy, curiously, said they valued line over machine drying on grounds of quality.[58] More curious still, many who owned dryers continued to use their lines regularly even after they had invested in a machine. Patricia Ronald discovered that only 14 per cent of women who had dryers in their homes used them year-round in 1968 in Fergus, Ontario, a town where laundry appliances were made. Martine Perrot, similarly, found strong qualitative judgments and patterns of seasonal appliance use in her ethnographic studies of the Haute-Lozère region of France. Many who spoke and wrote to me described such yearly variations and characteristic preferences.[59]

By one reading, this lack of correspondence between ownership and use shows dryers as paradigmatic modern mass consumption goods. Perhaps the dryer's commercially driven appearance of usefulness was so sufficient a justification, there was no need once the machine was in the home actually to run it. Ronald's conclusion that women in Fergus acquired dryers as 'status symbols' rather than tools is consistent with this reasoning.[60] Or might these selective patterns of use suggest resistance to the dryer's modernity and to the overbearing influence of technology in the home? This is what Perrot argues for the Haute-Lozère, that new domestic technology did not take command of and reorder household routines, but rather the reverse. New dryers (and freezers) were used *in tandem* with older technologies, labour patterns, and expectations, showing, she suggests, that these industrial objects did not impose a standardized mechanical order but rather were integrated and refeatured according 'to the rhythm of the seasons' and local ways.[61]

Some women, particularly those with full-time jobs outside the home, used their dryers as they used their stoves and refrigerators. Consistently, after the investment in equipment had been made, certain broad ranges of tasks belonged to certain machines. More frequently, women made judgments about whether the machine would be applied to the particular task at hand day by day, and garment by garment. Partly the specific decision about how much capital versus labour to use was a response to variations in the qualities of fibres and the resilience of construction, and thus similar for washing machines and dryers. Many women put cottons and linens outside to dry, hand washed and line dried woollen blankets, but ran all children's clothing through the machines. However, unlike washers and most other household appliances until dishwashers became common, each decision about whether to turn on the dryer also explicitly concerned running costs. Thus heavy articles such as sheets and towels, which actually finished better in the machine, were often line dried, or brought into the machine only when they were near dry. These practical accommodations to keep the electricity bill manageable were often described as 'my preference' or 'my routine.'[62] And about the use of the dryer, more than any of the first generation household appliances, hung dark imprecations about quality, not merely quality of laundry, but quality of life.

Women write poems about the smell of clothing crisp from the line, the clarity of white linens in the sun, the recognition at dawn that a particular clear dry day is meant for washing wool blankets.[63] Even those who habitually used their dryers expressed regret in letters and interviews for the sensual pleasures – the feel, the fragrance, the look – of laundry arrayed on the line.[64] Those who thought dryers were a negative influence used stronger language. Urging me to consider the significance of appliances for her generation in new ways, Elizabeth Perry at age seventy wrote from Calgary: 'In the days before [the advent of dryers], we women met over clothes lines, hanging out sheets and diapers, much as Arab women interact at wells. Our lives were displayed on clothes lines. As we did the chore we could call back and forth across 50 foot lots, and would comment on the weather for drying, the special washing we had done.' Perry thought the dryer brought the most significant change in household work, 'in my observation, a labor saver, but a social deprivation, in a way.' E.M. Botham, of Salt Spring Island, who bought an Inglis automatic washer in 1953, early for a Canadian, and an Inglis dryer in 1958, wrote in imagery of air and excavation: 'Why take so long to acquire one? I dunno. Expense wasn't the problem. More likely traditional patterns and thought were at work. Clothes dried in the fresh air did seem more pleasant than those excavated from a machine – the fact that it can rain in Vancouver six months of the year being beside the point.' The contrast, that the sun and air made clothes fresh, that the machine made clothes go round and round in the heat, was frequent and evocative throughout the interviews and correspondence.[65] These renderings of the natural and the mechanical as oppositions could not have been more different from the features the appliance makers and utilities had hoped to sell in their dryer campaigns.

The moral tone carried in this imagery – bright air and dark machine, pure breeze and dangerous heat – and the common attribution of cleanliness in clothes to the light of the line rather than the water of the wash raises an interpretive caution. Did women really not use their dryers, or use them as little as they claimed and claim? Were those who claimed loyalty to the clothes-line reporting what they actually did – that is, was line drying the *statistically* normal behaviour in the group? Or were they reporting the 'behaviour they considered morally normal or appropriate in the community'?[66] In the minds of purchasers, was the dryers' appearance of usefulness so separated from their functioning that even those who owned the machines could not own up to using them? Or did the latent purpose of the dryer campaign, to increase the revenues of the utilities, fortify householders' concerns about costs and waste, and thus overcome the manifest purpose of the power providers' initiatives to transform common drying technology? Did these campaigns have a perverse normalizing effect? The proportion of Canadian homes with dryers doubled between 1962 and 1968. Saturation levels at 36.8 per cent in 1968 were still comparatively low. But manufacturers were selling more machines.[67] For the utilities, seeking to sell more power, the campaigns must have seemed less successful.

In the next decade the costs, both market and non-market, of providing power mounted. The Science Council of Canada estimated in the 1970s that Canadians were using twice the energy they required. Broadly in the economy and the culture at large, the question, 'how much was enough?' began to be reconsidered. The distinction between using and consuming, between using and using up, grew more plain, not only in the moral economy of the household, where it had remained longer an issue, but in the public sector and industry as well. Resources and landfill sites pressed their sustainable limits. The consequences of growth supported by a commodity culture, which valued products built to replace over goods built to last, became more apparent and grave. Design for excess, trading up, and building load, which in the late 1950s had seemed reasonable accommodations for both individuals and firms to changes in the demography and the manufacturing economy of the nation, no longer were unambiguous corporate strategies or personal priorities. The romance of the clothes line remained in the realm of nostalgia, for time had become the most scarce household resource. The refrigerator, once sold and savoured for its modernist imagery, began to raise suspicions. The freon refrigerant, which had made it safe for the home kitchen, was discovered to have harmful atmospheric effects. The doors of these large cold boxes by the seventies bore two numbers as they stood in the showroom, the usable cubic feet of food they would hold, and the kilowatts of energy their operation would use up. Shared concerns about conservation, last compellingly articulated on the national level in wartime, three decades later once more became plausible.

Conclusion

'Characteristically more subdued' is how two British geographers, in a footnote to a recent international review of the literature, describe Canadian reactions to the sexualized spectacles of contemporary consumption.[1] Thus are we cast once more, by dry imperial understatement, as the most earnest and cautious among the ex-colonials. Apparently even the commercial excesses of the West Edmonton Mall cannot save us from this dull ignominy. In the end, I guess I must acknowledge that this book is about the values and constraints which made the Canadian culture of consumption, at least for household goods, and in the postwar years, 'characteristically ... subdued.' This is a group of stories about prudence and responsibility. Yet it is also about sensual delights, the pleasures of using tools well-suited to the task, about building and defining in a time when options might have seemed few and foreclosed.

This book is a beginning, a first attempt through a series of case studies to learn about the material, moral, and economic reasoning which governed Canadians' relationships to their domestic world of goods. By intention, the research questions were made specific to counterbalance the austere and aloof aspersions with which the practices of Canadian consumption have been cloaked, and products of Canadian design engineering have been dismissed.

Historical studies of consumption are new and few in Canada, as elsewhere. The issues at once blossom before the eye and elude the defining aspirations of the pen. These chapters were shaped as closely researched biographies of policies, institutions, and objects. Thus there is much work yet to be done, particularly to uncover regional and class differences within the nation. I hope that you will leave this book willing to grant this much: in the postwar period, household goods, mundane and homely as they may have been, were shaped by political processes and ethical judgments as much as by entrepreneurial imperatives and technological opportunities. Income, on its own, does not tell us much about spending. Consumption patterns were made in a complex arbitration among the political, moral, and household economies from which the entitlement to spend results. The physical postwar household, a highly local material world, was the outcome of these contentions between national and international producers, public and private claims to resources, and between purchased and communally generated sources of satisfaction. This form of material life was not determined 'down here,' by forces impelled from 'out there.' There has been space to refuse and remake and, the odds are, there still is.

In addition, these things, I think, we now know.

The workings of the political economy were nationally distinctive, and, in the world of goods, perceived and reinterpreted differently by citizens according to their gender and class. For the period on which this book focused, the influence of national governance on decisions by householders is most accessible and apparent. What made this so was the wartime emergency, the prolonged crises of reconstruction, and the yearning for the stability which Keynesian economics seemed to promise. These nationally articulated policies were based upon gender-specific assumptions which characterized household goods and household labour in particular ways. But householders lived both inside and outside the market, through material goods made for sale and goods they made at home. At the same time, they were seeking, and determinedly securing for themselves, their households, and their communities, goods which transcended and refused the material as their base. Homemaking was, and is, about this vexed and replenishing arbitrage. In this domestic work they practised what Michel Maffesoli lately has called the ethic of the everyday, the social will to live by adjusting 'to one another and to the natural environment.'[2] Householders were not autonomous. They did not live independent of their times. But neither were they so narrow in their judgments or so pliant in their responses as some economic theory and many polemics about consumption might leave us to believe.[3] Their portraits of themselves come to us as a mix of nostalgia and reasoned recollection. Yet in their stances of briskly accommodating resistance, they offer us firm grounds for reasoned hope.

Like ours, their times were neither easy nor simple. Who could have come through that depression and that war, to a new day where atomic clouds loomed, without bearing scars? In the forties, scarcity was accustomed, but no less inequitable or uncomfortable for being so. The elusive promised affluence threatened ironically and indifferently to excise both the worthy and the unlamented. The initiatives to build a more humane and ample international order through freer trade went awry. The Keynesian search for domestic economic stability foundered. The several buoyant and bumptious plans for an independent consumers' voice distilled to the least intervening and most mild. Access to consumer credit widened, but not in the hoped for ways which would have helped the most needy.

Yet within and despite these thickets of constraint hedged by disappointment, amidst the many detours from public and personal plans, people deliberately and with gusto led examined lives. They turned the goods of the market to their own purposes, attentive to implications the market left myopically unreckoned. They discounted the prodigal and savoured the suitable, mindful of their own priorities and their own sources of pleasure. They made do, and made things do for them, domesticating objects into interior landscapes which both anchored and nourished. They were agile and stalwart and, perhaps – to an observer distant and uninitiated – they were 'characteristically ... subdued.'

If their times were not simple, neither is their legacy. They grew up when the market governed less of social life. They lived in an era when having more was not transparently better than having less, when their newness made many new things both fascinating and intrusive, when the inevitability of many new technologies was less apparent than the accommodations they would demand, their promised benefits less certain than the costs they would entail. Trading in, trading up, and having more were recognizable as diversions as well as opportunities. It was more ordinary then, than now, to think beyond the market, to reckon the implications of excess, and, by accumulating evasion, to set a different course. Their practices belie the lingering din of commercial speech and offer precedents for a daily life quietly and creatively lived in a space neither the state nor the market could readily claim as its own.

In the forties and fifties it was easier to see, perhaps hardly possible but to see, social existence as teetering, hesitantly, 'at loose ends with itself,' rather than as integrated, overbearing, and resolved. By comparison, it is surely more difficult for us, than it was for them, to imagine ordinary practices of daily dissent in the presence of capitalist hegemony. We live amidst bold and willingly repetitive polemics about an increasingly 'global world.'[4] But in the wake of a global depression and a global war, they made discernible and discerning space for themselves outside the regulatory fictions of the market and the state. If theirs was a more materialist world than their parents', this was not a materialism unmodified in its reception. This was a materialism made fascinating by its novelty and elusiveness, and modest by the sceptical and self-protecting reflexes with which it was met. As the dreams in the big world for multilateral free trade, a more expansive welfare state, and more staunch standards of industrial citizenship foundered on contested claims nationally and abroad, householders shifted their horizons. As the visions of postwar utopias grew dimmer and more constrained, for many years in the little world of the household, citizens retained and elaborated a domestic consumer culture in which they enacted an alternative social and political agenda. Between the big world and the little world there are ancient and abiding ties. Recall how manufacturers and retailers, who, by these circumstances, were among the first to see this resistance, accommodated, making fewer, less colourful, and more stripped-down models to meet the habits of a Canadian consuming public more resiliently and 'characteristically ... subdued' than their neighbours to the south. Householders, as we noticed, in turn and in time, ceded plausibility to more of marketers' claims, for their needs and their circumstances were changing, most of all as more women entered the labour force and daily crossed the market boundary. Our individual and collective resources for practising accommodating resistance are surely different from theirs. If we choose to exercise prudence and responsibility as users of things, it will be in a material world made for us, and not much of our own making. For all our sakes, and for those who follow, let us hope that, in space the state and the market cannot readily claim as their own, we too will make grounds for reasoned and resisting hope.

APPENDIX 1

Households Equipped with Major Domestic Appliances, percentage, Canada (percentage, U.S.)

Year	Refrigerators	Washers*		Dryers	Ranges		Freezers	Dishwashers
		Auto	Wringer		Gas†	Electric		
1940	(44.1)				(54.2)			
1941	20.9					24.5		
1950	(80.2)				(59.6)	(15.0)		
1951	46.7	73.8			21.2	28.6		
1953	66.3	80.3			22.9	34.6	2.0	
1954	70.3	81.4			21.4	39.0	3.7	
1955	74.9	82.6			20.3	42.4	4.9	
1956	79.1	84.1			20.7	45.2	6.8	
1957	81.6	85.0			19.7	48.6	7.3	
1958	85.2	86.6			21.5	49.9	8.2	
1959	88.2	87.2			21.9	52.8	9.7	
1960	90.3	12.1	73.9	12.1	21.1		56.2	11.5
		(40.8)	(32.9)	(17.1)	(63.9)		(30.7)	(18.4)
1961	92.0	14.2	71.7	14.6	20.3	58.4	13.1	1.5
1962	93.3	16.5	70.1	18.5	19.5	61.6	15.6	1.7
1963	94.2	18.3	68.5	21.6	18.7	61.0	17.7	1.9
1964	95.0	20.7	65.9	23.9	18.2	66.6	20.4	2.2
1965	95.8	23.1	63.1	27.4	17.3	69.0	22.6	2.7
1966	96.5	25.6	59.4	30.1	17.2	70.7	24.8	3.2
1967	97.2	29.9	55.2	34.4	16.5	73.1	27.7	4.4
1968	97.4	32.0	51.6	36.8	15.1	75.3	29.2	5.1

*Electric or gas

†Includes both manufactured and natural gas

Source: Dominion Bureau of Statistics, *Household Facilities and Equipment*, 1953–68; *Census of Canada*, 1941, 1951

APPENDIX 2

Interviews and Letters

Industrial Designers and Industry Experts Interviewed

I sought out Canadian industrial designers as I got to know of their work through reading the trade journals and popular press of the forties and fifties. Veronica Nygren, a faculty member at the Konstfackskolan (National College of Art and Design), Stockholm, compiled the list of Swedish designers and provided me with introductions. Most interviews were taped, transcribed, and the transcriptions returned for amendment. For the Millar and Oliver interviews, there are only handwritten notes. Many designers gave me duplicate copies of drawings and advertising copy from their portfolios, and these will be deposited with the transcripts. The interviews with designers were life histories, directed by the priorities of the interviewee, usually guided by the contents and order of their retrospective portfolio of work.

Brita Akerman, Stockholm, Sweden, 22 October 1991
Monica Boman, Stockholm, Sweden, 30 October 1991
Arthur Hald, Gustavsberg, Sweden, 8 October 1991
Howard Hemphill, Stratford, ON, 21 November 1991
Jan Hyndman, Toronto, ON, 24 June 1992
Jan Kuypers, Toronto, ON, 16 September 1991
Lars Lallerstedt, Stockholm, Sweden, 9 October 1991
Lena Larsson, Lidingo, Sweden, 14 October 1992
Hugo Lindstrom, Stockholm, Sweden, 10 and 23 October 1991
Bea Millar, Vancouver, BC, 8 May 1996
Fred Moffatt, Thornhill, ON, 26 September 1991
Rune Mono, Taby, Sweden, 28 October 1991

John Murray, Mont Tremblant, QC, 6 April 1993
Leslie Oliver, Aurora, ON, 31 May 1996 and his letter 19 August 1996
Beryl Plumptre, Ottawa, ON, 26 November 1991
Peter Sansom, Stratford, ON, 21 November 1991
George Soulis, Waterloo, ON, 11 December 1992
Kirsten Wickman, Stockholm, Sweden, 11 October 1991

Homemakers Interviewed

These women, who furnished and equipped their houses between 1946
and 1968, came forward in response to requests made on my behalf
in newspaper columns by two sympathetic journalists (Frances Bula,
'Devices and Desires,' *Vancouver Sun*, 21 July 1993, A13; Deborah Pearce,
'Go Automatic? No Soap,' *Victoria Times-Colonist*, 15 Oct, 1993, C8). The
columns described the project and asked women to contact my university
office were they willing to write or talk about what they acquired and
why, and about what they thought about what they had chosen once they
got it home. Before writing her account, Bula had interviewed me about
the early stages of the research, which until that time had emphasized industrial design and manufacturing conditions. Pearce had attended a
lecture I gave, sponsored by the University of Victoria, on the production
and merchandising of washing machines.

The interviews were completed with help from Margaret-Anne
Knowles, an MA graduate in women's history and museum studies.
Knowles had experience doing oral history to document Parks Canada
domestic sites, and refined the interview schedule. We began the interviews by collecting date of marriage, dates of birth of children, work histories of wife and husband, and making lists of their places of residence
after marriage, with general descriptions of this accommodation, in
chronological order. We then asked each person to describe the appliances and furniture she had acquired once married, in order of acquisition, noting, when they could recall, whether these goods had come to
them as purchases, in trade, or as gifts. We tried to learn whether purchased goods had been bought for cash or credit, where, who had participated in what parts of the buying decision, and what factors had
informed the choice. We asked for descriptions of these objects as they
came into the home, and as they later were altered, and for judgments
about how these things worked as tools and as parts of the household
furnishings. We asked people to reflect on their priorities, as they
changed over the years, both in terms of what they acquired and what

they most valued in what they acquired, and to note conspicuous failures and successes.

The interviews were tape recorded. Elizabeth Hermann and Anita Mahoney transcribed the tapes, and the transcripts were returned to the volunteers for correction, amplification, and excision. In many cases this process resulted in an extended later correspondence. These letters have been added to the interview transcripts. Joan Coffey and Sally Tobe agreed to accept more tapes and on their own record more detailed commentaries on selected questions.

Marjorie Barlow: Interviewed in North Vancouver by Margaret-Anne Knowles, 3 March 1994. Married 1936. Office work, and after marriage insurance company service representative. Husband farmer and steam fitter. One child. From Manitoba farm to Winnipeg, 1953; to Vancouver, 1967.

Emma Boyd: Interviewed in Vancouver by Margaret-Anne Knowles, 27 January 1994. Married 1945. Teacher and legal secretary before marriage. Secretarial work after marriage. Husband farmer. Six children. From British Columbia farm to Vancouver, 1956.

Ann Brook (pseudonym): Interviewed in Mission by Joy Parr, 24 November 1994. Married 1953. Teacher-librarian to late sixties. Husband in navy, food services. Raised in Trail; after marriage around Victoria to 1969

Patricia Cliff: Interviewed in Victoria by Joy Parr, 16 June 1994. Married 1955. Retail work before marriage. Husband psychiatric nurse and stationary engineer. Three children. Daughter of British immigrants to Saskatchewan, 1925; family to Victoria, 1947.

Joan Coffey: Interviewed in Coquitlam by Joy Parr, 17 May 1994. Married 1940. Psychiatric nurse before marriage; supervisor for market research firm after marriage. Husband psychiatric nurse. Four children. Prairie-born daughter of British immigrants; family to Vancouver, 1931.

Winnifred Edwards (pseudonym): Interviewed in Vancouver by Joy Parr, 9 June 1994. Married 1940. Registered nurse; after marriage does accounts for husband's practice. Husband Canadian-born physician. Three children. Emigrated from Britain to Winnipeg, 1941; to lower mainland of BC, 1950.

Gerd Evans: Interviewed in Burnaby by Margaret Anne Knowles, 6 April 1994. Married 1948. Housekeeper and rooming house–keeper. Husband sawmill worker, fisherman, sprinkler fitter. Three children. Immigrated from Norway with parents. Lived up and down the BC coast until settled in Vancouver, 1955; Burnaby, 1957.

Harriet Fraser (pseudonym): Interviewed in Vancouver by Margaret-Anne Knowles, 14 April 1994. Married 1948. Teacher until married. Returned to teaching 1963. Husband secondary school teacher. Three children. Raised family in Burnaby.

Lily Hansen (pseudonym): Interviewed in Vancouver by Joy Parr, 25 May 1994. Married 1940, widowed 1956. Laundry worker before marriage, part-time retail to 1956, full-time secretarial work thereafter until retirement. Husband delivery van driver. Two children. Vancouver.

Gerry Kilby: Interviewed in North Vancouver by Margaret-Anne Knowles, 10 March 1994. Married 1953. Nutritionist before marriage; returns to this work in 1973. Husband health administrator. Four children. Vancouver to 1954; Ocean Falls, 1955–7; North Vancouver thereafter.

Mary Kippen (pseudonym): Interviewed in Vancouver by Margaret-Anne Knowles, 5 March 1994. Married 1957. Husband warehouseman. Three children. Raised family in New Westminster and Burnaby.

Pam McKeen: Interviewed in Colwood outside Victoria by Joy Parr, 15 June 1994. Married 1954. Office worker before marriage, bank teller and retail worker after marriage. Husband auto worker in Britain, structural steel manufacturing worker and business agent for union in Ontario. Three children. Immigrated from England to St Catharines Ontario, 1955. St Catharines until 1992.

Nettie Murphy: Interviewed in Mission by Joy Parr, 24 November 1994. Married 1957. Retail work after marriage, later chain man on survey crew, house cleaner. Husband to university after their marriage, then joins penitentiary service. One child. Immigrated with family from Holland, 1951. Raised family around Vancouver.

Greta Nelson: Interviewed in Burnaby by Margaret-Anne Knowles, 5 March 1994. Married 1946. BA in psychology. Teacher before and after marriage. Husband teacher and member of Parliament. Two children. Born in Swedish-speaking part of Finland. Raised family around Vancouver but for two years in late fifties at Woss Lake.

Joan Niblock: Interviewed at Fort Langley by Joy Parr, 26 May 1994. Married 1954. BSc in bacteriology. Worked as research technician until first child born. Husband electrical engineer. Three children. Raised family around Vancouver.

Mary Paine (pseudonym): Interviewed in Vancouver by Joy Parr, 17 May 1994. Married 1949. Office machine operator before marriage. Husband in retail sales. Three children. Calgary until 1967, to Vancouver, 1969.

Margaret Shortliffe: Interviewed in Victoria by Joy Parr, 16 June 1994. Married 1937. BA in French. School teacher before and after marriage. Husband professor of French. Three children. Alberta born. Raised family in Kingston, Ontario.

Allison Simpson: Interviewed in Delta by Joy Parr, 18 May 1994. Married 1955. Bachelor of Commerce, University of Alberta 1995. Husband with RCMP. Two children. Raised in NWT; after marriage lived in Saskatchewan: Meadow Lake, 1955–9; Moose Jaw, 1959–61; Lloydminster 1961–3; Outlook, 1963–6; Regina, 1966–73. Lived in Delta, BC, since 1973.

Ella Smith: Interviewed in Vancouver by Margaret-Anne Knowles, 1 February 1994. Married 1938. Husband factory worker. Two children. Raised family in Vancouver.

Lynn Stevens: Interviewed in Langley by Joy Parr, 26 May 1994. Married 1949. Secretary with law firm and airline until first child born; home sales of cosmetics thereafter. Husband in sales. Two children. Raised family around Vancouver.

Susan Taylor (pseudonym): Interviewed in Victoria BC, by Joy Parr, 10 May 1994. Married 1947. Social scientist in the federal civil service before marriage. Husband university teacher. Four children. Ontario migrant to Prairies.

Sally Tobe: Interviewed in West Vancouver by Joy Parr, 17 October 1994. Married 1955. Worked in parents' furniture store, Kitchener, Ontario. Bachelor of Fine Art, University of British Columbia, 1979; now practices as photographer and historian. Husband physician. Two children.

Tina Wall (pseudonym): Interviewed in Victoria by Joy Parr, 16 June 1994. Married 1954. Secretarial work before and after marriage. Husband engineer. Emigrated from north of England with brother after the Second World War and settled in Vancouver.

Letters from Homemakers

These letters arrived in response to the Bula and Pearce columns, either when they appeared in the *Vancouver Sun* and the *Victoria Times-Colonist,* or when they were reprinted across the country from national news services.

Anne Barber, Victoria, BC, 17 October 1993
Marjorie Barlow, North Vancouver, BC, 25 July 1993
Hazel Beech, Lake Cowichan, BC, 22 July 1993
Lorne and Cindy Bolger, Arris, ON, 25 July 1993
E.M. Botham, Ganges, BC, 16 October 1993
Joan Catlin, Burnaby, BC, 28 July 1993
Joyce Cunningham, Victoria, BC, 30 October 1993
Liz Forbes, Duncan, BC, November 1993
Kathy Grenswich, Kitchener, ON, 2 August 1993
Olive L. Kozicky, Calgary, AB, 14 September 1993
Sheila Maurice, Nanoose Bay, BC, 30 July 1993
M. McConnell, Aldergrove, BC, 9 August 1993
Pam McKeen, Victoria, BC, 18 October 1993
Nettie Murphy, Mission, BC, 21 July 1993
Greta Nelson, Burnaby, BC, 23 July 1993
Irene Newlands, Surrey, BC, September 1993
Bev Newmarch, Calgary, AB, 6 September 1993
Joan Niblock, Fort Langley, BC, 23 Jan 1994
Elizabeth Perry, Calgary, AB, 12 September 1993
Betty Robson, Calgary, AB, 15 September 1993
Margaret Shortliffe, Victoria, BC, 20 October 1993
Marilyn Ward, Victoria, BC, 10 August 1993
Martha Watson, Alma, ON, 24 July 1993

Notes

Abbreviations

AGO	Art Gallery of Ontario
AGOA	Art Gallery of Ontario Archives
BCHA	BC Hydro Archives
CAC	Canadian Association of Consumers (later Consumers' Association of Canada)
CB	*Canadian Business*
CCF	Cooperative Commonwealth Federation
CDNPA	Canadian Daily Newspaper Publishers Association
CEMA	Canadian Electrical Manufacturers Association
CHG	*Canadian Homes and Gardens*
CMA	Canadian Manufacturers' Association
CW	*Canadian Woodworker*
DRS	Department of Reconstruction and Supply
DTC	Department of Trade and Commerce (later Industry, Trade and Commerce)
EFIR	Employment Forecast Interview Report
EFSIR	Economic Forecast Survey Interview Report
HGR	*Home Goods Retailing*
IC	*Industrial Canada*
McMUA	McMaster University Archives
McGUA	McGill University Archives
MTPL	Metropolitan Toronto Public Library
NAC	National Archives of Canada
NFB	National Film Board
NGA	National Gallery of Canada Archives

NMA	National Manufacturers' Association
NIDC	National Industrial Design Committee (later National Industrial Design Council)
NSRCCB	Nova Scotia, Royal Commission on the Cost of Borrowing Money, Cost of Credit and Related Matters in the Province of Nova Scotia
OHA	Ontario Hydro Archives
QUA	Queen's University Archives
RAIC	Royal Architectural Institute of Canada
RCBF	Royal Commission on Banking and Finance
RCCEP	Royal Commission on Canada's Economic Prospects
ROM	Royal Ontario Museum
ROMA	Royal Ontario Museum Archives
SN	*Saturday Night*
UGA	University of Guelph Archives
WPTB	Wartime Prices and Trade Board
WS	*Westinghouse Salesman*

Introduction

1 Paul Glennie, 'Consumption within Historical Studies,' in Daniel Miller, ed., *Acknowledging Consumption* (London: Routledge, 1995) 190; Paul Willis, *Common Culture: Symbolic Work at Play in the Everyday Cultures of the Young* (Milton Keyes: Open University Press, 1990) 133–9; Mica Nava, *Changing Cultures: Feminism, Youth and Consumerism* (London: Sage, 1992) 167–8, 193; Alan Warde, 'Notes on the Relationship between Production and Consumption,' in Roger Burrows and Catherine March, eds., *Consumption and Class: Divisions and Change* (London: Macmillan and Sociological Association, 1992) 16, 20–6; Rachel Bowlby, *Shopping with Freud* (London: Routledge, 1993) 3; Rita Felski, *The Gender of Modernity* (Cambridge: Harvard University Press, 1995) 63; Laura Kipnis, *Ecstasy Unlimited* (Minneapolis: University of Minnesota Press, 1993) 29; Daniel Miller, 'Consumption as the Vanguard of History,' in Miller, ed., *Acknowledging Consumption*, 23–4; Robert Bocock, *Consumption* (London: Routledge, 1993) x; Mihaly Csikszentmihalyi and Eugene Rochberg-Halton, *The Meaning of Things* (New York: Cambridge University Press, 1981) 29. See also David Halle, *Inside Culture* (Chicago: University of Chicago Press, 1993), a clarifying critique of Pierre Bourdieu, *Distinction: A Social Critique of the Judgement of Taste* (Cambridge: Harvard University Press, 1984).
2 For guidance I suggest Juliet B. Schor, *The Overspent Americans* (New York:

Basic, 1998). Schor is a Harvard feminist and economist, writing in the tradition of J.K. Galbraith but arguing toward very different conclusions than Galbraith reached in his path-making works on consumption of the 1950s.

3 Lately, American writing for the period has changed emphasis as well. See Joanne Meyerowitz, *Not June Cleaver: Women and Gender in Postwar America, 1945–1960* (Philadelphia: Temple University Press, 1994), and Lizabeth Cohen 'From Town Center to Shopping Center: The Reconfiguration of Community Market Places in Postwar America,' in Roger Horowitz and Arwen Mohun, eds., *His and Hers* (Charlottesville: University of Virginia Press, 1998) 189–234.

4 Raymond Williams, *Keywords: A Vocabulary of Culture and Society* (New York: Oxford University Press, 1976) 68–70

5 Celia Lury, *Consumer Culture* (London: Routledge, 1996) 1

6 Warde, 'Notes,' 28–9

7 Judith Williamson, *Consuming Passions: The Dynamics of Popular Culture* (London: Marion Boyars, 1986) 226–7

8 Miller, 'Consumption as the Vanguard,' 26

9 Gary Cross, *Time and Money: The Making of Consumer Culture* (London: Routledge, 1993) 167

10 Warde, 'Notes,' 16–20, 28–9

11 Felski, *Gender of Modernity*, 61; Judy Attfield, 'FORM/female FOLLOWS FUNCTION/male: Feminist Critiques of Design,' in John Walker, ed., *Design History and the History of Design* (London: Pluto, 1989) 220

12 Ben Fine and Ellen Leopold, *The World of Consumption* (London: Routledge, 1993) 71; Bocock, *Consumption*, 20

13 Betty Friedan, *The Feminine Mystique* (New York: Norton, 1963); Vance Packard, *The Hidden Persuaders* (New York: D. McKay, 1957), and *The Waste Makers* (New York: D. McKay, 1960); J.K. Galbraith, *Affluent Society* (Boston: Houghton Mifflin, 1958), and *American Capitalism* (Boston: Houghton and Mifflin, 1958); Grant McCracken, *Culture and Consumption* (Bloomington: Indiana University Press, 1988) 72, 83, 88; T. Jackson Lears, *The Culture of Consumption* (New York: Pantheon, 1983); Roland Marchand, *Advertising the American Dream: Making Way for Modernity, 1920–1940* (Berkeley: University of California Press, 1985); Herbert Marcuse, *One Dimensional Man: Studies in the Ideology of Advanced Industrial Society* (Boston: Beacon, 1964); Theodore Adorno, *The Culture Industry: Selected Essays on Mass Culture* (New York: Routledge, 1991), and *The Authoritarian Personality* (New York: Harper and Row, 1950); Max Horkeimer, *Critical Theory: Selected Essays* (New York: Herder and Herder, 1972), and *Critique of Instrumental Reason* (New York: Seabury,

1974); William Leiss, *The Limits to Satisfaction: An Essay on the Problem of Needs and Commodities* (Toronto: University of Toronto Press, 1976)

14 Rob Shields, *Places on the Margin* (London: Routledge, 1991) 9; Fine and Leopold, *World of Consumption,* 67; Ben Fine, 'From Political Economy to Consumption,' in Miller, ed., *Acknowledging Consumption,* 138–9; Bowlby, *Shopping with Freud,* 4; Nava, *Changing Cultures,* 162–3, 185–9

15 Ellen Willis, '"Consumerism" and Women,' in Leslie B. Tanner, ed., *Voices from Women's Liberation* (New York: New American Library, 1971) 307–13. In the Canadian literature, Bryan D. Palmer, *Working Class Culture* (Toronto: Butterworth, 1983) 190–5, 230–1, and Suzanne Morton, *Ideal Surroundings* (Toronto: University of Toronto Press, 1995) 149–50, 154–6, are susceptible to this critique.

16 Nava, *Changing Cultures,* 190–1; Jennifer Scanlon, *Inarticulate Longings: The Ladies Home Journal, Gender, and the Promises of Consumer Culture* (London: Routledge, 1995) 230–1

17 Dick Hebdige, 'Object as Image: The Italian Scooter Cycle,' in his *Hiding in the Light* (London: Routledge, 1988) 86–7; Attfield, 'FORM/female'; P. Goodall, 'Design and Gender,' *Block* 9 (1983) 50–6; Angela Partington, 'Design Knowledge and Feminism,' *Feminist Art News* 2 (1985) 9–13; and considering sex rather than gender, Penny Sparke, *As Long as It's Pink: The Sexual Politics of Taste* (London: Pandora, 1995)

18 Alice T. Friedman, 'Domestic Differences: Edith Farnsworth, Mies van der Rohe and the Gendered Body,' in Christopher Reed, ed., *Not at Home* (London: Thames and Hudson, 1996) 190. The whole book bears reading on this theme.

19 Judith Williamson, 'Woman Is an Island: Femininity and Colonisation,' in Tania Modleski, ed., *Studies in Entertainment* (Bloomington: Indiana University Press, 1986) 101–6; Felski, *Gender of Modernity* 62–3

20 Fine and Leopold, *World of Consumption* 16–17; Jonathan Friedman, *Consumption and Identity* (Chur, Switzerland: Harwood, 1994) 5; Alan Warde, 'Consumers, Identity and Belonging: Some Reflections on Theses of Zygmunt Bauman,' in Russell Keat et al., eds., *The Authority of the Consumer* (London: Routledge, 1994) 66, 70–1; Ben Fine, 'From Political Economy to Consumption,' in Miller, ed., *Acknowledging Consumption,* 127–33

21 Glennie, 'Consumption within Historical Studies,' 167, 176, 191; Fine and Leopold, *World of Consumption,* 71, 136; Frank Mort, *Cultures of Consumption: Masculinities and Social Space in Late Twentieth Century Britain* (London: Routledge, 1996) 7, 12

22 Mike Featherstone, *Cultural Theory and Cultural Change* (London: Sage, 1992), *Consumer Culture and Postmodernism* (London: Sage, 1991), and *Undo-*

ing Culture: Globalisation, Postmodernism and Identity (London: Sage, 1995) 75–6; John Fiske, *Reading the Popular* (Boston: Unwin and Hyman, 1989), and *Understanding Popular Culture* (London: Routledge, 1989); Hebdige, *Hiding in the Light*; Keat et al., eds., *Authority of the Consumer*; Friedman, *Consumption and Identity*; many contributions to this literature appeared in two journals, *Block* and *Theory, Culture and Society*.

23 Paul Willis, *Common Culture: Symbolic Work at Play in the Everyday Cultures of the Young* (Milton Keynes: Open University Press, 1990) 133; Nava, *Changing Cultures*; Dick Hebdige, *Subculture: The Meaning of Style* (London: Methuen, 1979); Rob Shields, 'Spaces for the Subject of Consumption,' and Janice Williamson, 'Notes from Storyville North,' in Rob Shields, ed., *Lifestyle Shopping* (London: Routledge, 1992); Rob Shields, 'Social Spatialisation and the Built Environment: The West Edmonton Mall,' in *Environment and Planning D: Society and Space* 7 (1989) 147–64; Raj Anand, *Taskforce on the Law Concerning Trespass to Publicly-Used Property as It Affects Youth and Minorities* (Toronto: Ministry of the Attorney General, 1987); Sally Zukin, *Landscapes of Power* (Berkeley: University of California Press, 1991); Susan M. Ruddick, *Homeless in Hollywood* (New York: Routledge, 1996)

24 Mort, *Cultures of Consumption*; Victoria de Grazia, *The Sex of Things: Gender and Consumption in Historical Perspective* (Berkeley: University of California Press, 1996); John Goldthorpe, *The Affluent Worker in the Class Structure* (London: Cambridge University Press, 1969), and *The Affluent Worker: Industrial Attitudes and Behaviour* (Cambridge: Cambridge University Press, 1968); Colin Campbell, *The Romantic Ethic and the Spirit of Modern Consumerism* (Oxford: Blackwell, 1987) 205–6; Lury, *Consumer Culture*, 4; Bocock, *Consumption*, 5; Miller, 'Consumption as the Vanguard,' 26; and Glennie, 'Consumption within Historical Studies,' 181

25 In a fascinating study Erica Carter shows how young women in postwar Germany insisted on wearing nylon stockings to work as a protest against contemporary dearth and discipline. But she concludes with an appropriate caution that 'there are no simple connections to be made' between a well-honed dress sense of a young Berliner and the skills a homemaker needed to navigate the shoals in other parts of that straitened market. Erica Carter, 'Alice in the Consumer Wonderland,' in Angela McRobbie and Mica Nava, eds., *Gender and Generation* (London: Macmillan, 1984) 213, 196; Glennie, 'Consumption within Historical Studies,' 190

26 Scholars who have urged this are Miller, 'Consumption as the Vanguard,' 16, 17, 34; de Grazia, 'Introduction,' in *The Sex of Things*, 16; Fine and Leopold, *World of Consumption*, 72; Williamson, 'Woman Is an Island,' 101–3; and Tim Putnam, 'Beyond the Modern Home: Shifting Patterns of Residence,' in Jon

Bird et al., eds., *Mapping the Futures* (London: Routledge, 1993) 157; Alan Warde 'Afterword,' in Stephen Engell, Kevin Heatherington, and Alan Warde, *Consumption Matters: The Production and Experience of Consumption* (Oxford: Blackwell, 1996) 311

27 Gary Cross, *Time and Money: The Making of Consumer Culture* (London: Routledge, 1993) 165

28 Albert O. Hirschman, 'Industrialization and Its Manifold Discontents: West, East and South,' in his *A Propensity to Self-Subversion* (Cambridge: Harvard University Press, 1995) 208–10

29 Elaine Tyler May, *Homeward Bound: American Families in the Cold War Era* (New York: Basic Books, 1988) 16–20

30 Pamela W. Laird, 'Stories against the Current,' *SHOT Newsletter* no. 79, n.s., (April 1998) 2–3

Chapter 1: Domestic Goods in Wartime

1 In British Columbia, for example, 86.4 per cent of those receiving new driver's licences in 1945 were men; the figure was 72.2 per cent in 1950. In 1955, with 35 per cent women and 65 per cent men, the gender balance among new drivers stabilized: in 1965, 65 per cent of all automobile drivers in the province were male. British Columbia, *Report of the Superintendent of Motor Vehicles* 1945, 17; 1950, 19; 1955, 33; 1965, 8

2 F.H. Leacy, ed., *Historical Statistics of Canada*, 2nd ed. (Ottawa: Statistics Canada, 1983) A1, A248, A67–9, A249, B4; Alison Prentice et al., *Canadian Women: A History*, 2nd ed. (Toronto: Harcourt Brace, 1996) 351

3 Leacy, ed., *Historical Statistics*, H50, F83, F1, F82; Lizabeth Cohen, 'From Town Center to Shopping Center,' in Roger Horowitz and Arwen Mohun, eds., *His and Hers* (Charlottesville: University of Virginia Press, 1998); Meg Jacobs, 'How about Some Meat? The Office of Price Administration, Consuming Politics, and State Building from the Bottom Up, 1941–1946,' *Journal of American History* (Dec. 1997) 912; M.C. Urquhart and K.A.H. Buckley, eds., *Historical Statistics of Canada* (Toronto: Macmillan, 1965) B268

4 Note for example the oral history accounts of life in Ottawa in Heidi Henkenhaf, 'Women in the Canadian Federal Civil Service during World War II' (MA thesis, Memorial University of Newfoundland, 1990).

5 A.F.W. Plumptre, *Mobilizing Canada's Resources for War* (Toronto: Macmillan, 1941) 243; Jeff Keshen, 'One for All and All for One: Government Control, Black Marketing and the Limits of Patriotism,' *Journal of Canadian Studies* 29, 4 (winter 1994–5) 111–43; Laura Brown Webb, 'Wartime Changes in Consumer Goods in American Markets,' *Monthly Labor Review*, Nov. 1942, 892–3

6 NAC, RG 20, Industry, Trade and Commerce, 1452 A-10.9-4, 'Civilian Requirements: Consumer Durable Goods,' 8 Oct. 1943; Plumptre, *Mobilizing*, 243; NAC, RG 20, 325 T11555, Committee on Reconstruction, L.L. Lang, president of the Canadian Manufacturers' Association, 'Submission to the Chairman and members of the Senate Committee on postwar reconstruction and re-establishment by the CMA on postwar problems of manufacturing industry'

7 Webb, 'Wartime Changes,' 893; Richard R. Lingeman, *Don't You Know There's a War On: The American Home Front, 1941–1945* (New York: Putnam, 1970) 263

8 David Slater, *Consumption Expenditures in Canada*, study prepared for Royal Commission on Canada's Economic Prospects, 1957 (Ottawa: Queen's Printer, 1957) Table 15, p. 44; D'Ann Campbell, *Women at War with America: Private Lives in a Patriotic Era* (Cambridge: Harvard University Press, 1984) 169; John Morton Blum, *V Was for Victory: Politics and American Culture during World War II* (New York: Harcourt Brace Jovanovich, 1976) 92; Jacobs, 'How about Some Meat?' 931; Webb, 'Wartime Changes,' 891; Lingeman, *Don't You Know There's a War On*, 263 ; Harvey Mansfield, *A Short History of OPA* (Washington: Office of Temporary Controls, 1947) 201, 56, 80, 84, 149, 153. Galbraith, as director of the Price Division of OPA, had been in a good position to discern whether supply shortages had existed.

9 NAC, RG 64, WPTB, 1452 A-10-9-4, 'Age of household appliances owned, Summer 1940'; 'Civilian Requirements: Consumer Durable Goods,' 8 Oct. 1943, report by W.E. Duffett; and 'Lists of Durables in Short Supply,' Fall 1943. This last report also notes contemporary American investigations. The wartime income and spending figures were calculated from Leacy, ed., *Historical Statistics*, F85, 81, 83; Doug Owram, *Born at the Right Time: A History of the Baby Boom Generation* (Toronto: University of Toronto Press, 1996) 10.

10 On early experiments with collective household technology see Dolores Hayden, *The Grand Domestic Revolution* (Cambridge: MIT Press, 1981). On the choice between commercial and home laundries see Arwen Mohun, 'Why Mrs Harrison Never Learned to Iron: Gender, Skill and Mechanisation in the American Steam Laundry,' *Gender and History* 8, 2 (Aug. 1996) 231–51; on the refinement of small engines for domestic technology see Leslie Oliver, 'The Fractional Horsepower Motor and Its Impact on Canadian Society and Culture,' *Material History Review* 43 (spring 1996) 55–67.

11 NAC, RG 64, WPTB, 1452, 'Civilian Requirements: Consumer Durable Goods,' 8 Oct. 1943; 1411 A10-9-5, 'Furnishing and Equipment Owned by Urban Families, March 1942,' showing percentage owning by income

12 Blum, *V Was for Victory*, 93

13 NAC, RG 64, WPTB, 1445, Report to the Women's Regional Advisory Committee meeting in Montreal, 16 Nov. 1943

14 Laura Jamieson, *Women Dry Those Tears* (Vancouver: Broadway Printers, 1945) 2

15 NAC, RG 64, WPTB, 1452 A-10.9-4, 'Requirements of Domestic Washing Machines'; A-10.9-7, 'Civilian Requirements and Reconversion,' W.E. Duffett, Dec. 1943; estimating maximum repairable life at 15 years, 125,000 electric washing machines from existing stock would be worn out by the end of 1943, and a further 100,000 by the end of 1944; NAC, RG 64, WPTB, 1452 A-10-9-7, memo by J.F. Parkinson in Decontrol and Deconversion file, 20 Feb. 1944, defining washers as essential and 'most other items in the metal field ... as "conveniences."'

16 NFB, *Tomorrow's World* (1943); *Supper's Ready* (1944); *Stitch and Save* (1943); *No More Kitchen Sopranos* (1942); *Make It Over* (1943); *The Main Dish* (1943)

17 NAC, RG 64, WPTB, 1452 A-10-9-4, 'Civilian Requirements of Electric Ranges, over 35 amperes, electric rangettes and cooking plates,' M.L. Reid, 30 Nov. 1943. Some electric ranges were made, but none were distributed without a signed essentiality certificate establishing that existing equipment was unrepairable and that a coal, wood, or gas stove could not be installed.

18 NAC, RG 64, WPTB, 1446, Consumer Branch Labour Liaison, reports from the Niagara Peninsula in the fall of 1942

19 NAC, RG 64, WPTB, 1452 A-10-9-4, 'Civilian Requirements – electric refrigerators,' W.E. Duffett, 8 Nov. 1943. American controllers faced the same dilemma. Webb, 'Wartime Changes,' 893–4

20 Jacobs, 'How about Some Meat?' 915. U.S. controllers were anticipating a high wage, high volume economy before the war ended. Mansfield, *Short History*, 90

21 Owram, *Born at the Right Time*, 8–12; Doug Owram, 'Canadian Domesticity in the Postwar Era,' in Peter Neary and J.L. Granatstein, eds., *The Veterans Charter and Postwar Canada* (Montreal: McGill-Queen's University Press, 1998) 210; Doug Owram, *The Government Generation* (Toronto: University of Toronto Press, 1986), ch. 11

22 Jacobs, 'How about Some Meat?' 912, 920, 940; Blum, *V for Victory*, 101–4

23 Alvin Finkel, *Our Lives: Canada after 1945* (Toronto: Lorimer, 1997) 6, and similarly 76; Peter S. McInnis, 'Planning Prosperity: Canadians Debate Postwar Reconstruction,' in Greg Donahy, ed., *Uncertain Horizons: Canadians and Their World in 1945* (n.p.: Canadian Committee on the History of the Second World War, 1997) 231–2, 238, 252; James Struthers, 'Family Allowances, Old Age Security, and the Construction of Entitlement in the Canadian Welfare State, 1943–1951,' in Neary and Granatstein, eds., *Veterans Charter*, 186, 191, 198

24 *Canada's Market in Home Equipment* (Toronto: Maclean-Hunter, 1945) 3, 5, 6,

a survey of 1,526 housewives across the country, compared with NAC, RG 64, WPTB, 1452 A-10-9-4, apparent consumption figures for various appliances, 1926–42; *Hardware in Canada*, June 1945, 2, 26–7; March 1945, 17; McMUA, Westinghouse Collection, box 7, file 27, *WS*, July 1946, 11; July 1947, 8; Oct. 1947, 6–7. There was similar concern in the United States. See Arthur J. Pulos, *The American Design Adventure* (Cambridge: MIT, 1988) 44–5.

25 NAC, RG 64, WPTB, 1460 A-10-9-23, 'A Survey of Household Necessities,' and covering letter by J.D. Gibson, 10 May 1945

26 NAC, RG 20 756, 'Canada's Economic Development in the Transition Period, 1945–7,' 1947; Mansfield, *Short History*, 14

27 NAC, MG28 I 68 52, Ontario Farm Radio Forum, 'Rural Home Improvement,' 24 April 1944, responses from Wellington, Dufferin, Perth, Waterloo, Dundas, Grey, Bruce, Oxford, Lanark, and Rainy River. All but the Rainy River reports came from southern Ontario, many from prosperous agricultural districts.

28 Ibid., 28 Oct. 1946, 11 Nov. 1946. The quote comes from Lansdowne, Leeds, 28 Oct. 1946.

29 *A Guide to Farm Home Planning and Modernization* (Saskatoon: Department of Reconstruction and Rehabilitation, 1946) 5, 29, 33; *Your Modern Farm Kitchen* (Victoria: Rural Housing Advisory Committee for British Columbia, 1948) 7, 13

30 Jamieson, *Women Dry Those Tears*, 2

31 NAC, RG 64, WPTB, 1452 A-10-9-4, Research and Statistics, Civilian Requirements, 'Age of Household Appliances Owned, Summer 1940,' based on interviews with 6,524 persons by the Commercial Research Division of the Curtis Publishing Company; 'Civilian Requirements – electric refrigerators' W.E. Duffett, 8 Nov. 1943

32 QUA, New Democratic Party of Ontario, box 42, Grace MacInnis and Charles J. Woodsworth, 'Canada through CCF glasses'; William Irvine, 'Scarcity or Abundance, the People Must Choose' (Winnipeg: Contemporary Publishers, 1944); Jamieson, *Women Dry Those Tears*, 2, 4; Keith R. Fleming, *Power at Cost: Ontario Hydro and Rural Electrification, 1911–1958* (Montreal: McGill-Queen's University Press, 1992) 224

32 Jamieson, *Women Dry Those Tears*, 11

Chapter 2: Envisioning a Modern Domesticity

1 Another exhibition called *Design in Industry* sponsored by the National Film Board and the National Gallery, opened in Ottawa in 1946 and toured the country thereafter. See John Collins, '"Design in Industry" Exhibition, Na-

tional Gallery of Canada, 1946: Turning Bombers into Lounge Chairs,' *Material History Bulletin* 27 (spring 1988) 27–38; *Design in Industry* was mounted in the National Gallery in Ottawa, but thereafter the exhibition was presented in department stores: Henry Morgan's in Montreal, and Eaton's in Toronto, Winnipeg, Edmonton, Vancouver, and Calgary; NGA, 5.5–D, 'Design in Industry Exhibition,' 1946, itinerary; the two Toronto exhibitions discussed in this chapter are also analysed in Virginia Wright, *Modern Furniture in Canada, 1920–1970* (Toronto: University of Toronto Press, 1997) chap. 3.

2 Lovat Dickson, *The Museum Makers* (Toronto: ROM, 1986) 7, 40; Jay Cantor, 'Art and Industry: Reflections on the Role of the American Museum in Encouraging Innovation in the Decorative Arts,' in Ian Quimby and Polly Earl, eds., *Technological Innovation and the Decorative Arts* (Charlottesville: University of Virginia Press, 1974) 332–4, 342; Neil Harris, 'Museums, Merchandising and Popular Taste: The Struggle for Influence,' in his *Cultural Excursions* (Chicago: University of Chicago Press, 1990) 57–65, 76–78; Helen Rees, 'The Culture of Consumption: Design Museums as Educators or Taste-makers?' in Russell Keat et al., *The Authority of the Consumer* (London: Routledge, 1994) 154–65; Seth Koven, 'The Whitechapel Picture Exhibitions and the Politics of Seeing,' in Daniel Sherman and Irit Rogoff, eds., *Museum Cultures* (London: Routledge, 1994)

3 ROMA, curatorial records for 'Design in Industry,' 1945, exhibition announcement and flyer headed 'An Exhibition of Contemporary Design in Industry May 18th to June 10th, 1945'; Tony Bennett, *Birth of the Museum: History, Theory, Politics* (London: Routledge, 1995) 210–14; Carol Duncan, 'Art Museums and the Ritual of Citizenship,' in Ivan Karp and Steven D. Lavine, eds., *Exhibiting Cultures: The Poetics and Politics of Museum Display* (Washington: Smithsonian Institution, 1991) 94–5; Harris, 'Museums, Merchandising and Popular Taste,' 76–7; Gordon Fyfe, 'A Trojan Horse at the Tate: Theorizing the Museum as Agency and Structure,' in Shawn Macdonald and Gordon Fyfe, eds., *Theorizing Museums: Representing Identity and Diversity in a Changing World* (Oxford: Blackwell, 1996) 210, 212–13, 224; Robert Rydell, *World of Fairs: The Century of Progress Expositions* (Chicago: University of Chicago Press, 1993) 135; Jeremy Aynesley, *Nationalism and Internationalism: Design in the Twentieth Century* (London: Victoria and Albert Museum, 1993)

4 Ian McKay, *The Quest of the Folk: Antimodernism and Cultural Selection in Twentieth-Century Nova Scotia* (Montreal: McGill-Queen's University Press, 1994) chap. 3; Gloria Lesser, *École du Meuble, 1930–1950* (Montreal: Montreal Museum of Decorative Arts, 1989); Elaine Holowach-Amiot, *The Women's Art Society of Montreal* (Montreal: McCord Museum, 1994); Canadian Handicrafts

Guild Archives, Montreal, typescripts of minutes, 1905–29; McGUA records of the Black Whale Community Shop, Percé, Quebec, 1934–74, files 1–15; Maria Tippett, *Making Culture: English-Canadian Institutions and the Arts before the Massey Commission* (Toronto: University of Toronto Press, 1990) 104–5, 11

5 McGUA, RG 43 c236, Handicraft Department, 'Rural Handcraft Activities in Canada, a correspondence survey for study by the Sub-Committee on Agricultural Policy, prepared by the Interdepartmental Committee on Canadian Homecrafts,' 6 Sept. 1943, Deane H. Russell, 1–3, and his 'Hand Arts and Crafts in Canada, report of the Canadian Delegation to International Conference on Food and Agriculture, Hot Springs, Virginia,' 3. This volume also includes a boldly stated critique of the craft revival's potential to 'glorify, without qualifying, what our grandmothers made, and compare it with "shoddy machine made products"' and to become 'simply a production for market racket.' Extension Department, Saint Francis Xavier University, 'Problem of Arts and Crafts in Nova Scotia,' undated, c. 1941

6 NAC, RG 20, Trade and Commerce, 601 3:401, G.R. Heasman, 'Investigation into Canadian Handcraft Industry,' 21 Oct. 1940, with commentaries by A. McD. McBain, Public Relations Section, Foreign Exchange Control Board, D. Cole, New York, 6 Dec. 1940, and Floyd Chalmers, 5 Dec. 1940; H.G. Kettle, 'The Canadian Handicraft Movement,' *Canadian Forum*, July 1940, 112, 114. Copy in records of the Department of Finance, NAC, RG 20 601.

7 McGUA, RG 43 c236, Handicraft Department, 1946–8, J. Murray Gibbon, 'Submission to the Council of the Royal Canadian Academy,' 15 May 1943; Tippett, *Making Canadian Culture*, 168–71

8 Humphrey Carver, 'Home-Made Thoughts on Handicrafts,' *Canadian Forum*, March 1940, 386–7, copy in NAC, RG 20 601

9 The history of Eaton's relationship with the Canadian Handicrafts Guild is documented in AO, T. Eaton Company, series 69, vol. 13. In the same collection, see also the interview with O.D. Vaughan, series 221, vol. 2, 24 Feb. 1964; for reviews of the 1942 exhibition see *Financial Post*, 25 April 1942; *Globe and Mail*, 25 April 1942; CHG, June 1942, 18–21.

10 AO, T. Eaton Company, series 69, vol. 19, 'Design furniture and fabric design,' including M.A. Barter's 5 Sept. 1941 memo on modernism and small-scale lower-cost furniture, reports on the ROM lecture series, and a description of the wartime housing replica. See the same series, vol. 23, 'Homefurnishing Committee minutes' for descriptions of the 'Home-in-one room,' 7 Oct. 1944, and the 'Avenue of Small Homes,' 2 March 1945.

11 Susan M. Pearce, *Museums, Objects and Collections* (Leicester: Leicester University Press, 1992) 234; Dickson, *Museum Makers*, 69–71, 98

12 Mary Lowrey Ross, 'Design for Living,' SN, 14 May 1955, 66–7; ROMA, *Design*

in Industry, minutes of planning meetings, April 1946; Pearce, *Museums, Objects*, 236; Fyfe, 'Trojan Horse at the Tate,' 206; Harris, 'Museums, Merchandizing,' 59–63

13 ROMA, 'Design in Industry,' copy of captions for the exhibition; 'Exhibit Sets New Goals for Industrial Design,' *SN*, 2 June 1945; Dickson, *Museum Makers*, 67; Pearce, *Museums, Objects*, 136–7; Peter Vergo, 'The Reticent Object,' in Peter Vergo, ed., *The New Museology* (London: Reaktion, 1989) 46; and Ludmilla Jordanova, 'Objects of Knowledge: A Historical Perspective on Museums,' ibid., 23

14 Rydell, *World of Fairs*, 135; Harris, *Cultural Excursions*, 59–63; Burton Benedict, *The Anthropology of World's Fairs* (Berkeley, CA: Lowie Museum of Anthropology, 1983) 2, 3; Paul Greenhalgh, *Ephemeral Vistas* (Manchester: Manchester University Press 1988) 168

15 ROMA, 'Design in Industry, 1945,' 15-page retrospective assessment of the exhibition, unsigned, undated; on eye appeal as a priority in the retailers' conceptions of household goods, see AO, T. Eaton Company, series 69, vol. 30, O.D. Vaughan to G.W. Barber, Household Furnishings Merchandising Office, 26 April 1944.

16 Wellington Jeffers, 'Finance at Large,' *Globe and Mail*, 12 May 1945; 'Design,' *Board of Trade Journal*, May 1945, 10–11; ROMA, 'Design in Industry' report on attendance as 24,984 in 3-week run of exhibit, 10,597 over the corresponding weeks in 1944

17 Donald W. Buchanan, 'Design in Industry – A Misnomer,' *Canadian Art* 2 (summer 1945) 194–7

18 AGOA, 'Design in the Household curatorial files,' C.S.D. Band, Gutta Percha & Rubber Limited, 5 April 1945

19 AGO, 'Design in the Household,' proposed exhibition of industrial design, commentary on draft scheme

20 Thomas Fisher Rare Book Room, University of Toronto, Jarvis Collection, Council of Industrial Design, *Design Quiz* (London: Lund Humphries, 1946); Penny Sparke, ed., *Did Britain Make It?* (London: Design Council, 1946) 32

21 Duncan Cameron, 'The Museum: A Temple or the Forum,' *Journal of World History* 14 (1972); Pearce, *Museums, Objects*

22 Douglas Worts, 'Extending the Frame: Forging a New Partnership with the Public,' in Susan Pearce, ed., *Art in Museums* (London: Athlone, 1995) 165, 170, 187, 191

23 Gaby Porter, 'Seeing through Solidarity: A Feminist Perspective on Museums,' in Macdonald and Fyfe, eds., *Theorizing Museums*, 113; Pearce, *Museums, Objects*, 136–9; Ivan Karp, 'Culture and Presentation,' in Karp and Lavine, eds., *Exhibiting Cultures*, 22

24 Barbara Swann, 'The Design in the Household Exhibition,' *IC*, March 1946, 77–9

25 AGOA, 'Design in the Household Exhibition 1946,' memo on the meeting on the house and industrial design exhibition, of Friday afternoon in the library of the art gallery, and detailed breakdown of purpose, notation, and illustrations for exhibition title industrial design for the house, 17 pp.

26 NGA, 5.5-D, Design in Industry Exhibition, 1946, Humphrey Carver to H.O. McCurry, 10 Dec. 1945

27 AGOA, 'Design in the Household,' copies of researcher's letters of introduction, 4 Dec. 1945, and insurance lists, 22 Jan. 1946; Humphrey Carver, *Compassionate Landscape* (Toronto: University of Toronto Press, 1975) 78

28 Michael Baxandall, 'Exhibiting Intention: Some Preconditions of the Visual Display of Culturally Purposeful Objects,' 33–40; Susan Vogal, 'Always True to the Object, in Our Fashion,' 196; Svetlana Alpers, 'A Way of Seeing,' 27, 30, 31; Carol Duncan, 'Art Museums and the Ritual of Citizenship,' 180, all in Karp and Lavine, eds., *Exhibiting Cultures*; Margaret Hall, *On Display: A Design Grammar for Museum Exhibitions*, (London: Lund Humphries, 1987) 17; Pearce, *Museums, Objects and Collections*, 235

29 Barbara Swann, 'The Design in the Household Exhibition,' *IC*, March 1946, 77–9; AGO, Photographic Archives, nos. 158, 159, 160, 161, 162, 163, 164; 'What's New? Report to the Reader,' *CHG*, March 1946

30 Wright, *Modern Furniture*, 93; Martin Eidelberg, ed., *Design, 1935–1965: What Modern Was* (New York: Abrams, 1991) 25; Christopher Wilk, *Marcel Breuer: Furniture and Interiors* (New York: Museum of Modern Art, 1981) 129

31 Swann, 'Design in the Household Exhibition'; 'What's New'

Chapter 3: Gender, Keynes, and Reconstruction

1 On Canadian consumption expenditures, 1947–50, by comparison with the United States see David Slater, *Consumption Expenditures in Canada* (May 1957), study prepared for Royal Commission on Canada's Economic Prospects, tables 16, 45, and the fuller discussion by Jean Mann Due, 'Consumption Levels in Canada and the United States,' *Canadian Journal of Economics and Political Science* 21 (May 1955) 174–89.

2 NAC, RG 20 316, Canadian Reconstruction Committee, draft report of Economic Advisory Committee on report of the Reconstruction Committee, 17 Nov. 1943; on the context for Keynesian reasoning about postwar planning see Doug Owram, *The Government Generation: Canadian Intellectuals and the State* (Toronto: University of Toronto Press, 1986) chaps 11 and 12.

3 DRS, *Reconversion, Modernization and Expansion: Progress and Programs in Selected Canadian Manufacturing Industries, 1945–47, An Analysis of Reports Pro-*

vided by 643 Major Plants Formerly Engaged in War Production (Aug. 1946) 37–8, 10–11

4 *WS*, Oct. 1946, 11

5 'Westinghouse Halts Product Advertising,' *Marketing*, 26 Oct. 1946, 24; 'Westinghouse on Exhibition,' *WS*, Oct. 1947, 6–7; 'Telling Is Good Selling,' *WS*, July 1947, 8

6 'New Moffat "Handi-chef" Sets Pace in Appliance Merchandising,' *Sales Chef*, May–June 1946 1–4; 'Sounder Retail Methods Instilled by Training Courses of Dealers,' *Marketing*, 14 Dec. 1946, 2; 'Improvement in Product Provides Compelling Advertising Campaign,' ibid., 28 Feb. 1948, 2; *WS*, July 1949, 2–3, Feb. 1950; 'Cook with a Baby Stove,' *Chatelaine*, June 1950, 54–5

7 NAC, RG 20, DTC, 325 T11555, Committee on Reconstruction, L.L. Lang, president of Canadian Manufacturers' Association, 'Submission to the Chairman and members of the Senate Committee on postwar reconstruction and re-establishment ... on postwar problems of manufacturing industry,' 23 Feb. 1943

8 For a good self-portrait of an industry resisting product line and production line innovation see the 1946 appeal for tariff protection by Canadian stove makers, AO, T. Eaton Company, series 28, vol. 4, Guelph Stove Company file, Canadian Institute of Stove and Furnace Manufacturers, brief to Trade and Tariff Committee, 16 Jan. 1946, by representatives from Clare Bros, Findlays, General Steel Wares, and Gurney.

9 NAC, RG 20 167 26958, C.L. Burton, 30 Jan. 1946, opposing continuation of regulation postwar; Floyd Chalmers, opening University of Toronto lecture series on marketing, *Marketing*, 6 April 1946, 26, 61, 63, 69; as Peter McInnis notes, Burton's defence of free enterprise was made more staunch by the intimation of a labour organizing drive in retailing. Peter S. McInnis, 'Planning Prosperity: Canadian Debate Postwar Reconstruction,' in Greg Donahy, ed., *Uncertain Horizons: Canadians and Their World in 1945* (n.p.: Canadian Committee on the History of the Second World War, 1997) 242–3; F.H. Leacy, ed., *Historical Statistics of Canada*, 2nd ed. (Ottawa: Statistics Canada, 1983) F83, F85

10 DRS, *Reconversion*, 37–8, 10–11

11 NAC, RG 64 1452, file A-10-9-7, WPTB Research and Statistics – Decontrol and Deconversion, Parkinson, Proposals to remove the ceiling on or raise the prices of capital goods, 11 March 1944

12 David A. Wolfe, 'Economic Growth and Foreign Investment: A Perspective on Canadian Economic Policy, 1945–1957,' *Journal of Canadian Studies* 13, 1 (spring 1978) 5–6; Robert Campbell, *The Grand Illusion: The Keynesian Synthesis in Canada* (Peterborough, ON: Broadview, 1987) 87–8

13 DRS, *Encouragement to Industrial Expansion in Canada, Operation of Special*

Depreciation Provisions (Ottawa, 1948) 24–8, 36, 60; on the use of such allowances in Britain see J.C.R. Dow, *The Management of the British Economy, 1945–60* (Cambridge: Cambridge University Press, 1968) 205–7, 286–7.

14 DRS, *Encouragement*, summary table 5, 43

15 Ibid., 55

16 Department of Reconstruction, *Employment and Income with Special Reference to the Initial Period of Reconstruction* (April 1945) 1

17 Ibid., 4; John Maynard Keynes, *The General Theory of Employment, Interest and Money* (London: Macmillan, 1936)

18 Campbell, *Grand Illusion*, 57, 60, 203

19 Department of Reconstruction, *Employment and Income*, 14

20 Ibid., 15; NAC, Interview with Robert Bryce by Ian Stewart, Ottawa, Ontario, 28 Feb. 1989

21 Department of Reconstruction, *Employment and Income*, 9, 6

22 NAC, RG20 668–669–670, file 22168, Conferences: Postwar trade policy, UK, USA, Canada, 1942–66, report on meeting of Commonwealth representatives in London, 15–30 June 1943, and L.D. Wilgress to James A. MacKinnon, 31 July 1942; RG 20 265 34736, brief from CMA committee on postwar export trade to J.A. MacKinnon, 6 Oct. 1943

23 NAC, RG 20 325 T11555, Robert Bryce, 'Basic Issues in Post-war International Economic Relations' paper delivered to the meetings of the American Economics Association, New York, Dec. 1941, 5, 3

24 Department of Reconstruction, *Employment and Income*, 6–9

25 Ibid., 9, 11; NFB films portrayed the inflationary danger, for example *Buying Fever* (1945); *Money, Goods and Prices*, (1945); *Main Street* (1945).

26 Department of Reconstruction, *Employment and Income* 4, 5, 13, 14; NAC, RG 64 A-10-9-7, WPTB, Research and Statistics, Decontrol and Conversion, J.H. Parkinson, 'WPTB Controls and Policies after VE Day,' 18 April 1945

27 Department of Reconstruction, *Employment and Income*, 4

28 The foundations for and fallacies in this reasoning will be discussed with reference to specific consumption policies below, but for a general introduction to habits of thought of early Keynesians, see a book about the period by one of them: Dow, *Management of the British Economy*, 168, 180–3, 215, 290; and Sir Alex Cairncross, 'Reconversion, 1945–51,' in N.F.R. Crafts and N.W.C. Woodward, eds., *The British Economy since 1945* (Oxford: Clarendon, 1991) 40–1; on short notice see John Maynard Keynes, 'The Balance of Payments of the United States,' *Economic Journal*, June 1946, 187.

29 DRS, *Reconversion*, 24, 26

30 Jack Granatstein and Robert Cuff, and more recently Bruce Muirhead, have analysed this episode closely. R.D. Cuff and J.L. Granatstein, *American Dollars – Canadian Prosperity* (Toronto: Samuel-Stevens, 1978); B.W. Muirhead, *The*

Development of Postwar Canadian Trade Policy (Montreal: McGill-Queen's University Press, 1992); McInnis, 'Planning Prosperity,' 232

31 Muirhead, *Development*, 18; Cuff and Granatstein, *American Dollars*, 31; Hector Mackenzie, '*Justice* Denied: The Anglo-American Loan Negotiations of 1945,' *Canadian Review of American Studies* 26, 1 (winter 1996) 79–110

32 Cairncross, 'Reconversion,' 30

33 Hector Mackenzie, 'The Path to Temptation: The Negotiation of Canada's Reconstruction Loan to Britain in 1946,' *Historical Papers/Communications historiques* (1982) 196–220; a film on the topic is NFB, *Canada – World Trader* (1946); Douglas LePan, *Bright Glass of Memory* (Toronto: McGraw-Hill, 1979) 66, 67, 82, 105

34 Keynes, 'The Balance of Payments,' 186–7; Cairncross, 'Reconversion,' (42–3

35 Granatstein and Cuff, *American Dollars*, 31–5, 44–7; a frequent reference point in discussions about imports and domestic growth at this time was Hans Neisser, 'The Significance of Foreign Trade for Domestic Employment,' *Social Research* 13 (Sept. 1946) 310–11, 313, 323–5; Muirhead, *Development*, 12–46, 56–7; J.R. Petrie, 'Exports and National Policy,' *Canadian Business*, Aug. 1945, 24–6, 112

36 A.F.W. Plumptre, 'Detour into Controls,' *International Journal* 3, 1 (winter 1947–8) 3, 6–10; C.D. Howe, 'The Capital Goods Programme,' *IC*, Feb. 1948, 49–52; NAC, Interview of Robert Bryce by Ian Stewart, 31 March 1989

37 NAC, RG 20 668–70, file 22168, 'Conferences,' James Coyne brief, 20 Sept. 1946, 3; R.W. Lawson, 'The Role of Foreign Exchange Control,' *Public Affairs*, Dec. 1947, 1

38 Canada, House of Commons, *Debates*, 16 Dec. 1947, 323–35, 339

39 *Canada Gazette*, 26 Nov. 1947, 2190–9; 10 June 1948

40 NAC, RG 20 987, Canadian Reconstruction Committee file 34292, *Current Economic Conditions*, 10 May 1948, 8 June 1948, July 1948; RG 64 1384, Emergency Import Control, Geo. Freeman to K.W. Taylor, 8 May 1948; H.N. Addison to J.G. McKinnon, 7 Dec. 1948; RG 20 774 23-100-S26, EFSIR, Henry Morgan and Co., 10 Jan. 1949; BCHA, Hydro Oral History, Bea Millar, p. 4, on her short-lived career with Northland Automatic Appliances, a firm which had intended to build Bendix washers in Ontario; among Canadian stove makers, only Moffat made controls for their own ranges, McMUA, Moffats', *Sales Chef*, Jan.–Feb. 1952, 7

41 NAC, RG 64, WPTB, 1381, Emergency Import Control, 1948–51, Abbott broadcast transcript, 17 Nov. 1947; RG 20 DTC 987, Canadian Reconstruction Committee file 34292, Economic Research Branch, Preliminary Report on the Outlook on Employment and Income in 1948, 26 Nov. 1947

42 H.C. Eastman, 'Recent Canadian Economic Policy: Some Alternatives,' *Canadian Journal of Economics and Political Science* 18, 2 (March 1952) 139

43 NAC, RG 64 1382, Emergency Import Control, annual reports

44 NAC, RG 20 948 7–694, Foreign Exchange Control Board, 1948–57, Louis Rasminsky, 'Canada's International Financial Relations,' notes for a lecture at the National Defence College, Kingston, 30 Jan. 1948

45 Leacy, ed., *Historical Statistics of Canada*, F83, F85; House of Commons, *Debates*, 16 Dec. 1947, 365

46 Howe, 'Capital Goods Programme,' 52

47 House of Commons, *Debates*, 8 Dec. 1947, 18; Abbott, CBC broadcast of 17 Nov. 1947; *Hardware in Canada*, Nov. 1947, 9–10; Bryce interview, 31 March 1989

48 Leacy, ed., *Historical Statistics of Canada*, F83, F85; NAC, MG 28 I 200, Canadian Association of Consumers minutes of annual meeting, Sept. 1951 resolution from Nanaimo and report by president on action of national executive

49 *Hardware in Canada*, April 1952, 13, 54; Clarence Barber, *The Canadian Electrical Manufacturing Industry* (Sept. 1956), study prepared for the RCCEP, 15; House of Commons, *Debates*, 17 March 1952, 507; NAC, RG 20 774, EFSIR, Henry Morgan and Co., 21 June 1951

50 Personal savings as a percentage of disposable income: 1947, 5.6; 1948, 10.2; 1949, 7.9; 1950, 5.8; 1951, 9.8; 1952, 10.1; 1953, 8.3; 1954, 4.5; 1955, 4.2; 1956, 5.0; 1957, 4.6; 1958, 5.3. *National Income and Expenditure Accounts – Quarterly Estimates, 1947–86* (Ottawa: Statistics Canada, 1989) 54–5

51 NAC, RG 19 E2 C, vol. 32, file 101–102–17, M.W. Sharp, Memo to Cabinet, 'Re Control of Consumer Credit,' 31 Aug. 1950, cabinet document 210–50; George Glass to W.C. Clark, memo of consumer credit with commentary on appropriate current policy, 28 Aug. 1950

52 The October 1950 regulations established a minimum down payment for cars of $33\frac{1}{3}$ per cent, and for all other consumer goods of 20 per cent, with a common maximum repayment period of 18 months. NAC, RG 19 E2 C 32 101–102–17, Memorandum to the Minister: re consumer credit regulations, 25 Sept. 1950; draft press release, 19 Oct. 1950; *Canada Gazette*, 8 Nov. 1950, Consumer Credit (Temporary Provisions) PC 4993, 1387–95

53 NAC, RG 19 E2 C 32 101–102–17, Statement by the Minister on the introduction of PC 1249, 13 March 1951; *Canada Gazette*, 28 March 1951, 317–19; House of Commons, *Debates*, 16 May 1951, 3086–95; down payments were increased in March 1951 to 50 per cent for cars and $33\frac{1}{3}$ per cent on all else, with the repayment period reduced to a year. The minimum term was relaxed again to 18 months in January 1952. *Canada Gazette*, 23 Jan. 1952, PC 108, 54–6

54 House of Commons, *Debates*, 5 May 1952, 1855; 26 May 1952, 2577

55 House of Commons, *Debates*, 11 Sept. 1950, 571–5, 587; K.W. Taylor warned W.C. Clark that people setting up households for the first time were likely to protest the more strenuous regulations of March 1951, NAC, RG 19 E2 C 32 101-102-17, K.W. Taylor to W. Clark, Feb. 1951; *Toronto Star*, 9 Sept. 1950, 6

56 'Thought of Credit Curbs Disquieting to Retailers,' *Toronto Star*, 9 Sept. 1950, 14; NAC, RG 19 E2 C 32 101-102-17, H.C. Clark to K.W. Taylor, 3 May 1951, on meeting with Retail Credit Federation; 'Blame Credit Restrictions for Layoffs,' *Financial Post*, 16 June 1951, 1; 'This Market Isn't Saturated,' *Financial Post*, 21 July 1951, 2; 'Sales Volume 10 Per Cent Increase Expected by Companies,' *Marketing* 12 Jan. 1952, 4; 'Consumer Buying Essential to Development,' *Marketing*, 9 June 1952, 4; House of Commons, *Debates*, 12 March 1952, address by Donald Fleming, 371–2

57 NAC, RG 19, Finance, E2 C, vol. 32, file 101-102-17, Summary of the Consumer Credit Administration's operations, 1 Nov. 1952 to 6 May 1952; Notes on Effects of Consumer Credit Regulations, 2 Jan. 1952

58 Ibid.

59 Eastman, 'Recent Canadian Economic Policy,' 139

60 Clarence Barber, 'Ottawa Government Helps Our Capital Boom,' *SN*, 6 Nov. 1948, 30

61 Eastman, 'Recent Canadian Economic Policy,' 138

62 Plumptre 'Detour into Controls,' 11; Ian Drummond, 'Economic History and Canadian Economic Performance since the Second World War,' in John Sargent, ed., *Postwar Macroeconomic Development* (Ottawa: Supply and Services, 1986) 21; the export values cited are in 1946 dollars, calculated using Leacy, ed., *Historical Statistics of Canada*, G383 and G387.

63 O.J. Firestone, *Investment and Inflation with Special Reference to the Immediate Postwar Period* (Ottawa: Department of Trade and Commerce, Feb. 1949) 14, 17, 194, 197

64 Dow reaches this conclusion for Britain, *Management of the British Economy*, 211; see similarly for Canada, Irwin Gillespie, 'Postwar Canadian Economic Policy Revisited, 1945–75,' *Canadian Tax Journal* 27, 3 (May–June 1979) 265–76; H. Scott Gordon, 'A 20 Year Perspective,' in S.F. Kaliski, ed., *Canadian Economic Policy since the War* (Montreal: Canadian Trade Committee, 1966). Robert Will argues that in Canada 'both the magnitude and timing of the impact of changes in fiscal policy often left much to be desired,' and that 'it was the operation of built-in stabilizers, especially income tax and unemployment insurance, which contributed heaviest to economic stability in this period as a whole.' Robert M. Will, *Postwar Fiscal Policy in Canada*, staff report for the Royal Commission on Banking and Finance, Nov. 1962, 11–50; the quote is at 47.

Chapter 4: Consumer Sovereignty

1 Joan Robinson, *Economics: An Awkward Corner* (New York: Random House, 1967) 53–4
2 NAC, RG 64, WPTB, Consumer Branch, vol. 1445 founding documents, vol. 1448 Conferences, 21–3 Jan. 1946, Ottawa, 20–1 March Brockville, 1 Oct. 1946, central Ontario
3 MTTPL, Baldwin Room, Harriet Parsons Papers, Minutes of National Conference called by the National Council of Women, 16 April 1947, afternoon session, question by Miss Anna Speers and *Chatelaine's* Department of Consumer Relations, a memo to the national presidents of Canadian women's organizations from Byrne Hope Saunders, n.d., prepared for April 1947 conference; NAC, MG 28 I 200, annual meeting reports of 1951 and 1955, vol. 1, of 1956, vol. 2, and 1961, vol. 3
4 MTPL, Parsons Papers, 'National Council of Women Questionnaire, summary of replies received from 37 Consumer Branch Committees,' spring 1946; NAC, RG 64 1446, Standards Division file, memo from Mrs W.R. Lang, summarizing replies, 3 May 1946; ibid., 1448 Consumer Branch Conferences, Mrs Lois Dallamore on extension of standards work, Brockville ON, 20 March 1946; Parsons Papers, afternoon session of National Council of Women convened planning meeting, Toronto, 16 April 1947, Mrs W.R. Lang, 6
5 Norman Isaac Silber, *Test and Protest* (New York: Holmes and Meir, 1983) 17; Robert N. Mayer *The Consumer Movement* (Boston: Twayne, 1989) 20–1
6 John Martin and George W. Smith, *The Consumer Interest* (London: Pall Mall, 1968) 28–30; Erica Carter, 'Alice in the Consumer Wonderland: West German Case Studies in Gender and Consumer Culture,' in Angela McRobbie and Mica Nava, eds., *Gender and Generation* (London: Macmillan, 1984) 194–6
7 The Dominion Trade and Industry Commission Act of 1935, c. 39 (amended 1930, c. 17), which empowered the National Research Council to do this work, had established standards for hosiery and fur garments, but had not been functioning since 1941. The Canadian Engineering Standards Association, renamed in 1944 the Canadian Standards Association, had with joint government and industry funding been establishing production criteria for construction materials and electrical equipment including household appliances and lighting since 1919. *Canadian Standards Association: The Significance of Its Services to Canadian Industry and Consumer Interests* (Ottawa: Canadian Standards Association, 1945) 16–20, includes a list of the standards then in place. Copy found in AO, T. Eaton Company, series 28, vol. 4, file 1331A. Ross Willmot, 'Canada Sets a Standard,' *Canadian Business*, March 1947, 62–3, 72–4. In January 1946 the Consumer Branch regional representatives recommended a permanent Standards Division within the Department of

Trade and Commerce. MTPL, Parsons Papers, Brief soliciting government support for the formation of a national association of Canadian women to be known as the Canadian Association of Consumers, Aug. 1947, 6

8 Britta Lovgren, *Hemarbet som politik* (Stockholm: Almquist & Wiksell, 1993); Brita Akerman, ed., *Vi Kan, Vi Behovs* (Stockholm: Akademlitteratur, 1983), and *Kunskap for var vardag* (Stockholm: Akademillitteratur, 1984); for further references see Joy Parr and Gunilla Ekberg, 'Mrs Consumer and Mr Keynes in Postwar Canada and Sweden,' *Gender and History* 8, 2 (summer 1996) 212–30.

9 NAC, RG64 1446, WPTB Consumer Branch, Standards Division file, memo by Mrs W.R. Lang, drafted 3 May 1946, presented 3 June 1946. On the context within the National Council of Women, see N.E.S. Griffiths, *The Splendid Vision: Centennial History of the National Council of Women of Canada, 1893– 1993* (Ottawa: Carleton University Press, 1993) 236, 238.

10 MTPL, Parsons Papers, Minutes of the National Conference of 16 April 1947, afternoon session; NAC, RG 103, vol. 36, file SC47 3360–3 pt 1, 'Commodity Standards' Allan Gill to F.D. Tolchard, Toronto Board of Trade, 30 July 1947, on initiation of standards research

11 MTPL, Parsons Papers, 'Brief soliciting support for the formation of a National Association,' Aug. 1947, 3, 5–6

12 On the succession from Lang to Parsons, see Mrs R.J. Marshall opening the 16 April 1947 planning conference, Parsons Papers, Minutes of National Conference, 1. Parsons view of postwar priorities is clear in National Council of Women, *Annual Report* (1947), 'Report on Economics and Taxation' 65–8.

13 MTPL, Parsons Papers, Mrs R.J. Marshall, president of the National Council of Women, addressing the planning committee meeting, 17 March 1947

14 Parsons Papers, 'Charting the Course of Controls,' 2 Oct. 1946, written when Parsons was educational secretary, Consumer Branch

15 Only Parsons's plan that the early afternoon be spent considering how 'we women can promote understanding of Canada's economic problems' was set aside. Parsons Papers, Parsons to Mrs R.J. Marshall, president of National Council of Women, 25 March 1947

16 Parsons Papers, 'Address by Mr G.F. Towers,' 16 April 1946, 3, 6, 8, 9

17 Parsons Papers, Parsons to Marshall, 10 May 1947

18 Parsons Papers, 'Brief to the Minister of Trade and Commerce Soliciting Support from the Canadian Association of Consumers,' Aug. 1947

19 NAC, RG 64 1446, Consumer Branch Labour Liaison, report from Christine White, 25 April 1946; *Canadian Tribune*, 27 July 1946, 26 Oct. 1946, 2 Nov. 1946

20 NAC, CCF Records, vol. 198, Research 'Women 1946–8,' presentation of Western Housewives' Consumers Associations regarding price controls and food subsidies; UGA, McCready Papers, A0021, box 1, Consumer Education, Lily Phelps, Housewives' Consumers Association, to Douglas Abbott, undated, June 1947; *Financial Post*, 7 June 1947; *Globe and Mail*, 25 June 1947; *Toronto Star*, 25 June 1947. For the HCA in context in the Canadian Left, see Joan Sangster, *Dreams of Equality: Women on the Canadian Left, 1920–1950* (Toronto: McClelland and Stewart, 1989) chap. 6.

21 CCF Records, vol. 198, Research 'Women 1946–8,' presentation of Western HCA; McCready Papers, A0021, box 1, Phelps to Abott, June 1947

22 CCF Records, vol. 198, Research 'Women 1946–8,' presentation of Western HCA; McCready Papers, A0021, box 1, Phelps to Abott, June 1947

23 NAC, Marjorie Mann Papers, vol. 2 'Housewives' Consumers Association,' Lucy Woodsworth to Mann, 22 June 1947

24 The records on this controversy within the CCF are voluminous and rich in incident. See Mann Papers, particularly the files on the Housewives' Consumers Association and the CCF Ontario Women's Committee; NAC, CCF Records, MG 28 IV-1, vol. 60, Ontario Women's Committee, 1947–50; Parsons Papers, Marion Harrington, 'No CAC for Me,' *CCF News*, 25 March 1948. On the context see Sangster, *Dreams of Equality*, chap. 7, especially 220.

25 NAC, CCF Federal Records, MG 28 IV-1, vol. 60, Ontario Women's Committee, 1947–50, Marjorie Mann to David Lewis, 16 Feb. 1948, reporting on views of Macphail; NAC, Marjorie Mann Papers, MG 32 G12, vol. 1, brochure 'Women in peace as in war – protect your home'; Barbara Cass-Beggs to Mann, 20 Nov. 1949; Peg Stewart to Mann, 16 Nov. 1949; Dan Azoulay, 'Ruthless in a Ladylike Way: CCF Women Confront the Postwar Communist Menace,' *Ontario History* 89, 1 (March 1997) 23–52

26 *Ottawa Journal*, 9 July 1947; *Marketing*, 13 March 1948; *Canadian Tribune*, 24 April 1948; *Globe and Mail*, 15 April 1948

27 MTPL, Parsons Papers, file 'What later became CAC,' Parsons address to Local Council of Women, Montreal, 27 Nov. 1947; National Council of Women, *Annual Report* (1947), 'Report on Economics and Taxation,' 66; Parsons Papers, Founding Meeting of the Canadian Association of Consumers, Ottawa, minutes of the morning session, 30 Sept. 1947, 3–4

28 UGA, McCready Papers, A0021, box 1, Consumer Education, 'Your Questions and Answers – what is this new thing Canadian women are doing' (Ottawa: CAC, 1947) 5; NAC, MG 28 I 200, CAC, *The Canadian Consumer*, first bulletin, 20 Jan. 1948, 1; *SN*, 23 Aug. 1949, 20, a biographical sketch of Catherine Wright; 12 April 1949, sketch of Blanche Marshall, 30–1

29 House of Commons, Session 1947–8, 'Special Committee on Prices,' minutes

of proceedings and evidence, no. 23, Friday 12 March 1948, the quote is at p. 1079; UGA, McCready Papers, Box 1, Consumer Economics, 'What CAC Has Done' (pamphlet); *The Canadian Consumer*, no. 1 (Jan. 1948): 5, (Feb.–March 1948): 1–2; and no. 1 (1949); NAC, MG 28 I 200 2, CAC, file 26 'Review of CAC activities from 1947 to 1957,' 2; W.H. Heick, *A Propensity to Protect: Butter, Margarine and the Rise of Urban Culture in Canada* (Waterloo: Wilfrid Laurier University Press, 1991) 82–3

30 Mrs Marshall's presence at the National Council of Women in this period seems to have had the same effects. See Griffiths, *Splendid Vision*, 250.

31 June Callwood, 'She Leads the Housewives' Crusade,' *Maclean's*, 1 Oct. 1952, 8, 9, 60–2; NAC, MG 28 I 200, CAC, vol. 1, file 9, Biographical sketch of Mrs W.R. Walton, 24 Sept. 1952

32 NAC, MG 28 I 200, CAC, vol. 1, Walton addressing CAC annual meeting 20–1 Sept. 1951; CAC annual meeting 1952 presidential address and reports on thrift campaigns; Walton addressing the CAC annual meeting, 1953; see similarly for West Germany, Carter, 'Alice in Consumer Wonderland,' in Angela McRobbie and Mica Nava, eds., *Gender and Generation* (London: Macmillan, 1984) 195–6.

33 UGA, McCready Papers, box 1, Renée Vautelet, 'As I See It,' CAC *Bulletin*, Jan. 1955; NAC, MG 28 I 200, CAC, vol. 1, Vautelet address to CAC 1954 annual meeting; *Canadian Who's Who*, 1958–60, (Toronto, 1960) 1124; Harriet Hill, 'Knight Errant in Petticoats,' *Saturday Night*, 24 Oct. 1953, 40

34 NAC, Mann Papers, vol. 2, Adeline Haddow to Mann, 28 Jan. 1948; MTPL, Parsons Papers, file 'What Later Became CAC,' Harrington, 'No CAC for Me' Mann papers, vol. 1, Peg Stewart to Mann, 21 Nov. 1948 and Jan. 1950

35 John Kenneth Galbraith, *American Capitalism: The Concept of Countervailing Power* (Boston: Houghton Mifflin, 1956), *The Affluent Society* (Boston: Houghton Mifflin, 1958)

36 NAC, MG 28 I 200, vol. 2, CAC, Presidential Address, 1956 Annual Meeting; UGA, McCready Papers, CAC *Bulletin*, Oct. 1956; Vautelet, 'As I See It'; Martin and Smith, *Consumer Interest*, 2; Mark V. Nadel, *The Politics of Consumer Protection* (Indianapolis: Bobbs-Merrill, 1971) xix

37 MTPL, Parsons Papers, Elliott Haynes Ltd. 'Survey on Peacetime Consumer Organisation' Summer 1947, question 2; NAC, MG 28 I 200, CAC, vol. 1, annual meeting reports 1950–1 and 1951–2; vol. 2, Mrs W.C. Rean, 'Review of CAC Activities from 1947 to 1957' delivered at 1957 annual meeting; in their publicity, however, the CAC continued to claim wide representation. See, for example, NFB, 'Consumers Unite to Solve Shopping Problems,' *Eye Witness* 84 (1956).

38 Parsons Papers, Minutes of afternoon session, 16 April 1947; NAC, MG 28 I

200, CAC minutes of founding meeting, 30 Sept. 1947; S.P. Lewis, *Grace* (Madeira Park, BC: Harbour, 1993) 303

39 'Christine S. White OBE,' *Canadian Home Journal*, May 1947; Parsons Papers, Christine White to Harriet Parsons, 25 Oct. 1947, 29 Oct. 1947; Parsons to White, 30 Oct. 1947, 7 Nov. 1947; White to Aaron Mosher and Percy Bengough, 24 Oct. 1947 covering 'Report re formation of Canadian Association of Consumers' and film script for 'The Story of the Canadian Association of Consumers'; NAC, MG 28 I 200, CAC annual meetings of 1949, 1950, 1956; Callwood, 'She Leads the Housewives' Crusade,' 62

40 CAC *Bulletin*, no. 1 (Jan. 1948) 4

41 NAC, MG 28 I 200, vol. 1, file 8A, Milk Committee of the CAC, report, 20–1 Sept. 1951; Walton Presidential report, Annual Meeting, 1952; NAC, MG 28 I 68, National Farm Radio Forum, Ontario Farm Forum Findings, 'Frills in the Marketplace,' 3 Feb. 1964

42 NAC, MG 28 I 200, vol. 1, Report of Mrs Hugh Summers, Agricultural Convenor, to CAC annual meeting 1955; vol. 3, her report 1959; vol. 3, tariff discussion and resolution at 1957 annual meeting following report to executive meeting of 28 Nov. 1956 on tariff reference, 121, in vol. 2; Renée Vaudelet addressing 1955 annual meeting, in vol. 1

43 NAC, MG 28 I 200, vol. 1, Vautelet to mid-year board meeting, 19 April 1955; vol. 3 Aitkinson to annual meeting Sept. 1959; 'Business and Government Listen to This Consumers' Voice,' *Canadian Business*, Feb. 1956, 73; UGA, Helen Abell collection, 'Special Study of Ontario Farm Homes and Homemakers' Progress Report no. 1, Table 1, p 35

44 A comparison of the CAC treatment of manufacturing tariffs and marketing boards in their brief before the Royal Commission on Canada's Economic Prospects well illustrates this difference. NAC, RG 33, vol. 95, RCCEP, March 1956

45 On the shift in economists' attention from allocation to aggregates see Robinson, *Economics*, 38–40.

Chapter 5: Borrowing to Buy

1 Interviews: Ella Smith, Harriet Fraser, Susan Taylor, Patricia Cliff, Tina Wall; Letters: Hazel Beech, Sheila Maurice; see the classic work, Glen Elder, *Children of the Depression* (Chicago: University of Chicago Press, 1974).

2 Jacob Ziegel, 'Legal Aspects of the Regulation of Consumer Credit,' in *Consumer Credit and the Lower Income Family* (Ottawa: Canadian Welfare Council, 1970) 1; 'Final Report of the Select Committee of the Ontario Legislature on Consumer Credit,' *Ontario Sessional Papers* no. 85, 10 June 1965; Dian N.

Cohen, 'Consumer Credit: Strength or Weakness in a Changing Economy?'
CB, April 1958, 64; Canada, Special Joint Committee of the Senate and
House of Commons, (hereafter Joint Committee), *Hearings*, Appendix H,
Retail Council of Canada, 458; RCBF, Brief from Canadian Retail Federation,
31–2; 'Credit – Good or Bad?' *HGR*, 12 June 1957, 44; OHA, 570 – Corporate
Relations, 'Financial Assistance Sales Programs,' 29 Jan. 1965, 17; on this
transformation generally see Avner Offer and Sue Bowden, 'Gratification
and Prudence: The United States and Britain, 1945–1989' (unpublished
paper, Rutgers Center for Historical Analysis, Nov. 1991).

3 Durable consumer expenditures: 1948, $934 million, 1960, $2664 million;
consumer credit outstanding: 1948, $835 million, 1960, $4020 million, from
E.P. Neufeld, 'The Economic Significance of Consumer Credit,' in Jacob
Ziegel and R.E. Olley, eds., *Consumer Credit in Canada* (Saskatoon: University
of Saskatchewan, 1966) 13, Table II, based on Dominion Bureau of Statistics,
National Accounts – Income and Expenditure by Quarters, 1947–61, 20–7; Cana-
dian Consumer Council, 'Report to the Minister of Consumer and Corporate
Affairs on Consumer Credit,' 1969, 1; Debra Frazer and Janet McClaine,
Credit: A Mortgage for Life (Ottawa: Canadian Council for Social Development,
1981)

4 As a portion of GNP, Canadian consumer credit outstanding had been less
than in the United States through the late 1940s and the 1950s, but by the
early 1960s Canadian rates matched and then passed the American. As a
ratio of personal disposable income, Canadian consumer debt had been
notably lower through the fifties, but by 1963 Canadian and U.S. patterns
had converged. Joint Committee, *Report* (1967) 34; William C. Hood, *Financing Economic Activity in Canada*, prepared for the Royal Commission on Canada's Economic Prospects (Ottawa: Queen's Printer, 1958) chap. 5,
'Consumer Finance,' 134–5; Neufeld, 'Economic Significance,' 12–15, 19;
RCBF, *Report* (1964), 205; OHA, 570, Corporate Relations 'Credit & Expenditure on Consumer Durable Goods, Canada & USA'

5 Hood, *Financing Economic Activity*, chap. 4 and 130; RCBF, *Report* 14–15;
Neufeld 'Economic Significance,' 13; many such statements are attributed to
James Coyne, governor of the Bank of Canada from 1955 to 1961. See J.E.
Coyne, 'Strong Roots for New Growth,' remarks prepared for delivery at the
Annual Meeting of the Newfoundland Board of Trade, St John's, 31 Jan.
1961; the version Betty Lee transcribed was 'personal earnings might be
better spent in financing Canadian development rather than acquiring shiny
new cars and taking trips to the tropics.' QUA, Donald C. MacDonald Papers,
box 63, subject files

6 Interviews: Joan Coffey, Emma Boyd, Mary Kippen; Letter: Hazel Beech; the

consumer durables revolution Martha Onley documented for the United
States in the 1920s, the shift upward in demand at each income and price
level, appears to have happened in Canada thirty years later, Martha Onley,
Buy Now, Pay Later: Advertising, Credit and Consumer Durables in the 1920s
(Chapel Hill: University of North Carolina Press, 1991) 86, 182; Gerald
Fortin, 'The Social Meaning and Implications of Consumer Credit,' in Ziegel
and Olley, eds., *Consumer Credit*, 32; Joint Committee, *Report*, 32

7 Interviews: Mary Kippen, Emma Boyd, Lily Hansen

8 E.P. Neufeld, *Financial System of Canada* (Toronto: Macmillan, 1972) 105;
Interviews: Allison Simpson, Mary Kippen; the ceiling specified by the Bank
Act on personal loans was evaded by adding the 6 per cent to the opening
loan balance rather than recalculating the interest on the declining sum
owing as the loan was repaid.

9 Joan Coffey of Coquitlam, for example, overrode her husband's caution and
cashed or leveraged three separate insurance policies to finance their first
car in 1950. Interview: Joan Coffey

10 RCBF, *Report*, 204; Joint Committee, *Report*, 67; Neufeld, 'Economic Aspects,'
5–7; Neufeld, *Financial System*, 550, 105, 324, 339, 341; 'Panel on Sources of
Consumer Credit,' in Ziegel and Olley, eds., *Consumer Credit*, 57–8, 67; Ziegel,
'The Legal Regulation of Consumer Credit,' in ibid., 74; Ziegel, 'Legal Aspects,' 11, 37; NSRCCB, *Report*, 22 Feb. 1965, 150; Hood, *Financing Economic
Activity*, 132–3; 'Home Improvement Loans Now Being Promoted,' *HGR*,
16 April 1958, 8; Ann Finlayson and Sandra Martin, *Card Tricks* (Toronto: Penguin, 1993); NAC, RG 20 778, EFIR, 23–100–S26, Robert Simpson Co., Interview with T.L. Robinette, 4 June 1959, and with Morgan Reid, 30 July 1959

11 RCBF, *Hearings*, J.A. Sawyer, Canadian Retail Federation 5774–5 and Cana-
dian Retail Federation Brief 38; Royal Commission on Taxation, Brief of the
Consumers' Association of Canada, Nov. 1963, 17; 'Is Consumer Credit
Good?' *Marketing*, 14 Jan. 1955, 42; Ruth P. Mack, 'Trends in American Consumption and the Aspiration to Consume,' *American Economic Review* Proceedings and Papers, 46, 2 (May) 1956, 55–68, widely cited in submissions to
Canadian Royal Commissions in the 1960s; Robert Campbell, *The Grand
Illusion: The Keynesian Synthesis in Canada* 195 (Peterborough, ON: Broadview,
1987)

12 John Kenneth Galbraith, *The Affluent Society* (Boston: Houghton Mifflin,
1958) 205–6

13 Robert Ferber, *Factors Influencing Durable Goods Purchases* (Urbana: University
of Illinois University Press, 1955); F. Thomas Juster, 'Durable Goods Purchase Intentions, Purchasers and the Consumer Planning Horizon,' in Nelson Foote, ed., *Household Decision-Making* (New York: New York University

Press, 1961); George Katona and Eva Mueller, 'A Study of Purchase Decision,' in Lincoln H. Clark, ed., *Consumer Behavior: The Dynamics of Consumer
Reaction* (New York: New York University Press, 1955)

14 An influential review of these issues in the late 1950s was Warren L. Smith,
'Consumer Instalment Credit,' *American Economic Review* 47 (Dec. 1957) 966–
84; Neufeld, 'Economic Significance,' 17–19, 24–7; RCBF, Canadian Retail
Federation Brief, 41–7; 'Consumer Credit Situation Clarified in Over-all
Economy,' *Marketing*, 30 Jan. 1954, 14; Richard L. Edsall, 'Big Question in
Consumer Debt Is – How Much Is too Much?' *CB*, Aug. 1956, 32–6; Dian
Cohen provided a Canadian context for the U.S. Federal Reverse Board
Study reviewed in Warren Smith, above, in 'Consumer Credit: Strength or
Weakness in a Changing Economy?, *CB*, April 1958, 64–72; H.S. Houthakker,
'The Permanent Income Hypothesis,' *American Economic Review* 48 (June
1958) 396–404; Houthakker and L.D. Taylor, *Consumer Demand in the United
States* (Cambridge: Harvard University Press, 1970); Onley, *Buy Now*, 133

15 Elizabeth Ackroyd, 'Commentary' in Ziegel and Olley, eds., *Consumer Credit*,
83–4; RCBF, *Report*, 433, 476; Joint Committee, *Hearings*, 1964–5, Testimony
of Gerald Bouey, 96–7, 122–3; NAC, RG 33/35, vol. 50, file 3–31–1, RCCEP,
Secondary Industries, C.V. Fessenden to D.V. LePan, 27 Dec. 1955, and vol.
88, E.G. Burton, president of Simpson's Ltd., 'The Department Store in
Canada,' 2 Feb. 1956; 'Expect Credit Controls to Cut Down Sales,' *HGR*, 12
Dec. 1956; 'Credit Control on Consumers not in Sight,' *Financial Post*, 28 July
1956, 1; RCBF, Canadian Retail Federation Brief, 46–51

16 W. Irwin Gillespie, 'Postwar Canadian Fiscal Policy Revisited, 1945–1975,'
Canadian Tax Journal 27, 3 (June 1979) 274–6; Robert M. Will, 'Postwar Fiscal
Policy in Canada: A Study of Policy and Policy Lags,' Staff Study for RCBF,
Nov. 1962; H. Scott Gordon, 'A Twenty Year Perspective: Some Reflections
on the Keynesian Revolution in Canada,' in S.F. Kaliski, ed., *Canadian Eco-
nomic Policy since the War* (Montreal: Canadian Trade Committee, 1966);
Galbraith, *Affluent Society*, 228; CAC, Brief to the Royal Commission on Taxa-
tion, Nov. 1963 18–22; RCBF, *Report*, 524; Campbell, *Grand Illusion*, 201;
Offer and Bowden, 'Gratification and Prudence,' 23–5

17 Hood, *Financing of Economic Activity*, 192–4, 154–63; the quote is from 194;
'Confused Loan Interpretations Seen as a Major Hindrance to Built-in Appliances,' *HGR*, 13 June 1956, 1, 16; David E. Bond and Ronald A. Shearer, *The
Economics of the Canadian Financial System* (Scarborough: Prentice-Hall, 1972)
50–1

18 Joint Committee, *Hearings*, Appendix A, Brief by G.K. Bouey, chief of research for the Bank of Canada, 114–15, and his responses to questions, 88–9,
104; Appendix P, Brief by Fédération de Québec des Unions régionales des

Caisses populaires Desjardins, 606–7, all following closely the annual reports of the Bank of Canada for 1956 and 1957; EFIR 778 Robert Simpson Company, interview on response to Bank of Canada suasion by T.L. Robinette, 21 Feb. 1957; the final quote is from Joint Committee, *Report*, 80

19 As examples see *Hansard*, 5 March 1957, 'Interest Act, amendment to establish maximum rate' 1895–1903; 10 Jan. 1958, 3161–8; 5 June 1958, 857–93, and 27 June 1958, 1730–7; 12 Feb. 1959, 948–81, and 26 May 1959, 4029–36.

20 J. Harvey Perry, *A Fiscal History of Canada: The Postwar Years* (Toronto: Canadian Tax Foundation, 1989) 51–9; 161–5; Denis Smith, *Rogue Tory: The Life and Legend of John G. Diefenbaker* (Toronto: Macfarlane Walter and Ross, 1995) chaps 8–12; Campbell, *Grand Illusion*, 118–41; Bond and Shearer, *Economics of the Canadian Financial System*, 278–9

21 Dominion Bureau of Statistics, *Incomes, Assets and Indebtedness of Non-Farm Families in Canada 1963* Tables 47 and 58; ibid., 1958, Tables 39 and 50

22 Ibid., 1958, Table 18; RCBF, Canadian Retail Federation Brief, 3

23 UGA, Helen Abell, *Special Study of Ontario Farm Homes and Homemakers, 1959* Progress Report no. 7 (1960), 7–14, 28; H.C. Abell, *Rural Families and Their Homes* (University of Waterloo, School of Urban and Regional Planning, Nov. 1971) 18–22

24 See the bemused Toronto minutes of the New Canadian Committee which met during the retail downturn of 1957–8, AO, T. Eaton Company, series 69, box 27; Douglas L. Gibbs, 'Low Income and Opportunity' (University of Toronto, MSW thesis 1966) vi, x, 34, 59, 74; 'In-store Payments Crux of Credit Question,' *HGR*, 18 May 1964, 24; Cynthia Wright, 'Cross-border Shoppers: Eaton's and the Postwar "New Canadian" Consumer Market in Toronto' (unpublished paper)

25 NSRCCB, *Report*, 205, 331; BC Hydro Archives, BC Electric, *Consumer Attitude Survey* (May 1961) 13–15; Joint Committee, *Report* (1967) 82; RCBF, *Report* (1964) 21; Ziegel, 'Legal Aspects,' 11; Wing Ming Wai, 'Low Income and Opportunity' (University of Toronto, MSW thesis, 1966) 46–57. In the forties and still in the sixties, those who were asked what credit should or would be used for (as opposed to what they had bought on credit) noted conventional contemporary necessities, in the forties a refrigerator or washing machine, in the sixties education or medical bills; *Canada's Market for Home Equipment* (Toronto: Maclean-Hunter, 1945) 8; *CCLIF* 92

26 Ziegel, 'Legal Aspects,' 19; Betty Lee's articles on consumer credit are compiled in QUA, Donald C. MacDonald Papers, box 63, subject files.

27 Ziegel, 'Legal Aspects,' 14–15; Beryl Plumptre papers, private collection, Beryl Plumptre, 'The Role of Finance in Family Life,' address to the Conference on Social Welfare Papers, Vancouver, June 1966, 8; RCBF, *Report*, 31,

559; Joint Committee, *Report*, citing evidence from the Army Benevolent Fund Board, 84–5; Dorothy McArton, 'Problems in the Consumer Credit Field and Their Solution,' in Ziegel and Olley, eds., *Consumer Credit*, 92–3. McArton was director of the Family Bureau of Greater Winnipeg. The Fortin and Tremblay Quebec finding that 20 per cent of wage earners had credit problems was frequently cited. See Marc Adelard Tremblay and Gerald Fortin, *Les Comportements économiques de la famille salariée du Québec* (Quebec: Laval, 1967), especially chap. 9; an inquiry in Hamilton found that 25 per cent of families studied had histories of debt litigation, *CCLIF.*

28 On lending rates Moreira invoked Psalm 15, 'Lord who shall abide in thy tabernacle? who shall dwell in thy holy hill? ... He that putteth not out his money to usury, nor taketh reward against the innocent. He that doesth these things shall never be moved.' NSRCCB, *Report* 321, 323, 324, 331; McArton, 'Problems in the Consumer Credit Field,' 91

29 Renée Vautelet, 'The Final Arbitrator, Friend or Foe?' *IC*, July 1963, 107–10; Joint Committee, *Report*, ix, 16, *Hearings*, 1964–5, 502, testimony of J.S. Enns, MP for Portage-Neepawa, answering questions concerning the brief of the Family Bureau of Greater Winnipeg; McAnton, 'Problems in the Consumer Credit Field,' 106; the critique of the corrosive effects of luxury goods, especially for working people was, of course, not new. See David Monod, *Store Wars* (Toronto: University of Toronto Press, 1996) 238; Vance Packard, *The Waste Makers* (New York: David McKay, 1960); David Caplovitz, *The Poor Pay More* (Boston: Free Press, 1963)

30 'The Disclosure Controversy,' in Ziegel and Olley, eds., *Consumer Credit*, intervention by David Croll, 139; and in the same volume, Fortin, 'Social Meaning,' 34–6; and recommending redistribution, McAnton, 'Problems in the Consumer Credit Field,' 95; on the need for education, NSRCCB, *Report*, 330–1; 'Final Report of the Select Committee of the Ontario Legislature on Consumer Credit' (1965) 10; Joint Committee, *Hearings* (1964–5) 786; Plumptre, 'Role of Finance'; Joint Committee, *Report* (1967) 4, 26; Clifford Leeb, 'Financial Assistance in a Private Family Agency' (University of Toronto, MSW thesis, 1963); Ross A. McClellan, 'The Development of the Credit Counselling Service of Metropolitan Toronto' (University of Toronto, MSW thesis, 1967)

31 Joint Committee, *Hearings* (1964–5), Appendix P, Brief from Fédération de Québec des Unions régionales des Caisses populaires Desjardins, 599; testimony of Gerald Bouey, 80–1; both of Bouey's sceptical questioners were westerners: Nicolas Mandziuk, MP for the Manitoba riding of Marquette, and Wesley Stambaugh, a Senator from Bruce, Alberta.

32 The clear aim of the Canadian Retail Federation brief to the Royal Commis-

sion on Banking and Finance was to shift the discourse in this way. Note especially pages 8, 34, 46–7 of the brief. A.J. McKichan of the Retail Council of Canada, addressing the Saskatchewan Conference on Consumer Credit, 'The Sources of Consumer Credit,' in Ziegel and Olley, eds., *Consumer Credit*, 59 noted the negative consequences of the early 1950s 'diversion of income from the purchase of "domestic capital goods"' through credit controls; see similarly, 'Consumer Credit Is Essential to Stable Economic Growth,' *HGR*, 8 Oct. 1962, 1, 3; 'Cites Credit's Role in Increasing Sales,' *HGR*, 11 May 1960, 20; OHA, 570, Corporate Relations, 'Financial Assistance Sales Programs,' 29 Jan. 1965; on the inappropriateness of moral judgments about household investment decisions, Canadian Retail Federation Brief to RCBF, 35; RCBF, *Hearings*, testimony from Canadian Consumer Loan Association, 5520–1; Carne H. Bray, executive vice-president, Federated Council of Sales Finance Companies, 'Panel on the Sources of Consumer Credit,' 51.

33 *RCBF*, 559, 14
34 Royal Commission on Taxation, Brief by the CAC, Nov. 1963, 2–3, 12–13; NAC, MG 28 I 200 vol. 5, file 60A, CAC, Arthur J.R. Smith, director, Economic Council of Canada, to CAC Annual Meeting 2 June 1966, 6
35 Monod, *Store Wars*, 162–8
36 Interviews: Gerd Evans, Lily Hansen, Sally Tobe, Ella Smith
37 NSRCCB, *Report*, 182–3; revolving credit provided the retailer with the same advantages of regular contact, 'Revolving Credit Results Are Good,' *HGR*, 2 May 1956, 5; 'Merchants Approve Revolving Credit,' *FP*, 12 May 1956
38 Interviews: Joan Niblock, Ella Smith, Joan Coffey, Mary Kippen; NSRCCB, *Report*, 162–7, 317, 356–7, 409; Ziegel, 'Legal Regulation,' 75, 79, and Arthur Moreira, 'Problems in the Consumer Credit Field and Their Solution,' in Ziegel and Olley, eds., *Consumer Credit*, 114–15; Joint Committee, *Hearings* (1964–5), testimony of Jacob Ziegel, 391
39 NSRCCB, *Report*, 198–200
40 Hood, *Financing of Economic Activity*, 164–5; NSRCCB, *Report*, 197–205, 313–24; 'bribes' 320; 'false pretenses' 205; Canadian public discourse on this question was a good deal more explicit than in the United States, where Senator Paul Douglas, while campaigning for many years, and in the end effectively, for interest rate disclosure, remained for political reasons reluctant to make complicity between retailers and finance companies as issue for discussion. See Mark V. Nadel, *The Politics of Consumer Protection* (Indianapolis: Bobbs Merrill, 1971) 130–7.
41 Warren R. James, *The People's Senator* (Vancouver: Douglas and McIntyre, 1990); David Croll in discussion of 'The Disclosure Controversy,' 140
42 NSRCCB, *Report*, 310

43 Hood, *Financing of Economic Activity*, 196–7, 182 n. 61, 172; Joint Committee, *Report* (1967) 78–9; RCBF, *Hearings* (1962), J.A. Sawyer, University of Toronto School of Business questioned by James Douglas Gibson, expressing exasperation about 'misallocation of resources,' 28 Sept. 1962, 5752

44 NAC, MG 28 I 200 CAC, vol. 2, annual meeting 1957, executive minutes 1957; vol. 3 annual meeting 1959, presidential address and report of the economics committee, 1961; Beryl Plumptre papers, private collection, Beryl Plumptre requesting that Bill S-4 be referred to the Senate Banking and Commerce committee, 17 March 1961; Joint Committee, *Hearings* (1964–5),. Appendix E, Brief from CAC.

45 RCBF, *Hearings*, CAC testimony by Mrs W.T. Wilson, 25 Oct. 1962, questioned by W.A.C. MacIntosh, 6634–5; Joint Committee on Consumer Credit, *Report*, 54, *Hearings* (1964–5) 294–7, 514–15; 'Submission of the Consumers' Association of Canada to the Royal Commission on Banking and Finance' Aug. 1962; Neufeld, *Financial System of Canada*, 332, 550; Ziegel, 'Legal Aspects,' 13, 21; Royal Commission on Taxation, Brief of the CAC, Nov. 1963

46 RCBF, *Hearings*, testimony of R.W. Macaulay, 7163; the objections are summarized in Joint Committee, *Hearings* Appendix F, Brief of the Executive Council, Canadian Chamber of Commerce, 344–5, and are stated as well in briefs to both the RCBF and the Joint Committee by the Federated Council of Sales Finance Companies and the Consumer Loan Association, the two lobby groups for the consumer loan sector; see as well their representatives' contributions to the discussion, 'The Disclosure Controversy.'

47 Joint Committee, *Hearings* (1964–5), testimony by Mrs A.G. Brewer, National Advisory Committee, CAC, 283; June Menzies, participating in 'The Disclosure Controversy,' 158

48 Ziegel, 'Legal Aspects,' 20; Canadian Consumer Credit Council, 'Report to the Minister of Consumer and Corporate Affairs on Consumer Credit,' 1969, 4; RCBF, *Report*, 382, 562; Bond and Shearer, *Economics of the Canadian Financial System* (1972) 247, 327, (1995) 375; Neufeld, *Financial System of Canada*, 550; on the subsequent generation's dilemma with consumer credit, see Finlayson and Martin, *Card Tricks*. By 1991 consumer loan and sales finance companies accounted for only 7 per cent of consumer credit balances outstanding.

Chapter 6: Inter/national Style

1 Clive Dilnot, 'The State of Design History,' *Design Issues* 1, 1 (spring 1984) 11, 16

2 Tony Fry, 'A Geography of Power: Design History and Marginality,' *Design*

Issues 6, 1 (fall 1989) 24–5; a good array of the contrasting forms are presented in Jeremy Aynsley, *Nationalism and Internationalism* (London: Victoria and Albert Museum, 1993); a similar argument could be made about the appearance of abstract expressionism in Canada, David Howard, 'From Emma Lake to Los Angeles: Modernism on the Margins,' in John O'Brien, ed., *The Flat Side of the Landscape* (Saskatoon: Mendel Art Gallery, 1989) 41–9, or about nationalism and internationalism in New York modernism during the Second World War, Serge Guilbaut, *How New York Stole the Idea of Modern Art* (Chicago: University of Chicago Press, 1983) 59–99.

3 Virginia Wright, 'Design in Central and Eastern Canada,' in Robert McKaskell, et al., *Achieving the Modern: Canadian Abstract Painting and Design in the 1950s* (Winnipeg: Winnipeg Art Gallery, 1993) 121–2, and *Seduced and Abandoned: Modern Furniture* Designers in Canada – *The First Fifty Years* (Toronto: Art Gallery at Harbourfront, 1985) 3

4 Herbert Read, 'Introduction,' in *The Practice of Design* (London: Lund Humphries, 1946) 21; Philip Johnson, 'History of Machine Art,' in *Machine Art* (New York: Museum of Modern Art, 1934)

5 Alan Jarvis, *The Things We See Indoors and Out* (Harmondsworth: Penguin, 1947) 55

6 D.W. Buchanan, 'Design in Industry,' *IC* 47 (July 1946) 313–15; Virginia Wright, *Modern Furniture Design in Canada, 1920–1970* (Toronto: University of Toronto Press, 1997) 120, characterizes Buchanan's approach to modern design as reductive and dogmatic.

7 NAC, RG 20 997, NIDC General Correspondence, 1946–61, D.W. Buchanan, address to the CMA, 17 July 1946; Jarvis, *Things We See*, 62; Thomas Fisher Rare Book Room, Robarts Library, University of Toronto, Jarvis Collection, MS 171, box 22, Jarvis, 'What's All This Fuss about Modern Design,' *Target*, 9 Oct. 1945, 6–10; Peter Dormer, *The Meanings of Modern Design* (London: Thames and Hudson, 1990) 54

8 Jarvis, *Things We See*, 41

9 Robin Kinross, 'Herbert Read's *Art and Industry*: A History,' *Journal of Design History* 1, 1 (1988) 38–9, 44–5, 48–9

10 Read, 'Introduction,' 9; Jarvis, *Things We See*, 27

11 Peter Wollin, *Raiding the Icebox* (London: Verso, 1993) 104

12 Alfred Barr, foreword in Johnson, *Machine Art*; Peter Dormer, *Design since 1945* (London: Thames and Hudson, 1993) 199–201

13 Herbert Read, *Art and Industry* (London: Faber and Faber, 1953) 51, 52, 54; Humphrey Carver, *Compassionate Landscape* (Toronto: University of Toronto Press, 1975) 78

14 Robert Fulford, 'What Is a Designer Anyway? And Why Is He Fighting in

Your Living Room?' *CHG*, Sept. 1958, 22; Jane Fiske McCullough, 'New Problems of Style in Design,' *Industrial Design*, 7 March 1960, 36–7; Arthur B. Gallion, 'The Industrial Designer and the Arts,' RAIC *Journal* 28 (Jan. 1951) 3–4; Alan Colquhoun, 'Typology and Design Method,' *Arena*, June 1967, 13; Kinross, 'Herbert Read's,' 37; Jonathan M. Woodham, 'Managing British Design Reform I: Fresh Perspectives on the Early Years of the Council of Industrial Design,' *Journal of Design History* 9, 1 (1966) 55–64

15 Read, *Art and Industry*, 55

16 Marshall Berman, 'The Experience of Modernity,' in John Thackara, *Design after Modernism* (London: Thames and Hudson, 1988) 45; David Pye, *The Nature and Aesthetics of Design* 1978 (London: Barrie and Jenkins, 14, 89; Fran Hannah and Tim Putnam, 'Taking Stock in Design History,' *Block* 3 (1980) 31; John Heskett, *Industrial Design* (London: Thames and Hudson, 1980) 104

17 In Donald Buchanan, industrial design had an advocate with powerful political patrons. As the son of a Liberal senator, he was well connected in governing circles. After a decade in the city he knew something about how official Ottawa worked and, through his experience with the National Film Society, about building cultural institutions. Gloria Lesser, 'Biography and Bibliography of the Writings of Donald William Buchanan (1908–1966),' *Journal of Canadian Art History* 5, 2 (1981) 129–31; John B. Collins, 'Design in Industry,' *Material History Bulletin* 27 (spring 1988) 7; Thomas Fisher Rare Book Room, Jarvis Collection, Tape 9, Interview with Alison Grant Ignatieff by Elizabeth Chisholm; Interview with Beryl Plumptre, by Joy Parr, Ottawa, 26 Nov. 1991

18 Claxton was interested in Canadian art. He had become a member of the Art Association of Montreal in the 1920s. Through his sister-in-law, the painter Anne Savage, and her friend A.Y. Jackson, and through private study, he developed his knowledge of the Group of Seven. He had a particular interest in the Montreal painter James Morrice, whose biography Buchanan had published in 1936. Later in life, his interventions helped effect the Massey Commission. He served as the first chairman of the Canada Council. David Jay Bercuson, *True Patriot: The Life of Brooke Claxton, 1898–1960* (Toronto: University of Toronto Press, 1993) 54, 57, 111, 141, 200, 275; NGA, 7.4–D Design in Industry, file 1, Claxton to McCurry, 10 April 1946

19 NIDC, General Correspondence, 997 13–2, vol. 1, Donald Buchanan, 'Design in Industry,' 3 pp, n.d., but referred to in surrounding correspondence of April 1946. Peter Day states that this proposal was commissioned in June 1947 and delivered in 1948, but both the Department of Trade and Commerce and the National Gallery files locate the work in the early spring of 1946. Day uses Norman Hay's writing in the late 1970s, and recollections in

the 1980s, as evidence that Buchanan wanted industrial design to be under the purview of the National Research Council and considered the Department of Trade and Commerce or the National Gallery as second choices. Peter Day, 'The Future Can Be Ours,' in Peter Day and Linda Lewis, *Art in Everyday Life* (Toronto: Summerhill Press, 1988) 133–4, 149

20 NGA, Design in Industry, file 1, C.J. Mackenzie to Brooke Claxton, 17 April 1946

21 Ibid., McCurry to Claxton, 16 April 1946

22 NIDC, General Correspondence 997, notes by copy of Buchanan's address to CMA, 4 June 1946; Buchanan speech to CMA, 4 June 1946, 5 pp.; Buchanan's and Jarvis's speeches were both summarized in *IC* 47 (July 1946) 313–7; 1 John B. Collins, 'Design for Use, Design for the Millions: Proposals and Options for the National Industrial Design Council, 1948–1960' (MA thesis, Carleton University, 1986) 14; G.R. Heasman to Buchanan, 15 June 1946; K.E. Chamberlain, *Design by Canadians: A Bibliographic Guide* (Richmond, BC: privately published, 1994)

23 NGA, Design in Industry, file 1, H.O. McCurry to Read, telegram 29 March 1946; McCurry to Buchanan, telegram 5 April 1946; reference in Read report to letter from Buchanan 15 April 1946; NGA, Design in Industry, file 1, Herbert Read, 'The Future of Industrial Design in Canada: A Preliminary Review of the Problem,' 12 June 1946, 2, 3

24 NGA, Design in Industry, file 1, James MacKinnon to Buchanan, 22 March 1947; C.D. Howe to Buchanan, 11 April 1947

25 D.W. Buchanan, 'Canadian Design Index,' *IC*, Jan. 1948, 141, for his title; on the small allocation for an industrial design department at the gallery, D.W. Buchanan, *How Industrial Design Can Help Your Business* (Ottawa: NIDC, 1949) copy in NAC, RG 77/88/89/045, vol. 6, file 3–12–N4–2, pt 10, and similarly Charles Tisdall, 'Industrial Design in Canada,' *CW*, June 1952, 30

26 Donald Buchanan, 'Design Index,' *Canadian Art* 5 (Christmas 1947) 87–9; Buchanan, 'Canadian Design Index,' 141; *Canadian Art* 5, (spring 1948) 194–5; Wright, *Modern Furniture*, 114, 116; Donald Buchanan, 'Completing the Pattern of Modern Living,' *Canadian Art* 6 (spring 1949) 112; Buchanan, 'Design in Industry: The Canadian Picture,' RAIC *Journal* 24 (July 1947) 235; for Jarvis on the same theme, see *Things We See*, 59.

27 Council of Industrial Design, *Design Quiz* (London: Lund Humphries, 1946). There is a copy in Jarvis Collection, MS 171, Box 22; NGA 5.5–D Design Centre Exhibition, 1948, *Design Quiz, A Chance to Test Your Taste* (Ottawa: National Gallery, 1948); NAC, RG 20 A 4 1433 file George Englesmith, George Englesmith to Donald Buchanan, 11 Sept. 1947

28 Donald W. Buchanan, 'Design for Selling and Selling Design,' *Food for*

Thought 11 (April 1951) 8; NGA, Design in Industry, file 2, D.B. Cruickshank, 'Industrial Design: What Are Canadians Doing About It?' speech dated 7 June 1949; *Canadian Art* 6 (Christmas 1948) 59

29 NGA, 5.5–D 'Design in Industry Exhibition,' 1946, commentary by Jocelyn Moore Classey, dated 28 Jan. 1946, but by context likely 1947; Jarvis, *Things We See*, 3, 5, 30, inside back fly leaf; the similar organization in France had a broader educative compass, merging design education with consumer education generally. See Martine Segelan, 'The Salon des Arts Menagères, 1923–1983,' *Journal of Design History* 7, 4 (1994) 267–75.

30 The brief of the Association of Canadian Industrial Designers states this position, see Paul Litt, *The Muses, the Masses, and the Massey Commission* (Toronto: University of Toronto Press, 1992) 84–96.

31 Dick Hedbige, 'Towards a Cartography of Taste,' *Block* 4 (1981) 53; this is not how Buchanan read the sellers' market, 'Design in Industry,' 235

32 The grant was passed as a supplementary appropriation for $9500. NIDC, General Correspondence, 997 file 5–1112, 'Canada Needs More Industrial Designers', 3, enclosure in W.O. McCurry to M.W. Mackenzie, 2 Feb. 1948

33 T.E. Matthews, 'Design in Industry: A Canadian Designer's Picture,' RAIC *Journal* 24 (July 1947) 241; Buchanan, 'Design in Industry,' 236; NGA, Design in Industry, Association of Industrial Designers of Canada statement, 3 July 1947; Buchanan, 'Design for Selling,' 8–9; NGA, Design in Industry, file 3, 2-page statement by Buchanan on foreign competition with Canadian products, marked 'Dec. 1950?;' Paul Reilly, 'The Challenge of Pop,' *Architectural Review*, Oct. 1961, 255–6; Thomas Fisher Rare Book Room, Jarvis Collection, MS 171, tape 12, Dorothy Cameron on the internationalism of Alan Jarvis; Allan Collier, 'Design in Western Canada,' in McKaskell et al., *Achieving the Modern*, 103; Penny Sparke, *Consultant Design* (London: Pembridge Press, 1983) 58; Christine Morley, 'Homemakers and Design Advice in the Postwar Period,' in Tim Putnam and Charles Newton, eds., *Household Choices* (London: Futures, 1990) 89; 'Progress in Design Promotion,' *Food for Thought* 12 (April 1952) 19; Collins, 'Design for Use,' 18; Paddy Maguire, 'Designs on Reconstruction: British Business, Market Structures, and the Role of Design in Post-War Recovery,' *Journal of Design History* 4, 1 (1991) 15–29

34 National Gallery, *Design for Use*, a survey of design of Canadian manufactured goods for home and office, for sports and outdoors, including for the Design in Industry exhibition, 1947, 24

35 NIDC, *How the Industrial Designer Can Help You in Your Business* (Ottawa, NIDC: 1949) 5 (note the handi-chef described as 'a Canadian portable cooker' featured on p. 22 by the caption, 'manufacturers can give practical encouragement to industrial designers'); NIDC, *The Story behind the Design Centre:*

Encouraging Better Design in Canadian Products (Ottawa NIDC: 1955) 2; Charles Tisdall, 'Industrial Design in Canada,' *CW*, June 1952, 30; NIDC, *The Story of Canadian Design* (Ottawa NIDC: 1952)

36 NIDC, General Correspondence, 997 file 5–2190, Vincent Massey, Chairman, National Gallery of Canada, to Alphonse Fournier, Minister of Public Works, 23 March 1948; ibid., file 5–1112, H.O. McCurry to M.W. Mackenzie, 2 Feb. 1948; for budgets see ibid., and NGA, Design in Industry, files 1 and 5

37 NIDC, General Correspondence, 997 file 5–112 'Canada Needs to Encourage Its Industrial Designers,' 1, appended to H.O. McCurry to M.W. Mackenzie, 2 Feb. 1948; AO, T. Eaton Company, series 69, vol. 19, Merchandise Department minutebooks, Dec. 1947, ibid., box 19, Design Index and Awards; NIDC 1946–60, B.E. Mercer on meeting about NIDC, 21 Feb. 1949; 'Editorial,' RAIC *Journal*, July 1947; T.E. Matthews, 'Design in Industry: A Canadian Designer's Picture,' ibid., July 1947, 241; 'Industrial Design Session,' *IC* 50 (July 1949) 217; H.C. Eastman, 'Recent Canadian Economic Policy: Some Alternatives,' *Canadian Journal of Economics and Political Science* 18, 2 (March 1952) 144

38 Moffat was a man of modernist sympathies who, as an associate of the Royal Photographic Society, exhibited his art photography internationally. Charles L. Moffat, 'Design in Industry: A Canadian Industrialist's Picture,' RAIC *Journal* 24 (July 1947) 250–1; D.W.B., 'Introducing Manufacturers to Designers,' *Canadian Art* 7 (Christmas 1949) 55–7; *How the Industrial Designer Can Help You in Your Business* (Ottawa: NIDC, 1949), Foreword and 3, 9; NGCA, Design in Industry file 2, James Ferguson and John Low-Beer, 'Survey of Design Requirements and Conditions in the Canadian Furniture Industry,' 12 July 1950, summarized in 'Cooperate with Industry in Promoting Design Sources,' *CW* (Sept. 1950) 30, 52, 66, 77; Wright, *Modern Furniture*, 129–30

39 'Industrial Design Competition Announced,' *Foreign Trade* 8 (25 Nov. 1950) 898; 'Design: To Sell Canada,' *SN*, 6 March 1951, 12

40 NIDC, General Correspondence 997, jury report on 1951 competition signed by Serge Chermayeff, 27 March 1951; the report was summarized in Donald Buchanan, 'Reflections on a Competition for Product Designs,' *Canadian Art* 8 (summer 1951) 168, and 'Canadian Design,' *CB*, May 1951, 76, 94; the jury consisted of Ernest Cormier, architect and engineer; L.V. Randell, professor of art, University of Montreal; J.K.E. Cox, from Alcan; W.J. Le Clair from the Lumberman's Association; and Chermayeff: *CW*, April 1951, 66–7

41 Buchanan, 'Reflections,' 168, 170; NGA, Design in Industry, file 3, E.J. Allaire, G.L. Patton, and W.B. Miller, letter of 23 April 1951; 'Canada Seeks Design Values,' *CW*, June 1951, 27

42 'National Industrial Design Competition,' RAIC *Journal* 28 (Oct. 1951) 313–14; NIDC, General Correspondence 997, 1952 competition; 'Progress in Design Promotion,' *Food for Thought* 12 (April 1952) 18–19

43 NGA, Design in Industry, file 3 W.A. Trott, 'Report on Possible Development of Regional Activities and Consolidation of the NIDC,' received 17 May 1951; Collins, 'Design for Use,' 40

44 NIDC, General Correspondence 997, Report of Walter Bowker, attached to letter to Floyd Chalmers, Chair of NIDC, 4 Aug. 1951; notes on discussions between Bowker and B.C. Butler, Aug. 1951

45 NAC, MG 28 I230, vol. 116, CMA, file on Industrial Design, 1950–4, J.T. Sirrett, General Manager to Hugh Crombie, President, 18 Sept. 1951; results of 1952 questionnaire on industrial design; memo of meeting of Whitelaw, Frechette, and Chalmers, 3 Feb. 1954, and Chalmers' reply 25 Feb. 1954; NIDC, General Correspondence, 997 file 13–2 vol. 7, report on reorganization of NIDC, 1953; ibid., 997, O.J. Firestone reporting on Oct. 1953 NIDC meetings; Collins, 'Design for Use,' 39

46 Henry Finkel, 'Architecture and Industrial Design: A Relative Study,' RAIC *Journal* 27 (Nov. 1950) 369; 'Design' 55 Top Winners,' *CHG*, May 1955, 29

47 David Fulton, 'Henry Finkel: Total Solutions,' *IC*, Jan. 1963, 33–4; Interview: Fred E. Moffatt; 'A Designer Decorates His own Living Room,' *CHG*, April 1954, 14–15; David Fulton, 'Sid Bersudsky: The Mathematics of Design,' *IC*, Oct. 1962, 40, 42; Allan Fenton, 'Product Design for Profit,' *CB*, May 1963, 40–50; 'Sid Bersudsky Slide Viewer Wins the $4,000 Top Prize,' *Canadian Plastics* (Jan. 1965) 26–7; Interview: John Murray

48 *How Can We Sell More Modern Furniture* (Ottawa: NIDC, Oct. 1954) 5, 6, 13, 14, quote is from 13

49 Ibid., 24; Rhodri Windsor Liscombe, *The New Spirit: Modern Architecture in Vancouver, 1938–63* (Vancouver: Douglas and McIntyre, 1997) 114–19, 129, 131, 135, 179

50 RCCEP, *Report* (Ottawa: Queen's Printer, 1957); Glen Williams, *Not for Export* (Toronto: McClelland and Stewart, 1983)

51 On the implications of short runs for the design of Canadian products, 'Industrial Design Conference,' *IC*, July 1953, 139–44; 'What the Winners Say,' *IC*, Jan. 1955, 55; 'Changing to Canadian Designs to Meet Canadian Needs,' *IC*, July 1952, 171, 173; 'Canadian Designs Solve Canadian Problems,' *Hardware in Canada*, Aug. 1952, 13; Victor Koby, 'Industrial Design: It's Losing Out in Import Race,' *Financial Post*, 5 Dec. 1953, 19; Ernest Orr, 'Creativity, Mainspring of Product Development,' *IC*, Jan. 1955, 62

52 NGA, Design in Industry, Miscellaneous Publications, report by Norman Hay on NIDC annual meeting, 2–3 April 1958; L.G. McIntosh, 'What Is Wrong

with Canadian Industrial Design?' *Product Design and Engineering,* June 1958, 22–3

Chapter 7: Maple as Modern

1 'Industrial Design Conference,' *IC,* July 1953, 142–4; Donald B. Strudley, 'Town Planning at Work,' RAIC *Journal,* Nov. 1946, 270–1; Interviews: Jan Kuypers, Howard Hemphill, and Peter Sansom; see 'Canadian Design,' *CB,* Sept. 1951, 50 for an example of Strudley's work; Virginia Wright, *Modern Furniture Design in Canada, 1920–1970* (Toronto: University of Toronto Press, 1997) 112–13 and fig. 135

2 'Imperial History,' typescript, files of Krug Furniture plant, Trinity Street, Stratford, ON; *CW,* July 1949, 56; NAC, RG 20 A4 1434, National Industrial Design Conference, McGill University, 18 Oct. 1952, Donald B. Strudley, 'Design as a Function of Management, remarks on the experiences of his own company'; Snyders of Kitchener, Ontario, in the 1930s made a line called 'Modern Maple,' by the acclaimed American industrial designer Russell Wright. Wright, *Modern Furniture,* 68 and plate 6.

3 John R. Seeley, R. Alexander Sims, and E.W. Loosely, *Crestwood Heights: A Study of the Culture of Suburban Life* (Toronto: University of Toronto Press, 1956) 58; the Musée des Arts Décoratifs de Montréal exhibition catalogue, *Design, 1935–1965: What Modern Was. Selections from the Liliane and David M. Stewart Collection* (New York: Abrams, 1991), does not mention maple, but neither does it include any Canadian designer or maker; Virginia Wright, *Seduced and Abandoned: Modern Furniture Designers in Canada – The First Fifty Years* (Toronto: Art Gallery at Harbourfront, 1985) 4; Wright, 'Design in Central and Eastern Canada,' in Robert McKaskell et al., *Achieving the Modern: Canadian Abstract Painting and Design in the 1950s* (Winnipeg: Winnipeg Art Gallery, 1993) 119; Jean Duruz, 'Laminex Dreams: Women, Suburban Comfort and the Negotiation of Meaning,' *Meanjin* 53, 1 (1996) 99; as John Heskett suggests, noting the similarity of German and British airplane and furniture design in the 1940s, design aesthetics and political ideals are not automatically associated, and 'similarities in the repertoire of forms and their functional capabilities do not imply ... that the political philosophies and social aims of the combatants were identical.' *Industrial Design* (London: Thames and Hudson, 1980) 194–5

4 Edgar Kaufmann, *Prize Designs for Modern Furniture from the International Competition for Low Cost Furniture Design* (New York: Museum of Modern Art, 1950) 14–15, 19–23; Hans Wegner, 'Furniture,' in Kathryn B. Hiesinger et al., *Design since 1945* (Philadelphia: Philadelphia Museum of Art, 1983)

118–19; Peter Dormer, *Design since 1945* (London: Thames and Hudson, 1993) 117–29

5 See the discussion in 'Inter/national Style,' Chapter 6 above.

6 Wright, *Seduced and Abandoned*; Wright, 'Design in Central and Eastern Canada,' and Allan Collier, 'Design in Western Canada,' in McKaskel et al., *Achieving the Modern*; Gloria Lesser, *École du Meuble, 1930–1950* (Montreal: Le Château Dufresne, 1989); Robert Fones, *A Spanner in the Works: The Furniture of Russell Spanner, 1950–53* (Toronto: Power Plant Art Gallery, 1990)

7 Tim Putnam and Charles Newton, eds., *Household Choices* (London: Futures, 1990), especially John Murdoch, foreword, 5; John Fiske, *Understanding Popular Culture* (London: Routledge, 1989), and *Reading Popular Culture* (London: Unwin Hyman, 1989)

8 J-C Agnew, 'Coming Up for Air: Consumer Culture in Historical Perspective,' in John Brewer and Roy Porter, eds., *Consumption and the World of Goods* (New York: Routledge, 1993) 19–39; David Halle, *Inside Culture* (Chicago: University of Chicago Press, 1993) 3–7, 159–70, 193–202, especially 193–6.

9 Michel de Certeau, *The Practice of Everyday Life* (Berkeley: University of California Press, 1984) 166

10 These questions will be addressed in more detail in chapter 8. See on 'popular productivity,' Fiske, *Understanding Popular Culture*, 142, 146; Fiske, 'Cultural Studies and the Culture of Everyday Life,' in Lawrence Grossberg et al., eds., *Cultural Studies* (New York: Routledge, 1992) 160–1; on the potentially radical politics of consumption, Judith Williamson, *Consuming Passions: The Dynamics of Popular Culture* (London: Marion Boyars, 1986) 229–32

11 Interviews: Jan Kuypers, Howard Hemphill, Peter Sansom; Robert Judson Clark, 'Cranbrook and the Search for Twentieth-Century Form,' 21, 24 and Davira Taragin, 'The History of the Cranbrook Community,' 35, 38, both in Clark and Andrea Belloli, *Design in America: The Cranbrook Vision, 1925–50* (New York: Abrams, 1983); the Imperial Saarinen photographs and price list are in the historical files at Krug Furniture, Stratford. See the Saarinen seating also in the Imperial Loyalist catalogue, no 16, 26 and 29 in the Krug collection. John Collins notes that this furniture was shown in the Robert Simpson 'Apartments of Today' display in 1940. Collins, 'Design in Industry,' *Material History Bulletin* 27 (spring 1988). The attribution to Eero is in Donald W. Buchanan, 'Design in Industry: The Canadian Picture,' RAIC *Journal* 24 (July 1947) 235. Virginia Wright states that the line was drawn by Eliel rather than Eero, but she includes no references to her source. Wright, *Modern Canadian Furniture*, 74

12 Strudley, 'Design as a Function of Management.'

13 'Natural Birch Wins High Praise among Modern Cabinet Woods,' *Furniture*

and Furnishings, March 1946; 'Where Does Atlantic Lumber Go?' *CW,* July 1953, 20; Interviews: Jan Kuypers, Howard Hemphill, Peter Sansom; 'Introduction of "Spiced Maple" Sparks Excitement,' *Canadian Wood Products Industries,* April 1965, 30

14 'Introduction of "Spiced Maple,"' 30; 'Here a Leading Furniture Manufacturer Talks about Synthetic Finishes,' *CW,* Nov. 1959, 30–2; Interviews: Howard Hemphill and Peter Sansom; AO, T. Eaton Company, series 69, Mercantile, vol. 16, 'Complaints, furniture' correspondence in July 1952 concerning the delay of the Vilas furniture company in meeting orders for light finishes because of materials limitations. At Imperial's Stratford plant, a conveyor belt carried the furniture into ovens where heat fused the several coats of finish and transformed their molecular structure so as to resist the solvents with which they had been applied.

15 Strudley, 'Design as a Function of Management'; Strudley, 'Report re the Incorporation of Some Design Content in the Management Training Course at the University of Western Ontario,' spring 1952 in NGA, 7.4D, Design in Industry, file 4; Strudley's later 'Report on Summer Course' in the same file refers to a 22-page brochure from which the Imperial case was taught. I have not been able to locate the brochure in Stratford, London, or Ottawa; NAC, RG 77, Acc 88–89/045, National Research Council, box 3, file 3–12–N4–2, parts 1 and 2, 'NIDC of NG' report on Western case on industrial design problems; 'Industrial Design Conference,' address by Strudley, *IC,* July 1953, 142–3.

16 Interview: Jan Kuypers

17 An article on Morris, featuring Canadian birch chairs, was reprinted in Canada as Strudley was formulating his plans for a design department. Neil Morris, 'New Trends in Furniture,' *CW* Jan. 1948, 22, 23, 44

18 Note the mixture of historical and modern forms in the Kuypers' own home, including the table, made from a new rounded triangular top and a refinished pedestal base, shown on p. 17 of 'Seven Good Low-Cost Houses,' *CHG,* Feb. 1958, 16–18, 23; on front parlour elegance, 'Seven Canadian Designs for Living: Jan Kuypers,' *CHG,* Sept. 1958, 17

19 Interview: Jan Kuypers; see similar comments by other designers about Britain in 1951, Sally MacDonald and Julia Porter, 'Mid-Century Modern,' in *Putting on the Style: Setting up Home in the 1950s* (London: Geffrye Museum, 1990) unpaginated.

20 Martin Eidelberg, 'Modern Historicism,' in *What Modern Was,* 120–1; Clive Wainwright, 'The Legacy of the Nineteenth Century,' 26–40, and Gillian Naylor, 'Swedish Grace ... or the Acceptable Face of Modernism,' 164–83 both in Paul Greenhalgh, ed., *Modernism in Design* (London: Reaktion, 1990);

Eileen Boris, '"Dreams of Brotherhood and Beauty": The Social Ideas of the Arts and Crafts Movement,' in Wendy Kaplan, ed., *The Art That Is Life'* (Boston: Little, Brown, 1987) 208–11, 216–17; Peter Wollin, *Raiding the Icebox* (London: Verso, 1993) 104, 29; Gillian Naylor, 'The Survival of the Craft Ideal,' in Jocelyn de Noblet, ed., *Industrial Design: Reflection of a Century* (Paris: Flanmarion, 1993) 110–18; Bengt Nystrom, 'Fran Status till Borgerlig Vargag,' 50, 57, 61–3, Anne-Marie Ericsson, 'Brytningstid for Fattig och Rik,' 105–11, 116–25, and Sigrid Eklund Nystrom, 'Funktionalism i Folkhemmet,' 163, 215–21, all in Monica Boman, ed., *Svenska Mobler, 1890–1990* (Lund: Bokforlaget Signum, 1991); Ake Haldt, 'Grandeur vs Comfort in the Home,' *Form* 6 (1953) 1233–5; Ulf Hard af Segersted, *Modern Scandinavian Furniture* (Stockholm: Nordisk Rotogravyr, 1963) 22; Witold Rybczynski, *Looking Around* (New York: Viking, 1992) 177; Penny Spark, *Consultant Design* (London: Pembridge Press, 1983); Jan Kuypers, 'Why Hasn't Real Mass Production Been Achieved in the Furniture Industry,' *CW*, June 1960

21 Bruno Zevi, *Towards an Organic Architecture* (London: Faber and Faber, 1949) 66–76; Hiesinger, 'Introduction,' *Design since 1945*, x; Jeffery Daniels, ed., *Utility Furniture and Fashion, 1941–1951* (London: Inner London Education Authority, 1974) xii, xiv, 25; Harriet Dover, *Home Front Furniture: British Utility Design, 1941–51* (London: Scolar Press, 1991) 20, 31–3; Sparke *Consultant Design*, 38; Ake Haldt, 'Craftsmanship in the Plastic Age,' *Kontur*, 1963–4, 52–4; Interviews: Lena Larsson, Monica Boman; Lena Larsson, 'Elias Svedberg,' and Karin Winter, 'Lena Larsson' both in Boman, ed., *Svenska Mobler*, 246–7, 386–7, 289; R. McFadden, *Scandinavian Modern Design, 1880–1950* (New York: Abrams, 1982) 148; Pat Kirkham, *Charles and Ray Eames: Designers of the Twentieth Century* (Cambridge: MIT, 1995) 6, 46, 169–76, 183, and on folk hearts 218; Interview with Jehan Burns Kuhn, by Joy Parr, Cambridge, MA, 13 March 1992

22 Interview: Jan Kuypers; see examples in *What Modern Was*, 123, 141, 136, 186–7, 189–90.

23 Interviews: Kuypers, Sansom, and Hemphill; Krug Manufacturing, Stratford, *Imperial Loyalist Catalogue No. 16* (late 1940s) and 'Imperial History' typescript

24 Donald Strudley speaking from the chair, National Industrial Design Council conference, 'How Can We Sell More Modern Furniture?' 30 Oct. 1954, Toronto (typescript found in Toronto Public Library) 2. Conference delegates visited the touring exhibition *Design in Scandinavia* then on display at the ROM.

25 Interviews: Howard Hemphill, Jan Kuypers; on the relationship between

design and marketing staff in the development of new lines, Jan Kuypers, 'Must Break Away from Regional Approach, Manitobans Are Told,' Manitoba Design Council Seminar *CW*, June 1965; 'Furniture Market News,' *CHG*, March 1959, 1

26 Don Wright, 'Significant Trends in Canadian Furniture Mart,' *CW*, Feb. 1956, 25

27 Jan Kuypers, 'What Next in Canadian Design?' *Furniture and Furnishings*, May 1960, 28; Jan Kuypers, 'Excitement Lacking in Mart Furniture,' *Canadian Wood Products Industries/Furniture Production edition*, Feb. 1965, 28; Robert Fulford, 'What Is a Designer Anyway? And Why Is He Fighting in Your Living Room?' *CHG*, Sept. 1958, 90; Interview: Kuypers

28 Letter: Jan Kuypers, Okano Kuypers, Toronto, to author, 15 Jan. 1997

29 Krug Furniture, Stratford, Imperial catalogues; *Svenska Mobler*, 138, 246–7, 289; *What Modern Was*, 187, 192

30 Thibault: 'A New Tested Line of Canadian Modern,' *Furniture and Furnishings*, Jan. 1958, 28; on Donald Lapp's designs for Thibault, 'Donald Lapps's Doodles Are Different,' ibid., Dec. 1956, 40; *CHG*, March 1958, 10, April 1958, 21, lower left; Vilas: *CHG*, May 1950, 114; *Furniture and Furnishings*, July 1954, 21; *CHG*, May 1957, 100; on Paul McCobb joining Vilas as designer *Furniture and Furnishings*, Jan. 1959, 36, 38, 46; Barbara Reynolds, 'Canada's Own Colonial Gets a Big Welcome,' *Chatelaine*, March 1961, 124–6; James Warren, 'Our Design Poverty,' *Furniture and Furnishings*, April 1962, 37; *CW*, Dec. 1966.

31 Bunny Cosway, 'Forecasts in Wood and Design at the Mart,' *CW*, Jan. 1957, 26; *Furniture and Furnishings*, Feb. 1960, 39; May 1960, 29; Oct. 1960, 46–7; Jan. 1961, 32–3; Margaret Daly, 'What's Killing Canadian Borax?' ibid., April 1962, 27–30

32 Harold Stanfield exhibit, *Marketing*, 26 April 1952, 67; Imperial advertisements, *CHG*, April 1945, 47; June 1945, 63; Aug. 1945, 45; Sept. 1945, 57; Oct. 1945, 61

33 *CHG*, May 1947, 77; Nov. 1947, 79

34 Craft/design: *CHG*, March 1946, 45; Aug. 1946, 49; Nov. 1946, 57; principle/homily: *CHG*, Aug. 1945, 45; Sept. 1945, 57

35 Krug Company, Stratford, catalogues, Imperial Loyalist 5, 1955, Imperial Loyalist 29, 1959, Sampler 19, 1959; *CHG* cover, ad 38, and 'Our Guide to New Furniture,' April 1959

36 'Good Design in Furniture Basis of Survey,' *CW*, Aug. 1950, 28

37 Stratford Perth Archives, Imperial Furniture, 'Values of Goods Placed with Retailers, by Month'; Interviews: Howard Hemphill and Pete Sansom

38 *Why People Don't Buy Furniture* (Indianapolis: Mills Advertising, 1928) 23, 30,

31; 81 per cent expressed no, or little, interest in period design, 80 per cent were little, or not, interested in exclusive design. Copy in Baker Library, Harvard University

39 Christine Morley, 'Homemakers and Design Advice,' in Putman and Newton, eds., *Household Choices*, 96

40 Pierre Bourdieu, *Distinction: A Social Critique of the Judgement of Taste*, trans. Richard Nice (Cambridge: Harvard University Press, 1984), see the discussion 'Class Condition and Social Conditioning,' 101–14, and 'Classes and Classifications,' 466–84.

41 David Halle, *Inside Culture* (Chicago: University of Chicago Press, 1993) 7–9, 225

42 Tim Putnam, 'Introduction: Design, Consumption and Domestic Ideals,' in Putnam and Newton, eds., *Household Choices*, 15

43 Interview: Ann Brook

44 Interview: Joan Coffey

45 Interview: Winnifred Edwards

46 Interview: Sarah Brown Tobe

47 Harrison addressing NIDC conference, 'How Can We Sell More Modern Furniture?' Oct. 1954, 16; Letter: Sheila Maurice; Jan Kuypers, 'Why Hasn't Real Mass Production Been Achieved in the Furniture Industry?' *CW*, June 1960, 33

48 Interview: Mary Kippen

49 Interviews: Ann Brook, Winnifred Edwards; 'The Canadian Story in Home Furnishings,' *Furniture and Furnishings*, April 1950, 60–1; furniture report, *CW*, Feb. 1954, 26–7; Letters: Hazel Beech, Joan Catlin

50 *The Furniture Buying Habits of Canadians: A Canadian Homes and Gardens Report* (1957), 22, 15, 21, found in AO, T. Eaton Company, series 69, vol. 25, Market Research 1953–60

51 Imperial Loyalist ad, 'For Junior Men,' *CHG*, July 1946, 47; Interviews: Tina Wall, Mary Paine; Sally Tobe, West Vancouver, response to interview transcript, 10 June 1995

52 Interviews: Pam McKeen, Ann Brook; 'What the Women Want,' *CHG*, March 1955, 56; consider, for example, affinities between high modernist forms and the parlour furniture Katherine C. Grier discusses in 'Orthodox as the Hymn Book: The Rhetoric of Parlour Furnishing,' in *Culture and Comfort: People, Parlors and Upholstery, 1850–1930* (Amherst: University of Massachusetts Press, 1988).

53 Interviews: Winnifred Edwards, Mary Paine, Joan Coffey; Halle, *Inside Culture*, 11; AO, T. Eaton Company, series 69, vol. 31, Sales Promotion, Report by G.S. Screaton on Chicago and Grand Rapids furniture markets, 1954

Chapter 8: Domesticating Objects

1 The narrative here follows Daniel Bell, *The Cultural Contradiction of Capitalism* (New York: Basic, 1976), 'From the Protestant Ethic to the Psychedelic Bazaar,' 55–75; but see similarly Grant McCracken, *Culture and Consumption* (Bloomington: Indiana University Press, 1988) 52–3,104; Albert O. Hirschman, *Shifting Involvements* (Princeton: Princeton University Press, 1982) 38; David Lockwood, 'Sources of Variation in Working-Class Images of Society,' in Martin Bulmer, ed., *Working-Class Images of Society* (London: Routledge and Kegan Paul, 1975) 22–3; Stuart Ewan, *All Consuming Images* (New York: Basic Books, 1988); Richard Wrightman Fox and T.J. Lears, eds., *The Culture of Consumption* (New York: Pantheon, 1983), and the critique of this work in Jean-Christophe Agnew, 'Coming Up for Air: Consumer Culture in Historical Perspective,' in John Brewer and Roy Porter, eds., *Consumption and the World of Goods* (New York: Routledge, 1993), and Geraldine Pratt, 'The House as an Expression of Social Worlds,' in James S. Duncan, ed., *Housing and Identity* (London: Croom Helm, 1981).

2 Mary Douglas and Baron Isherwood, *The World of Goods* (New York: Norton, 1979), discuss this problem in Chapter 2, 'The Uses of Goods'; see especially 59–62.

3 Robert Lane published this work first in 'Markets and the Satisfaction of Human Wants,' *Journal of Economic Issues* 12, 4 (Dec. 1978), the material here is from 803, 805, and 821. The analysis is elaborated in his *The Market Experience* (New York: Cambridge University Press, 1991) chap. 27; see also Albert O. Hirschman, *Shifting Involvements: Private Interest and Public Action* (Princeton: Princeton University Press, 1982) 20.

4 Mihaly Csikszentmihalyi and Eugene Rochberg-Halton, *The Meaning of Things* (New York: Cambridge University Press, 1981) 231–2

5 Steven Sheffrin, 'Habermas, Depoliticization and Consumer Theory,' *Journal of Economic Issues* 12, 4 (Dec. 1978) 786–9

6 Ibid., 792–4; this argument is developed in sections 4, 5, and 6 of Jurgen Habermas, *The Structural Transformation of the Public Sphere*, trans. Thomas Burger (Cambridge: MIT Press, 1991) 89–236.

7 Douglas and Isherwood, *World of Goods*, 127, drawing on Herbert Simon, 'Decision-Making in Economics,' in *Resource Allocation*, Surveys in Economic Theory, vol. 3 (New York: St Martins, 1966) 1–28

8 Douglas and Isherwood, *The World of Goods* 4, 10; John Fiske, *Understanding Popular Culture* (London: Routledge, 1989) 105; Fiske, *Reading the Popular* (London: Unwin Hyman, 1989) 24, 28

9 J.K. Gibson-Graham, *The End of Capitalism (As We Knew It): A Feminist Critique*

of Political Economy (Oxford: Blackwell, 1996) 2, 3, 14–15, 35, 116–17, 260, 263

10 Kathleen Stewart, 'Nostalgia – A Polemic,' *Cultural Anthropology* 3, 3 (1988) 228; Christopher Lasch, *Haven in a Heartless World* (New York: Basic, 1977)

11 Daniel Horowitz, *The Morality of Spending* (Baltimore: Johns Hopkins University Press, 1985) 168–70

12 Alan Ehrenhalt, *The Lost City* (New York: Basic Books, 1995) 26

13 Stuart Hall, 'Notes on Deconstructing "the popular,"' in Raphael Samuel, ed., *People's History and Socialist Theory* (London: Routledge, 1981) 232–3

14 Note Fox and Lears, *Culture of Consumption,* and the critique by Agnew, 'Coming Up For Air'.

15 Poststructuralist writing of the early 1990s risked this interpretation. See for example Fiske's widely read *Understanding Popular Culture* and Mike Featherstone, *Consumer Culture and Postmodernism* (London: Sage, 1991).

16 There are similar studies attempting to refine the poststructuralist critique of household consumption for Glasgow, Scotland, and Sydney, Australia, though neither considers 'nation' explicitly as a category of analysis. See Ruth Madigan and Moira Munro, '"House Beautiful": Style and Consumption in the Home,' *Sociology* 30, 1 (Feb. 1996) 41–57, and Jean Duruz, 'Laminex Dreams: Women, Suburban Comfort, and the Negotiation of Meanings,' *Meanjin* 53, 1 (1996) 99–110. I am grateful to Cynthia Wright and Gail Reekie, respectively, for these references.

17 This passage draws on Doug Owram, 'Canadian Domesticity in the Postwar Era,' in Peter Neary and J.L. Granatstein, eds., *The Veterans Charter and Postwar Canada* (Montreal: McGill-Queen's University Press, 1998) 207, 212–13; and his *Born at the Right Time* (Toronto: University of Toronto Press, 1996).

18 James Struthers, 'Family Allowances, Old Age Security, and the Construction of Entitlement in the Canadian Welfare State, 1943–1951,' in *Veterans Charter,* 186, 198–9

19 Richard Sennett, *The Fall of the Public Man* (New York: Random House, 1974) 220

20 Ehrenhalt, *Lost City,* 24–5

21 Martine Perrot, 'The Domestication of Objects,' in Jocelyn de Noblet, ed., *Industrial Design: Reflection of a Century* (Paris: Flammarion, 1993) 365–71; Tim Putnam, 'Beyond the Modern Home: Shifting Parameters of Residence,' in Jon Bird et al., *Mapping the Futures* (London: Routledge, 1993) 152–5

22 Hannah Arendt, *The Human Condition* (Chicago: University of Chicago Press, 1958) 137

23 Owram, 'Canadian Domesticity,' 207

24 National Industrial Design Council, *How Can We Sell More Modern Furniture,* Oct. 1954, 16

25 The concern is repeated frequently in Canadian Furniture Manufacturers Association meetings. For the sleeping giant imagery see *CW,* Jan. 1956, 24–5.

26 Interview: Tina Wall

27 Sally MacDonald and Julia Porter, *Putting on the Style: Setting up Home in the 1950s* (London: Geffrye Museum, 1990) in chapter 'Traditional Values,' no pagination; McCracken, *Culture and Consumption,* chap. 8, 'Diderot Unities and the Diderot Effect'; Hirschman, *Shifting Involvements,* 37–8

28 Interview: Patricia Cliff; Letter: Cindy Bolger

29 Interviews: Winnifred Edwards, Gerd Evans

30 Interview: Allison Simpson

31 Clare Cooper Marcus, *House as a Mirror of Self* (Berkeley: Conari Press, 1995) 10–11

32 John Seeley, Alexander Sims, and E.W. Loosley, *Crestwood Heights* (Toronto: University of Toronto Press, 1956) 57, 60; Letter: Bev Newmarch

33 Interviews: Joan Coffey, Pam McKeen; British interwar evidence from working people is similar: Gary Cross, *Time and Money* (London: Routledge, 1993) 170, 270.

34 Tim Putnam 'Introduction,' in Tim Putnam and Charles Newton, eds., *Household Choices* (London: Futures, 1990) 7; similar to the Household Choices project, but focusing on information technologies, is Roger Silverstone and Eric Hirsch, eds., *Consuming Technologies* (London: Routledge, 1992).

35 Douglas and Isherwood, *World of Goods,* 68; Tomas Maldonado, 'The Idea of Craft,' *Design Issues* 8, 1 (fall 1991) 35–43; James Yandell, 'Introduction,' to Marcus, *House as a Mirror,* xiv

36 J.A. Davis, 'Living Rooms as Symbols of Social Status: A Study in Social Judgement' (PhD diss., Harvard University, 1955); B. Junker, 'Room Compositions and Life Styles' (PhD diss., University of Chicago, 1954); E.O. Laumann and J.S. House, 'Living Room Styles and Social Attributes: The Patterning of Material Attributes in a Modern Urban Community,' *Sociology and Social Research* 54, 3 (1970) 321–42; Pratt, 'House as an Expression'; Marcus Felson, 'The Differentiation of Material Life Styles, 1925–1966,' *Social Indicators Research* 3 (1976) 397–421

37 'Why Isn't the Consumer Spending More on Home Furnishings?' *Furniture and Furnishings,* Oct. 1958, 52

38 Csikszentmihalyi and Rochberg-Halton, *Meaning of Things,* especially chaps 4 and 5

39 Jennifer A. Gonzalez, 'Autotopographies,' in Gabriel Brahm and Mark

Driscoll, eds., *Prosthetic Territories: Politics and Hypertechnologies* (Boulder, CO: Westview, 1995) 136

40 See, for example, Pat Kirkham's discussion of Aalto's appraisal of wood and chrome in *Charles and Ray Eames: Designers of the Twentieth Century* (Cambridge: MIT Press, 1995) 204.

41 Csikszentmihalyi and Rochberg-Halton, *Meaning of Things*, chap. 7; Fiske, *Understanding Popular Culture*, 34–7; Fiske, 'Cultural Studies and the Culture of Everyday Life,' in Grossberg et al., *Cultural Studies* (London: Routledge, 1992) dialogue with Linda Charnes, 171–2; for a Norwegian reading of the big world/little world boundary see Marianne Guilestad, 'Home Decoration as Popular Culture,' in Stevi Jackson and Shaun Moores, eds., *The Politics of Domestic Consumption* (London: Prentice-Hall, 1995) 321–35; Duruz, 'Laminex Dreams,' 101–2; Madigan and Munro, '"House Beautiful,"' 41, 43; Interviews: Pam McKeen, Mary Paine

42 Interviews: Ella Smith, Mary Kippen; Joan Coffey to Joy Parr, revising interview, 23 Feb. 1995

43 Interviewees often remarked on the detail with which they could recall their purchases in the 1940s and 1950s, when purchases were few and made after deliberation and delay. See similarly, Judy Attfield, 'Inside Pram Town: A Case Study of Harlow House Interiors, 1951–61,' in Judy Attfield and Pat Kirkham, eds., *A View from the Interior: Feminism, Women, and Design* (London: Women's Press, 1989) 225. Christine Morley, 'Homemakers and Design Advice in the Postwar Period,' in Putnam and Newton, *Household Choices* 92; MacDonald and Porter, *Putting on the Style*, section 'You Have Your Love to Keep You Warm' in chapter 'Make Do and Mend'; Pratt finds a similar preference for gradual accretion of goods among her Shaughnessy interviewees in the late 1970s, who stressed that furniture they bought themselves had been acquired 'slowly,' 'bit by bit,' 'over time,' and that 'Living in a room furnished all at once would "feel like being in a capsule."' Pratt, 'The House as an Expression,' 161

44 Michel de Certeau, *The Practice of Everyday Life* (Berkeley: University of California Press, 1984) 32

45 Helga Ditmar, 'Meanings of Material Possessions as Reflections of Identity,' in F.W. Rudmin, ed., *To Have Possessions: A Handbook on Ownership and Property*, special issue of *Journal of Social Behaviour and Personality* 6, 6 (1991) 165–86; Susan M. Pierce, *On Collecting: An Investigation into Collecting in the European Tradition* (London: Routledge, 1995) 207–10; Russell W. Belk and Melanie Wallendorf, 'Of Mice and Men: Gender Identity in Collecting,' in Susan M. Pierce, ed., *Interpreting Objects and Collections* (London: Routledge, 1994) 240–53; Cross, *Time and Money*, 173

46 Alison Ravetz, 'A View from the Interior,' 201–2, and Angela Partington,

'The Designer Housewife in the 1950s,' 212, both in Attfield and Kirkham, eds., *A View from the Interior*

47 Interview: Joan Coffey; Cross, *Time and Money*, 170
48 Duruz, 'Laminex Dreams,' 102, 107
49 These were Hoggart's terms describing English forms chosen to ensure confirmation of belonging and community. Richard Hoggart, *The Uses of Literacy* (London: Chatto and Windus, 1957) 30–5
50 Katherine Grier argues in this way, and against Veblen's emulation hypothesis, in *Culture and Comfort: People, Parlors and Upholstery, 1850–1930* (Amherst: University of Massachusetts Press, 1988) 13.
51 Interviews: Gerd Evans, Lily Hansen, Pam McKeen, Nettie Murphy; Madigan and Munro, '"House Beautiful"' 48
52 Morley, 'Homemakers and Design Advice,' 96
53 Interview: Sally Tobe, Harriet Fraser, Emma Boyd; Letter: Nettie Murphy; on British suites, see Judy Attfield, '"Give 'em Something Dark and Heavy": The Role of Design in the Material Culture of Popular British Furniture,' *Journal of Design History* 9, 3 (1996).
54 Duruz, 'Laminex Dreams,' 101; Gibson-Graham, *End of Capitalism*, 207
55 Gonzalez, 'Autotopographies,' 134–5; Stewart, 'Nostalgia,' 234; Jennifer Gonzalez, 'The Rhetoric of the Object: Material Memory and the Artwork of Amalia Mesa-Bains,' *Visual Anthropology Review* 9, 1 (1993) 82–92; Cross, *Time and Money*, 174
56 Interviews: Tina Wall, Margaret Shortliffe
57 McCracken, *Culture and Consumption*, 51
58 Tim Putnam, 'Regimes of Closure: The Representation of Cultural Process in Domestic Consumption,' in Silverstone and Hirsch, *Consuming Technologies*, 203; M. Segalen, ed., *Etre bien dans ses meubles* (Paris: Institut d'Ethnologie Française 1990); Gertrude Øllgaard, 'Consumption as an Act of *Bricolage*,' in David Nye and Carl Pedersen, eds., *Consumption and American Culture* (Amsterdam: Vu University Press, 1991) 191
59 Interviews: John Murray, George Soulis
60 Interviews: Mary Paine, Margaret Shortliffe
61 Interviews: Susan Taylor, Emma Boyd; Csikszentmihalyi and Rochberg-Halton, *Meaning of Things*, 168
62 Interview: Joan Niblock
63 Interview: Allison Smith; Pratt, 'House as an Expression,' 159
64 Interviews: Nettie Murphy, Mary Paine, Joan Niblock, Greta Nelson
65 Suilio Venchiarutti as told to Doris McCubbin, 'How Women Drive Architects Crazy,' *Chatelaine*, May 1954, 36; see symmetrically, Elizabeth Gaylord, 'I'm a Fugitive from a Postwar Home,' *Canadian Home Journal*, May 1948, 6, 7, 76.

66 Commentaries on interview transcripts by Joan Coffey, Coquitlam, 23 Feb. 1995, and Sally Tobe, West Vancouver, 10 June 1995

67 Csikszentmihalyi and Rochberg-Halton, *Meaning of Things*, 28; on the capacity of colour and material to invoke moods, Interviews: Pam McKeen, Lynn Stevens, Winnifred Edwards, Nettie Murphy, Joan Coffey; on decorating as process and art, J.E. Hiss, 'Domestic Interiors in Northern Mexico,' *Heresies* 3 (1981) 30–3; and Pauline Hunt, 'Gender and the Construction of Home Life,' in Graham Allan and Graham Crowe, eds., *Home and Family* (Basingstoke: Macmillan, 1989)

68 Gonzalez, 'Rhetoric of the Object,' 83–4

69 Fiske, 'Cultural Studies,' 158

70 Virginia Woolf, *A Room of One's Own* (New York: Harcourt Brace Jovanovich, [1929] 1991) 95

71 Gonzalez, 'Autotopographies,' 146–7; 'Rhetoric of the Object,' 82, 86, 89; McCracken, *Culture and Consumption*, 136; Stewart, 'Nostalgia,' 232; Perrot, 'Domestication of Objects,' 370; Øllgaard, 'Consumption as an Act of *Bricolage*,' 191–2; for an example of the process in a more recent Canadian setting see Annamma Joy and Ruby Roy Dholakia, 'Remembrances of Things Past: The Meaning of Home and Possessions of Indian Professionals in Canada' in Rudmin, '*To Have Possessions*,' 396.

72 This effect is widely observed. See Albert O. Hirschman, *Shifting Involvements* (Princeton: Princeton University Press, 1982) 37; Tibor Skitovsky, *The Joyless Economy* (New York: Oxford University Press, 1992); Fiske, *Understanding Popular Culture*, 15; Marcus, *House as Mirror*, 54.

73 Letter: Bev Newmarch; Interviews: Mary Kippen, Marjorie Barlow, Ella Smith, Lily Hansen, Greta Nelson, Harriet Fraser

74 Joy and Dholakia, 'Remembrances of Things Past,' 395

75 Morley, 'Homemakers and Design Advice,' 92

76 Interview: Mary Kippen

77 Interviews: Greta Nelson, Gerry Kilby, Emma Boyd, Allison Simpson

78 Interview: Marjorie Barlow

79 Interviews: Margaret Shortliffe, Nettie Murphy

80 Csikszentmihalyi and Rochberg-Halton, *Meaning of Things*, 62; Stewart, 'Nostalgia,' 234–6

81 Interview: Allison Simpson

82 Susan Stewart, *On Longing: Narratives on the Miniature, the Gigantic, the Souvenir, the Collection* (Baltimore: Johns Hopkins University Press, 1984)

83 Interviews: Ella Smith, Mary Kippen; Letters: Sheila Maurice, Joan Catlin

84 Interview: Tina Wall; see similarly Morley, 'Homemakers and Design Advice,' 95.

Chapter 9: Shopping for a Good Stove

1 'Cultivate the Ladies,' *Hardware in Canada,* Aug. 1946, 26, 28; Frank Wright, 'Woman the Nation's Purchasing Agent,' *CB* Aug. 1946, 132; AO, T. Eaton Company, series 69, Merchandise Office, vol. 12, 'Business Conditions and Forecasts, 1940–52,' B.E. Mercer to W. Park, 9 Feb. 1950, summarizing talk at the Retail Federation by Edythe Fern Melrose and article in *Hardware Metal and Electrical Dealer,* 4 Feb. 1950. The study Mercer and Park used was published by Paul Converse and Merle Crawford as "Family Buying: Who Does It? Who Influences It?" in *Current Economic Comment* 11 (Nov. 1949) 38–50. Mirra Komarovsky compared a number of postwar studies showing similar outcomes in 'Class Differences in Family Decisionmaking on Expenditures,' in Nelson N. Foote, ed., *Household Decisionmaking* (New York: New York University Press, 1961) 255–65. On the male shadow see Wright, 'Woman'; on the impatient husband, 'Mrs Consumer Speaks Out on Design,' *IC,* Jan. 1955, 78. The literature on women's level of autonomy in various types of decision making is well summarized in Rosemary Scott, *The Female Consumer* (New York: John Wiley, 1976) 119–25.

2 For positive views of women in appliance sales, see McMUA, Moffats' *Sales Chef,* Jan.–Feb. 1952, commentaries by C.A. Winder, General Sales Manager, p. 2, and by Elaine Collert in her column, 'The Woman's Angle.' The negative view is from a male sales consultant, 'More Selling, Less Crying,' *Marketing,* 18 March 1955, 24. For contending views on why commission appliance sales is a men's job in the United States see 'Women's History Goes on Trial: *EEOC* v. *Sears, Roebuck and Company,*' *Signs* 11, 4 (summer 1986) 751–79, and Ruth Milkman, 'Women's History and the Sears Case,' *Feminist Studies* 12, 2 (summer 1986) 375–400.

3 For example McMUA, Westinghouse Collection, box 7, file 27, *WS,* May 1948, 2 'Eight Sound Rules for Selling,' and on Moffat, 'Virile Salesmanship and Advertising Built World-Wide Canadian Business,' *Marketing,* 2 Oct. 1948, 56.

4 McMUA, Westinghouse Collection, Charles Pearce, 'Watch Your Language!' and 'Why True-temp Is Better,' *WS,* July 1947, and G.I. Harrison, 'I Lost the Sale Because ...,' *WS,* June 1948; McMUA 'The Woman's Angle,' *Sales Chef,* March 1951; 'Would-be Purchasers Still Getting Brush-off, This Customer Declares,' *Marketing,* 13 April 1946, 10

5 'The Sales Clinic,' *CB,* Jan. 1948, 92; 'I Lost the Sale Because ...'; 'Life with Buy-ology,' *WS,* July 1951, 8–9; 'Selling via Demonstrations,' *Marketing,* 30 July 1949, 8; 'Manufacturer's Retailers' Guide Promotes Many Competing Products,' ibid., 16 Sept. 1950, 18; 'Canadian Women Want Product Facts,' ibid., 12 Dec. 1951, 18

6 Robert M. Campbell, 'You Can't Wash Dishes with Aesthetics!' *CB*, June
   1951, 41
7 *Sales Chef*, Dec. 1950, 5; 'Women's Views of Moffat News,' ibid., Nov. 1948;
   July 1950, 7; March–April 1950, 6; *WS*, April 1951, 11; Campbell, 'You Can't
   Wash Dishes,' 41
8 On selling an appliance as a redefinition of a task, Carolyn Shaw Bell, *Consumer Choice in the American Economy* (New York: Random House, 1967) 224;
   Sales Chef, Nov. 1948, Feb.–March 1951, 17, July-Aug. 1947. Suzette Worden
   sees this pattern in interwar Britain: 'Powerful Women: Electricity in the
   Home, 1919–40,' in Judy Attfield and Pat Kirkham, eds., *A View from the Inte-
   rior: Feminism, Women and Design* (London: Women's Press, 1989) 140. Keith
   Walden describes a similar campaign by manufacturers to turn attention
   from local skills toward goods sold in national markets in 'Speaking Modern:
   Language, Culture and Hegemony in Grocery Window Displays, 1887–1920,'
   Canadian Historical Review 70, 3 (Sept. 1989) 296, 308–9.
9 The quote is from 'Help Yourself to Future Range Sales,' *WS*, Sept. 1950;
   'Practical Ideas for Advertisers in Cultivating Women Customers,' *Marketing*,
   11 Dec. 1948, 14; 'Would-be Purchasers,' 10
10 'Service Page,' *Sales Chef*, Sept. 1946 and Nov. 1948, *Marketing*, 30 Nov. 1948,
   18; Peter J. McClure and John K. Ryans, 'Differences between Retailers' and
   Consumers' Perceptions,' *Journal of Marketing Research* 5 (Feb. 1968) 37;
   NGA, 7.4 'Design in Industry' file 2, D.B. Cruickshank, 'Industrial Design,
   What We Are Doing about It' speech, c. 7 June 1949. Scott, *Female Consumer*,
   67–8; On appliance gadgets and sales in other settings see Judy Wajcman,
   Feminism Confronts Technology (University Park: Pennsylvania State University
   Press, 1991) 103–4, and T.A.B. Corley, *Domestic Electrical Appliances* (London:
   Jonathan Cape, 1966) 136.
11 *Sales Chef*, March-April 1950, Nov. 1952; *Marketing*, 15 Aug. 1953, 3; McMUA,
   'The Farmer's Wife,' *WS*, Feb. 1948, 9
12 See, for example, Norton Calder, 'Women Are Lousy Housekeepers,' *Liberty*,
   Nov. 1954, 15; 'Wasted Effort,' *SN*, 30 Oct. 1954, 3
13 'Women Best Ad Readers, Shrewder Buyers: Long,' *Marketing*, 29 April 1955,
   8
14 '50% of Ranges 10 Years Old Basis for McClary Campaign,' *Marketing*,
   8 Oct. 1954, 6, 8; Dianne Dodd notes that in the interwar period in Canada,
   advertisers responded to this concern by emphasizing the benefits of labour-
   saving domestic appliances to the whole family, Dodd, 'Women in Advertising: The Role of Canadian Women in the Promotion of Domestic Electrical
   Technology in the Interwar Period,' in Marianne Ainley, ed., *Despite the Odds:
   Essays on Canadian Women and Science* (Montreal: Véhicule, 1990) 144–5;

Corley suggested similarly in the British case that women might fear being thought lazy if they had too many appliances, or might have preferred to agree that money be spent on items more immediately pleasing to their husbands. Corley, *Domestic Electrical Appliances*, 133. See similarly Vance Packard, *Hidden Persuaders* (New York: David McKay, 1957) 62, and Maxine L. Margolis, *Mothers and Such* (Berkeley: University of California Press, 1984) 167.

15 On this point see Harrison White, 'Where Do Markets Come From?' *American Journal of Sociology* 87 (Nov. 1981) 543–4, and Susan Strasser, *Satisfaction Guaranteed* (New York: Pantheon, 1989) 289.

16 See 'Would-be Purchasers,' 10; 'Canadian Women Want Product Facts,' 18; and 'Women's Purchasing Viewpoints Explained ...,' *Marketing*, 19 Jan. 1952, 4.

17 'Charting the Course for Selling ...,' *Marketing*, 30 Nov. 1946, 2; 'Selling via Demonstrations ...,' 12; *WS*, July 1951, 9; 'Mrs Consumer Speaks Out,' 78; Eaton Collection, series 69, Merchandise Office, vol. 12, M Park to B.E. Mercer, 12 Feb. 1951, A.E. Nurse to B.W. Smith, 15 Feb. 1951; Park to Smith, 20 Feb. 1951. William H. Whyte invokes this dilemma well in 'The Web of Word of Mouth,' *Fortune*, Nov. 1954, reprinted in *Consumer Behavior*, vol. 2, (New York: New York University Press, 1955) 118–20.

18 Campbell, 'You Can't Wash Dishes,' 40–1; similar patterns are observed from Britain and Australia: see Corley, *Domestic Electrical Appliances*, 52, and Wajcman, *Feminism Confronts Technology*, 100–3; note the analogies with microwave design and sales, Cynthia Cockburn and Susan Ormrod, *Gender and Technology in the Making* (London: Sage, 1993) especially chap. 3.

19 Thomas Fisher Rare Book Room, Robarts Library, University of Toronto, Alan Jarvis Collection, MS 171, box 22, 'What's All This Fuss about Modern Design?' *Target*, 9 Oct. 1945, 10; NGA, Design in Industry, 7.4–1, Statement by the Affiliation of Industrial Designers of Canada, 3 July 1947; on the priority of materials and promise of Canadian production, ibid., 5.5–D, speech by C.D. Howe, Minister of Reconstruction, opening Design in Industry Exhibition, 1946; John B. Collins, 'Design for Use, Design for the Millions: Proposals and Options for the National Industrial Design Council, 1948–1960' (MA thesis, Carleton University, 1986), chap. 2; McMUA, Westinghouse Collection, *Westinghouse News*, 2 June 1948; Stuart Ewen, *All Consuming Images* (New York: Basic, 1988) chap. 9.

20 Donald Buchanan, preface to NIDC, *Design for Use* (Ottawa: King's Printer, 1947) 5; on acting the part see NGA, 5.5D, 'Design Centre Exhibition 1948,' Dora de Pedery to H.O. McCurry, 23 Sept. 1948. De Pedery, a sculptor who had been instrumental in wartime initiatives to establish a postwar design

council, may have been influenced in her view about the representation of function by the American critics Sheldon and Martha May Chandler, who argued in 1936 for 'functional expressiveness' as a central industrial design principle: *Art and the Machine* (New York: McGraw-Hill, 1936) 14–15; the emphasis on being 'true to materials' and signifying usefulness is strong in *It Pays to Buy Articles of Good Design* (Ottawa: National Gallery and CAC, 1951); *IC*, Jan. 1948, 141; D.W. Buchanan, 'Completing the Pattern of Modern Living,' *Canadian Art* 6 (spring 1949) 112; *Foreign Trade*, 25 Nov. 1950, 898; for similar issues in Britain in the postwar see Isabelle Anscombe, 'The Return to Normalcy,' in her *A Woman's Touch* (New York: Viking, 1984) 185–90.

21 AO, Eaton Company series 69, box 19, 'Design Index and Awards, 1946–60,' B.W. Smith from Eaton's Merchandising Office on 25 Feb. 1953; Henry Dreyfuss, 'The Silent Salesman of Industry,' *IC*, July 1952, 65; Dreyfuss, *Designing for People* (New York: Simon and Schuster, 1955) 65–6, 202; NAC, RG 20, A4 1434, file 2, National Industrial Design McGill Conference, 'Design as a Function of Management,' 18 Oct. 1956, commentary on paper by C.H. Linder, unpaginated.

22 NAC, RG20 997, vol. 2, minutes of the NIDC, 23 and 24 April 1951; ibid., vol. 1429, National Design Branch and CAC, file 1000 240/C27, extracts from the annual meeting of the CAC, 29 Sept. 1954

23 NIDC and CAC, *It Pays to Buy Articles*

24 NAC, MG28 I 200, vol. 1, CAC, Design Committee Report, mid-year report, April 1955, report to annual meeting, 5, 6 Oct. 1955, ; NGA, 7.4, file 7, Design in Industry, Mrs K.E. Harrison, Chairman of Design Committee, to Executive of CAC, 26 Feb. 1955; NAC, RG 20, vol. 1429, file 1000 240/C27, Mrs C. Breindahl, CAC Ottawa, to Donald Buchanan, requesting performance testing, 15 April 1955, and reply by Buchanan, 20 April 1955, describing the change in award specifications, and Kathleen Harrison on behalf of CAC to Donald Buchanan, 23 April 1955, stating that volunteers are overburdened and do not feel they constitute a valid testing unit. This file also includes the home-testing questionnaire formulated by the Ottawa branch and their April 1956 report on their work in 1955. An unsigned confidential memo for the consumer relations council of the NIDC, written around October 1955, summarizes the history and work of the CAC from the perspective of the Design Council.

25 There were 896 responses in total, 366 of them from Ontario. NAC, RG 20, vol. 1429, file 1000 240/C27, 'Review of the 1954 NIDC–CAC contests for suggestions for the improvement of household goods'

26 'Mrs Consumer Speaks Out,' 76, 78, and 80

27 'What the Women Want,' *CHG*, Jan. 1955, 36; NFB, *Designed for Living*, 1956

28 Barbara Swann, 'The Design in the Household Exhibition,' *IC*, March 1946, 77–8

29 There are clear illustrations of early Canadian high-oven ranges in a fine article by Hillary Russell, '"Canadian Ways": An Introduction to Comparative Studies of Housework, Stoves and Diet in Great Britain and Canada,' *Material History Bulletin* 19 (spring 1984) 1–12; NAC, RG 20, A4, vol. 1433, National Design Branch, file 'George Englesmith, architect,' Buchanan to Englesmith, 16 Sept. 1947, 14 Nov. 1947, and 21 Nov. 1947; Donald Buchanan, 'Take Another Look at Your Kitchen Range' *Canadian Art* 5 (spring–summer 1948) 182–3; J.B. Craig, F. Dawes and J.C. Rankin, 'A Cooperative Problem in Industrial Design,' RAIC *Journal* 25 (May 1948), 154–5. Buchanan on streamlining: 'Design in Industry: The Canadian Picture' ibid., 24 (July 1947) 234–5, 'Good Design and "Styling" – The Choice Before Us,' *Canadian Art* 9, (Oct. 1951) 32–5; "These Are the Ones the Experts Picked," ibid., 6 (Christmas 1948) 59–60, shows the University of Toronto mock-up and a British Maxwell Fry design; NGA, 7.4 'Design in Industry,' file 2, D.B. Cruickshank, 'Industrial Design: What Are Canadians Doing about It?' June 1949.

30 June Callwood, 'She Leads the Housewives' Crusade,' *Maclean's*, 1 Oct. 1952, 60; NAC, MG 28 I 200, vol. 1, file 10, CAC, report of the consumer relations committee, 20–1 Sept. 1951; Mrs R.G. Morningstar, 'Survey of Time and Motion Studies for Household Equipment' report no. 23, 1952; NGA 7.4-D, Design in Industry, file 4, minutes of the NIDC meeting, 15 and 16 April 1952

31 NAC, RG 20, vol. 1429, file 1000 240/C27, 'Review of the 1954 NIDC-CAC Contest,' 4; UGA, M.S. McCready Collection, A0021, 'From Modernity to Convenience,' *CAC Bulletin*, Jan. 1955; NAC, MG28 I 200, vol. 1, CAC, 1952 annual meeting, 'National Industrial Design Report' by Mrs G.J. Wherrett and Design Committee Report by Mrs W.F. Harrison, April 1955, 13–14 June 1955 and 5–6 Oct. 1955; *Furniture and Furnishings* (April 1955) 83; on early export performance, NAC, RG 20 998 13–2, D.G.W. Douglas to J.P.C. Gauthier, Department of Trade and Commerce report, 15 July 1955, 5; note the women examining the Hy-Oven in NFB, *Designed for Living*.

32 NAC, MG28 I 200, vol. 1 CAC, 1952 annual meeting, report by Mrs G.J. Wherrett, Design Committee; 'What the Women Want,' *CHG*, Jan. 1955, 36; Dreyfuss, *Designing for People*, 69; NIDC Conference, 'Design as a Function of Management,' Donald Daley on U.S. high-oven experiments

33 On the 'characteristics' of goods, Jean-Christophe Agnew, 'The Consuming Vision of Henry James,' in Richard Fox and T.J. Jackson Lears, eds., *The Culture of Consumption* (New York: Pantheon, 1983) 67–74; on the assertion of Jean Baudrillard that 'the real effect of consumption has been to herald "the

passage from use value to sign value,'" Tomlinson, introduction in Alan Tomlinson, ed., *Consumption, Identity and Style: Marketing, Meanings and the Packaging of Pleasure* (New York: Routledge, 1990) 18–21. Baudrilliard makes this argument in 'The Ecstasy of Communication,' in Hal Foster, ed., *The Anti-Aesthetic: Essays on Postmodern Culture* (Port Townsend, WA: Bay Press, 1983) 126–33; on consumer reinterpretation of designs, Cheryl Buckley, 'Made in Patriarchy: Toward a Feminist Analysis of Women and Design,' *Design Issues* 3, 2 (fall 1986), 11, and Phillipa Goodall, 'Design and Gender,' *Block* 9 (1983) 50–61; on reciprocity between the values goods bring to users and users bring to goods, see Penny Sparke, *Electrical Appliances* (London: Unwin Hyman, 1987) 6, and Susan Strasser, *Satisfaction Guaranteed: The Making of the American Mass Market* (New York: Pantheon, 1989) 15.

34 Margaret Hobbs and Ruth Roach Pierson, '"A Kitchen that Wastes no Steps ..." Gender, Class and the Home Improvement Plan, 1936–40,' *Histoire sociale/Social History* 21, no. 41 (May 1988) 9–37

35 McMUA Westinghouse Collection, box 8, file 21, 'Canadian Westinghouse Presents,' broadcast script for 11 Feb. 1951; J.K. Edmonds, 'The Mechanized Household,' *Marketing*, 5 Nov. 1954, 17

36 On the ambiguous messages carried by factory and laboratory imagery see Stuart Ewen, 'Marketing Dreams: The Political Elements of Style,' in Tomlinson, ed., *Consumption, Identity and Style*, 48–9, and Ewen, *All Consuming Images*, 215–16.

37 'Kitchens,' *CHG*, Oct. 1958, 30

38 'Long Range Planning for Tomorrow's Kitchens,' *Design*, Aug. 1957, 50

Chapter 10: What Makes Washday Less Blue?

1 NAC, RG 20 767, EFIR, 'Canadian Westinghouse,' Hamilton, 5 May 1959; 'Thor Gathers Speed after U.S. Agreement,' *Marketing*, 24 April 1959, 8

2 EFIR 765, Canadian General Electric, 7 Oct. 1958, 6 Dec. 1962; Zimmerman's comments are in NAC, RG 20 767, 6 May, 1959; for Kelvinator, see EFIR 773.

3 Susan Strasser, Never Done (New York: Pantheon, 1982); Ruth Schwartz Cowan, *More Work for Mother* (New York: Basic, 1983). Judy Wacjman suggests in her study of refrigerators, however, that Cowan reduced housewives to the role of consumers, responsive only to price, and told the story as a rivalry between manufacturing interests in which user preferences did not figure. Judy Wacjman, *Feminism Confronts Technology* (University Park: Pennsylvania State University Press, 1991) 102. It is worth considering whether the precedence of price over use values in consumer decision making may have been

more marked in the United States than in other North Atlantic economies in the 1950s.

4 Strasser, *Never Done*, 267–8, Cowan, *More Work*, 94

5 Cowan, *More Work*, 128–43

6 *HGR*, 23 Jan. 1967, 1, 7, 23. NAC, RG 20 1755 8001–404/34, 'Domestic Appliances: Canadian Manufacturing + Imports – Exports' for 1965 and 1966

7 T.A.B. Corley, *Domestic Electrical Appliances* (London: Jonathan Cape, 1966) 131–6; Penny Sparke, *Electrical Appliances* (London: Unwin Hyman, 1987) chap. 7; the best British article on women and laundry technology is Christine Zmroczek, 'Dirty Linen: Women, Class and Washing Machines, 1920s-1960s,' *Women's Studies International Forum* 15 (1992) 173–85. The statistics used in this paragraph are drawn from Zmroczek, tables 2 and 1.

8 Zmroczek, 'Dirty Linen,' 182; Robert Frost, 'Machine Liberation: Inventing Housewives and Home Appliances in Interwar France,' *French Historical Studies* 18 (1993) 128; Cynthia Cockburn and Ruza Furst Dilic, Introduction to *Bringing Technology Home: Gender and Technology in a Changing Europe* (Buckingham: Open University Press, 1994) 17

9 There is a fine discussion of this issue in Wajcman, *Feminism Confronts Technology*, chap. 4.

10 'Are We "Selling" the Company to the Consumer?' *IC*, July 1958, 140

11 Peter J. McClure and John K. Ryans, Jr, 'Differences between Retailers' and Consumers' Perceptions,' *Journal of Marketing Research* (Feb. 1968) 35–40; the discussion of retailers' understandings of consumer valuation of automatic washers is at 36–7.

12 For example, see the discussion of product engineering in a 1980 Spanish washing machine firm, M. Carme Alemany Gomez, 'Bodies, Machines and Male Power,' in Cockburn and Dilic, eds., *Bringing Technology Home*, 132–3.

13 Slavenka Drakulic, *How We Survived Communism and Even Laughed* (New York: HarperCollins, 1993) 53. The whole chapter 'On Doing Laundry,' 43–54, is compelling reading for those interested in these questions. Thanks to Dana Frank for this reference.

14 Zmroczek, 'Dirty Linen,' 183; Wajcman *Feminism Confronts Technology*, 102

15 Interviews: Lily Hansen, Tina Wall; Letters: Martha Watson, Irene Newlands

16 Interviews: Allison Simpson, Joan Coffey, Mary Paine, Patricia Cliff, Marjorie Barlow, Lynn Stevens, Nettie Murphy, Gerry Kilby, Ella Smith; 'Better Care Longer Wear,' (*CHG*, Oct. 1950), 68–9; Jane Monteith, 'Planning a laundry for Today and Tomorrow,' *Chatelaine*, Feb. 1949, 37

17 Interviews: Mary Paine, Allison Simpson, Pam McKeen, Winnifred Edwards; *Chatelaine* noted as advantages for automatic over wringer machines in November 1951, that 'Your hands never touch the water; weight of wet clothes

does not have to be lifted up and down; no dripping water to clear up after-ward' and emphatically, 'No worry about children playing around the auto-matic machine'; Susan Sellers, 'Mechanical Bride: The Exhibition,' *Design Issues* 10, 2 (summer 1994) 76

18 Interview: Allison Simpson
19 Ruth Schwartz Cowan, 'The Consumption Junction: A Proposal for Research Strategies in the Sociology of Technology,' in Wiebe K. Bijker et al., *The Social Construction of Technological Systems: New Directions in Sociology and the History of Technology* (Cambridge: MIT Press, 1987) 263, 278
20 Sigfried Giedion, *Mechanization Takes Command* (New York: Oxford University Press, 1948)
21 A.B. Blankenship, Blankenship, Gruneau Associates, 'The Consumer of the Sixties,' *Texts of Papers Presented at the 3rd Annual Appliance Marketing Seminar*, CEMA, 9 June 1960 (CEMA, 1960) 33–4
22 F.W. Mansfield, 'A Discussion of the Principles of Marketing Research and How They Can be Used by the Appliance Industry,' in *The Next Fifty Years Belong to Marketing: Texts of Papers Presented at the 2nd Annual Appliance Market-ing Seminar*, CEMA, 3 June 1959 (CEMA, 1959) 6, 8, 13
23 Sparke, *Electrical Appliances*, 6; Cockburn and Dilic, Introduction, *Bringing Technology Home* 11; Frost, 'Machine Liberation,' 127, at n. 44, citing Bruno LaTour and Madeleine Akrich; Susan Ormrod, '"Let's Nuke the Dinner": Discursive Practices of Gender in the Creation of a New Cooking Process,' in Cockburn and Dilic, eds., *Bringing Technology Home*, 42–58
24 Frost, 'Machine Liberation,' 129
25 'The Beautiful McClary Washer,' *Chatelaine*, April 1951, back of front cover; the Connor pitch is described in 'Hookers Used in Connor Campaign,' *Marketing*, 15 May 1954, 16; 'Housewives Like Color Washers: Beatty Adds Color Sales Curve with Cromatic Line,' *Marketing*, 11 Nov. 1955, 20; 'Mothers of All Ages Choose Beatty Copperstyle,' *Chatelaine*, March 1958, 53
26 Strasser, *Never Done*, 267
27 'The Easy Way to Sell – Coax Man on Store Floor to 'Romance' Your Prod-uct,' *Marketing*, 30 Aug. 1957, 20–2
28 R.J. Woxman, 'The Consumer Needs and Wants – How Can the Appliance and Home Entertainment Industry Meet the Challenge?' *Proceedings of the 5th Annual Appliance Marketing Seminar*, CEMA, 17 May 1962 (CEMA, 1962) 41
29 A.L. Vincent, 'The Retailers Viewpoint on Marketing Appliances,' *CEMA 1959* 53–4
30 'Change Washday into Playday! The New Easy Combination ...,' *CHG*, Nov. 1956, 45; 'Now the New Beatty Washer Saves You,' *CHG*, June 1952, 34; 'Bendix Introduces '53 Line,' *Marketing*, Jan. 1953, 1; OHA, Live Better Elec-

trically file 570, 1958 ad for automatic washer showing mother with toddler in high chair, washer behind them, and cover line 'Less time for your laundry, more time for your family'

31 Marie Holmes, 'Look What's Happening to Washday,' *Chatelaine*, May 1953, 78; Strasser, *Never Done*, 268

32 Ads for automatic washers, 1959 and 1960, OHA 'Live Better Electrically' 570.1; the advantages Australian women found in daily laundry are described by Kereen Reiger, 'At Home with Technology' *Arena* 75 (1986) 115–16, 117–18.

33 '"Twins for Twins" Promotion,' *Marketing*, 21 Feb. 1953, 1; 'Practical and Emotional Appeals Feature This Consumer "Contest,"' ibid., 21 March 1953, 2; 'Laundry Dealership Told "Babies Mean Business,"' ibid., 5 Sept. 1958, 46

34 Marshall McLuhan, a philosophy professor at St Michael's College, University of Toronto, ponders this elision in *The Mechanical Bride: Folklore of Industrial Man* (New York: Vanguard Press, 1951). Dianne Newell pointed out to me this aspect of these essays, particularly apparent in McLuhan's choice of illustrations; see similarly, Richard Sennett, *The Fall of Public Man* (New York: Vintage, 1974), 20; Mariana Valverde, 'Representing Childhood: The Multiple Fathers of the Dionne Quintuplettes,' in Carol Smart, ed., *Regulating Women* (New York: Routledge, 1992) 119–46; special Dionne issue of *Journal of Canadian Studies* (winter 1994–5)

35 OHA, 570.1 'Living Better Electrically' 1959 automatic washer ad; 'Buy a Washer, Save a Wife: Promotion Soaps Up Husbands,' *Marketing*, 11 July 1958, 30; 'After the Wedding: A Washer Inglis Ads Aimed at Husbands,' ibid., 3 April 1959, 6. The latter campaign ran in both *Maclean's* and *La Patrie*. The *Marketing* stories describe the advertising campaign and the advertiser's rational for its design.

36 In 1954 the four largest makers of automatics commanded 91 per cent of the market. That year the four largest firms producing wringers made only 52 per cent of the machines offered for sale. See Clarence Barber, *The Canadian Electrical Manufacturing Industry*, RCCEP (Ottawa: Queen's Printer, Sept. 1956) 43; *Major Household Appliances: Production, Consumption and Trade: Selected Countries* (United States Department of Commerce, 1960) 9, 14; on Beatty's history in the field see 'The Costs Are the Same but Value Greater Now,' *Financial Post*, 17 May 1958, 28; NAC, RG 20 1755 404/34, 'Major Appliance Industry Plan' Domestic Appliance Plan 1965–8; EFIR 763, Beatty Brothers, 22 Oct. 1963; EFIR 773, Kelvinator Canada, April 1956.

37 Barber, *Canadian Electrical*, 29, 51–2, 54; H.C. Eastman, 'Electrical Appliances Industry,' 5, in NAC, RG 20 1755 8001–404/35

38 Barber, *Canadian Electrical*, 10; EFIR 763, Beatty Brothers, interview with R.L.

Kerr, 20 May 1964; EFIR 767, Canadian Westinghouse, interview with C.H. McBain and K.E. Waugh, 6 June 1962; J.H. Connor and Son produced wringer machines in two versions, one for rural and northern markets using cast iron, steel, and heavy aluminum for maximum durability at a higher price, the other using more light metals and plastics for urban users. H.E. English reporting on visit to J.H. Connor and Son Ltd, 12 April 1956. NAC, RG 33 52, RCCEP, 3–13–8

39 Eastman, 'Electrical Appliances Industry,' 5, 8, 12; NAC, RG 20 1755 P8001–404/35, comments on Eastman by G.Q. Rahm, chief, Appliance and Commercial Machine Division, Trade and Commerce, 4 Feb. 1966, and by Ralph Barford, General Steel Wares, 23 Feb. 1966. There is a longer discussion about optimal plant size by Barford, of Beatty and General Steel Wares in NAC, RG 20 P8001–270/G47, P.C. Fredenburgh site visit 5 Jan. 1967. Plants which used more out-sourcing – that is, purchased rather than produced parts – would have been efficient at a smaller scale, but here the national boundary loomed as an obstacle, for even firms with Canadian subsidiaries confined parts manufacture to the United States.

40 Gomez, 'Bodies, Machines and Male Power,' 132

41 'Laundry Appliance Firms Sign Agreement,' HGR, 15 May 1959; NAC, RG 20, 1755 8001–404/41, vol. 2, P.C. Fredenburgh 'Comparison of US and Canadian Major Appliance Plants,' 22 March 1968, 23

42 David Sobel and Susan Meurer, Working at Inglis: The Life and Death of a Canadian Factory (Toronto: Lorimer, 1994) 115, 141, 149–53

43 Major Household Appliances, 14; Barber, Canadian Electrical, 62; NAC, RG 20, vol. 1755 P8001–404/46 'Major Appliance Study,' chap. 3, Input prices

44 Fredenburgh, 'Comparison of US and Canadian Major Appliance Plants,' 22

45 For a discussion of the different ways in which manufacturers using mass and batch production methods feature, and attend to, consumers see Philip Scranton, 'Manufacturing Diversity: Production Systems, Markets, and an American Consumer Society, 1870–1930,' Technology and Culture 35 (1994) 476–505.

46 Interview: Joan Coffey; Letter: Martha Watson

47 See the warnings to salesmen in 'Charting Course for Selling,' Marketing, 30 Nov. 1946, 2; 'Selling Via Demonstrations,' ibid., 30 July 1949, 8, 12.

48 Interviews: Patricia Cliff, Margaret Shortliffe, Winnifred Edwards, Nettie Murphy; see Zmbroczek 'Dirty Linen,' 183 on the British equivalent of wet wash called bag wash. A recent discussion of commercial laundries in the U.S. is Roger Miller, 'Selling Mrs Consumer: Advertising and the Creation of Suburban Socio-spatial Relations, 1910–1930,' Antipode 23 (1991) 278.

49 McLuhan, Mechanical Bride, 32, 33; William Christian, George Grant (Toronto:

University of Toronto Press, 1993) 177, 250. Grant's best-known writings are *Lament for a Nation* and *Technology and Empire.*

50 Interviews: Margaret Shortliffe, Ann Brook, Susan Taylor, Joan Niblock; Letter: Bev Newmarch, M. McConnell

51 Letters: Olive L. Kozicky, Bev Newmarch, Elizabeth Perry

52 Interviews: Margaret Shortliffe, Winnifred Edwards; Letter: Liz Forbes

53 'Laundry's No Problem,' *CHG,* Oct. 1950, 91; 'How to Choose Your Next Big Appliance,' *Chatelaine,* Nov. 1956, 22; EFIR 765, 'Canadian General Electric,' 9 June 1965; Tanis Day, 'Substituting Capital for Labour in the Home: The Diffusion of Household Technology' (PhD diss., Queen's University, 1987) 185. The 1966 prices cited from Day are in 1971 dollars.

54 Jean Mann Due, 'Consumption Levels in Canada and the United States, 1947–50,' *Canadian Journal of Economics and Political Science* 21 (May 1955) 174–81

55 Nancy Folbre and Heidi Hartmann, 'The Rhetoric of Self Interest: Ideology and Gender in Economic Theory,' in Arjo Klamer et al., *The Consequences of Economic Rhetoric* (New York: Cambridge University Press, 1988) 184–203; Paula England, 'The Separative Self: Androcentric Bias in Neoclassical Assumptions,' in Marianne A. Ferber and Julie A. Nelson, eds., *Beyond Economic Man: Feminist Theory and Economics* (Chicago: University of Chicago Press, 1993) 37–53

56 The least spent for refrigerators was $342, the most $353; for stoves the range was between $205 and $219, both narrower differences, on larger sums, than the $35 gap for washers. AO, T. Eaton Company, series 69, vol. 25, Market Research 1953–60, 'Purchasing of Furniture, Household Appliances and Homes Furnishings – Toronto – By Age Groups, 1949–50–51 and 32 weeks of 1952'

57 AO, T. Eaton Company, series 165, box 2, file 5.1. 'Purchasing of home furnishings and appliances by new home owners' Controller's Office, 2 Sept. 1958

58 Interviews: Pam McKeen, Joan Niblock, Joan Coffey, Gerd Evans; Letters: Mrs A.B. Botham, Hazel Beech

59 This seems to have been the case for Ontario in the 1950s. See Nora Cebotarev, 'From Domesticity to the Public Sphere: Farm Women, 1945–86,' in Joy Parr ed., *A Diversity of Women: Ontario 1945–1980* (Toronto: University of Toronto Press, 1995) 203, 207. In Quebec, aspiration for domestic comfort (247) took greater precedence, Yves Tremblay, 'Équiper la maison de ferme ou la ferme, le choix des femmes québécoises, 1930–1960,' *Bulletin de l'histoire de l'électricité* 19–20 (1992) 235–48.

60 Katherine Jellison, *Entitled to Power: Farm Women and Technology, 1913–63*

(Chapel Hill: University of North Carolina Press, 1993) 109; Corlann Gee Bush, '"He Isn't Half so Cranky as He Used to Be": Agricultural Mechanization, Comparable Worth, and the Changing Farm Family,' in Carol Groneman and Mary Beth Norton, eds., *'To Toil the Livelong Day': America's Women at Work, 1780–1980* (Ithaca, NY: Cornell University Press, 1987) 228

61 UGA, Helen Abell Papers, AOS6076, 'Report of Findings Concerning Consumer Information; Crafts and Hobbies; Housing (The Farm Home)' Progress Report no. 7, 'Special Study of Ontario Farm Homes and Homemakers 1959,' 11, 12, 28

62 J.K. Edmonds, 'Keep a Sales Eye on the Farmer's Wife,' *Marketing*, 24 May 1957, 28

63 Proportion of automatic washing machines among electric washing machines in Quebec homes (%): 1960 – 13, 1961 – 15.6, 1962 – 18.4, 1963 – 21.6, 1964 – 25.4, 1965 – 28.3, 1966 – 32.7, 1967 – 38.8; *Household Facilities and Equipment* (Ottawa: Dominion Bureau of Statistics, 1960–7); Jellison, *Entitled to Power*, 180, 185

64 The interviews included questions about how buying decisions were made. The response usually was that decisions were arrived at jointly. It was usually difficult to discern whether or how patriarchal privileges or status as breadwinners influenced buying priorities. In the analysis of the transcripts and correspondence, I have taken women at their word. Interviews: Patricia Cliff, Nettie Murphy

65 J.K. Edmonds, 'An Expanding Durable Goods Market: Aim Ad Pitch to Working Wife,' *Marketing*, 28 Oct. 1960, 42; 'The Working Wife – Appliances Target,' *Marketing*, 24 Dec. 1958, 8; Vance Packard, *The Hidden Persuaders* (New York: David McKay, 1957) 62; Maxine Margolis, *Mothers and Such* (Berkeley: University of California Press, 1984) 167; Joan Sangster bases her finding on detailed studies by the Women's Bureau of the Federal Department of Labour. See her 'Doing Two Jobs: The Wage-Earning Mother, 1945–70,' in Parr, ed., *Diversity of Women*, 100, 120; UGA, RE1 MAC AO135, Mary E. Singer and Sue Rogers, 'Survey of Child Care and Housekeeping Arrangements Made by Homemakers Who Are Employed outside the Home,' June 1966, 22, 25; Letters: Bev Newlands, Joyce Cunningham.

66 'The Working Wife – Appliances Target,' *Marketing* 24 Dec. 1958 8; Edmonds, 'Expanding Durable Goods Market'; Lee Maguire, 'Canadian Consumer Buying Intentions: A Study of Provincial and Socio-economic Differences' (MBA thesis, University of Windsor, 1967) 34. A copy of this thesis is in the University of Guelph Library.

67 UGA, Abell Collection, Helen Abell and Frank Uhlir, 'Rural Young People

and Their Future Plans: Opinion and Attitudes of Selected Rural Young People Concerning Farming and Rural Life in Alberta, Ontario and Quebec, 1951–2,' Canada, Department of Agriculture, 1953

68 UGA, Margaret McCready Collection, AO13518 and 13519, Margaret McCready, 'Science in the Home,' Feb. 1946, and 'Whither Home Economics,' Nov. 1954

69 Anne-Jorunn Berg, 'A Gendered Socio-technical Construction: The Smart House,' 173–4, and Andjelka Milic, 'Women, Technology and Societal Failure in Former Yugoslavia,' 156, both in Cockburn and Dilic, eds., *Bringing Technology Home*

70 *Housing Plans of Canadians* (Toronto: Maclean-Hunter, Aug. 1945) 7; Lever Brothers, *Canadian Homes. A Survey of Urban and Farm Housing* (Toronto, 1945) 7. The regional variations were considerable. See D.R. White, 'Rural Canada in Transition,' in M.A. Trembley and W.J. Anderson, eds., *Rural Canada in Transition* (Ottawa: Agricultural Economics Research Council, 1966) 39–41. In 1961 two-thirds of prairie farm homes still did not have inside running water.

71 White, 'Rural Canada,' 39–41

72 The association between use of wringer technology and the absence of municipal water systems in apparent in the United States as well. See James A. Carman and J.D. Kaczor, 'Ownership Patterns for Major Household Appliances,' in James A. Carman, *Studies in the Demand for Consumer Household Equipment* (Berkeley: University of California Press, 1965), 118.

73 Interviews: Gerd Evans, Emma Boyd, Gerry Kilby, Allison Simpson, Lily Hansen; Letter: Kathy Grensewich

74 F.H. Leacy, ed., *Historical Statistics of Canada*, 2nd ed. (Ottawa: Statistics Canada, 1983) E49. Women who remembered the 1950s as a time when they struggled to get by, retrospectively often dated their own postwar prosperity from 1962.

75 In 1964, three-quarters of wringer sales were to households with incomes greater than $5000. G.D. Quirin, R.M. Sultan, and T.A. Wilson, 'The Canadian Appliance Industry,' University of Toronto, Institute for Quantitative Research in Social and Economic Policy, 1970, 36, 77; NAC, RG 20, vol. 1755 P8001-4404/46, 1964 – Major Appliance Study, sales of wringer washers, 203,000; of automatics, 162,900: 75.3 per cent of wringer sales were to replace wringers; 59.6 per cent of automatic sales were conversions from wringers; 1964 sales by types of transactions.

76 Sparke, *Electrical Appliances*, 6; Rosemary Pringle, 'Women and Consumer Capitalism,' in Cora Baldock and Bettina Cass, eds., *Women, Social Welfare and*

the State in Australia (Sydney: Allen Unwin, 1983) 100; Susan Strasser, *Satisfaction Guaranteed* (New York: Pantheon, 1989) 15; David Nye, *Electrifying America* (Cambridge: MIT Press, 1990) 281; John Fiske, *Reading the Popular* (Boston: Allen and Unwin, 1989) 2

77 Nye, *Electrifying America*, 281; Mihaly Csikszentmihalyi and Eugene Rochberg-Halton, *The Meaning of Things* (Cambridge: Cambridge University Press, 1981) 53

78 The comment from Mrs Barr and similar one by Mrs G.F. Grady of Peterborough are in 'Housewives' Ideas for Better Washers,' *CHG*, June 1955, 66; the filling system of the 7 rinse Inglis automatic is described in NAC, MG 28 I 200, vol. 1, CAC, Mrs R.G. Morningstar, 'Survey of Time and Motion Studies for Household Equipment,' report 23, 1952; 'Look What's Happening to Washday,' *Chatelaine*, May 1953, 79, 81; 'Today's Household Equipment,' ibid., Nov. 1951, 90; 'Buying Public Loves Laundry "Automation,"' *HGR*, 25 March 1963, 18; 'Laundry Market Accelerating Fast in Canada,' *HGR*, 7 March 1966; Nye, *Electrifying America*, 303; Letters: Cindy Bolger, Liz Forbes.

79 Suzette Worden, 'Powerful Women: Electricity in the Home, 1919–40,' in Judy Attfield and Pat Kirkham, eds., *A View from the Interior: Feminism, Women and Design* (London: Women's Press, 1989) 140; Rosemary Pringle, 'Women and Consumer Capitalism,' 100–1

80 Corley, *Domestic Electrical Appliances*, 136; Giedion, *Mechanization Takes Command*, 570; Walton before CEMA 1962 16; Interview: Greta Nelson; Letters: E.M. Botham, Bev Newmarch

81 Letter: Elizabeth Perry; for reactions to Canadian women's 'doubts and prejudices' about automatics, Margaret Meadows, 'What to Look for When Buying an Automatic Washer,' *Chatelaine*, May 1951, 84; 'Working up Sales Lather – Market Was Made Sure – It Was Westinghouse,' *Marketing*, 22 Feb. 1957, 7; 'Guarantees Washer for Twelve Years,' *Marketing*, 28 March 1958, 1; BCHA, BC Electric Marketing Division, 'Consumer Attitude Survey – Fuels and Household Appliances,' May 1961, 5, 39, 41; Interview: Bea Millar; Millar, head of BC Electric Home Services, noted that the first automatics needed to be bolted to a good cement foundation because the spinning tub caused the washer cabinet to shift.

82 Frost, 'Machine Liberation'; on freedom, technological complexity, and processes of consumption, with intermittent reference to washing machines, see Zygmunt Bauman, *Thinking Sociologically* (Oxford: Blackwell, 1990) 196, 201, 204; and commentary on this argument by Alan Warde, 'Consumers, Identity and Belonging: Reflections on Some These of Zygmunt Bauman,' in Russell Keat et al., *The Authority of the Consumer* (London: Routledge, 1994) 67–72.

Chapter 11: A Caution of Excess

1 On microwaves, Cynthia Cockburn and Susan Ormrod, *Gender and Technology in the Making* (London: Sage, 1993); on saturations, Appendix 1 below; G.D. Quirin, R.M. Sultan, and T.A. Wilson, 'The Canadian Appliance Industry,' University of Toronto, Institute for Quantitative Research in Social and Economic Policy, 1970, Appendix V-C, pp. 38–49; BCHA, Sales Research Department, 'Residential Appliance Saturations, Appliance Use Survey as at November 30, 1957,' 1; there were two-door refrigerators in 10.6 per cent of Ontario households by 1962 and in 33.3 per cent by 1968. Tanis Day, 'Substituting Capital for Labour in the Home: The Diffusion of Household Technology' (PhD diss., Queen's University, 1987) 176

2 'Appliance Manufacturers Told: "Next Boom in 1960s,"' *Marketing*, 23 May 1958, 33; 'CDNPA Survey, Big Sales Future Cooking for Appliances,' ibid., 8 March 1957, 14, 16, 18

3 NAC, RG 20 765 23–100–C27 CGE, EFIR, 16 Jan. 1956; 'Appliances – Sales to Increase 34%,' *Marketing*, 9 Nov. 1962, 34–7; 'Watch the Age Group Pattern,' ibid., 8 June 1962, 79–81; 'Luxury Appliance Sales Hold up Hard Market,' ibid., 17 March 1961, 20; F.H. Leacy, ed., *Historical Statistics of Canada*, 2nd ed. (Ottawa: Statistics Canada, 1983) Series B81 and A350

4 'Canadian Appliance Industry,' chap. 2, p. 45 and Appendix fig. 49, p. 85; CEMA, 'Appliance Marketing Seminar,' 1962, opening remarks by D.C. Marrs, 1–2; 'Not Interested in Selling Tombstones,' *Marketing*, 30 Aug. 1957, 20, 22; Lundy to CEMA 'Appliance Marketing Seminar,' 1960, 63.

5 'Dryers, Polisher, Freezers Top Want List,' *Marketing*, 7 Oct. 1960, 74; 'Canadian Appliance Study,' Appendix, figs 27 and 30, pp. 54, 57; Leacy, ed., *Historical Statistics of Canada*, E168, S186; 'Appliances – Sales to Increase 34%,' 34–7

6 T.A.B. Corley, *Domestic Electrical Appliances* (London: Jonathan Cape, 1966) 54; George Katona, *The Powerful Consumer* (New York: McGraw-Hill, 1960) 48–9; EFIR 774 Moffat, EFIR 767 Canadian Westinghouse, both reports for 1960; EFIR 778 Robert Simpson Company interview with Morgan Reid, 29 Aug. 1959

7 'Canadian Appliance Industry,' chap. 5, charts 2A-G, 63–9, chap. 1, 5; Lee Maguire, 'Canadian Consumer Buying Intentions' (MBA thesis, University of Windsor, 1967) 30, a study based on 1963–6 Gruneau data; 'Husband May Insist on New Appliances,' *HGR*, 2 Dec. 1963, 15; 'Suggests Replacement Market Best Bet for 1961 Retailing,' *HGR*, 4 Jan. 1961, 53

8 Pat Armstrong and Hugh Armstrong, *The Double Ghetto: Canadian Women and Their Segregated Work* (Toronto: McClelland and Stewart, 1978) 152

9 Penny Sparke, *As Long as It's Pink* (London: HarperCollins, 1995) 86–7

10 This transition is analysed cogently as a reconsideration of the reservation wage by Tanis Day in 'Capital-Labor Substitution in the Home,' *Technology and Culture* 33, 2 (1992) 323–5; Susan Willis treats the transformation as a weighing of use and exchange values in *A Primer for Daily Life* (London: Routledge, 1991) chap. 8; on postwar debates concerning economic and social implications of reckoning only the market consequences production see Joy Parr and Gunilla Ekberg, 'Mrs Consumer and Mr Keynes in Postwar Canada and Sweden,' *Gender and History* 8, 2 (July 1996) 212–30.

11 Day, 'Capital-Labor,' 323–5

12 'Keep a Sales Eye on the Farmer's Wife,' *Marketing*, 24 May 1957, 27–8; 'Aim Ad Pitch to Working Wife,' ibid., 28 Oct. 1960, 42; 'The Women Who Works Needs a Streamlined System for Housekeeping,' *Chatelaine*, Jan. 1965, 24–5

13 Willis, *Primer*, 98

14 Sue Bowden and Avner Offer, 'Household Appliances and the Use of Time: The United States and Britain since the 1920s,' *Economic History Review* 47, 4 (1994) 725–48

15 Interview: Mary Kippen; Letter: Leslie G. Oliver, Aurora, Ontario, to author, 19 Aug. 1996

16 'Consumers Will Be Tougher but They'll Be Better' *Marketing*, 3 April 1959, 12; 'Four Easy Ways to Be Wrong about Women Shoppers,' ibid., 19 Feb. 1965, 20; 'Sex Even Controls the Cheques' ibid., 15 Feb. 1963, 3; J.K Edmonds, 'The Powerful Man in the Middle,' ibid., 3 Dec. 1954, 6, 8; EFIR 771 General Steel Wares, report by S.W. Allen, 25 Oct. 1960; on the United States, see similarly Carolyn Shaw Bell, *Consumer Choice in the American Economy* (New York: Random House, 1967) 224; and for Australia, Kereen Reiger, 'At Home with Technology,' *Arena* 75 (1986) 117–18.

17 Percentage of homes cooking with gas or electricity, 73.4: CDNPA, *Canadian Consumer Survey*, 1947, 'Comparison between 1941 Census and Can. Consumer Survey,' vii; see summary of saturations, Appendix 1.

18 Letter: Irene Newlands

19 This transition occurred in three steps. 'The evolution was ... from noxious sulfur dioxide to less noxious but potentially explosive and inflammable methyl chloride ... to odorless, non-toxic, noninflammable fluorinated hydrocarbons.' Letter: Oliver

20 Don Wallace, *Shaping America's Products* (New York: Reinhold, 1956) 74; Stuart Brownlee, a pioneer in Canadian General Electric's product design department addressing the Canadian Council of Appliance Manufacturers, in 'New Appliance Materials Ad Theme of the Future?' *Marketing*, 25 Oct. 1963, 9; NAC, RG 20, A4 1434, NIDC Conference, McGill University, 18 Oct.

1956, Clarence H. Linder, vice-president Engineering Services, General Electric USA, 'Accent on the Optimum,' 5

21 Richard S. Tetlow, *New and Improved* (New York: Basic Books, 1990) 308–13, 326; Ruth Swartz Cowan, *More Work for Mother* (New York: Basic Books, 1983) 131–43

22 Penny Sparke, *Electrical Appliances* (London: Unwin Hyman, 1987) 54, 79–81; Tetlow, *New and Improved* 318, 322; Wallace, *Shaping America's Products* 72

23 'Frigidaire Presents 1950 Line,' *Marketing*, 25 Feb. 1950, 1; 'I-H "Decorator" Campaign,' ibid., 14 Feb. 1953, 1; Letter: Leslie G. Oliver; 'Creating Dealer Enthusiasm "Must" in Putting New Sales Points Across,' Marketing, 7 March 1953, 2–3; 'Jet Floating Sells Frig.,' ibid., 4 June 1965, 2, 29; 'Refrigerators Go High Fashion,' *HGR*, 5 April 1965, 1, 26; '"Floating" Refrigerator Developed in Canada,' ibid., 31 May 1965, 23

24 CDNPA, *Canadian Consumer Survey*, 1956, 1963

25 EFIR 771, T.W. Fenton to R.S. Cook, 20 Oct. 1953; S.W. Allen to Cook, 20 June 1961

26 'Canadian Appliance Industry,' chap. 7, Table 2, p. 5; Clarence L. Barber, *The Canadian Electrical Manufacturing Industry*, Study for RCCEP, Sept. 1956, 50–1; EFIR 771 General Steel Wares, T.W. Fenton to Cook, 20 Oct. 1953; EFIR 767 Canadian Westinghouse, J.E. Cassidy and Ian Malcolm, 7 Oct. 1953; EFIR 765 CGE, Roy Phillips, 11 Feb. 1960; EFIR 773 Kelvinator, J.P. Ryan to R.S. Cook 23 Sept. 1957; EFIR 770 Frigidaire, L.N. Gill to Cook, 14 Aug. 1957; 'Week's Pay Buys Twice as Much as 10 Years Ago,' *HGR*, 17 Oct. 1956, 32; EFIR 774 Moffat, Quirk to Cook, 10 March 1958. The number of refrigerators exported into Canada from the United States increased by 11 per cent between 1957 and 1958. U.S. Department of Commerce, *Major Household Appliances – Production, Consumption, Trade*, Sept. 1960, 13

27 'Revolutionary Concept – GM Shows Kitchen of Tomorrow,' *Marketing*, 7 Dec. 1956, 46; EFIR 771 Frigidaire, Gill interviewed by Cook, 7 Jan. 1957; NIDC Conference, McGill University, 1956, Clarence H. Linder, vice-president Engineering Services, General Electric USA, 'Accent on the Optimum,' 7

28 EFIR 771 General Steel Wares, T.W. Fenton to R.S. Cook, 27 May 1958 and 17 Dec. 1958

29 EFIR 767 Canadian Westinghouse, William Campbell to R.S. Cook, 14 March 1957; EFIR 770 Frigidaire, L.N. Gill to R.S. Cook, 14 Aug. 1957 and 31 March 1958; CDNPA, *Canadian Consumer Survey*, 1957, 1958

30 Interview: Leslie Oliver

31 EFIR 771 General Steel Wares, T.W. Fenton to R.S. Cook, 27 May 1958; EFIR 765 Canadian General Electric, Wylie and Jacques Lefebvre, 9 June 1965;

NAC, RG 20 1755 P8001-404/46, Harold Crookell, 'Marketing Appliances in Canada,' Sept. 1969, 7–12; 'Canadian Appliance Industry,' chap. 1, p. 9; chap. 5, p. 11; Gibson, Roy, McClary, Admiral, and Moffat combined market share percentage, 1961 – 11, 1963 – 11, 1963 – 13, 1967 – 15, CDNPA, *Canadian Consumer Survey* 1961, 1963, 1965, 1967

32 Interviews: Joan Coffey, and her later notes on the transcript; Susan Taylor, and her later transcript notes; Tina Wall, Leslie Oliver, Bea Miller; University of British Columbia Special Collections, Bea Millar Papers, 1-18, BC Hydro publicity for freezers, 'Freeze 'n Save'

33 Interviews: Ann Brook, Nettie Murphy, Ella Smith; Stuart Brownlee, president of Canadian Admiral, formerly product engineer with CGE, 'New Appliance Materials as Theme of the Future' on the limitations of new materials 'prematurely' employed, *Marketing*, 25 Oct. 1963, 8

34 Alan Tomlinson, ed., *Consumption, Identity, and Style* (London: Routledge, 1990) 21, quoting Mike Featherston, 'Consumer Culture, Symbolic Power and Universalism' (unpublished paper, Sept. 1985) 4; Willis, *Primer*, 47–8 and 7, following Wolfgang Haug, *Critique of Commodity Aesthetics* (Cambridge: Polity Press, 1986); Richard Sennett, *The Fall of Public Man* (New York: Random House, 1974) 20; Morgan Reid, 'The Revolution in Retailing,' *Financial Post*, 27 June 1953, 24, in AO, T. Eaton Company, series 69, Merchandise Office, vol. 12, 'Business Conditions and Forecasts, 1940–52'

35 'Manufacturers to Blame for Slow Growth – Keyes,' *HGR*, 30 Nov. 1955, 36; Corley, *Domestic Electrical Appliances*, 135, 113; EFIR 770 Frigidaire, L.N. Gill to R.S. Cook, 7 Jan. 1957; D.C. Marrs, Canadian Westinghouse, 'Call for All-Out Consumer Campaign,' *HGR*, 11 Oct. 1961, 1; CEMA, 'Appliance Marketing Seminar,' 1962, R.J. Woxman, Kelvinator, 41; the classic contemporary analysis of this change in design reasoning is Reyner Banham, 'A Throw-Away Aesthetic,' originally published in *Industrial Design* (1960), reprinted in *Design by Choice* (New York: Rizolli, 1981) 90–3.

36 'Will Stress Trade-Sale,' *HGR*, 2 March 1960, 15; 'Dealers Eye Trades for Cottage Selling,' *HGR*, 30 March 1960, 16; Dominion Bureau of Statistics, *City Family Expenditures*, 1957, 22; 'How High Is Your Refrigerator?' *HGR*, 23 Sept. 1963, 20; 'Store Gets Modest Response to Test-as Promotion,' *HGR*, 29 June 1964, 15; 'Trade-in Handling and Pricing Criticized,' *HGR*, 10 Aug. 1964, 23; Day, 'Capital-Labor,' 313

37 'Canadian Appliance Industry,' chap. 2, pp. 31–5, 57–8; officials from Canadian Westinghouse reported early in the drive for replacement sales that while buyers were keen to have larger refrigerators, 'extras at additional cost were not received favourably.' EFIR 767, Canadian Westinghouse, E.P. Zimmerman, 6 May 1959

38 'Price War for Refrigerators?' *Marketing*, 26 Oct. 1956, 39; 'Coloured Appliances Not Popular,' *HGR*, 5 Oct. 1955, 54; 'Electrical Manufacturers Set Up Sales Drive,' *HGR*, 17 Oct. 1956, 1, 30; EFIR 765 CGE, 26 March 1957; 'It's Still White Goods Business in Canada,' *HGR*, 17 June 1963, 20; 'Confusion Over Terms Holds Back New Items,' *HGR*, 15 June 1964; Interview: Winnifred Edwards

39 Interview: Hugo Lindstrom

40 Corley, *Domestic Electrical Appliances*, 138; see similarly for Australia, another small market, Ann Game and Rosemary Pringle, *Gender at Work* (London: Pluto, 1984) 27; CEMA, 'Appliance Marketing Seminar' 1962, address by Dorothy Walton, 18, 22; NAC, RG 20 1435 Industrial Development Branch, 'National Consumer-Producer Conference,' Toronto, 14 March 1963, address by Beryl Plumptre

41 'Canadian Appliance Industry,' chap. 5, pp. 38–40; EFIR 770 Frigidaire L.N. Gill to R.S. Cook, 15 Jan. 1959; R. Woxman, president Kelvinator, addressing CEMA, 'Appliance Marketing Seminar' 1962, 40

42 'Canadian Appliance Industry,' chap. 8 and passim; NAC, RG 20 2070 P8001-270/G47, 'Report by P.C. Fredenburgh on interview with Ralph Barford,' et al., General Steel Wares, 5 Jan. 1967; Harry Eastman, 'Canadian Appliance Industry – Study of Optimum Size,' NAC, RG 20 1755 P8001-404/35, and comments by Ralph Barford; affidavit of Ralph Barford, 13 July 1992, as contained in court file no. B178/92 in the case of *GSW Inc.* v *General Electric Company and General Electric Canada Inc.* (1992) (Ont. C.J. [Gen. Div.] unreported).

43 Judith Williamson, *Consuming Passions: The Dynamics of Popular Culture* (London: Marion Boyars, 1986) 225

44 Adrian Forty, *Objects of Desire* (New York: Pantheon, 1986) 184–5; CEMA, 'Appliance Marketing Seminar' 1960, G.H. Henry, Manager of Residential Sales, Hydro Electric Power Commission of Ontario, 'Marketing Partners in the Sixties,' 26

45 Forty, *Objects of Desire*, 185, Day, 'Capital-Labor,' 308; OHA, 570 Marketing and Utilisation,' 'Suggested Educational and Public Programmes re: Electric Living in Ontario, 4 June 1957,' 3; BCHA, 455, George Hargreaves, 'Changes in Marketing Policy, BC Electric – BC Hydro, 1936–1976,' 2

46 Ruth Swartz Cowan, 'The Consumption Junction: A Proposal for Research Strategies in the Sociology of Technology,' in Wiebe K. Bijker et al., eds., *The Social Construction of Technological Systems* (Cambridge: MIT, 1987) 275

47 G.M. McHenry, 'Marketing Partners in the Sixties,' CEMA 'Appliance Marketing Seminar,' 1960, 26; Paul McKay, *Electric Empire* (Toronto: Between the Lines, 1983) 37; OHA, 570.71 Electricity vs Gas, memo on gas competition,

1 Nov. 1957, and Special Studies and Surveys, 'The Effect of Competition from Natural Gas on Demand for Electricity in Ontario, 1958–70,' report to the premier of Ontario by Jas S. Duncan, chair of Ontario Hydro, 20 Jan. 1959

48 Leacy, *Historical Statistics*, Q102–6; Jean Barman, *The West beyond the West* (Toronto: University of Toronto Press, 1991) 283–4; McKay, *Electric Empire*, 35–7; Neil B. Freeman, *The Politics of Power* (Toronto: University of Toronto Press, 1996) 105; Hargreaves, 'Changes in Marketing Policy'; BCHA, HOO76, Research and Planning Department, Memo from J. Davis to Members of the Management Committee, 19 Nov. 1959

49 McMUA, Westinghouse box 9, file 21, J.D. Adams, 'Notes on Canadian Electrical Manufacturing Industry,' c 1958, speech notes for C.H. McBain, president of Westinghouse as this campaign was instituted; McHenry to CEMA, 'Appliance Marketing Seminar,' 1960

50 'Hydro, Bank Help Sell White Goods,' *HGR*, 30 Aug. 1961, 1, 24; Hargreaves, 'Changes in Marketing Policy,' 4, 5; BCHA, Oral History Collection, 'Bea Millar, Home Services: "What on Earth Would an Electric Company Do with a Dietician?"'; OHA 570, Marketing and Utilization, 1959–64; BC Hydro, *the tie-in* 1958–68; BCHA, BC Electric, 'Consumer Attitude Survey – Fuels and Household Appliances,' May 1961; Leacy, *Historical Statistics*, Q102–6

51 BC Hydro, *the tie-in*, Dec. 1957, 3; March 1960, 2; Nov. 1960

52 Ibid., Oct. 1959; Sept. 1958; Feb. 1959; March 1959

53 Ibid., Oct. 1959 (ultraviolet); Feb. 1959 (sprinkling); Sept. 1958; OHA 570.1, 'Live Better Electrically' ad copy for 1958–60; on the array of possible dryer features, 'Should Your Next Appliance Be a Dryer?' *Chatelaine*, April 1959, 142

54 *Canadian Home Journal*, June 1952, 51; Sept. 1952, 41; Feb. 1953, 39; March 1953, 22–3, 45; 'Laundry's No Problem Now,' *CHG*, Oct. 1950, 91; 'Planning a Laundry for Today and Tomorrow,' *Chatelaine*, Feb. 1949, 37; 'Today's Household Equipment,' ibid., Nov. 1951, 92; 'Look What's Happening to Washday,' ibid., May 1953, 78; 'Learn How to Launder Nylon,' ibid., Aug. 1953, 28–9; 'How to Choose Your Next Big Appliance,' ibid., Nov. 1956, 23

55 Interviews: Ann Brook, Pam McKeen, Lynn Stevens, Harriet Fraser; J.A Carman and J.D. Kaczor, 'Ownership Patterns for Major Household Appliances,' in J.A Carman, *Studies in the Demand for Household Equipment* (Berkeley: ISER, 1965) 120

56 Letters: Olive Kozlicky, Joyce Cunningham, Joan Catlin, M. McConnell; Interviews: Winnifred Edwards, Lynn Stevans, Mary Kippen, Joan Coffey, Gerd Evans, Ella Smith

57 Interview: Bea Millar; *Marketing*, 7 Oct. 1960; University of British Columbia Special Collections; Bea Millar Papers, 1-23 Kitchen and Laundry Planning,

'A Guide to Wise Buying: Use and Care of Automatic Laundry Equipment';
Interviews: Lily Hansen, Pam McKeen, Tina Wall

58 'Consumer Attitudes Survey, May 1961,' 44; of those not buying a dryer,
21 per cent preferred to dry outside, 11 per cent were satisfied drying their
clothes in the basement, 14 per cent thought dryers impractical; 34 per cent
thought dryers too expensive.

59 Patricia Ronald, 'Factors Influencing Preferences for Household Tasks' (MSc
thesis, University of Guelph, 1969) 19; Ronald worked with a stratified sample of 63 persons, 60 per cent of whom owned dryers, a high saturation rate
for the time. Beatty, an appliance manufacturer, employed many in town.
Martine Perrot, 'The Domestication of Objects,' in Jocelyn de Noblet, ed.,
Industrial Design: Reflection of a Century (Paris: Flammarion, 1993) 367

60 Ronald, 'Factors Influencing Preferences,' 44

61 Perrot, 'Domestication of Objects,' 367

62 Interviews: Susan Taylor, Lynn Stevens, Mary Paine, Pam McKeen; Letter:
Betty Robson; see an account of similar reasoning in Australia in Jean Duruz,
'Laminex Dreams: Women, Suburban Comfort and the Negotiation of Mean-
ings,' *Meanjin* 53, 1 (1996) 99–110.

63 Helen Potrebenko, 'Almost Morningside,' in her *Hey Waitress and Other Stories*
(Vancouver: Lazara, 1989) 51; Helen Potrebenko, 'Housework,' in her *Riding
Home* (Vancouver: Talonbooks, 1995) 43–5; Beth Powning, *Seeds of Another
Summer* (Toronto: Penguin, 1996) 17, 28, 37, 128

64 Interviews: see notes 57 and 62 above, and Greta Nelson

65 Letters: Elizabeth Perry, E.M. Bothom, Pam McKeen, Betty Robson; on display see similarly, Judy Attfield, 'Inside Pram Town: A Case Study of Harlow
House Interiors, 1951–61,' in Judy Attfield and Pat Kirkham, eds., *A View from
the Interior* (London: Women's Press, 1981) 233–4

66 Bruce Hackett and Loren Lutzenhiser, 'The Unity of Self and Object,' *Western Folkflore* 44, 4 (1985) 318, considering how Californians reported using,
and were observed to use, their refrigerators.

67 See Appendix 1.

Conclusion

1 Peter Jackson and Nigel Thrift, 'Geographies of Consumption,' in Daniel
Miller, ed., *Acknowledging Consumption* (London: Routledge, 1995) 230

2 Michel Maffesoli, *The Time of the Tribes: The Decline of Individualism in Mass
Society* (London: Sage, 1996) 20

3 Daniel Miller, 'Consumption as the Vanguard of History,' in Miller, ed., *Acknowledging Consumption*, 33–9; Roger Silverstone, Eric Hirsch, and David

Morley, 'Information and Communication Technologies and the Moral
Economy of the Household,' in Silverstone and Hirsch, eds., *Consuming
Technologies* (London: Routledge, 1993) 15–31; David Cheal, 'Strategies of
Resource Management in Household Economies: Moral Economy or Politi-
cal Economy,' in Richard R. Wilk, ed., *Reconsidering the Domestic Mode of Pro-
duction* (Boulder, CO: Westview, 1989) 11–22

4 J.K. Gibson-Graham, *The End of Capitalism (As We Knew It): A Feminist Critique
of Political Economy* (Oxford: Blackwell, 1996) ix, 2, 3

Illustration Credits

British Columbia Electric, *the tie-in*, March 1960: 'Sell Her a Dryer' (260); October 1960: 'Dryer Buyer Days' (261)

Canadian Art, Summer 1951, 170: The honouring of geometric forms could be carried to extremes (134); Autumn 1949, 36: Floor lamp designed and manufactured by W.A. Trott (135)

The Canadian Consumer, no. 1, 20 January 1948, 1: Canadian Association of Consumers logo (94)

Canadian Business, July 1945, 53: 'Our Export Customers Need Our Products but They Have Not the Funds with Which to Buy Them' (76)

Canadian Homes and Gardens, May and November 1947: Stanfield advertisements for Imperial Loyalist (158, 159); October 1955, 56: Findlay Hy-Oven range (215); January 1955, 36: A resolution to the high oven/low oven dilemma (216); November 1956, 45: 'Change Washday into Playday' (228)

Chatelaine, March 1958, 53: 'Mothers of All Ages Choose Beatty Copperstyle' (225)

Council of Industrial Design (Britain) *Design Quiz* (London: Lord Humphries, 1946): Points to watch, comparing lamps and chairs (130)

Design in the Household exhibition, 25 January–28 February 1946, Toronto Art Gallery. Art Gallery of Ontario, LN-414: Room 1 (53); LN-411: Room 2 (54); LN-410: Fine ceramics (56); LN-69: The last three rooms mimicked retail conventions (57); LN-412: Woman visitor points an accusing finger (59); LN-415: Room 5 (60); LN-409: Scandinavian bedroom suite (62)

Design Quiz: A chance to test your taste (Ottawa: National Gallery, 1948): 'Which do you prefer,' comparing lamps and chairs (131)

Industrial Canada, January 1955, 60: 'Canada Can Make It,' Canadian Manufacturers' Association logo (141)

Irvine, William. *Scarcity or Abundance, the People Must Choose* (Winnipeg: Contemporary Publishers, 1944) 39. Queen's University Archives, Ontario NDP, box 42 campaign literature: CCF campaign literature (36)

Jamieson, Laura E. *Women Dry Those Tears* (Vancouver: Broadway Publishers, 1945) cover: Laura Jamieson's 1945 proposal (38)

Krug Furniture Company, Stratford, Ontario: The first modern furniture made by Imperial, Imperial Saarinen (147); Imperial Loyalist line before Jan Kuypers's redesign, from late 1940s catalogue (153); Jan Kuypers's redesign of Imperial Loyalist, from 1955 catalogue (154); Kuypers's Sampler Collection, from 1959 catalogue (155)

MacDonald, Elizabeth: Two young British Columbians in a Vilas maple chair (162); Ian and the chocolate pudding (175)

Marketing, 11 November 1953, 20: 'An Old Friend in New Dress' (226); 21 March 1953: 'Blessed Event' (229); 3 April 1959, 6: 'Is Your Bride Still Waiting for Her Inglis?' (230); June 1965, 2: 'Jet Floating Sells Frig.' (249)

McCollum, W.H. *Who Owns Canada?* (Ottawa: Woodsworth House, 1947) 74: 'Consumers Enchained' (92)

McMaster University Archives, Westinghouse Collection. *Westinghouse Salesman,* January 1947, 11: 'No he isn't proposing ... he's trying to get Miss Lovelace to sell him one of our demonstrators' (67); July 1951, 8–9: Salesmen and women customers (203); February 1948, 8–9: 'The Farmer's Wife' (206); *Westinghouse News* 2 June 1948, 9: 'That's what comes of having a production man for a husband' (209); *Moffats' Sales Chef,* November 1948, 8: 'Giant "handi-chef" focuses attention of crowd' (68); February 1946, cover: Bahaus plant and steam ranges headed overseas (75); March 1953, cover: Business suits and bathing suits (201)

Metropolitan Toronto Public Library, Parsons Collection. Edith Lang, *Consumers' Opinions Count,* cover: Women in hats meeting around dining room table (88); 'Women of Canada, This Concerns You' (98)

Murray, John: Snyders furniture (139)

Nelson, Greta: Interwar wood-frame rocker, Burnaby 1952 (177); Nelson family's first bedstead (190); The Nelsons' first wood stove, 1950, and their second, 1952 (210); A wringer washer in use in a Vancouver apartment (222); The wood pile behind the Nelsons' home (263)

Paine, Mary: The bottom half of an Imperial Loyalist bunkbed with side rail (162); The living room of a Canadian Mortgage and Housing Small Home in Calgary, 1953 (184)

Shortliffe, Margaret: Home-made rocking horse (191); A round-cornered refrigerator, 1950 (252)

Simpson, Allison: One of a pair of mid-nineteenth-century side chairs (193)

Your Modern Farm Kitchen (Victoria: Rural Housing Advisory Committee for British Columbia, 1948) 13: British Columbia postwar pamphlet (34)

Index